STUDIES IN IMPERIALISM

general editor John M. MacKenzie

Established in the belief that imperialism as a cultural
phenomenon had as significant an effect on the dominant
as on the subordinate societies, Studies in Imperialism
seeks to develop the new socio-cultural approach which
has emerged through cross-disciplinary work on popular
culture, media studies, art history, the study of education
and religion, sports history and children's literature.
The cultural emphasis embraces studies of migration and
race, while the older political and constitutional,
economic and military concerns will never be far away.
It incorporates comparative work on European and
American empire-building, with the chronological focus
primarily, though not exclusively, on the nineteenth and
twentieth centuries, when these cultural exchanges were
most powerfully at work.

Imperial cities

MANCHESTER
UNIVERSITY PRESS

AVAILABLE IN THE SERIES

Imperial cities

LANDSCAPE, DISPLAY
AND IDENTITY

edited by Felix Driver
and David Gilbert

MANCHESTER
UNIVERSITY PRESS
Manchester and New York

distributed exclusively in the USA by
PALGRAVE

Copyright © Manchester University Press 1999

While copyright in the volume as a whole is vested in Manchester University Press, copyright in individual chapters belongs to their respective authors, and no chapter may be reproduced wholly or in part without the express permission in writing of both author and publisher.

Published by **MANCHESTER UNIVERSITY PRESS**
OXFORD ROAD, MANCHESTER M13 9NR, UK
and ROOM 400, 175 FIFTH AVENUE, NEW YORK, NY 10010, USA
www.manchesteruniversitypress.co.uk

Distributed exclusively in the USA by
PALGRAVE
175 FIFTH AVENUE, NEW YORK, NY 10010, USA

Distributed exclusively in Canada by
UBC PRESS, UNIVERSITY OF BRITISH COLUMBIA,
2029 WEST MALL, VANCOUVER, BC, CANADA V6T 1Z2

British Library Cataloguing-in-Publication Data
A catalogue record for this book is available from the British Library

Library of Congress Cataloging-in-Publication Data applied for

ISBN 0 7190 5413 3 *hardback*
ISBN 0 7190 6497 X *paperback*

First published 1999
First published in paperback 2003

10 09 08 07 06 05 04 03   10 9 8 7 6 5 4 3 2 1

Typeset in Trump Medieval
by Northern Phototypesetting Co Ltd, Bolton
Printed in Great Britain
by Bookcraft (Bath) Ltd, Midsomer Norton

CONTENTS

CONTENTS

ILLUSTRATIONS

GENERAL EDITOR'S INTRODUCTION

When the *Studies in Imperialism* series was founded in 1985, it was dedicated to the study of the effects of empire and imperialism upon the home societies in Europe. While the focus has inevitably been principally upon Britain, the series has also been concerned to demonstrate the manner in which imperialism was a Europe-wide phenomenon and the extent to which these reciprocal influences had to be carried well beyond the conventional climax of the First World War. This volume triumphantly vindicates such an approach.

It arises from a stimulating conference on imperial cities which was held at Royal Holloway in early May 1997. It turns the spotlight on a whole range of urban characteristics associated with imperialism, relating not only to the built environment but also to display, ceremony, exhibitions, engineering, clothing and gardening. It also spans France, Italy, Austria, Spain and Great Britain. The contributions illustrate the range and depth of the effects of empire upon metropolitan cultures, exploring fresh aspects of the visible manifestations of imperialism through appropriate multi-disciplinary eyes.

It is a striking characteristic of the arguments of many of the chapters that the full effect of imperialism upon the urban environment, in all its forms, was not felt until relatively late in the imperial story. The reconstruction of Paris during the Second Empire is a famous early example, but it was soon followed in late nineteenth and early twentieth-century Vienna and Rome, in the twentieth-century expositions in Seville, Marseilles and Glasgow, and in the imperialisation of the architecture, pageantry and layout of London in Edwardian times and the inter-war years. Metropolitan cultures seem to have been particularly influenced by imperialism in the era of imperial decline. If new capital cities and a fresh syncretic imperial architecture were being forged throughout the colonial world in this period, so too were the imperial states reassuring themselves of their continuing power and influence by a late flowering of imperial forms. In these ways an imperial culture often fails to march in step with the economic and political realities which have too often been identified by historians as marking out the chronology of imperial rule. It seems to be at its most imperial just at the moment when the forces of anti-imperialism (as at the Pan-African Conference of 1900 in London) are gathering within its portals.

I trust that readers will experience some of the excitement these and other studies aroused at the Imperial Cities conference. Since much of the work is pioneering as well as innovative, the book should be of interest to practitioners in a wide variety of disciplines. It should also stimulate much more research upon similar lines.

John M. MacKenzie

NOTES ON CONTRIBUTORS

David Atkinson is lecturer in Geography at the University of Hull. His research interests include the histories of geographical thought and geopolitical theory: his publications include the co-edited collection *Geopolitical Traditions* (2000). He also works upon the historical and cultural geographies of Liberal and Fascist Rome, and upon Italian colonialism in Africa. He was a member of the Leverhulme Imperial Cities research project team.

Iain Black is Lecturer in Geography at King's College London. He has written on the economic, social and architectural transformation of the City of London in the eighteenth and nineteenth centuries. He is currently working on a project, funded by the British Academy, concerning the commercial architecture of Sir Edwin Lutyens in late-imperial London.

Christopher Breward is Professor in Historical and Cultural Studies at the London College of Fashion. His publications include *The Culture of Fashion* (1995), *The Hidden Consumer* (1999) and co-edited collections *Material Memories* (1999) and *The Englishness of English Dress* (2002). He is currently working on the history of fashion in London.

Denis Cosgrove is Humboldt Professor of Geography at UCLA, and a Visiting Professor at Royal Holloway, University of London. His publications include *The Palladian Landscape* (1993), *Social Formation and Symbolic Landscape* (1998), *Mappings* (1999) and *Apollo's Eye: A Cartographic Genealogy of the Earth in the Western Imagination* (2001). He was a co-director of the Leverhulme Imperial Cities project.

Felix Driver is Professor of Human Geography at Royal Holloway, University of London. His books include *Geography Militant: Cultures of Exploration and Empire* (2001), *Power and Pauperism* (1993) and *Nature and Science* (1992), edited with Gillian Rose. He was a co-director of the Leverhulme Imperial Cities project, and has recently been involved in a creative arts project at Royal Holloway on the theme of 'Visualising Geography'.

Yaël Simpson Fletcher is visiting Assistant Professor of History at the University of the South. Her work explores questions of immigration, race, and national identity in twentieth-century France and Algeria. She is preparing a book manuscript, "Contesting Frenchness: City, Nation, and Empire in Marseilles, 1919-1939," and has contributed chapters to *Domesticating the Empire: Race, Gender, and Family Life in French and Dutch Colonialism, 1830–1962* and *Gender, Sexuality and Colonial Modernities*.

David Gilbert is Senior Lecturer in Geography at Royal Holloway, University of London. He has worked on the influence of imperialism on modern London, particularly in relation to urban planning and the representation of London in travel writing and tourist guides. He has also written on the histories of community and industrial protest. His publications include *Class, Community and Collective Action* (1992), and *The Atlas of Industrial Protest* (1996). He was a co-director of the Leverhulme Imperial Cities project.

Anthony Gristwood recently completed his Ph.D. in Geography at the University of Cambridge. His teaching and research interests are in urban, cultural and political geography, the historical geography of Spain and the use of ICT in geographical education. He lectures on contemporary Europe, cities and development at the International Study Centre of Queen's University (Canada), Herstmonceux Castle, Sussex.

Claire Hancock is maitre de conferences at the University of Paris-XII-Val de Marne. Her doctoral work concerned representations of Paris and London in tourist guides and travel literature. More recent work has explored European representations of New York, and the wider issue of urban and travelling identities in Europe and the Americas.

Andrew Hassam convenes the Australian Studies degree programme at the University of Wales, Lampeter. He has held research fellowships in Canberra, Melbourne, Brisbane, Adelaide and Sydney. His publications include *Sailing to Australia* (1994) and *No Privacy for Writing* (1995). His most recent book is *Through Australian Eyes: Colonial Perceptions of Imperial Britain* (2000).

John MacKenzie is Professor Emeritus of Imperial History at Lancaster University and Honorary Professor in the Research Institute of Irish and Scottish Studies at Aberdeen University. His many books include *Propaganda and Empire, The Empire of Nature* and (as editor) *Imperialism and Popular Culture* and *Imperialism and the Natural World*.

Anna Notaro is a Research Fellow in Visual Culture at the University of Nottingham, working on a project on 'Literary and Visual Representations of Three American Cities (New York, Chicago, Los Angeles), 1870-1930'. She was a research fellow on the Leverhulme Imperial Cities project at Royal Holloway.

Rebecca Preston is a freelance researcher and writer on the history of gardening. Her PhD at Royal Holloway on the culture and politics of gardening in nineteenth-century Britain was completed in 1999. Her published work explores the relationship between the practice of gardening and social identity.

Deborah Ryan is Postdoctoral Research Fellow in the School of History and International Affairs at the University of Ulster at Jordanstown. Her publications include *The Ideal Home Through the Twentieth Century* (1997), and she is currently researching the life and pageants of Frank Lascelles, 1875–1934. She was a research fellow on the Leverhulme Imperial Cities project at Royal Holloway.

Jonathan Schneer is Professor of History at the Georgia Institute of Technology. He has written books on *Ben Tillett: Portrait of a Labour Leader, Labour's Conscience: the Labour Left 1945–51,* and *George Lansbury*. His most recent book is *London 1900: The Imperial Metropolis* (1999). He is currently writing a biography of the river Thames.

Bill Schwarz is an editor of *History Workshop Journal, Cultural Studies* and *New Formations*. He has edited *Crises in the British State 1880–1930* (1985) and *The Expansion of England: Race, Ethnicity and Cultural History* (1996). He teaches at Goldsmiths College, University of London.

Tori Smith is an Assistant Professor of History at Trent University in Ontario, Canada. She is working on a book based on her PhD dissertation at Rutgers on the representation of Queen Victoria in the British Empire.

Jill Steward is Senior Lecturer in the School of Art and Social Sciences at the University of Northumbria at Newcastle. She is joint editor of *The City in Central Europe, Culture and Society* and has published on the history of tourism, spas and popular travel writing.

ACKNOWLEDGEMENTS

The chapters in this book explore the role of imperialism in shaping the land-scapes of modern European cities. The book has its origins in a research project at Royal Holloway, University of London, concerned with the relationship between imperial culture and urban space in London and Rome, between the mid-nineteenth century and the mid-twentieth. The formal part of the project was concluded with a major international conference on the theme of imperial cities in May 1997. Earlier versions of most of the chapters were presented at the conference.

We have incurred many debts in the preparation of the volume. First and foremost, we thank the Leverhulme Trust for supporting the Imperial Cities research project over two years. We must also acknowledge the participation of other members of the Imperial Cities research team – David Atkinson, Denis Cosgrove, Anna Notaro and Deborah Ryan – who contributed in a variety of ways to the making of the book. We are also grateful to the staff and graduate students at Royal Holloway who assisted with the running of the conference and with the management of the project; to Rick Mitcham and staff of the Mitchell Library, Glasgow, for help with picture research for chapters 12 and 14; and to Luciana Martins for compiling the index. Thanks are also due to the participants in conferences, seminars and workshops during which the ideas in the book were developed, including those held at Royal Holloway, the Open University, Birkbeck College, Exeter University and the British School at Rome, whose facilities were made available to us for a memorable visit to Rome. We are also grateful to a number of individuals who have given valuable advice at various stages of the project, including John Agnew, Morag Bell, Tim Barringer, Stephen Daniels, Jim Duncan, John Dickie, Catharine Edwards, Mica Nava, Javier Pes, James Ryan and Bill Schwarz. Finally, we would like to thank all the contributors for their efficiency and good humour in meeting the deadlines we imposed on them.

F.D.
D.G.
Royal Holloway, University of London

CHAPTER ONE

Imperial cities: overlapping territories, intertwined histories

Felix Driver and David Gilbert

In 1932 a poster for the Underground Electric Railway Company invited the people of London to 'Visit the Empire'. All that was required to embark on a tour of the 'wealth, romance and beauty of the empire' was a ticket for the London Underground: Australia could be reached via Temple or the Strand, India via Aldwych, and much of the rest of empire via South Kensington (Figure 1).[1] In this vision of empire, the familiar logo of the London Underground was transformed into a belt around the world, connecting the urban landscape of the imperial capital with the far-flung territories of empire. The dome of St Paul's became a beacon illuminating the imperial landscapes of the globe, each represented as a stop on a trans-metropolitan line. It was as if empire, once so distant and alien, had come home, its products and peoples absorbed into the very fabric of modern urbanism.

Such imagery was neither novel nor exceptional. A 1913 poster entitled 'Trade follows the All Red Route', had encouraged advertisers to use the London omnibus network to sell their wares: 'Just as the flag links the empire's commerce, so does the General link up the world's greatest city'. Other London Underground posters promoted visits to military, naval and explorers' memorials as 'pilgrimages of empire', and a similar rhetoric was exploited in publicity for exhibitions at Wembley, the Science Museum and the Imperial Institute ('the empire under one roof'). If in this rhetoric Whitehall was 'the high-street of empire', South Kensington or Kew Gardens were the places to see its more exotic features. A traveller in London could 'span the globe' in the course of a day: one could even see 'The Tropics by Underground'. Such imagery projected a distinctive imaginative geography on to the landscapes of the modern metropolis, the world exhibited for the Underground passenger. In this vision, London was not merely the heart of a global empire: it was the place in which an enormous variety of imperial sights could be seen. Particular aspects of empire –

Figure 1 'Visit the empire', by Ernest M. Dinkel (1932)

political authority, commercial power, cosmopolitan consumption, scientific progress, popular display – were represented by different sites such as Westminster, the City, Oxford Street, South Kensington or Wembley. And the Underground itself was represented as the means of rendering these diverse sites accessible, the metropolitan equivalent of the global 'All Red Route' across the seas or the burgeoning network of Imperial Airways. In these images the rhetoric of modernity – of mass leisure and consumption – mapped the empire on to the city: if the imperial city was at the centre of the world, the empire was now at the heart of the urban experience.

Images like this fix the 'overlapping territories' and 'intertwined histories' of modern imperialism in a particularly striking manner.[2] Indeed, their rhetoric and iconography need to be situated within a much wider history of cross-mappings between empire and the modern European city. This wider history may be approached from a variety of perspectives, and this book brings together contributors from several disciplines, including imperial history, geography, cultural studies, literature and the history of art and design. Their essays consider a range of urban settings, including capital cities such as London, Paris and Rome, and other major European cities, including Glasgow, Marseilles and Seville. In some chapters a specific monument or exhibition provides the main focus; others explore the ways in which imperial identities were composed, reproduced and contested. But common to all is a conviction that the form, use and representation of modern European cities have been shaped by the global history of imperialism in ways that continue to matter even in an apparently post-imperial age. Even today many of these cities display unmistakable signs of their imperial past, not only in their architecture and monuments but also in the ways in which they are imagined by their inhabitants and visitors. While the modern traveller may be unmoved by the representation of a journey across London as a trip round the empire, there are still other stories to tell about the global history of the imperial city.[3]

Imperial cities: rethinking the city, relocating empire

As the title indicates, we are concerned with the ways in which the experiences of empire and urbanism intersect; more specifically, we want to explore the role of imperialism in the cultural history of the modern European metropolis. *Imperial Cities* focuses mainly on the impress of nineteenth and twentieth-century forms of imperialism, rather than on that of their predecessors, because we believe this dimension of urban history has been neglected in comparison with the impact of early modern, medieval or ancient empires. This neglect may reflect a common assumption that modern forms of urbanism, in contrast to those associated with absolutist states, are shaped less by political than by economic processes; indeed, where political processes are considered in relation to the making of the modern city, they are more often associated with the politics of class or citizenship than with those of empire. A partial exception is, of course, generally admitted in the case of the modern totalitarian state, whose power was inscribed on to the urban fabric of much of Europe during the twentieth century.[4] The urban legacy of fascism and state socialism is undoubtedly significant, and surely deserves greater attention. Nevertheless, we would suggest that other forms of modern imperialism have also left their mark on the architecture and design of European cities, and it is these which are the primary concern of this volume.

Our focus on the modern imperial city requires further justification, if only because the experiences of urban modernity and of empire are usually assumed to belong to two distinct domains, one claimed by urban sociologists, the other by imperial historians. The strange neglect of the modern imperial city as an object of study contrasts markedly with the substantial literature which exists on the formation of the colonial city, where the articulation of global modes of production and exchange with the spatial structure of the city has been a major focus of attention for urban theorists for more than two decades.[5] Yet the modern European city has, until recently, escaped such an analysis, its development interpreted largely in terms of the evolution of capitalism, urban planning and social movements. In writing of 'imperial cities', then, we argue for a different perspective on the history of European cities: to interpret their landscapes, at least in part, as hybrid products of the cultural history of modern imperialism. This is emphatically not to argue that the history of modern capitalism or of urban planning is not of critical importance for an understanding of the modern city. It is rather to offer a new context for understanding an important yet neglected aspect of the European urban landscape.[6]

This rethinking of the history of the modern European city is inspired in part by recent writings on the identity of places, most notably those of the geographer Doreen Massey.[7] In a series of essays Massey has argued that the identity of places in the modern world is constituted as much by their relation with other places as by anything intrinsic to their location. It is impossible, for example, to understand the economic geography of Manchester in the mid-nineteenth century, of Chicago in the early twentieth century, or of Los Angeles today, without considering the ways in which their urban economies were integrally related to a wider global economic system. This argument finds a parallel in the cultural geography of modern cities – that is, the ways in which the identities of urban places are imagined, represented and performed. Massey herself famously uses the example of the Kilburn High Road in London, significantly a rather less glamorous site than those more usually claimed as exemplars of (post) modern urbanism, to develop an argument about the hybridity of place. The identities of urban places, as much as those of individuals or nations, are multiple and complex; they are formed and re-formed through networks of relationships across space and time. In this perspective, a place is less an origin than a meeting point; the city as a whole becomes less a centre than a crossroads.

The idea that places and cultures are becoming increasingly interconnected is, of course, a major theme in the substantial literature on what is termed 'globalisation'.[8] From our perspective, this literature offers a potentially useful perspective on the constitution of places in the past as well as in the present. Rather than regarding the city as the product of some inexorable process of organic growth, only contingently connected with broader systems or structures, we are encouraged to consider the ways in which these systems help to shape the city; or rather, the ways in which the city and the system are mutually constitutive. However, it is a common complaint that writings on globalisation are often characterised by a profoundly unhistorical account of the modern world system. They tend to treat contemporary processes of globalisation as both revolutionary and unprecedented, without paying much attention to their complex histories; they too rarely consider the different and sometimes contradictory spatial forms which globalisation may take. In this context, the work of Anthony King provides a particularly useful corrective. In his book *Colonial Urban Development* (published well before the rise to prominence of the term 'globalisation'), King not only argued for the significance of the global economy in shaping the spatial structure of cities like New Delhi or Cairo; he also paid particular attention to the influence of the cultural forms of empire on the landscapes of these cities. In his more recent work King has offered a novel perspective on the development of modern London as a global city, paying particular attention to the significance of British imperial history for the constitution of metropolitan spaces. The central issue for King 'is whether the real development of London or Manchester can be understood without reference to India, Africa and Latin America [and, we would add, other First World cities] any more than can the development of Kingston (Jamaica) or Bombay be understood without reference to the former'.[9]

King's observation is echoed in recent writing on the cultural

[5]

dynamics of imperialism. In *Culture and Imperialism*, for example, Edward Said draws attention to the ways in which the cultural history of empire became a genuinely global process during the nineteenth and twentieth centuries, creating hybrid landscapes and identities across the globe. 'Who in India or Algeria today,' asks Said, 'can confidently separate out the British or French component of the past from present actualities; and who in Britain or France can draw a clear circle around British London or French Paris that would exclude the impact of India and Algeria upon these two imperial cities?'[10] A similar argument could be extended to other cities discussed in this volume, such as Rome, Vienna, Glasgow, Marseilles and Seville. Our focus on the 'imperial city' is thus intended to raise questions about the ways in which the global processes of imperialism were absorbed and re-presented in the urban context. At this point, further questions begin to intrude. Precisely how, for example, did the experience of empire help to shape the urban landscapes of these cities? The answer is necessarily complex. (Indeed, if it were not, there would be little point in reading further.) In our own work on London, for example, we have argued that existing studies of 'imperial London' have been overwhelmingly concerned with the public, architectural face of empire, and especially the ceremonial landscapes constructed during the brief moment of high imperialism between 1880 and 1914, that golden age of invented traditions.[11] But we also need to consider other ways in which empire was expressed in the urban landscape: for example, in the London docks, that 'nexus of empire' where lives were shaped by the ebb and flow of goods and people,[12] in the permanent and temporary displays at South Kensington, the Crystal Palace or Wembley, and in the miniature and domestic expressions of imperial culture to be found in and around suburban homes.

The symbolism of even the most bombastic of landscapes in the imperial city was more fragile than it appeared, as several contributors to this volume show. Certainly, the ways in which monuments and landscapes were actually used and understood frequently departed from the intentions of their designers. Furthermore, it is possible to find contrasting emphases and even contradictions in the work of those architects and urban planners involved in reshaping the imperial city. For example, Aston Webb, the architect of the Victoria memorial and Admiralty Arch, was also the editor of *London of the Future* (1921), a volume containing eighteen essays on subjects as various as railway construction and public parks. An aerial photograph of the Mall and Buckingham Palace, predictably captioned 'Heart of the Empire', formed the frontispiece of the book. The imperial theme was also the subject of a chapter by the Earl of Meath, creator of Empire Day and a host of other schemes for imperial education. However, rather than proposing grand architectural schemes for London's ceremonial core, Meath used his chapter to promote other ways to make the city fittingly imperial: by co-opting dominion representatives on to local government bodies, by training its ordinary citizens to be more healthy, and by creating 'rings of beauty' in the form of parks and gardens around its suburbs. These proposals are a reminder of the ways in which the imperial project was an influence on many developments in planning theory; modernist planning, with its emphases on functional zoning, green belts and the creation of a healthy urban environment, was stimulated in part by the desire to create a fitting centre for the empire. Meath sought to make London 'a *real home* for the children of the empire', arguing that London's 'homeliness' was its most distinctive feature as an imperial capital.[13] For Meath and his colleagues, 'imperial' sentiment was not identified with extravagant architectural display: it was as much about the suburbs as the centre, about ordinary lives as much as patriotic spectacles, about mothers and children as much as soldiers and politicians.

The representation of London as the 'home city of empire' directs our attention to the ways in which notions of 'home' and empire could be mutually constitutive rather than mutually exclusive. The idea of empire has often been regarded in Europe as a matter of diffusion, extension and expansion: as something which happens over 'there' rather than close to home. Recent work inspired by the 'post-colonial' turn in literature and the humanities has suggested a shift in our angle of perspective, towards the impact of imperialism 'at home'. From this perspective imperialism is understood as a necessarily hybrid though still uneven experience, shaping the identity of the colonisers as much as that of the colonised. This approach raises questions about the intertwining of the 'domestic' and 'imperial' histories of modern Europe.[14] Such questions are of critical importance, not least because the impact of empire was prominently displayed within the built environment of all the major cities of Europe as they came (in different ways) to play the role of regional, national and imperial centres.

Yet the post-colonial perspective has until recently promised more than it has delivered, at least as far as the study of the city is concerned. Post-colonial critics have concentrated their attention on written texts, especially the canonical works of European literature. With a few notable exceptions,[15] they have yet to explore the diverse relations between imperial culture and the production, consumption and representation of urban space. In order to understand the variety of ways in which cultures of imperialism were represented and negotiated in the European city, it is necessary to move beyond maps and texts to consider the relationship between different kinds of spaces – architectural, spectacular, performative and lived. Many of the spaces of the imperial city, from exhibitions to public thoroughfares, were spaces in movement, shaped at least in part by the crowds who passed through them. Any discussion of the iconography of ceremonial spaces such as Trafalgar Square in London or the Piazza Venezia in Rome, for example, must pay attention to the complex of meanings surrounding their representation and use.[16] And, alongside these public and often spectacular performances, it is important to consider the more domestic, informal and even private performances that were going on elsewhere in the city. Empire could be found in the most unlikely of places and activities: even, as Rebecca Preston shows, in the choice of species planted in the borders of suburban lawns.

The relationship between imperial culture and urban space worked out very differently in different European cities. Indeed, the nature of that relationship was defined partly in relation to European as much as to non-European 'others'. To speak of 'European', even French, British or German, imperialism as a homogeneous and unitary discourse is to obscure the very questions which were at stake in debates over imperial policy and urban planning: how to be imperial, how to reconcile competing versions of the imperial project, and how to define a national imperialism against other national imperialisms. As the chapters in this book demonstrate, these questions were answered in different ways in different times and places. One of the limitations of post-colonial theory in this context is its tendency to underestimate the historical diversity and the geographical heterogeneity of imperial cultures. Any account of the culture of imperial urbanism must therefore pay due attention to the particularities of time and place. It is for this reason that we have collected together in one volume essays on very different kinds of imperial city. The experience of London was different from that of Rome or Paris, that of Marseilles from that of Glasgow or Seville: teasing out the comparative aspects of the history of imperial urbanism is one of the key aims of the book.

Yet this emphasis on the specificity of imperial cultures in different times and places also has its limits. The history of European imperial cities needs to be situated in the wider context of intellectual and architectural discourses which extended beyond local and national boundaries. The great European cities were not merely isolated sites, each articulating a different vision of empire; they were also part of a wider economic, geopolitical and (not least) cultural system. As David Atkinson, Denis Cosgrove and Anna Notaro point out in Chapter 3, the collective memory of the classical imperial city, pre-eminently Rome, had a marked impact on urban design across the globe. While mid-nineteenth-century Rome itself was little more than a provincial town with some impressive ruins, the idea of Rome was ubiquitous.[17] Such memory took shape in a variety of ways, from the iconography of individual buildings and public statuary, through the shape and form of public spaces, both permanent and ephemeral, to the planning of whole cityscapes. While there were often nuanced discussions about the most appropriate classical models, as Claire Hancock shows in her discussion of the development of Paris, there was little doubt that material memories of Rome haunted the landscape of most European imperial cities.

In what was effectively a pan-European discourse on the imperial city, national models were implicitly and explicitly defined in relation to other national models, in a spirit of competition as much as emulation. For example, while theorists looked to Rome or Athens for their models of what empire should be, professional architects and planners in Britain followed developments in cities such as Paris or Brussels for their modern precedents. Through publications, conferences, exhibitions, personal contacts and travel writing of all kinds, a network – or rather a series of networks – was put in place, creating a kind of European market in urban ideas, strategies and models. In the wake of the Paris International Exhibition of 1855, for example, the prize-winning designs in the competition for new Foreign and War Offices in Whitehall bore a close resemblance to Parisian models, including the new Louvre and the redesigned Hôtel de Ville.[18] Half a century later we find a young Patrick Abercrombie writing in *The Architectural Review* on Léopold II's rebuilding of Brussels, including not only the grandiose Palais de Justice but also numerous royal residences, gardens, boulevards and colonial museums.[19] In the case of London, as elsewhere, this process of cultural exchange was frequently an anxious one. Late Victorian planners frequently complained that London lagged behind its rivals in the imperial city stakes. For example, the liberal positivist Frederic Harrison (speaking on behalf of the new London County Council) claimed in 1892 that 'London, with the grandest river of any capital in Europe, with a rich and glorious history, with boundless energy, wealth and culture, suffers itself to be put to shame by Paris, Berlin, Vienna, Rome, Chicago and New York, and is content with its narrow lanes and hugger-mugger traditions of street architecture'.[20] The absence of state-sponsored projects to parallel Haussmann's rebuilding of Paris or Léopold's grand plans for Brussels has led some historians to cast London as a failed imperial city. As Jan Morris puts it, 'London was not, like [ancient] Rome, paved with the spoils and trophies of Empire'.[21] But this observation masks a more complicated story; there were, and are, many ways of being an imperial city.

Imperial landscape, display and identity

The chapters of this book explore the role of imperialism in shaping the history and geography of a variety of modern European cities. They are grouped in three parts, each of which focuses on distinct, though related, aspects of this theme. Part I, 'Imperial landscapes', considers some of the ways in which the design of urban landscapes articulated competing visions of the imperial city, including large-scale planning and architectural schemes, urban design and public monuments. Part II, 'Imperial Display', considers the role of various forms of visual display, including spectacular pageants, imperial exhibitions and suburban gardens, in the cultural life of metropolitan imperialism. Finally, Part III, 'Imperial Identities', is primarily concerned with the associations between imperial identities and the history of urban space in a variety of European cities.

In considering the impact of empire on the urban landscapes of modern Europe, it should be noted that many of the techniques of urban design now commonly attributed to authoritarian or totalitarian regimes were not exclusive to them. In his foreword to *Art and Power*, concerned with the twentieth-century totalitarian state, Eric Hobsbawm identifies three 'primary demands' which the state makes on public art and architecture: the first is to glorify power itself, which in the European context usually involved the construction of victory arches and columns on the Roman model; the second is the organisation of art as a public drama, by means of ceremonial avenues and spaces designed for spectacular performances; the third is the use of art in the service of education or propaganda.[22] As Hobsbawm's account suggests, classical forms of urban design – the theatre, the circus, the avenue, the arch – have long played an important role in the exercise of political power. The exploitation of such forms in the architecture and design of fascist urbanism may have been extravagant, but it was certainly not unique. While we would not want simply to equate fascist imperial urbanism with the urban discourse of liberal imperialism, it is important to recognise that connections undoubtedly exist between them.

In Chapter 2, on the Queen Victoria Memorial, Tori Smith shows how imperial preoccupations entered into debates over the reconstruction of a key ceremonial site at the heart of London in the opening years of the twentieth century. As she and several other contributors demonstrate, there was considerable debate over how precisely to make London a fitting capital for empire; in the process, comparisons and contrasts were repeatedly drawn with other major European cities. The representation of Paris as an imperial capital, as Claire Hancock shows, was an important dimension of Napoléon III's rebuilding of the city, as well as of the series of international expositions sponsored by the French state. Still more grandiose attempts to represent the achievements of the Italian nation in architectural terms are discussed by David Atkinson, Denis Cosgrove and Anna Notaro in their study of Rome. While it is often assumed that explicitly imperial themes came to prominence only with the coming to power of Mussolini, they argue the liberal project to remake the city as the capital of a united Italy drew directly upon the imaginative and material heritage of ancient Rome, as well as more modern ideologies of European imperialism. While such allusions to classical Rome were commonplace in the public architecture of modern European states, they must always be interpreted in context: as Iain Black shows in his careful reading of the iconography of the Bank of England, imperial motifs were articulated with national, commercial and cosmopolitan themes, in this case reflecting a particular moment of late imperialism.

Many of the landscapes considered in this book were explicitly designed for grand displays of imperial prestige and prowess. As Claire Hancock and Jill Steward show in Chapters 4 and 5, on Paris and Vienna, the form these landscapes took also reflected the growing significance of modern forms of tourism and the 'tourist gaze'.[23] In both cases, the promotion of the city as a tourist spectacle was a significant feature of urban design. The associations between modern European imperialism and what has been called 'the exhibitionary complex' are addressed explicitly in the second section of this book, concerned with a variety of forms of display in the imperial city.[24] Yet exhibitions of empire involved more than merely the imaginative projection of an imperial image of the world: such acts of display need to be located within the context of the city in which they take place. For example, Yaël Simpson Fletcher's account of the 1922 Colonial Exposition in Marseilles pays close attention to spatial forms of inclusion and exclusion which characterised the social geography of the city as much as the exhibition. Deborah Ryan's study of the Pageant of London of 1911 shows the ways in which public celebrations of empire were not simply triumphal demonstrations of national or racial superiority; they also provided opportunities for the expression of civic pride. In other cases, as Anthony Gristwood shows in his study of Seville, exhibitionary events were designed to celebrate past imperial glories, in this case recasting the story of the Spanish diaspora in modern terms.

It is important to recognise that the 'world exhibition' was only one means through which empires and imperial cities were represented. Moreover, the world exhibitions themselves worked through a variety of different technologies of display: there was no single way of seeing the world. In Chapter 10 Andrew Hassam emphasises the instabilities at the heart of the exhibitionary project. The very structures erected to contain and fix the 'world as exhibition' were mobile and temporary; their story as told by Hassam is less one of imperial centrality than one of instability and uncertainty. In Chapter 11, on the culture of exotics in British gardening, Rebecca Preston also emphasises the ways in which imperial culture was refracted in shaping even the most ordinary forms of display. In this account, our attention is directed away from the ceremonial spaces of the imperial city and towards less familiar territory: the suburban garden as a site for the negotiation of imperial, national and gender identities.

Questions of imperial identity are addressed throughout the book. Projects to design imperial landscapes or to display the fruits of empire necessarily implicated assumptions about national and imperial identity: how to be imperial, and how to reconcile different versions of the imperial project, were, as we have argued, integral to the discourse on imperial cities. Part III addresses the issue of imperial identities directly. In Chapter 12, John MacKenzie considers the cultural history of Glasgow, once renowned as the 'second city' of the empire, examining the complex interplay of imperial, British, Scottish and civic identities. What is striking about this case is the divergence between the evidently imperial image of the city and the neglect of its imperial past in most histories of Glasgow. The question of the invisibility of the imperial in urban history is taken up by Christopher Breward in his account of masculine identities in late Victorian and Edwardian London. Breward's chapter demonstrates the extent to which imperial themes infiltrated all sorts of aspects of metropolitan cultural life – in this case, the performance of masculinity through the dress code of lower middle-class men. As Breward shows, anxieties about empire found their way into expressions of gender identity: there is more to fashion than meets the eye.

Many of the contributors draw attention to the heterogeneity of attitudes towards empire, and the tensions between competing conceptions of the imperial city. In Britain, for example, the increasing stridency of claims to imperial prowess in the late nineteenth century masked growing anxiety about the condition of the metropolis. Allusions to the past glories of Rome in late Victorian and Edwardian writings on the British empire had a distinctly unsettling edge, especially given the intensification of commercial and political competition from rival imperial powers. The sense that London's pre-eminence might pass – indeed, that, like ancient Rome, it might sink into corruption and decay – was never far from the surface. Anxiety about the social, moral and environmental fabric of the modern metropolis was an endemic feature of public debate throughout Europe during the late nineteenth and early twentieth centuries. Cities like London, Glasgow, Berlin or Rome were portrayed by critics less as hearts of empire than as cancers within the imperial organism, sites of decay and neglect offering an implicit contrast, or even a rebuke, to the glamour of imperial enterprise overseas. Some liberal intellectuals, such as Charles Masterman or J. A. Hobson, regarded popular imperialism as itself part of the dark side of modern urban life. In this perspective the 'jingoism' of the crowd was a positively demoralising force which brought uncontrollable desires to the surface, threatening to engulf the very moral and physical fabric of society.[25]

There is, of course, a difference between anxiety over empire and resistance to imperial rule. Yet the imperial capitals of Europe have also, perhaps ironically, provided the setting for significant displays of anti-imperial sentiment in the twentieth century. The history of African and Indian nationalism, for example, cannot be fully understood without some consideration of the role of London as a site for the development of an anti-imperialist politics. This role is explored by Jonathan Schneer in Chapter 14, which focuses mainly on the first Pan-African Conference of 1900. As Schneer demonstrates, London provided a site – among many others – for the emerging discourse of pan-Africanism. Schneer's emphasis on the significance of anti-imperial politics in the imperial city has wider implications for interpretations of imperial urbanism. In periods of mass political unrest, spaces which had been consciously designed to symbolise imperial power could also become sites of challenge and resistance. Rodney Mace has provided a particularly compelling account of the ways in which Trafalgar Square, designed as a imperial space during the nineteenth century, became appropriated as a site of political demonstration and protest.[26] These two dimensions of the square's history were of course related: its officially monumentalised status as an 'emblem of empire' provided the rationale for its use by those who challenged the nature of the imperial order. While Mace emphasises socialist and anti-fascist protest, the square was also a prime site for explicitly anti-colonial protests, such as those of the India League and Indian Freedom Campaign in the decade before Indian independence. More recent demonstrations outside South Africa House during the apartheid era provide a further instance of the ways in which imperial politics continued to haunt the landscape of central London.

New maps of the imperial city

In this book we seek to demonstrate that the culture of imperialism left a substantial imprint on the histories and landscapes of the modern European city. The chapters which follow consider not just those cities which have long proclaimed their imperial role but others which are not usually thought of as 'imperial'. Our general aim is to illuminate some of the ways in which empire made a difference 'at home': in the streets, offices and homes of Europeans themselves. The difference that empire made is, of course, open to question, and there is clearly great scope for comparative studies of the cultural significance of empire in the modern history of other European cities, such as Brussels, Berlin or Lisbon. Our purpose in this book is less to provide a universal survey of the imperial city, even were such a survey possible, than to open up a new agenda for students of urbanism and imperialism.

We began this chapter with a singular example of the representation of the European metropolis as an imperial spectacle, in which the sights of empire were mapped on to the sites of the city, and we conclude with some thoughts on alternative ways of mapping the imperial city. It should be clear from the chapters in this book that such efforts to represent the world in or from a single vantage point – the heart of empire – are always and necessarily partial. In the case of London, for example, there was always a number of sites rather than a single pivot, each reflecting a rather different version of empire. In a sense, the Underground posters of the inter-war period made a virtue of this multiplicity of 'centres': the imperial capital was represented through its transport networks rather than a single site, offering the visitor an experience that could be gained only through movement between them. Yet such maps were themselves partial: not simply because they failed to mark the routes of visitors coming from other directions – the Chinese dock worker, the Jamaican immigrant or the returning soldier, for example – but also because they positioned London solely in relation to the British empire. For, as we have seen, the process by which images of the imperial city were constructed was as much a product of relations *between* the imperial powers as of the power of metropolitan rule over an extra-European empire. If we examine debates over the architecture and design of European cities in the period between the mid-nineteenth century and the mid-twentieth we find a common experience of emulation and competition, a kind of struggle for urban primacy which set London against Paris, Rome against Berlin; and the same applies to the experience of image makers in non-capital cities, such as Glasgow, Marseilles or Seville, which was inevitably influenced by their relationship with these capitals. The anxiety which constituted the dark side of triumphal expressions of imperial might was also marked by this national and European frame

[14]

of reference. Fears about the presence of 'aliens' in the capital cities of Western Europe before the 1950s were focused not on the empire but on those ethnic 'others' within Europe itself: the Jew, the Slav and the Gypsy. It is clear, in sum, that national debates over imperial urbanism were conditioned not simply by understandings of the global reach of European empires but also by attitudes towards social, cultural and political change within Europe itself.

This is perhaps an unexpected conclusion to reach. After all, our own journey through the landscapes of modern imperial London has taken us not simply to India, Canada, Australia or Africa – places on the imaginative itinerary of the Underground – but also to Paris, Rome and Brussels. In the process, moreover, we have encountered new territories, relatively unexplored by the imperial historian, including the mundane office landscapes of the city or the gardens of its suburbs. A key theme running throughout this book is the association of different aspects of empire not only with different cities, but with different parts of cities. The metropolis appears here as a heterogeneous but material space, in which manifestations of urban spectacle shape, and are shaped by, the locations in which they take place. Future excavations of the material geographies of the imperial city should pay close attention to this differentiated landscape of empire: though they may have been connected by transport networks of various kinds, from rivers to underground trains, these sites were not all the same. The imperial city, in other words, had a geography which mattered.

And, finally, how can we revisit the imperial city today? One route through its past may be via the sort of maps with which we began, treating them as clues to the cultural history of urban image-making. Another may be through the material forms which urban landscapes take, from the ceremonial design of their central places to the iconography of their built forms. Alternatively, we might begin to trace other trajectories through the imperial city, by listening for other voices, such as those of the migrant worker, the refugee or the colonial tourist.[27] The social history of European cities is in part a history of movement and migration, sometimes voluntary, sometimes forced, and this history cannot fully be appreciated without some understanding of these cities' imperial role. While the cities of Europe have provided homes for non-Europeans for as long as they have been cities, it is in the social composition of the post-imperial city – in Glasgow and Marseilles as much as London and Paris – that the impact of empire can most readily be appreciated. The hybridity of these places, their overlapping territories and intertwined histories, testifies to the enduring legacy of empire.

Notes

1 The poster was one of a pair produced by Ernest Dinkel; the other showed British colonies in the Americas and New Zealand, with Underground stations including Holborn ('For the British Museum') and Camden Town ('For the Zoo'). These posters, together with those mentioned in the following paragraph, are available in the Resource Centre of the London Transport Museum, Covent Garden.

2 These terms are borrowed from Edward Said, *Culture and Imperialism* (London, Chatto & Windus, 1993).

3 In 1998 a poster campaign for London Transport directed at restaurant-goers announced that 'the simplest way to get to the Khyber Pass, New Delhi or the Taj Mahal is by bus'. In the 1950s the organisation had itself voyaged out into the empire, setting up offices in the Caribbean to recruit drivers, guards and cleaners.

4 See especially D. Ades, T. Benton, D. Elliott and I. Boyd White (eds), *Art and Power: Europe under the Dictators, 1930–45* (London, Thames & Hudson, 1995); A. Gentes, 'Memorable irony: the life, death and resurrection of the Cathedral of Christ the Saviour, 1812 to the present', *History Workshop Journal*, 46 (1998) 63–95.

5 See especially A. D. King, *Colonial Urban Development* (London, Routledge, 1976); N. Al Sayyad, *Forms of Dominance: On the Architecture and Urbanism of the Colonial Enterprise* (Aldershot, Avebury, 1992); B. Yeoh, *Contesting Space: Power Relations and the Urban Built Environment in Colonial Singapore* (Kuala Lumpur, Oxford University Press, 1996).

6 This argument is developed in F. Driver and D. Gilbert, 'Heart of empire? Landscape, space and performance in imperial London', *Environment and Planning D: Society and Space*, 16 (1998) 11–28.

7 D. Massey, 'A global sense of place', *Marxism Today*, June 1991, pp. 24–9, reprinted in S. Daniels and R. Lee (eds), *Exploring Human Geography* (London, Arnold, 1996); D. Massey, 'The conceptualisation of place', in D. Massey and P. Jess (eds), *A Place in the World? Places, Cultures and Globalization* (Oxford, Oxford University Press, 1995); D. Massey, 'Places and their pasts', *History Workshop Journal*, 39 (1995) 182–92.

8 In addition to Massey's work, cited above, see, for example, J. Eade (ed.), *Living the Global City: Globalization as Local Process* (London, Routledge, 1996); M. Featherstone (ed.), *Global Culture* (Newbury CA, Sage, 1990); A. D. King (ed.), *Culture, Globalization and the World System* (London, Macmillan, 1991); R. Johnston, P. Taylor and M. Watts (eds), *Geographies of Global Change: Remapping the World in the Late Twentieth Century* (Oxford, Blackwell, 1995); D. Morley and K. Robins, *Spaces of Identity: Global Media, Electronic Landscapes and Cultural Boundaries* (London, Routledge, 1995).

9 A. D. King, *Urbanism, Colonialism and the World Economy: Cultural and Spatial Foundations of the World Urban System* (London, Routledge, 1990), p. 78. King's other works include *Colonial Urban Development* (London, Routledge, 1976), *The Bungalow: The Production of a Global Culture* (London, Routledge, 1984) and *Global Cities: Post-imperialism and the Internationalization of London* (London, Routledge, 1990).

10 Said, *Culture and Imperialism*, p. 19.

11 See Driver and Gilbert, 'Heart of empire?', on which this section is based.

12 J. Schneer, 'London's docks in 1900: nexus of empire', *Labour History Review*, 59 (1994) 20–33; L. Tabili, *We ask for British Justice: Workers and Racial Difference in Late Imperial Britain* (Ithaca NY, Cornell University Press, 1994).

13 Earl of Meath, 'London as the heart of empire', in A. Webb (ed.), *London of the Future* (London, Unwin, 1921), pp. 251–60 (quote from p. 260, emphasis in the original). On Meath's various schemes for urban improvement and imperial education see F. Aalen, 'Lord Meath, city improvement and social imperialism', *Planning Perspectives*, 4 (1989) 127–52.

14 See R. Samuel, 'Empire stories: the imperial and the domestic', in R. Samuel, *Island*

Stories: Unravelling Britain, Theatres of Memory II, (London, Verso, 1998), pp. 74–97.

15 See especially J. Jacobs, *Edge of Empire: Postcolonialism and the City* (London, Routledge, 1996).

16 On the former see R. Mace, *Trafalgar Square: Emblem of Empire* (London, Lawrence & Wishart, 1976); on the latter, D. Atkinson and D. Cosgrove, 'Urban rhetoric and embodied identities: city, nation and empire at the Vittorio Emanuele II monument in Rome, 1870-1945', *Annals of the Association of American Geographers*, 88 (1998) 28–49.

17 Chapter 3 of this volume. See also R. Betts, 'The allusion to Rome in British imperialist thought of the nineteenth and early twentieth centuries', *Victorian Studies*, 15 (1971) 149–59; C. Edwards, *Writing Rome*, Cambridge (Cambridge University Press, 1996).

18 M. H. Port, *Imperial London: Civil Government Building in London, 1851–1915* (New Haven CT, Yale University Press, 1995), p. 169. See also E. Morris, 'Symbols of empire: architectural style and the government offices competition', *Journal of Architectural Education*, 32 (1978) 8–13.

19 P. Abercrombie, 'Leopold II and Brussels', *Architectural Review*, 32 (1912) 114–25.

20 F. Harrison, 'London improvements', *New Review*, 7 (1892) 414–21 (quote from p. 414).

21 J. Morris, *Pax Britannica: The Climax of an Empire* (Harmondsworth, Penguin, 1979), p. 454.

22 E. Hobsbawm, 'Foreword', in Ades *et al.*, *Art and Power*, pp. 11–15.

23 J. Urry, *The Tourist Gaze* (London, Sage, 1990). On urban spectacle more generally see G. Kearns and C. Philo (eds), *Selling Places: The City as Cultural Capital, Past and Present* (Oxford, Pergamon Press, 1993).

24 T. Bennett, *The Birth of the Museum* (London, Routledge, 1995).

25 Driver and Gilbert, 'Heart of empire?', pp. 24–6.

26 Mace, *Trafalgar Square*.

27 On London see, for example, N. Merriman and R. Visram, 'The world in a city', in N. Merriman (ed.), *The Peopling of London: Fifteen Thousand Years of Settlement from Overseas* (London, Museum of London, 1993); Tabili, *We ask for British Justice*; A. Burton, 'Making a spectacle of empire: Indian travellers in *fin-de-siècle* London', *History Workshop Journal*, 42 (1996) 127–46; A. Wollacott, '"All this is the Empire, I told myself": Australian women's voyages "home" and the articulation of colonial whiteness', *American Historical Review*, 102 (1997) 1003–29; D. Gilbert, 'London in all its glory: imperial London in its guidebooks', *Journal of Historical Geography*, 25 (1999).

PART I

Imperial landscapes

CHAPTER TWO

'A grand work of noble conception': the Victoria Memorial and imperial London

Tori Smith

At the beginning of the twentieth century, as at its end, Britons grieved the loss of a royal icon. In the aftermath of Victoria's death, as after Diana's, thoughts turned quickly to the question of commemoration. Only weeks after the Queen died in January 1901, a committee was established to consider a national memorial. But the plan it eventually adopted was an attempt to do more than just commemorate Victoria. The planning committee and its supporters used the occasion of the Queen's death to propose the creation of a new imperial space in London: a 'grand work of noble conception'.[1]

In the closing years of the nineteenth century, it seemed to some observers that the built environment of London was inadequate to its role as an imperial city. The Queen Victoria Memorial, which comprised both a monument to the Queen in front of Buckingham Palace and the redesign of the Mall to incorporate the new Admiralty Arch, was intended as one step towards redressing that inadequacy. As conceived and executed by its proponents and planners, the memorial is an important element in the history of London as an imperial city. Its features suggest that, for Edwardians, imperial space was a fluid concept shaped by Britons' relationship with Europe as well as with the empire. Significantly, the advocates of the memorial, who included architects, journalists, civil servants and politicians, looked chiefly to the Continent for inspiration. Moreover, as they defined it, imperial space was inextricably linked with performance and with the monarchy. By building a processional way, elevating the stature of Buckingham Palace, and enshrining the memory of Victoria, the memorial's planners inscribed the monarchy in a new way onto the landscape of London. In its representation of the Queen as a triumphant empress the memorial enshrined a vision of an imperially styled monarch. Yet while the statue of the Queen, the processional way and the triumphal arch gestured to imperial power, the significance of the colonies themselves was barely acknowledged in the design, despite their substantial financial contribution. Indeed, the final shape of the memorial suggests an oddly tenuous relationship between the creation of imperial space and the representation of the empire itself.

1901: commemorating the Queen and changing London

In retrospect, it seems inevitable that Queen Victoria should have been memorialised after her death in 1901. The building of monuments was a favoured means of celebrating national figures during the nineteenth century, and this fondness for permanent memorials did not abate with the dawn of the new century.[2] Military heroes, writers, philanthropists and politicians all had their statues, so it is not surprising that after her death attention quickly turned towards commemorating the Queen. Indeed, the national memorial in London was only one of many; after Victoria's death over thirty statues were erected throughout Britain.[3]

The interest in memorials to the late Queen was heightened by her unique position in turn-of-the-century British culture. She had become a ubiquitous and beloved figure, and following her death many people expressed a sense of personal loss. Moreover, Victoria's long reign was often associated by her contemporaries with stability, progress and imperial growth. One observer remarked that the news of her death 'fell upon the whole nation like a thunderclap'.[4] For many men and women, especially elites, Victoria's death seemed to heighten the anxieties occasioned by growing international competition, fears of national decline, and the war in South Africa. Lord Esher was not alone when he wrote after the Queen's funeral, 'So ends the reign of the Queen – now I feel for the first time that the new regime, so full of anxieties for England, has begun.'[5]

While the significance of the Queen's death and the affection people felt for her all but ensured her formal commemoration, other concerns affected the ultimate shape of the London memorial. Shortly after her death the new King appointed a non-partisan committee to begin organising a memorial.[6] The committee met in February 1901 and decided on the general principles that the memorial should be in London and that it should be 'monumental in character'.[7] With this decision the committee rejected suggestions from the public and some of the press that a philanthropic fund or institution should be established as a memorial.[8] Structural memorials, they argued, were 'the only things that last'.[9]

Responsibility for drawing up a plan for a such a memorial was delegated to a small executive committee, which included an architect, a sculptor, the Lord Mayor, a representative of the King, and Lord Esher, Secretary of the Office of Works.[10] The committee considered sites near Westminster as well as the area in front of Buckingham Palace, quickly settling on the latter. In March, after consulting the Office of Works and the King, the committee presented its plan for a memorial comprising both a monument to Victoria and the redesign of the Mall.[11] To proceed, they divided the project into sculptural and architectural components. The sculptural component, consisting of a monument to the Queen in front of the palace, was placed in the hands of Thomas Brock, who had executed several statues of Victoria. The committee decided to hold a limited competition between five architects to select the final design for the space around the monument, the Mall and the entry into Charing Cross.[12] In July they announced their selection of Sir Aston Webb's entry.[13] Webb's plan involved the widening of the main carriageway through the Mall, the creation of circular 'place' at the Charing Cross end, and a semicircular enclosure in front of the palace (Figure 2).

It is unclear who first put forward the redesign of the Mall as a suitable memorial for Victoria. Lord Esher claimed credit, and probably played a pivotal role.[14] Further elaboration of the idea was provided by the Office of Works.[15] Nevertheless, it was not an entirely original idea. As soon as the Memorial Committee announced its intention to locate a monument in London, *The Times* suggested that the Mall 'might be developed in a truly regal and Imperial manner'.[16] Indeed, in choosing this project, the committee was attaching the memory of the Queen to a long-advocated city improvement.[17] The Mall's history stretched back to the seventeenth century, when it had replaced Pall Mall as the favoured place for royal and aristocratic recreation.[18] Evolving into a tree-lined boulevard popular for promenading, it ended unassumingly at Spring Gardens. By making an opening into Charing Cross, advocates believed, they could substantially relieve traffic in Pall Mall and even Piccadilly.[19] Such a change would also provide an outlet from

Figure 2 Aston Webb's plan for the Queen Victoria Memorial and reconstruction of the Mall. *The Builder*, 2 November 1901

Trafalgar Square, a move which was advocated by the Royal Institute of British Architects in 1897.[20] Opening up the Mall had aesthetic implications as well as practical advantages. Also writing in 1897, the editor of *The Builder*, H. H. Statham, noted that opening the Mall into Charing Cross would bring 'the vista of the long avenue of trees into connection with one of the most crowded corners of London'. But Statham also noted pessimistically that improvement of the Mall was an idea 'still being talked about and nothing done'.[21] The popular support for a memorial to Victoria finally provided an opportunity to accomplish this project, using public subscriptions to do so.

The decision to incorporate a redesigned Mall within the Victoria Memorial was made in the context of wider concerns over planning and architecture. To many critics, London seemed to fall short of what a great city should be. There were ongoing fears that the metropolis's increasing traffic and crowding would lead to paralysis.[22] In addition, there was increasing embarrassment over the metropolis's 'dowdiness and disorder'.[23] This dissatisfaction grew in tandem with admiration for the wide avenues and grand government buildings of Continental cities, such as Rome, Paris and Vienna. Although the city had its defenders, it seemed to many Londoners that, in an era of growing international competition, their city was losing ground to Continental cities.[24] In H. H. Statham's opinion, the metropolis was almost 'entirely devoid of the qualities of spaciousness and stateliness'. Without these qualities, London was 'not so much like a capital city as like a very large and overgrown provincial town'.[25]

In the last decades of the nineteenth century shifts in government policy facilitated some architectural improvement of the city.[26] In 1888 the metropolis's first municipal government, the London County Council, was inaugurated and undertook a handful of major projects.[27] Then, in the 1890s, a 'flourishing treasury' combined with a strong Ministry prompted the government to embark on an extensive building programme.[28] These efforts were shaped by a growing self-consciousness of London's imperial role. As M. H. Port suggests, the great buildings housing the machinery of government – including the War Office, the Admiralty and new Public Offices – were all designed during this period to reflect a renewed sense of imperial grandeur.[29] Even the new London County Council, which was driven largely by a progressive agenda, was also 'eager' to execute projects in an 'imperial spirit'.[30]

The sense of London as an imperial city was, however, a fluid concept. Indeed, it is hard to define just what contemporaries meant when they described London as 'imperial'. Certainly there was a growing consciousness that the city was the centre of a huge empire, and that its public architecture needed to reflect that role. At the same time, the 'imperial' concept was used to invoke less tangible qualities, which had to do less with London's role as capital than with its historic world position. The writer and Indian administrator Lepel Griffin suggested, for example, that a city's rank as 'imperial' depended primarily on its 'antiquity, and world interest, and the fact of being today, or having been in the past, the centre of national, intellectual, political and social life'.[31] While London's imperial position was important, its boosters believed that the city had a significance beyond the empire. London after all was, according to *The Times* and many others, 'the greatest city of the world'.[32]

When the Victoria Memorial Committee embarked on its project in 1901, it provided one answer to the question of what imperial London should look like. The memorial was envisaged both as a central point in a vast empire and as lying squarely within a European context. Yet, while it was to be an imperial monument and space, the question of how to represent the empire proved problematic. The planning, eventual design and subsequent use of the memorial shed light on the various ways in which Edwardians imagined their imperial city.

The elements of an imperial space

Advocates of the Victoria Memorial regarded it first and foremost as embodying the qualities which they admired in Continental cities, especially Paris. Prime Minister Arthur Balfour, who sat on the organising committee, hoped that instead of 'a mere monument to the Queen' the committee could effect 'some great architectural and scenic change'. Balfour described the chosen plan as 'of a kind of which other nations have shown examples, which we may well imitate and easily surpass'.[33] Supporters in the press looked to the avenues of Paris as the ideal to which the redesigned Mall should aspire. The *Daily Mail* wrote that 'by these designs London has at last an opportunity of creating a noble thoroughfare almost Parisian in its depth and beauty'.[34] More confidently, the *Pall Mall Gazette* predicted that, once finished, the Mall 'will have no reason to fear comparison with the Champs Elysées'.[35]

For architectural critics the lack of vistas was one of London's key problems. Commentators hoped that the memorial would 'stand where it can be seen from a distance'.[36] Although London possessed imposing buildings, it was often noted that there were no impressive approaches to them. Art critic M. H. Spielmann complained, 'we approach buildings sideways ... you cannot drive straight up to the ... Mansion House, to the Bank'. He praised Aston Webb's winning submission for 'bringing a fine road straight up to the great feature to be viewed'.[37]

This desire for grand vistas reflects the value that nineteenth-century European elites had long placed on the theatricality of their metropolises. In her examination of Regency London, Deborah Nord suggests that urban improvements resulted in 'not only a more easily navigable city but a city more easily viewed as an enormous stage'.[38] At the end of the century the association of London and spectacle still flourished, albeit in new forms. Lavish spectacle thrived in theatres across London, in the West End's new commercial spaces and in the streets themselves, with events like the Diamond Jubilee.[39] Like Regent Street and the Parisian boulevards, the Mall was in part conceived of as a stage, one on which the power of the British empire could be displayed for mass spectatorship, and indeed the whole world. [40]

While the redesigned Mall would give London a space comparable to the avenues of European capitals, planners hoped that the central monument would rectify another of London's defects. Great cities, they implied, must physically embody their history. Yet London, despite dozens of statues, lacked the sort of impressive architectural memorials found on the Continent. 'No metropolis in Europe,' one writer complained, 'is so poverty-stricken in the matter of ... impressive monuments as the centre of the British empire.'[41] Speaking in favour of the Victoria Memorial, William Harcourt noted that 'though this nation has not been poor in great characters, it has not been distinguished in the manner in which it has commemorated them.' He continued that he 'hardly [knew] of one even in this great metropolis – the greatest City in the world – which is deserving either of the greatness of the Empire or the greatness of this City'.[42] There were exceptions to this, most notably the Albert Memorial in Hyde Park and Nelson's Column in Trafalgar Square.[43] But, for inspiration, commentators and advocates looked again to the Continent. Amid doubts that British sculpture was up to the task, the memorial committee even hinted, in vain, that the sculptor Thomas Brock might travel to see the 'great examples of monumental sculpture of Europe'.[44] In the press grandiose European memorials, such as those to Frederick in Germany and Catherine the Great in Russia, were discussed as possible models.[45] M. H. Spielmann suggested that inspiration could be found in the memorial to Vittorio Emanuele II under construction in Rome, 'the most noteworthy of all modern monuments'. [46]

The inscription of national and imperial history onto the urban landscape was intended to involve more than a monument to the Queen. There was some thought in the planning stages that the Mall might be a suitable site for a large number of statues, and various subjects were proposed. One of the architects competing for the commission, Rowan Anderson, included statues of Queen Elizabeth, William the Conqueror and King Alfred in his plan.[47] Another architect suggested statues up and down the length of the Mall.[48] Eventually the committee decided that extra statuary should depict the expanse of Britain's empire. There were to be four groups in the Mall, one each representing India, Africa, Canada and Australia. Together these would be a visible representation of the empire in the city's centre.[49] This decision was significant because it was an attempt to relate the memorial specifically to Britain's imperial possessions. As one advocate argued, the 'Empire must have a capital, and all citizens whether they belonged to the United Kingdom, to India, or to the colonies ... ought to be proud of that capital, and try and ensure that it had monuments in it of that which was great and memorable in the history of the Empire.' [50]

Among those involved with the memorial, the Colonial Secretary, Joseph Chamberlain, perhaps felt most strongly the need for some physical expression of imperial unity. Chamberlain, the pre-eminent advocate of imperial federation, had first proposed a memorial which would consist of a group of chapels, each built by a different colony.[51] Although his idea was rejected, Chamberlain remained a vocal supporter of the memorial. Speaking at a memorial meeting, he emphasised 'the extraordinary, the unparalleled position which Queen Victoria occupied in ... the Empire.' It was 'impossible', Chamberlain claimed, 'to overestimate the influence which was exerted by the character and the personality of the Queen in securing the unity of the Empire'. [52]

Chamberlain's assertion of the importance of the Queen for imperial unity underscored a significant aspect both of the memorial plan and of the imagined contours of imperial London. In several ways the planners of the memorial attempted to enshrine a particular vision of the monarchy. In location, purpose and design the memorial reified a ceremonial monarch at the heart of the empire. By opening the Mall into Charing Cross, by widening it, and by embellishing it architecturally, the Memorial Committee transformed what had been a fashionable promenade into a regal procession route. Moreover, in choosing to locate the memorial at Buckingham Palace, the committee elevated the importance of the London residence of the monarch. The palace itself had little historical importance, dating back only to George III, who had built it as a private residence. In the 1820s George IV had ordered it to be rebuilt, but Victoria had been the first monarch actually to live in the new palace. Even after reconstruction the palace was widely criticised. *The Times* referred to it as the 'shabbiest Royal

Palace in Europe'.[53] The Queen herself had never especially liked the palace, far preferring to spend time at Windsor, Osborne House or Balmoral. Yet the Victoria Memorial Committee gave the palace greater prominence, remaking it as a focal point for the metropolis and connecting it symbolically with Trafalgar Square and Whitehall.

The Memorial Committee also designated a new purpose for the Mall and the palace. The success of the great ceremonial events in the latter part of Victoria's reign – especially her two jubilees – had convinced officials and royals not only that such grand ceremonies were popular but also that they could be used to celebrate the imperial idea. Bringing troops from each part of the empire together for the first time, the Diamond Jubilee seemed to many to have been a triumphant expression of imperial unity. Yet London was ill prepared for such massive demonstrations. Its narrow streets provided neither adequate room for crowds of spectators nor a grand setting for spectacle.[54] Lord Esher, secretary of the Memorial Committee, would have been keenly aware of this fact, since he had participated in planning the London celebrations of the Diamond Jubilee.[55] In addition, both he and King Edward, who took an active interest in the memorial, had great appreciation of ceremonial spectacle. June 1897 loomed large in the minds of many others as they remembered the Queen in 1901. In the climate of anxiety occasioned by – among other things – the South African War, the memory of the Diamond Jubilee seemed especially poignant. One writer compared 'the "tumult" and the "shouting"' of 1897 with 1901's 'war and khaki, sickness, wounds and death'.[56] It was in this context that the committee conceived of the new Mall and its monumental centrepiece as both a stage and a backdrop to further grand performances.

As the memorial's creators enshrined the memory of the Diamond Jubilee, they also shaped the memory of Victoria to reflect a particular vision of empire. Throughout the last years of her life the Queen was repeatedly depicted in two idealised images.[57] The first was of a resplendent monarch, shown in allegorical drawings and staged spectacles of grandeur. In the year of the Diamond Jubilee this Victoria was often the centre of an imagined scene of imperial unity in which colonial soldiers paid tribute to the throne. A second, more common image, however, portrayed Victoria as humble, kindly and maternal. This motherly queen was celebrated in poetry and popular biography, and in countless illustrations and advertisements which showed the Queen comforting her subjects or enjoying domestic pleasures. Both images of the Queen were equally idealised: in the latter, her compassion was exaggerated to superhuman proportions, while the former image bore little if any resemblance to the small woman who in reality eschewed the trappings of royalty.

Both the regal and the domestic Victoria found their way into Thomas Brock's statuary. Dominating the memorial was a huge and regal empress-queen who stared sternly down the length of the Mall. But behind and at the sides of this figure were three allegorical arrangements intended to represent 'those qualities which made our Queen so ... much beloved.'[58] At the sides, mythical winged women represented Truth and Justice, while at the back a young, seated woman with children at her knees and an infant in her arms represented Motherhood (Figure 3). Allusions to Truth and Justice were common in public statuary, but the figure of Motherhood was more unusual, and was found in only a handful of monuments, including those dedicated to Victoria in Manchester and Sheffield. By including this figure in the London memorial Brock imported a sentimental, domestic scene into an imperial space. While it alluded directly to Victoria's alleged nature and 'great love for her people', it also served a wider purpose.[59] For late Victorians and Edwardians, ideas about motherhood were central to ideas about imperial strength.[60] Moreover, the image of the Queen as motherly ruler was one which imperialists often used to naturalise the empire by describing it as a family.

Just as the figure of Motherhood was idealised, so was the figure of Victoria on the front of the monument. The manner in which this was done was not pleasing to all eyes.[61] George Bernard Shaw, for example,

Figure 3 'Motherhood', detail from the Queen Victoria Memorial, London, Thomas Brock

complained that the Queen was 'represented as an overgrown monster'.[62] But for the sculptors who executed public memorials to the Queen a 'literal personal resemblance' was less important than the overall effect.[63] Like Brock, George Frampton had portrayed Victoria several times. He believed that a 'statue of the Queen should be ... a symbol of her exalted position, and of the greatness of the realm over which she ruled'.[64] By changing her proportions, and making her appear regal, sculptors like Brock and Frampton gave body to a vision of imperial grandeur. On Brock's memorial, symbolic ornamentation heightened the impact. Mermaids, tritons, and figures representing the navy, the army, Peace, Progress, Labour, Agriculture and Manufacture adorn the fountain and steps which surround the central monument. Towering over the arrangement is a gold figure of Victory. The effect of the whole memorial was to transform the diminutive and dowdy Queen into an empress triumphant.

The transformation of Victoria was further accentuated by the architectural style of the setting. Aston Webb's winning submission, as well as the other competition entries, reflected the ascendancy in the late 1890s of neoclassical styles for public buildings in Britain, such as the War Office and the new Public Offices.[65] Neoclassical styles were also used for major colonial buildings, including the Union Buildings in Pretoria, the Victoria Memorial in Calcutta and the buildings of New Delhi.[66] For these buildings, and for London's Victoria Memorial, classical forms evoked a connection with the Roman empire. As Thomas Metcalf explains in his study of imperial architecture, 'classical styles ... were the architectural medium through which Europeans always apprehended empire'.[67] Metcalf also notes, however, that it was equally important to British architects that their style should seem authentically national. To this end, Edwardian architects used baroque forms which harked back to Christopher Wren and his school.[68] In the Victoria Memorial, Webb used neoclassicism, drawing especially on baroque and eighteenth-century styles, to provide an ideal backdrop to the ceremonial enactments of empire.[69]

For its planners and its advocates the Victoria Memorial provided an opportunity to carve out an imperial space in the heart of London. Its salient features lay in its similarity to the avenues of the great Continental cities, its evocation of imperial grandeur, its theatricality and its reification of a ceremonial monarchy. Like a great stage set, the long processional route was styled with allusions to classical Rome and presided over by an imposing empress-queen. Depictions of the empire's different regions, which were imagined united in their devotion to her memory, were also intended. Yet, while planners had imagined an imperial space, the actual execution of their plans involved a less direct means of representing the empire. Nor did they foresee what the real focal point of the space would become.

1911: the monument unveiled

The main components of the Victoria Memorial were completed in only ten years. Edward, who had been an active proponent of the project, did not live to see its completion in 1911. Instead, the memorial was finished just in time to serve as a processional setting a month later at the coronation of George V. Meanwhile the metropolis also hosted a conference of colonial Premiers and, at the Crystal Palace, the 'Festival of Empire and Pageant of London'. [70]

The coronation of George V was, in many ways, the ideal event to launch the Victoria memorial as an imperial space. George, like Edward before him, embraced the pomp and ceremony which Victoria had disdained. Travelling in a gilded state carriage, the new King passed the great statue of Victoria and processed down the Mall on his way to and from Westminster Abbey. Participating in the procession were colonial troops and ornately uniformed Premiers. Observers declared the new Mall and monument a great success as the backdrop for the pageant of the coronation. The *Illustrated London News* highlighted the moment when George V passed by the statue of Victoria with an elaborate illustration captioned 'George the imperialist at the memorial to Victoria the Good' (Figure 4). [71]

It had been only a month since the central monument was unveiled amid similar pomp, but that event had a different emphasis. A large crowd heard the King speak of Victoria as the 'most honoured woman and beloved queen'. The monument, he asserted (reading a speech written for him by Esher), served 'to revive for us and convey to our descendants the lustre and fame which shine upon that happy age'. Voicing the hopes of the Memorial Committee, he depicted the memorial standing 'for ever ... to proclaim the glories of the reign of Queen Victoria, and to prove to future generations the sentiments of affection and reverence which Her People felt for Her and Her Memory'. [72] He then knighted Thomas Brock for his accomplishment.

The press, for the most part, praised both the statue and the King's words. *Lloyd's Newspaper* declared that the speech was a 'call to the nation ... a voice from the Queen who will never die in the affection of the English-speaking races, bidding us make our lives worthy of the high position to which we are called by divine providence'. [73] Both the King and the press also portrayed the memorial as truly imperial. It was, in the words of the *Illustrated London News*, 'a great imperial and national ideal wrought in marble'. [74] 'The Dominions and Colonies'

Figure 4 The coronation procession of King George V: 'George the imperialist at the memorial to Victoria the Good'. *Illustrated London News*, 1 July 1911

had, the King claimed, 'united to enshrine Her Memory; and this Monument represents races and regions more various than have been combined before upon a common purpose'.[75]

Despite the King's declaration, the colonies did not have a high profile either in the monument itself or at its unveiling. Although illustrations of the day echoed depictions of the Diamond Jubilee, the cast of players was very different (Figure 5). Neither colonial Premiers nor troops took part in the ceremony. Instead, the guest of honour was the Queen's grandson, Kaiser Wilhelm II. Indeed, in the context of tense relations between Britain and Germany, his presence in London was deemed the most newsworthy aspect of the day. Even an ardent supporter of the empire, who was visiting from Canada, reported that 'the most memorable incident ... was that of the placing of a wreath at Queen Victoria's feet by her grandson, Kaiser Wilhelm'.[76]

The focus on the Kaiser's attendance serves as a reminder that London's imperial spaces, and its imperial performances, were defined and understood within the context of Europe as well as of the empire. Moreover, the final form of the memorial suggests that the planners did not regard the details of the representation of the colonies as an integral part of marking imperial space. By the time the Victoria Memorial was completed, the committee and the architect, in fact, had

Figure 5   George V and Kaiser Wilhelm II unveiling the Queen Victoria Memorial, London. *The Graphic*, 20 May 1911

made significant changes to their original designs. The changes were in part related to funding problems, but they also reveal much about how the planners imagined imperial space in London.

Funding had been an important factor in planning the memorial from the outset. As with most memorials to Victoria, the committee chose to raise money from the public by subscription.[77] This method presented practical problems, since committees had to begin planning before knowing how much money they could spend. The Victoria

Memorial Committee dealt with the handicap by scaling down some of the architectural embellishment which Webb had proposed for the space around the monument. More significantly, they delayed the execution of some stages of the monument, in particular the groups of statuary on the Mall, by which Webb had proposed to represent the colonies.[78]

When the committee chose, early in the process, to build an imperial memorial to Victoria, they also decided that the empire should bear some of its cost. This was one way in which the committee distinguished the memorial as imperial rather than national; as representing, in the Prime Minister's words, the loyalty of 'the citizens of this great Empire, whose growth ... has so mightily expanded during the course of [Victoria's] reign'.[79] While the desire to include the colonies was no doubt genuine, the committee may have been motivated by the need to raise the large sums required to complete the plan. With this in mind, the planners pressed colonies to donate by announcing that any colony which did not contribute would not be represented on the memorial. Colonial governments responded by contributing about £130,000, nearly a third of the total cost of the memorial.[80]

Despite the substantial colonial contributions and, ultimately, a budget surplus, the colonies did not feature prominently on the monument itself. Initial plans called for groups of statuary on the Mall but specified few details. In the end, the colonies were represented either by urns or by cherubs carrying shields and national symbols, which surmount gateposts surrounding the monument.[81] These gateposts were the last portion of the monument to be completed, in 1924, and formed a small and inconspicuous part of the memorial layout. Moreover, a significant part of the empire was omitted entirely. As the Viceroy, Lord Curzon, had decided to build an Indian Victoria Memorial rather than contribute to the London fund, India was not directly represented on the memorial at all. This was a striking omission, given that the popular image of Victoria as mother of the empire prominently included India as one of her charges. Indeed, the figure of Victoria as mother-empress alluded to the presence of India among her 'children'. Yet the absence of India from the colonial iconography highlights the contradictions which emerged in this attempt at creating imperial space for an empire with little coherence.

While the representation of the colonies shrank to near invisibility in the finished memorial, in other ways the memorial as a whole became more imperial as building progressed. Among the many construction projects undertaken by the government in the last years of the nineteenth century were new offices to house the Admiralty. Beset with problems, this large project had advanced slowly. This fact was turned to the advantage of the Victoria Memorial when the planners arranged to include a great arch as part of the Admiralty offices. They had earlier discussed erecting an arch leading from the Mall into Charing Cross but had found it too expensive. By integrating an arch with the Admiralty buildings, the memorial's planners found a way to have the government pay for it.[82]

The Admiralty Arch, which was also designed by Aston Webb, further added to the sense of the Mall as a processional route. Echoing other triumphal arches, such as the Arc de Triomphe in Paris, it formed a grand entry into the redesigned Mall. Looking from Buckingham Palace, it provided a visual endpoint to the long avenue. The concept of the arch, combined with Webb's use of neoclassicism, prompted *The Builder* to praise the project as 'essentially Roman'.[83] The connection with the ancient empire was underscored by a Latin inscription dedicating the arch to Victoria's memory. As with the monumental sculpture at the far end of the Mall, the arch, adorned with figures representing Gunnery and Navigation, cast Victoria in the role of triumphal empress-queen.[84]

For some observers the Victoria Memorial seemed like the first step towards the remaking of London as the capital city of a new imperial federation. Encouraged both by George V's coronation and the belief that the empire was 'inevitably tending' towards federation, *The Builder* published a plan for 'Imperial London' in January 1912. This plan called for the development of an Imperial Quarter comprising a new imperial parliament, palace and processional way. The Victoria Memorial was to be pivotal, with avenues radiating out from it, and the Mall forming the 'principal approach' to a new imperial palace.[85] Of course, neither imperial federation nor the rebuilding of London took place. Nor did the Mall become the prime location for memorials which some of its planners had envisioned. A few monuments with imperial significance were placed in close proximity to the Admiralty Arch. A statue of Captain Cook sponsored by the British Empire League was unveiled in 1914, and memorials to those killed fighting in South Africa and China were erected by the Royal Marines and the Royal Artillery.[86] But in the wake of the First World War, the major memorials to the nation's dead were located in Whitehall or at Hyde Park Corner rather than the Mall.

One last addition to the Victoria Memorial was made in 1913 when the facade of Buckingham Palace was reconstructed. Throughout the planning stages, and after completion of the memorial, many observers commented upon the architectural inadequacy of the palace. With surplus funds, the Memorial Committee commissioned Aston Webb to design a new facade, which he executed in the same style as the Admiralty Arch. Although advocated by *The Builder*, this change foreshadowed a different focus to the Mall than the one they, or the planners, envisaged. Once imagined as a backdrop to the memorial, the palace itself became the focus of attention.

Significantly, King George V insisted that the new facade should leave the central balcony open to public view.[87] It had been from this balcony that he had waved to the crowds on his coronation day. Rather than a mere backdrop, the palace balcony became the stage on which the King and Queen appeared at moments of national crisis and celebration, most notably the eve and end of the First World War. For these events the nation – rather than the empire – was represented by huge crowds which filled the area around the monument to Victoria. Although the growing symbolic importance of the palace and its balcony did not entirely overshadow the Mall, which remained the route of royal processions to and from Westminster, the connection of the whole project with Victoria's memory was largely forgotten. Moreover, the central monument to the Queen faded into a kind of prominent obscurity. While still embodying imperial glory, it came to serve chiefly as a vantage point from which to peer into the domestic abode of the late twentieth-century monarchy.

Notes

I would like to thank Erika Rappaport, Maureen McCarthy, Paul Deslandes, and Felix Driver for their very helpful suggestions on this chapter, and John Gillis for his support and assistance.

1 *Art Journal*, quoted in Elizabeth Darby and Michael Darby, 'The nation's memorial to Victoria,' *Country Life*, 16 November 1978, p. 1648.

2 See Benedict Read, *Victorian Sculpture* (New Haven CT, Yale University Press, 1982); Alison Yarrington, *The Commemoration of the Hero, 1800–64: Monuments to the British Victors of the Napoleonic Wars* (New York, Garland, 1988); Rodney Mace, *Trafalgar Square: Emblem of Empire* (London, Lawrence & Wishart, 1976).

3 See Elisabeth Susan Darby, 'Statues of Queen Victoria and Prince Albert: A Study in Commemorative and Portrait Statuary', Ph.D. dissertation, Courtauld Institute of Art, University of London, 1983; Victoria R. Smith, 'Constructing Victoria: The Representation of Queen Victoria in England, India and Canada, 1897–1914', Ph.D. dissertation, Rutgers University, 1998.

4 Selina (Lady) Southwark, *Social and Political Reminiscences* (London, Williams & Norgate, 1913), p. 283.

5 Esher to his son, *Journals and Letters*, in Maurice Brett (ed.), *Journals and Letters of Reginald Viscount Esher* (London, Nicholson & Watson, 1923), p. 278.

6 The committee members included the Marquess of Salisbury (chairman), Aretas Akers-Douglas (First Commissioner of Works), A. J. Balfour, Lord Balfour of Burleigh, Joseph Chamberlain, Sir Henry Fowler, Lord George Hamilton, Earl Cadogan, the Earl of Kimberley, the Earl of Rosebery and the Lord Mayor of London. Arthur Bigge was originally the secretary, but he resigned and was replaced by Lord Esher, secretary of the Office of Works.

7   *The Times*, 28 February 1901, p. 9.
8   Many members of the public and some members of the press advocated memorials which would reflect the Queen's compassionate character. The *Pall Mall Gazette*, for example, argued that a philanthropic memorial would symbolise Victoria's 'love for and interest in the people' (12 February 1901, p. 2).
9   A. J. Balfour, memorial meeting reported in *The Times*, 27 March 1901, p. 8.
10 Besides Esher the committee members were Lord Windsor, Lord Redesdale, Edward Poynter, William Emerson, Sidney Colvin and Arthur Ellis.
11 The King was reported to have visited several possible sites (*Pall Mall Gazette*, 5 March 1901, p. 2). The plan was approved by the full committee on March 19 (*The Times*, 20 March 1901, p. 9).
12 The press, architects, and sculptors criticised the limited nature of the competition: see Darby and Darby, 'The nation's memorial', p. 1647.
13 *The Times*, 27 July 1901, p. 14
14 Esher, letter to his son, 26 February 1901, *Journals*, p. 287.
15 A draughtsman, Richard Allison, drew up plans: M. H. Port, *Imperial London: Civil Government Building in London, 1850–1915* (New Haven CT, Yale University Press, 1995), p. 24.
16 *The Times*, 28 February 1901, p. 9. The *Pall Mall Gazette* concurred, favouring the Mall over some 'remote corner' near the House of Lords.
17 In the 1850s Albert had advocated some sort of route through St James's Park to meet the needs of the growing population in the area: Port, *Imperial London*, p. 20.
18 Steen Eiler Rasmussen, *London: The Unique City* (London, Jonathan Cape, 1937), p. 95.
19 *The Times*, 27 July 1901, p. 14.
20 Port discusses their proposal, which focused on opening the square into Whitehall: *Imperial London*, pp. 22–3.
21 H. H. Statham, 'London as a jubilee city', *National Review*, 29 (1897) 594–603 (quote from p. 599).
22 James Winter, *London's Teeming Streets, 1830–1914* (London, Routledge, 1993).
23 *Ibid.*, p. 20. Port notes that London's architectural journals began advocating more Parisian-style planning in the 1860s: *Imperial London*, p. 13. See also Donald J. Olsen, *The Growth of Victorian Cities* (New York, Holmes & Meier, 1976).
24 Lepel Griffin, 'An imperial city', *Pall Mall Magazine*, 1 (1893) 656–68.
25 Statham, 'London as a jubilee city', p. 595, quoted in Felix Driver and David Gilbert, 'Heart of empire? Landscape, space, and performance in imperial London', *Environment and Planning D: Society and Space*, 16 (1998) 11–28 (quote on p. 16).
26 An early project was the Thames embankment, completed in 1870: Port, *Imperial London*, p. 13; Winter, *London's Teeming Streets*, pp. 27–33.
27 See Susan Pennybacker, *A Vision for London, 1889–1914: Labour, Everyday Life and the LCC Experiment* (London, Routledge, 1995).
28 Port, *Imperial London*, p. 16.
29 *Ibid.*, pp. 2–3, 233–51.
30 Frederic Harrison, quoted in Driver and Gilbert, 'Heart of empire?', p. 20.
31 Griffin, 'An imperial city', p. 657.
32 *The Times*, 23 June 1897, p. 9.
33 *Ibid.*, 27 March 1901, p. 8.
34 *Daily Mail*, 28 March 1901, p. 1.
35 *Pall Mall Gazette*, 23 August 1904, clipping. Public Record Office, London, Work 20/20.
36 *Ibid.*, 5 March 1901, p. 2.
37 M. H. Spielmann, 'On the Queen Victoria Memorial', *Royal Institute of Great Britain Proceedings*, 17 (13 May 1904) 540–6 (quote from p. 542).
38 Deborah Epstein Nord, 'The city as theater: from Georgian to early Victorian London', *Victorian Studies*, 31:2 (1988) 159–88 (quote from p. 165). While the planners of the Victoria Memorial looked to Paris for inspiration, the redesigners of Paris had emulated the development of Regent Street.

39 Asa Briggs notes that theatrical spectacle became more lavish towards the end of the century: *Victorian Things* (London, Batsford, 1988), p. 104. See also Michael Booth, *Victorian Spectacular Theatre, 1850–1910* (Boston MA, Routledge, 1981), p. 3. On the West End see Erika Rappaport, *Shopping for Pleasure: Gender, Commerce and Public Life in London's West End, 1860–1914* (Princeton NJ, Princeton University Press, forthcoming).

40 See Tori Smith, '"Almost pathetic ... but also very glorious": the consumer spectacle of the Diamond Jubilee', *Histoire Sociale/Social History*, 24:58 (1997) 333–56.

41 *Daily Mail*, 28 March 1901, p. 7.

42 Memorial meeting reported in *The Times*, 27 March 1901, p. 8.

43 On Nelson's Column see Mace, *Trafalgar Square*.

44 *The Times*, 15 May 1911, p. 10.

45 *Daily Mail*, 8 February 1901, p. 7.

46 Spielmann, 'On the Queen Victoria Memorial', p. 541. On the Italian monument itself see Chapter 3 of this volume.

47 *The Times*, 31 October 1901, p. 8.

48 *The Builder*, 2 November 1901, p. 377.

49 This plan was reminiscent of the figures on the Albert Memorial, which represented not merely the empire but the whole world: see Stephen Bayley, *The Albert Memorial: The Monument in its Social and Architectural Context* (London, Scolar, 1981).

50 Duke of Devonshire, Westminster memorial meeting, reported in *The Times*, 27 April 1901, p. 10.

51 'The national memorial to the Queen', *Review of Reviews*, 23 (1901) 245–51 (quote from p. 247).

52 *The Times*, 27 March 1901, p. 8.

53 *Ibid.*, 31 October 1901, p. 8.

54 David Cannadine notes this in 'The context, performance and meaning of ritual: the British monarchy and the "invention of tradition", *c.* 1820–1977', in Eric Hobsbawm and Terence Ranger (eds), *The Invention of Tradition* (Cambridge, Cambridge University Press, 1983), p. 128.

55 For assessments of Esher's role in the Diamond Jubilee see Jeffrey Lant, *Insubstantial Pageant: Ceremony and Confusion at the Court of Queen Victoria* (London, Hamish Hamilton, 1979), pp. 224–5; Smith, 'Constructing Victoria', p. 27.

56 Anon., *Our Queen in Memoriam* (London, Marshall, 1901), Collection of Elegies, etc., 1901, British Library.

57 On images of the Queen see Smith, 'Constructing Victoria'; Dorothy Thompson, *Queen Victoria: Gender and Power* (London, Virago, 1990); Adrienne Munich, *Queen Victoria's Secrets* (New York, Columbia University Press, 1996).

58 Statement by Thomas Brock, *The Times*, 15 May 1911, p. 10.

59 *Ibid.*

60 Anna Davin, 'Imperialism and motherhood', *History Workshop Journal*, 5 (1978) 9–65; Pat Thane, 'Late Victorian Englishwomen', in T. R. Gourvish and Alan O'Day, (eds), *Later Victorian Britain, 1867–1900* (London, Macmillan, 1988), p. 183.

61 *The Times*, 17 May 1911, p. 12.

62 Quoted in Stanley Weintraub, *Victoria: An Intimate Biography* (New York, Dutton, 1988), pp. 641–2.

63 Meeting of the General Committee, 12 February 1903, *Queen Victoria Memorial Minute Book*, Atkinson Library, Southport, Lancashire.

64 *Ibid.*

65 Port, *Imperial London*, passim.

66 Thomas R. Metcalf, *An Imperial Vision* (Berkeley CA, University of California Press, 1989), pp. 177–80.

67 *Ibid.*, pp. 178–9.

68 *Ibid.*, p. 179.

69 Richard Fellows notes that although Webb had control over each element of the Victoria Memorial, the style changed from baroque in the work first completed, around the monument itself, to a more restrained eighteenth-century style for the arch and

the refronting of the palace: see *Edwardian Architecture: Style and Technology* (London, Lund Humphries, 1995), pp. 34–5.

70 See Chapter 7 of this volume.

71 *Illustrated London News*, 1 July 1911, pp. 6–7.

72 Queen Victoria Memorial Committee, *Queen Victoria Memorial Report, 1901–11*, p. 7.

73 *Lloyd's Newspaper*, 21 May 1911.

74 *Illustrated London News*, 20 May 1911, p. 735.

75 *Queen Victoria Memorial Report*, p. 6.

76 Edith Nordheimer, President of the Imperial Order of the Daughters of the Empire, *Echoes*, June 1911, p. 17. Public Archives of Canada.

77 Thousands of individuals and businesses made donations which totalled nearly £200,000. Account Books, Queen Victoria Memorial Fund, Corporation of London Record Office.

78 Esher to Lord Knollys, *Journals*, p. 302.

79 *Ibid.*, 27 March 1901, p. 8.

80 The largest amounts came from the settler colonies. Canada, for instance, gave £30,000, while the Cape Colony donated £20,000. Statement of Account, Queen Victoria Memorial Fund, Corporation of London Record Office.

81 *Queen Victoria Memorial Report*, p. 6.

82 The practical function of the arch was threatened by a disagreement over who should fund the creation of an access route to Trafalgar Square. Only three months before the coronation the LCC, Westminster City Council and the Office of Public Works agreed to share the cost: *The Times*, 10 April 1911, p. 6.

83 *The Builder*, 29 April 1905, p. 456.

84 Webb's original design included the possibility of monumental sculpture surmounting the arch. However, this idea seems to have been discarded. See perspective drawing, Darby and Darby, 'The nation's memorial', p. 1648.

85 *The Builder*, 5 January 1911, pp. 11–12.

86 The Royal Marines memorial erected in 1903 antedates the Admiralty Arch; the Royal Artillery memorial at the north-east corner of St James's Park was erected in 1910.

87 Port, *Imperial London*, p. 250.

CHAPTER THREE

Empire in modern Rome: shaping and remembering an imperial city, 1870–1911

David Atkinson, Denis Cosgrove and Anna Notaro

In his 1930 essay 'Civilisation and its discontents', Sigmund Freud contrasted the human mind with the city of Rome. In the Eternal City, he wrote, the 'remains of ancient Rome are found dovetailed into the jumble of a great metropolis which has grown up in the last few centuries since the Renaissance. This is the manner in which the past is preserved in [such] historical sites ...'.[1] Unlike the human mind, which in Freud's view almost inevitably functioned as a repository of multiple memories and past identities, a city could sustain a series of historical identities, or 'historical sequences', only in adjacent spaces: 'the same space cannot have two different [historical] contents'.[2] In this chapter we suggest otherwise. Our focus is on various attempts by successive Italian governments from 1870 until 1911 to articulate the imperial identities of antiquity together with the contemporary imperial pretensions of the modern Italian kingdom in the reworked landscapes of central Rome. We argue that the making of modern Rome was informed and shaped to a significant degree by this dual imperative to celebrate – in the same spaces – an Italian imperialism at once ancient and modern. The unique status of Rome as both a glorious capital city in antiquity and the new capital of modern Italy with its colonial empire meant that Italian efforts to invoke the memory of classical Rome involved not only metaphorical allusion but also the literal excavation and replanning of the extant remains of ancient Rome in the service of a contemporary imperialism.

Whilst doubting Freud's claim that urban spaces are incapable of hosting plural and multiple histories and identities, we accept his point that tensions inevitably arise in any efforts to realise such a juxtaposition. It is the various attempts to express this dual identity through the landscapes of Rome from 1870 to 1911, and, more briefly, their incorporation into public performance and ritual, that concern us in this chapter. We consider the development of a national architectural style, the creation (from 1882) of a national monument at the centre of Rome and the imperial claims that were made through its positioning and decoration, and, briefly, the 1911 celebrations of the fiftieth anniversary of the modern Italian state. We situate these examples within the wider context of the cultural history of 'Liberal Italy' (1861-1922) and its nation-making project prior to the Fascist period. We argue that ideas of empire and *romanità* (the Roman Spirit) were crucial and continuing elements of Italian efforts to frame a new and national identity from the late nineteenth century, and that these ideas inevitably found expression in the urban fabric of the Eternal City.

Memories of empire and imperial cities

Historically, the classical world has exercised an enormous influence over the cultures of European and 'Western' societies.[3] From the seventeenth century the 'Grand Tour' which culminated in Rome became well established as the most fitting conclusion to the education of European elite society.[4] Classical scholarship frequently enjoyed government favour, while classical literature, philosophy and languages occupied as much as 80 per cent of lesson time in the public schools of mid-nineteenth century England.[5] For many emerging imperial powers, ancient Rome provided a yardstick against which they might measure themselves and their own civilisation. Even the early history of nations which were not wholly subsumed within the Roman empire (including Germany) was outlined by reference to their struggles against Rome.[6] Moreover, from the earliest French and American revolutionary attempts to construct a modern territorial state, the memory of ancient Rome was invoked to legitimate republicanism and, later, a new imperialism. Although the material remains of classical Rome comprised, by the eighteenth and nineteenth centuries, little more than a few surviving buildings and a series of archaeological ruins and artefacts, in terms of memory and culture Rome was to be found everywhere.

The cultural significance of classical Rome to 'Western' societies found visible and lasting expression in the landscapes of nineteenth-century European and North American capital cities. Towards the close of the nineteenth century, in particular, Beaux Arts architecture became a key international style for major national monuments, monumental statuary, and public buildings and institutions.[7] In its decorative motif and iconography this style made constant reference to Augustan Rome and its public rhetoric of empire. Much of the styling of public statuary, notably the figure of the heroic equestrian, was derived from Roman precedents, while architectural structures emphasised gigantism in the scale of their columns, pediments, barrel vaults and triumphal arches, all combined within the parameters of the Corinthian and Composite classical orders.[8] Usually constructed of marble or white limestone, they were frequently decorated with friezes, mosaics and a muscular statuary consciously echoing the structures and motifs of first and second-century Rome.

In the United States, for example, the early twentieth-century reconstruction of central Washington DC abandoned the republican style of the Jeffersonian city for grander, more imperial forms, consistently and explicitly referencing memories of ancient Rome.[9] The main concourse of Union Station at Columbus Circle supports an immense coffered vault, while the station facade adopts the iconography of a Roman triumphal arch, inscribed with texts celebrating the progress of modern power over space and nature. Elsewhere, the neoclassical temple on the Mall which commemorates Abraham Lincoln flanks the seated hero with two *lictor fasces*, symbols of Roman authority that now signalled America's guardianship of the classical tradition.[10] At the Mall's eastern end, America's own 'Capitol' hill overlooks the federal capital. The French too had inscribed key icons of their post-revolutionary capital with Roman imperial motifs. From the Arc de Triomphe commemorating the triumphs of Napoleon's Grande Armée and the Madeleine, through the styling of Garnier's Opéra of 1875, to the boulevards of the Second Empire, the intention was to demonstrate that republican, and later imperial, France was the natural heir to the glories of Rome. [11]

Non-republican powers also found in ancient Rome a model for their colonial aspirations and the design of their newly imperial capitals. In Budapest the central railway station (1884) replicated classical styling to announce the imperial status of the Austro-Hungarian Dual Monarchy. In Brussels the Place Royale celebrated the imperial status of the Belgians in the columnar structures of the museums and halls which surround its central equestrian statue. And while conjuring a global Pax Britannica as the modern equivalent of the ancient Pax Romana, the British redesigned and decorated key spaces of London with reference to classical Rome.[12] The ceremonial route of 1911 reaching from Admiralty Arch along the Mall to the Victoria Memorial and the refaced Buckingham Palace was designed to be the public axis of British imperialism, concretising its global reach in the allegorical statuary surrounding the seated figure of the *regina-imperatrix*, and alluding to Rome as an imperial precedent through the replication of Roman building forms and neoclassical architecture. In many respects, therefore, classical Rome remained an enduring influence upon the landscapes of practically all other major European capitals.

In marked contrast, for two-thirds of the nineteenth century Rome itself remained a relatively small and largely unmodernised city, dominated iconographically by the dated baroque architecture of seventeenth-century papal imperialism and boasting practically nothing of the commercial, bureaucratic, industrial or imperial significance of those cities that imitated the forms of its classical ruins.[13] When the five-year occupation by Napoleonic France ended in 1814, control of the city reverted to the Papacy and the city's long-established aristocratic families. Traditional Roman life continued as it had for centuries, supported largely by the income flowing into the Church, from land rents and from the agriculture of the hinterland, which was still organised along feudal lines. Social change was often resisted: Rome's Jews were still confined to a ghetto and subject to oppressive restrictions until 1870, while industrial development was discouraged by a conservative Papacy, nervous of the social changes which might accompany such innovation.[14] The Vatican continued to administer global Catholicism whilst other holy orders ministered to the pilgrim faithful. Hoteliers, restaurateurs, traders and beggars survived from the expenditure of these religious visitors and of other tourists drawn by the ruins, history, art and architecture of the city.[15] The landscapes of Rome saw little of the modernity or architectural interventions which transformed other major European cities and – ironically, given developments elsewhere in Europe – modern interpretations of ancient empire were virtually absent from its urban spaces.

This began to change with the incorporation of Rome into the Italian state in 1870. From 1859, nationalists had been gradually uniting the provinces and principalities of Italy, and the new nation state was proclaimed in 1861. The Risorgimento was complete when troops occupied the papal city on 20 September 1870 and Pope Pius IX retreated into the Vatican. This final part of the peninsula to be brought into the new kingdom was also the most symbolic. The cultural authority of Rome, the political centre of Italy in antiquity and heart of classical empire, ensured that it was the only realistic choice as national capital.[16] Within ten days of its capture, and with the recognition that parliament, monarchy, state administration and national institutions would have to relocate from Florence, a parliamentary commission of engineers and architects was established to consider 'the expansion and embellishment of the city'.[17] From the start, the new government recognised the crucial importance of remaking the papal city as a renewed, dignified, grand and Italian national capital.

Although various different strategies, issues, themes and ideas informed the debates and controversies which attended the remaking of Rome,[18] our particular focus lies in the fact that, for the next seventy

years, state and municipal urban policies, and the spectacles and performances enacted in various spaces and locations across Rome, make
insistent and conscious reference to the motifs and rhetoric of ancient
empire. Furthermore, central to this discourse was the idea of *romanità* (literally Romanness or the Roman spirit): the idea that the spirit
and potential of ancient Rome had been reborn and revived in the new
Italy, and that the state was the inheritor of classical Roman moral and
political virtues.[19] *Romanità* appealed particularly to romantic nationalists, and, from 1922 onwards, the term was enthusiastically
embraced by Italian Fascism. Romke Visser has argued that, for Mussolini's regime at least, the cult of *romanità* functioned as a coherent
cultural strategy developed in order to secure the support of Italy's educated middle and upper classes through the decade of consensus from
1926.[20]

However, the celebration of *romanità*, and the invocation of the
Roman empire in particular, was by no means confined solely to the
Fascist period (1922–43); indeed, it was clearly evident in the preceding
Liberal regime of post-Risorgimento Italy. For the young nation, the
idea of imperial Rome proved a useful common denominator in several
ways. It provided a rhetoric of shared historical legitimacy for a state
facing overt hostility from the Catholic Church and struggling to command the affections of citizens whose affiliations were traditionally
local and regional. It offered a glorious national heritage, a sense of
trans-historical unity, and suggested an essential 'Italianness' which
arched across the intervening centuries of so-called 'clerical decadence'. It was also a precedent for the centralised state, recalling the
prior unity of the peninsula's regions and cities under the authority of
Rome. And, finally, it hinted at longevity and cultural pre-eminence
for an Italy trying to establish its credibility amongst Europe's established nineteenth-century imperial powers. In the rhetoric of liberal
nationalism, the people – fired by historical example – would reject the
Papacy and their provincial identifications, and invest emotionally in
a new national project. In the rest of this chapter we consider some of
the ways in which this agenda was realised through the physical landscapes of Rome, and through the performance and spectacle which
marked the material spaces of the city. From 1870 the city that had
been the template for so many other 'imperial cities' was itself cast as
an imperial city reborn.

Liberal Italy: appropriating Rome

The 1870 commission, constituted to plan the new Rome, was charged
with creating a capital city for Italy which would be appropriately

grand, impressive, efficient and modern but which would also preserve, albeit selectively, the multiple layers of its long and illustrious
history. The imperial heritage of ancient Rome was a key element in
the infant state's attempts to design a national capital that could both
unify the nation and bear comparison with the capitals of other European powers. If this agenda appeared demanding in theory, the remaking of Rome was in practice dogged by numerous logistical problems,
financial crises, absence of consensus amongst the parties involved,
and the failure to agree a clear vision for the planned growth of the
city.[21]

The new government's most immediate problem was the so-called
'Roman question', which crystallised around Pius IX's refusal to recognise the incorporation of the papal city into Italy. A self-styled 'Pris-
oner of the Vatican', Pius periodically issued instructions banning
Catholics from participation in the civic life of the state.[22] This in turn
provoked an ever more stridently anticlerical response from the secular authorities. Widespread appropriation of Church properties in
Rome provided temporary space for the apparatus of government and a
new royal palace. In new residential and commercial quarters, streets
and bridges were named after the regions, rivers and cities of Italy.
Risorgimento battles and members of the royal family were commemorated. Such interventions were not uncontested: a mainly pro-clerical
city council and the Vatican itself frequently managed to intervene in
projects and alter plans, while the city's poor resented the decline of
benefits previously provided by ecclesiastical patronage and their
replacement with national taxes and conscription.[23] In the most
extreme instance, at the 1899 inauguration of the statue to Giordano
Bruno – the sixteenth-century 'heretic' burnt by the Church for his
advocacy of rational science – a pro-papal mob violently disrupted the
ceremonies in the Campo de' Fiori.[24] However, notwithstanding such
events, from the 1870s onwards the process had begun whereby the
city was gradually marked with the iconography of a secular, national,
Liberal state.[25]

The government's programme for a secular, modern Rome, a 'Third
Rome' that was distinct from those of the Caesars and the Popes, was
broadly entitled 'Roma-Capitale'. Although inevitably beset by problems and delays, the programme prompted a debate about the best
ways to manage and direct the growth of the city, and a series of master
plans in 1873, 1883 and 1909.[27] However, these plans were soon overtaken by circumstances. Following the transfer of government business to Rome in 1871, the legion of government deputies, bureaucrats
and national institutions that descended on the city soon outstripped
all available space. With the court, the diplomatic corps and the mili-

tary also seeking suitable new accommodation, the finances provided by the Italian state for Rome proved woefully insufficient to meet the cost of providing new infrastructure, residential quarters, government complexes and other national edifices. Development was inevitably piecemeal and largely unregulated, driven in large measure by speculative developers attracted by the demand for property, inadequate and poorly enforced building regulations and the failure to impose the strictures of the master-plans. Consequently, while the city expanded enormously in population and area from the 1870s until the financial slump of the late 1880s, weak government stymied broader visions of a modern, capital city.[28]

Yet, despite the failure to control the city's overall development, the fluctuating relations between successive Liberal governments and the city authorities nevertheless began to produce a set of public spaces, monuments and buildings through which the new kingdom succeeded in the limited but significant task of marking its possession of Rome at key sites in the urban fabric. Myths of empire and *romanità* played a significant role both in individual architectural schemes which made explicit or coded reference to the Roman empire, and in ceremonies and rituals which the Liberal state inaugurated in Rome. Moreover the Liberal state's attempts to recapture an ancient imperial identity were juxtaposed in the same city spaces with the monuments of modern Italy. Our principal examples in what follows are the emergence of a national architectural style; the national celebrations which accompanied the fiftieth anniversary of the Italian state in 1911; and, finally, the design and construction of the Vittorio Emanuele II monument on the Capitoline Hill. In each case, a key element of the design of these events and buildings is the notion of ancient empire, reborn in the present.

Building styles and building a nation

Architecture, planning and the 'national style'
In a heated parliamentary debate of 1881 concerning the funding of national architectural projects in Rome, future Prime Minister Francesco Crispi directly challenged those deputies sceptical of the 'ostentation' and expense of national, monumental building.[29] He claimed that 'Governments and institutions must not only concern themselves with the well-being of nations but also have the obligation to perpetuate themselves in marble and monuments'.[30] Three years later, he re-emphasised his point that the new Rome should both complement and rival classical Rome:

Whoever enters this great city finds the synthesis of two great epochs, the one more marvellous than the other. The monuments which celebrate these epochs are the pride of the world; they are for Italians a powerful reminder of their duty ... It is necessary for us also to establish and heighten monuments of civilisation in Rome, so that posterity can say we were great like our fathers.[31]

Crispi's position proved persuasive: parliament agreed to continue the Roma Capitale programme through a further series of monumental architectural set pieces.[32] This was architecture designed to articulate the ambitions and imagined identity of the Liberal state; in virtually every case the structures were designed in what was considered the new 'national style'.[33] An interpretation of Beaux Arts form, conceived on a gigantic and overbearing scale, this genre worked to associate the new state simultaneously with the modern and ancient Roman worlds in general, often with the addition of details and statuary specific to Rome. The 'national style' reproduced the genre of neoclassical design and decoration common throughout Europe but departed from previous Roman urban conventions in two key respects. First, in colour: the buildings were usually constructed of paler materials than the ochre tones of medieval and baroque Roman fabric, being faced with dazzling white marble or limestone, as in the case of the Vittorio Emanuele II monument. Second, they were built at a scale which overwhelmed neighbouring buildings, competing with ancient ruins such as the Colosseum or the Basilica of Maxentius and Constantine.[34] In these respects too, despite its references to classical Rome, the Liberal state's 'national style' was intended to announce the arrival of the new nation, its legitimacy and its permanence.

One of the most spectacular of these projects was the vast new Palace of Justice, or the Palazzaccio as it was popularly dubbed by the Romans, designed by Guglielmo Calderari, on the banks of the Tiber in 1899 and completed in 1911.[35] In common with many of the other major new monuments of the Liberal capital, the realisation of the Palace of Justice was slow and dogged by political delays.[36] Nevertheless, it was explicitly intended as 'the seat and the symbol of Italian justice, now re-established and centralised in Rome, and one of the greatest constructions in the capital, assuming a clear position in the political and architectural panorama of Roma Capitale'.[37]

Finished in blinding white stone and decorated by classical figures proclaiming justice as the foremost virtue, the massive edifice was sited at the very edge of the Vatican, beside the Castel Sant' Angelo (formerly the mausoleum of the emperor Hadrian). It was a blunt and unequivocal statement of the victory of the secular state over the Papacy, and the substitution of the legal and moral codes of Liberal

Italy for the Catholic jurisdiction in Rome. Its colouring and its huge bulk dominated the townscape within the city's historic core, where previously only church domes had broken the skyline. For the classically educated bourgeoisie of the new capital, the palace's architectural style and decoration indicated a direct and unequivocal connection between Italian and ancient Roman justice. The tableaux of the classically garbed virtues and the personifications of Victory on the facade and in a bronze chariot atop the portico reinforced this architectural message. Similarly, both on the facade and in the interior courtyard, allegorical personifications of Justice were juxtaposed with the civic iconography of the ancient city. Modern Romans would recognise the legendary she-wolf which suckled the city's founders, Romulus and Remus, and also the initials SPQR, signalling 'Senatus Populusque Romanus' (the Senate and people of Rome), indicating the supreme authority of the ancient city. Statues of Cicero and Brutus on the facade pressed home these associations, while interior hallways continued the styling and decoration.[38] Aside from its resonances of empire, therefore, the building also referred to ancient Roman principles of civic virtue as well as the contemporary authority of the Italian state.[39] The 'national style' marked explicit connections between the fashionable neoclassical Beaux Arts architecture adopted throughout the imperial capitals of Europe, and also a symbolic vocabulary that belonged exclusively to Rome.

Elsewhere in the city, the state inscribed streets and squares with its presence, by constructing new, imposing buildings to house the business of government. The papal Quirinale Palace was appropriated for the Italian royal residence, and the Ministry of Foreign Affairs was sited on the other side of the Piazza Quirinale. In the Via XX Settembre a series of imposing government offices was constructed: the Ministry of War was completed in 1885, the Ministry of Finance in 1887, and the Ministry of Agriculture in 1914. Inspired initially by Quintino Sella, the national Finance Minister (1869–73), who aspired to a 'rational', non-industrialised Italian capital to direct the growth of a modern, industrialised Italy, these structures were intended to represent the authority of the new secular government, not least through their large scale.[40] At the same time, though, the hybrid architectural form and styling combined modern building methods with neoclassical Roman motifs, again emphasising the ancient and modern Italianness of the new state through its monumental architecture.[41]

Like the Papacy, the Liberal government was wary of encouraging the industrialisation of Rome and the emergence of an urban working class.[42] However, it welcomed nineteenth-century consumer capitalism to the city. The broad, straight Via Nazionale (National Avenue) which connected the grandiose, columnated circle and fountain of the Piazza dell'Esedrae (now the Piazza della Repubblica, built 1896-1902) with the zone of the imperial fora near the Capitoline Hill was lined with the plate-glass windows of commercial stores and offices.[43] This self-consciously modern route was nevertheless planned to exemplify both the modern and the ancient qualities of *italianità*. It was punctuated by two more weighty examples of the 'national style': the Bank of Italy building and the National Exhibition Hall (opened in 1882). Meanwhile, each end of the Via Nazionale was anchored by major monuments to Rome's imperial past: the third-century Baths of Diocletian occupied one side of the Piazza dell'Esedrae on the hills to the east of central Rome, and the cleared and restored remains of Trajan's markets, Trajan's Forum and the column which commemorated his defeat of the Dacians marked the western terminus of the avenue in the historic centre. Such urban interventions and their associated monuments were perhaps the most enduring way in which the Italian state marked its arrival in the Eternal City.

Performing the nation: the fiftieth anniversary of Italy, 1911
The historian Emilio Gentile argues that a key element of the project to forge Italian citizens lay in the Liberal governments' efforts to create a 'patriotic' or 'civil' religion: a collective consciousness and shared national identity developed, in part, by the observance of myths, rituals and ceremonies.[44] On a national scale, schools, sporting societies and the army were the first focus of largely unsuccessful government efforts to inculcate a sense of nationhood.[45] These initiatives were followed by the creation of national holidays which recalled the unification of Italy or the capture of Rome and commemorated the Risorgimento and the monarchy through military parades and the illumination of public buildings.[46] Given the symbolic importance of Rome to the entire Risorgimento project, the new national capital became a site of particular importance to the pursuit of this 'patriotic religion'.

Liberal governments commonly appropriated and altered the meanings of rituals and celebrations associated with papal Rome for secular purposes. The tradition of giant *girandoli* (firework displays) at Castel Sant' Angelo or at the Pincio (a public park featuring newly installed busts of Risorgimento heroes) became an occasion for national rather than ecclesiastical celebration.[47] On other occasions pre-Christian, pagan festivals were revived, as in the 1902 Festival of Palilia, during which thousands of Romans paraded through the city in classical costume.[48] Although Bruno Tobia highlights the extent of mass participation in some of these events, Gentile argues that they generally failed to spread patriotism amongst the Italian citizenry, being undermined by the persistent fractures which beset the young state, the governments' distrust of mass politics, and the concomitant failure to exploit ritual and ceremony effectively.[49] Yet these celebrations of the modern nation consistently proposed direct connections across history with the Rome of antiquity. Notwithstanding Gentile's caveats, we want to highlight here the role of ideas of empire and, crucially, their articulation through the urban fabric in the celebration of the fiftieth anniversary of Italy in 1911.

Among the earliest large-scale attempts to display the classical heritage of Rome through the material landscapes of the city were the excavations of the Roman Forum and Trajan's Forum undertaken during the Napoleonic administration. This work was continued by the Liberal governments on their arrival in the city.[50] The ruins of the ancient city were mapped and uncovered systematically from the 1880s onwards, in part as proof of the *romanità* of Romans and Italians. In 1911, on the fiftieth anniversary of the Italian state, the Passegiata Archaeologica was formally opened. Originally planned in 1887, it was a stretch of open land to the south of the Colosseum and the Palatine Hill that was scattered with ancient imperial palaces, baths, stadia and monuments. The parkland preserved these extant classical ruins in a green space for modern Romans to reflect upon their imperial heritage. Nearer the heart of the city, the Roman forum was also cleared for public display.[51]

The 1911 anniversary also prompted the use of other ruins for 'national' purposes. Since 1889 the Baths of Diocletian at the eastern end of the Via Nazionale had housed a National Museum of Antiquities.[52] In 1911 they hosted an 'Exhibition of the Provinces of the Roman Empire'. As Eugenie Strong, the noted British antiquarian and deputy director of the British School at Rome, reported, the Italians

> decided to mark the occasion in Rome herself by an exhibition that should not merely display the growth of present Italian art and industries, or afford hospitality to the art of other nations, but should set forth besides in visible monuments the former glory of Rome, the wide range of empire ruled by the eternal city, which, again a capital, is the centre of strong national life. [53]

The fiftieth anniversary was therefore another occasion to celebrate modern Italy alongside ancient Rome. The exhibition was intended to function as a place where 'Italian youth may seek inspiration for all those virtues which rendered Rome, morally as well as materially, the mistress of the world'.[54] Meanwhile, outside the exhibition, the contemporary international profile of the nation was expressed through the inaguration of further modern building and engineering works across the capital. The Palace of Justice was formally opened after twenty-three years of construction, as were two new bridges over the Tiber, all designed in the 'national style'. [55]

Finally, the 1911 world's fair held in Italy was supposed to demonstrate simultaneously the classical and the modern grandeur of the nation. Planned as early as 1878 to rival the international exhibitions of other European capitals, the 1911 international exhibition made much of the classical heritage of Rome. While the exhibitions of industry and technology were held in Turin, Rome was reserved for the arts and humanities, history and archaeology.[56] In the Valle Giulia a national gallery of modern art was constructed in the national Beaux Arts style to host an international art exhibition.[57] Nearby, further pavilions housed the displays of other nations, including the neoclassical facade of the British pavilion, designed by Edwin Lutyens.[58] Meanwhile, regional and ethnographic exhibitions were held in the Piazza d'Armi; archaeological displays were at the Baths of Diocletian; the Risorgimento exhibition was held in the Vittorio Emanuele II monument; and an historical exhibition was held in the Castel Sant' Angelo, including a full-scale replica of a Roman galley which served as the setting of ceremonial banquets for visiting international figures and delegates to the many international conventions held in Rome in 1911.[59] The Liberal state seems to have been consistent in its promotion of the contemporary vitality of Italy, linked with the classical inheritance which was considered a vital ingredient of Italy's modern national consciousness. In myriad ways, Rome's reworked landscapes were constantly interwoven with references to the idea of empire, metaphorically and literally.

This theme reached a spectacular apotheosis in the most self-consciously referential symbol of the Liberal state – its national monument, dedicated on 4 June 1911 to the memory of the first king of a united Italy, Vittorio Emanuele II (Figure 6). While public and national memorialisation is inevitably contested and plural,[60] we shall concentrate here upon the intended meanings and associations which the Vittorio Emanuele II monument suggests through its siting, design and decoration.

Imperial symbolism
Vittorio Emanuele II, crowned the first king of the reunited Italy in 1861, died in January 1878. As one of the few widely recognised icons of the infant nation, the government decided it was appropriate to commemorate him with a monument. A commission to organise the project was established in May 1878, and private donations supplemented

Figure 6 Aerial view of the Vittorio Emanuele II monument. The Campidoglio is directly behind the monument and to the right. The Roman Forum stretches out beyond it towards the Passegiata Archaeologica

allocated government funds.[61] Although an international architectural competition was announced in 1880, the victorious French architect Paul-Henry Nénot saw the result annulled owing to allegations of derivative design and political interference.[62] When the competition was reopened in December 1882 a new set of parameters was announced. The monument was to be built in Piazza Venezia on the northern slope of the Capitoline hill, a location that was symbolic in several respects. The Capitoline had been the site of the mid-fourteenth century Roman Republic that had briefly resisted the rule of the Vatican. More crucially, the Capitoline was the ancient acropolis where Rome was first established. As such it was perhaps the most sacred site of the cult of Roman antiquity. The siting of the monument here, amid a complex of classical ruins which included Trajan's column, the Theatre of Marcellus and the Roman Forum and the still unexcavated imperial fora (exposed from 1924 onwards), was an explicit attempt to associate the Liberal state with ancient Rome. Moreover the revised rules also prescribed 'an equestrian statue with architectural backdrop and suitable stairs',[63] which defined a form similar to the ancient altars with which imperial Rome commemorated its victories. The monument was thus designed to be a highly rhetorical symbol whose message of unity and rebirth was directed at all Italy, and whose very location declared a blatant connection between the national altar of modern Italy and the classical empire once founded on the same hill.

The architect who eventually won the commission was an Italian, Giuseppe Sacconi. Construction began in 1885 to a design that epitomised the Beaux Arts 'national' style and its imperial referents. The structure was built of Brescian *botticino* marble whose intense whiteness contrasted sharply with the surrounding buildings.[64] The thematic inspiration of the monument is Michelangelo's design of the adjacent Campidoglio (the complex of city hall and museums which crowns the summit of the Capitoline hill). At one end of this piazza is a statue of Dea Roma, the mythical goddess and spirit of the city, before the city hall, flanked by fountains representing the Nile and the Tiber. She stands guard over the material fragments of imperial Rome gathered in the Capitoline museums and looks across the piazza at the great equestrian statue of the emperor and philosopher Marcus Aurelius. In its effort to rehearse the *romanità* of the Liberal state, the Vittorio Emanuele II monument replicates this iconography precisely.

At the base of the Vittoriano (as the monument became known), flanking the broad central stairway demanded by the second competition, two fountains represent the Adriatic and the Tyrrhenian seas which define the east and west coasts of the Italian peninsula. Adjacent to the fountains, and the only buildings to survive the demolition of the surrounding seventeenth-century fabric (to make way for a grand piazza), were the remnants of two ancient Roman structures. Parts of an ancient tomb and a Roman dwelling, these were isolated and framed against the Vittoriano to emphasise the trans-historical connection between Rome ancient and modern. The remainder of the monument is an acropolis composed of three levels. The lowest of the three is an altar to Dea Roma, with another, larger statue of the goddess gazing out over Piazza Venezia (Figure 7). The second level was devoted to the commemoration of the late king, whose heroic equestrian statue echoes that of Marcus Aurelius and surmounts the plinth against which Dea Roma stands. The third level was a great stylobate comprising a portico of sixteen composite columns. The two pavilions at each end bore gold lettering that proclaimed the twin secular goals of *civium libertas* (a city freed) and *patriae unitas* (a nation united), in

Figure 7   Dea Roma, on the Vittorio Emanuele II monument. From I. S. Munro, *Through Fascism to World Power* (London, 1933)

overt defiance of the Papacy, and the Catholic domes and towers of Rome. [65]

Besides its references to the adjacent Campidoglio, the key axis of the monument is the vertical connection between the martial figure of Dea Roma and the statue of Vittorio Emanuele II positioned directly above the Goddess of Rome. As Marina Warner points out, part of the allegorical symbolism of Dea Roma was as 'the figure who personifies the claims of the state to be free ... [and as such] the goddess had to appear heroic, resisting, chaste and strong'.[66] If Dea Roma represents the strength and liberty of classical Rome, the connected figure of Vittorio Emanuele II suggests that the liberty and unity of Italy under Roman dominion were revived in modern Italy. Moreover the geographical unity and the supposed civic virtues of the revived Italy are referenced by the figural decoration of the monument. Sixteen figures in classical dress, representing the sixteen regions of the nation state, top the columns of the portico. Below them, around the plinth supporting Vittorio Emanuele II, the leading Italian cities are represented by figures in medieval costumes resonant of the cities' periods of political eminence. Meanwhile, to either side of Dea Roma, figures in classical garb representing Justice, Philosophy and War develop the monument's rhetorical construction of *romanità* as a moral discourse which had found new expression in Liberal Italy. [67]

The monument thus narrates an heroic Italian history which revolves around an imperial destiny, expressed through the recurrent motif of the human body.[68] The direct visual analogies with Michaelangelo's nearby urban scheme lay claim to the spirit of classical Rome, as does the location upon the symbolic space of the Capitoline hill with its surrounding imperial and Roman fora. The inscribed invocations to city and nation reflect the secular, national goals of Liberal Italy, whilst the statues personifying the cities and regions of Italy together record the Risorgimento project of uniting traditionally independent polities into a single nation. The brilliant white of the massive ensemble towers high above the Roman skyline, providing a spectacular backdrop to public ceremonies in Piazza Venezia, and effectively placing the Italian state in direct competition with the dome of St Peter's basilica across the Tiber.

In this iconographic reading of the monument we have thus far concentrated upon the notions of empire and *romanità* which are expressed through the location, styling and form of the Vittoriano. However, the construction and design of the monument were beset by numerous disagreements, controversies and problems besides those that we have mentioned. These ranged from the rivalries of Sacconi and some of the many sculptors and artists employed on the work,

through accusations about the award of contracts, other political interference and recurrent problems with funding, to unclear design plans,
strikes by the work force and cracks in the foundations.[69] The exterior
decoration of the structure was not finished until 1927, by which time
Sacconi had been dead for twenty-two years.[70] The interior spaces were
not completed until the mid-1930s.[71] Our focus upon the imperial
dimensions of the monument is not intended to foreclose upon these
other aspects of the story; neither do we wish to deny that there were
numerous understandings of the Vittoriano and its meanings upon its
opening in 1911.

For example, the intended message that Italy was once again an
imperial power was obviously not received uniformly and uncritically
by the Italian people. The Risorgimento was a project propelled mainly
by the northern elite of Piedmont. For many Italians, especially in the
south, the creation of a new 'national' government simply redirected
their taxes to different coffers, and meant that legislation now emerged
from a new authority in Rome. Moreover, despite their partial
attempts to nurture a 'national' religion, the ruling classes of Liberal
Italy did not trust ordinary Italians with the vote in this period: universal male suffrage was introduced only in 1913.[72] Nevertheless, for
the opening of the Vittoriano, the masses were encouraged to participate, and so reduced train fares were organised to tempt Italians to the
capital from the provinces.[73] This strategy met with varying success. A
cartoon from the satirical weekly *Il Bastone*, for example, portrays a
number of Romans attending the opening not for patriotic reasons but
for social or political gain, to avoid school for the day, or to show off the
latest fashions (Figure 8). Likewise, the socialist newspaper *Avanti!*
contrasted the exaggerated monumentalism of the structure with the
social problems which still faced the rest of the nation. However, even
Avanti! was forced to admit the enthusiasm of the crowds,[74] and the
Roman paper *Il Messaggero* confirmed these reports.[75] In this respect,
at least, the monument appears to have been partially successful in
forging some popular enthusiasm for the national project.

To one well informed British observer of Rome the monument was
certainly successful in its attempt to forge a connection between the
imperial forms of antiquity and its own reworked neo-imperial style.
In his account of the legacies of Roman art and architecture in the
modern world, G. Rushforth (sometime Director of the British School
at Rome) noted that:

[in terms of] great monuments and imposing architecture ... there is an
affinity between, for instance, the Septizonium of Septimius Severus [an
ancient monument], the conceptions and imaginations of Piranesi or the
Italian scenery designers of the eighteenth century, and the marble

Perchè si va all'inaugurazione

dell'altare della Patria!!!

Figure 8 'Why we're going to the inauguration of the altar of the nation!'.
Front page of *Il Bastone*, 4 June 1911

masses of the Monumento Nazionale which now towers over Rome from the Capitol, the lineal descendent of the monuments of Imperial Rome.[76]

Similarly, the Fascist regime of Benito Mussolini also celebrated the monument as the 'Altar of the Nation' in its presentation of imperial Rome to Adolf Hitler in May 1938.[77] For the Führer's visit the

[57]

Vittoriano was floodlit as a key icon of modern Rome, with search-lights reaching into the night sky from the roof of the monument's vast portico (Figure 9).[78] Aside from its function as a central element of Fascist urban spectacle, the monument was also regarded as a clear and legible statement of the ancient imperial heritage of Italy, which Mussolini doubtless sought to emphasise to his German guests.[79] Such examples help to demonstrate that the Vittorio Emanuele II monument was interpreted and used in the decades after its inauguration as an icon of Italy's imperial heritage. As the memorial to Italy's first monarch and altar to the nation (*ara nationis*), the Vittorio Emanuele II monument represented not only a modern, contemporary, European Italy but also one which was raised literally and metaphorically from the ruins and memories of the ancient Roman empire.

Conclusion

Sigmund Freud concluded his musings upon Rome by noting that 'Demolitions and replacement of buildings occur in the course of the

Figure 9 Postcard of the Vittorio Emanuele II monument floodlit for the visit to Rome of Adolf Hitler, May 1938. The ruins of Trajan's Forum are in the foreground

most peaceful development of a city'.[80] As he wrote this in 1930 Rome was in the midst of the violent transformations initiated by Mussolini's Fascist regime, when *romanità* became a still more pronounced element of Italian urban policy and Italy claimed a still more self-consciously 'imperial' profile.[81] The replanning and rebuilding of Rome under Fascism would culminate in Mussolini's efforts to forge close connections between his own expansionist rule and that of the emperor Augustus. In memory of Augustus, his *ara pacis* (the altar of peace, signifying the universal peace provided by Roman rule), and his *res gestae* (the valedictory text recording his achievements, triumphs and divine deeds) would be reconstructed and reinscribed at the site of his mausoleum by the Tiber.[82] Mussolini intended his own final resting place to be there, next to Augustus. Finally the bi-millennial anniversary of Augustus's birth was celebrated in 1937–38. A huge exhibition was held in the national Exhibition Hall on the Via Nazionale, its 'Liberal' styling masked by a modernist, Fascist facade which referred to the form of an ancient triumphal arch.[83] The materials collected for this exhibition are today housed in the grandest expression of Mussolini's dream of a resurrected imperial Rome, the EUR site planned to celebrate twenty years of Fascism in 1942, and intended to extend a metropolis of 20 million people to the shores of the Mediterranean and to re-establish Rome's global centrality.[84] To this day the urban landscapes of Rome bear the marks of a twentieth-century imperial imagination, not only in their modern structure but in the presences, the absences, and the very presentation of the ruins of antiquity themselves.

Rome thus became a still more consciously designed imperial city after the Fascist seizure of power in 1922. Liberal Italy's imperialism was perhaps not as aggressive as Mussolini's. Nevertheless, some historians draw connections between the patriotism and nationalism prompted by the 1911 celebrations, the opening of the Vittorio Emanuele II monument, and Italy's renewed imperialism, which began with the September 1911 invasion of Tripolitania and Cyrenaica in Libya.[85] As with the remaking of Rome under the Liberal regime, this expansion across the Mediterranean was interpreted by politicians and popular cultures alike as Italy retrieving its Roman heritage and imperial destiny in North Africa.[86] While Liberal Italy may have been less destructive than Fascism in exploiting imperial themes in its urbanism and its foreign policy, its projects within Rome itself were equally implicated in conflating and confusing visions of empire, past and future.

Notes

This chapter emerges from the Leverhulme Trust project 'Imperial Cities: Landscape, Space and Performance in London and Rome, 1850–1950'. Our thanks to Alistair Crawford for providing a copy of Figure 9. The errors are ours, as are the translations (unless otherwise indicated).

1 S. Freud, 'Civilisation and its Discontents', in *The Standard Edition of the Complete Psychological works of Sigmund Freud*, XXI (London, Hogarth Press and Institute of Psycho-analysis, 1961), pp. 64-145 (quotation from p. 70). See also P. Jacks, *The Antiquarian and the Myth of Antiquity: The Origins of Rome in Renaissance Thought* (Cambridge, Cambridge University Press, 1993), pp. 1–2.

2 Freud, 'Civilisation and its Discontents', pp. 70–1.

3 C. Edwards, 'The roads to Rome', in M. Liversidge and C. Edwards (eds), *Imagining Rome: British Artists and Rome in the Nineteenth Century* (Bristol, Bristol City Museum and Art Gallery, 1996), pp. 8–19.

4 J. Black, *The British and the Grand Tour* (London, Croom Helm, 1985); J. Black, *The British Abroad: The Grand Tour in the Eighteenth Century* (Stroud, Alan Sutton, 1982); C. Hibbert, *The Grand Tour* (London, Weidenfeld & Nicolson, 1969); B. Barefoot, *The English Road to Rome* (Upton-upon-Severn, Images, 1993), especially pp. 81–134.

5 M. J. Heffernan, 'A state scholarship: the political geography of French international science during the nineteenth century', *Transactions of the Institute of British Geographers*, 19 (1994) 21–45; Edwards, 'The roads to Rome', p. 8.

6 Edwards, 'The roads to Rome', p. 8. On the Germans and Rome see S. Schama, *Landscape and Memory* (London, Harper Collins, 1995), pp. 81–100.

7 On the expression of this style at the 1893 Chicago World's Fair see J. Gilbert, *Perfect Cities: Chicago's Utopias of 1893* (Chicago, University of Chicago Press, 1991).

8 J. Onians, *Bearers of Meaning: The Classical Orders in Antiquity, the Middle Ages, and the Renaissance* (Princeton NJ, Princeton University Press, 1988); G. M. Rushworth, 'Architecture and art', in C. Bailey (ed.), *The Legacy of Rome* (Oxford, Clarendon Press, 1924), pp. 385–427; G. Giovannoni, 'Building and engineering', in C. Bailey (ed.), *The Legacy of Rome* (Oxford, Clarendon Press, 1924), pp. 429–74.

9 D. E. Cosgrove, *Social Formation and Symbolic Landscape* (London, Croom Helm, 1984), pp. 181–3.

10 The *lictor fasces* was an axe surrounded by a bound bundle of rods. In Republican Rome it symbolised that executive authority (the axe) was controlled and wielded by the citizens and the Senate (the rods). The symbols were later appropriated by French and American revolutionaries, and, later still, by Italian Fascism.

11 H. T. Parker, *The Cult of Antiquity and the French Revolutionaries* (Cambridge, Cambridge University Press, 1982); P. Woolf, 'Symbol of the Second Empire: cultural politics and the Paris Opera House', in D. Cosgrove and S. Daniels (eds), *The Iconography of Landscape* (Cambridge, Cambridge University Press, 1988), pp. 214–35.

12 On ideas of London as an imperial capital see F. Driver and D. Gilbert, 'Heart of empire? Landscape, space and performance in imperial London', *Environment and Planning D: Society and Space*, 15 (1998) 11–28, and, on comparisons between British imperialism and ancient Rome, R. Betts, 'The allusion to Rome in British imperialist thought of the nineteenth and early twentieth centuries', *Victorian Studies*, 15 (1971) 149–59; Edwards, 'The roads to Rome'.

13 A. Caracciolo, *Roma Capitale: dal Risorgimento alla crisi dello Stato liberale*, fourth edition (Rome, Riuniti, 1993), especially pp. 27–59; J. Agnew, *Rome* (Chichester, Wiley, 1995), especially pp. 14–22.

14 R. Hilberg, *The Destruction of the European Jews* (London, Weidenfeld & Nicolson, 1985), pp. 9–11; Agnew, *Rome*, especially pp. 18–22; Caracciolo, *Roma Capitale*, especially pp. 129–68.

15 J. Buzard, *The Beaten Track: European Tourism, Literature and the Ways to Culture, 1800–1918* (Oxford, Oxford University Press, 1993), pp. 88–90, 172–88, 205–8.

16 Caracciolo, *Roma Capitale*, especially pp. 44–62; I. Insolera, *Roma: immagini e*

realtà dal X al XX secolo (Bari, Laterza, 1980).

17 S. Kostof, *The Third Rome, 1870–1950: Traffic and Glory* (Berkeley CA, University Art Museum, 1973), p. 43.

18 For discussion of these debates see I. Insolera, *Roma moderna: un secolo di storia urbanisticà* (Turin, Einaudi, 1971); R. C. Fried, *Planning the Eternal City: Roman Politics and Planning since World War II* (London, Yale University Press, 1973), especially pp. 19–40; Kostof, *The Third Rome*; Agnew, *Rome*, pp. 28-47; Caracciolo, *Roma Capitale*, pp. 75–267.

19 R. Visser, 'Fascist doctrine and the cult of the *romanità*', *Journal of Contemporary History*, 27 (1992) 5–22.

20 *Ibid.*, pp. 7–12.

21 Agnew, *Rome*, pp. 14–47; Fried, *Planning the Eternal City*, pp. 19–40; Caracciolo, *Roma Capitale*, pp. 169–239.

22 Caracciolo, *Roma Capitale*, pp. 129–68.

23 Fried, *Planning the Eternal City*, p. 26.

24 Kostof, *The Third Rome*, p. 21

25 M. Birindelli, *Roma italiana: come fare una capitale e disfare una città* (Rome, Palombi, 1978); S. von Falkenhausen, *Italienische Monumentalmalerei im Risorgimento 1830–90. Strategien nationaler Bildersprache* (Berlin, Winkler, 1993).

26 Caracciolo, *Roma Capitale*; F. Borsi, *L'architettura dell'unità d'Italia* (Florence, Le Monnier, 1963); F. Borsi (ed.), *Arte a Roma dalla Capitale all'Età Umbertina* (Rome, Editalia, 1980).

27 Kostof, *The Third Rome*, pp. 43–8.

28 Fried, *Planning the Eternal City*, p. 24.

29 B. Tobia, 'Urban space and monuments in the "nationalization of the masses"', in S. J. Woolf (ed.), *Nationalism in Europe. 1815 to the present* (London, Routledge, 1996), p. 181.

30 *Ibid.*, p.181; B. Tobia, *Una patria per gli Italiani: spazi, itinerari, monumenti nell'Italia unita, 1870–1900* (Bari, Laterza, 1991), p. 26.

31 F. Chabod, *Storia della politica esterna italiana dal 1870 al 1896* (Bari, Laterza, 1965), I, p. 297. R. Bosworth, 'The opening of the Victor Emmanuel monument', *Italian Quarterly*, 16 (1975) 78–87 (p. 79).

32 Kostof, *The Third Rome*, p. 26; Fried, *Planning the Eternal City*, p. 23.

33 Tobia, 'Urban space and monuments'; Tobia, *Una patria per gli Italiani*.

34 Borsi, *L'architettura dell'unità d'Italia*; Borsi, *Arte a Roma dalla Capitale all'Età Umbertina*.

35 F. Boco, T. Kirk and G. Muratore (eds), *Guglielmo Calderini dai disegni dell'Accademia di Belle Arti di Perugia: un architetto nell'Italia in costruzione* (Perugia, Accademia di Belle Arti di Perugia, Guerra Edizioni, 1995), especially pp. 29–38.

36 T. Kirk, 'Biografia di un architetto del nuovo Stato italiano', in F. Boco, T. Kirk and G. Muratore (eds), *Guglielmo Calderini dai disegni dell'Accademia di Belle Arti di Perugia* (Perugia, Accademia di Belle Arti di Perugia, Guerra Edizioni, 1995), pp. 32–47, especially pp. 29–37; see also T. Kirk, *The Politicization of the Landscape of Roma Capitale and the Symbolic Role of the Palazzo di Giustizia*, Mélanges de l'Ecole Française de Rome (Rome, Ecole Française, 1985).

37 Kirk, 'Biografia di un architetto del nuovo Stato italiano', p. 29.

38 *Ibid.*, pp. 34–8.

39 E. Gentile, *The Sacralization of Politics in Fascist Italy*, trans. K. Botsford (Cambridge MA, Harvard University Press, 1996), p. 7.

40 E. Schroeter, 'Rome's first national state architecture: the Palazzo delle Finanze', in H. A. Millon and L. Nochlin (eds), *Art and Architecture in the Service of Politics* (London, MIT Press, 1978), pp. 128–49, especially pp. 143–5; C. Aymonino *et al.*, *Roma Capitale, 1870–1911: architettura e urbanisticà, uso e trasformazione della città storica* (Venice, Ateneo, 1984).

41 Schroeter, 'Rome's first national state architecture', pp. 143–5.

42 Fried, *Planning the Eternal City*, p. 21.

43 M. Tafuri, 'La prima strada di Roma moderna: Via Nazionale', *Urbanisticà*, 27 (1959)

95–108; M. Scattareggia, 'Roma Capitale: arretratezza e modernizzazione, 1870–1914', *Storia Urbana*, 42 (1988) 37–84.

44 Gentile, *The Sacralization of Politics in Fascist Italy*, especially pp. 1–18; E. Gentile, 'Fascism as political religion', *Journal of Contemporary History*, 25 (1990) 229–51. See also F. Cammarano, 'The nationalization of politics and the politicization of the nation in Liberal Italy', in R. Lumley and J. Morris (eds), *The New History of the Italian South: The Mezzogiorno revisited* (Exeter, Exeter University Press, 1997), pp. 148–55.

45 Gentile, *The Sacralization of Politics in Fascist Italy*, pp. 7–9.

46 *Ibid.*, pp. 9–10.

47 R. B. Williams, 'An unsung protagonist of Roma Capitale: the Ministry of Public Instruction and its documents at the Archivio Centrale dello Stato', *Annali Academici Canadesi*, 8 (1992) 97–105, here p. 104.

48 A. Notaro, *Telling Imperial Histories: Contests of Narrativity and Representation in post-Unification Rome, 1870–1911*, Royal Holloway, University of London, Department of Geography, Imperial Cities Project working paper No. 1 (1996), p. 12; M. Venturoli, *La Patria di Marmio* (Pisa, Nistri-Lischi, 1957), pp. 220–1.

49 Gentile, *The Sacralization of Politics*, pp. 11-12. Tobia ('Urban space and monuments', p. 178) disagrees, claiming that the 1884 pilgrimage of 76,000 Italians to Vittorio Emanuele II's tomb was a success, albeit one compromised by class divisions.

50 R. Ridley, *The Eagle and the Spade* (Cambridge, Cambridge University Press, 1991); C. Springer, *The Marble Wilderness: Ruins and Representation in Italian Romanticism, 1775–1850*, (Cambridge, Cambridge University Press, 1987), pp. 64–97.

51 Kostof, *The Third Rome*, p.22

52 Williams, 'An unsung protagonist of Roma Capitale'.

53 S. A. Strong, 'The exhibition illustrative of the provinces of the Roman empire, at the Baths of Diocletian, Rome', *Journal of Roman Studies*, 1:1 (1911) 1–49 (p. 1).

54 *Ibid.*, p. 49.

55 A. M. Racheli, 'Le sistemazioni urbanistiche di Roma per l'Esposizione Internazionale del 1911', in G. Piantoni (ed.), *Roma 1911* (Rome, De Luca, 1980), pp. 229–64.

56 Piantoni, *Roma 1911*, especially pp. 7–68; G. Cassetti and L. Callari, *Il Giubileo della Patria* (Milan, Angeli, 1911).

57 S. Pasquarelli, 'Il concorso per il Palazzo per l'Esposizione di Belle Arti', in Piantoni, *Roma 1911*, pp. 279–84.

58 S. Pasquarelli, 'I padiglioni stranieri', in Piantoni, *Roma 1911*, pp. 265–78. Lutyens's contribution was preserved as the facade of the British School at Rome.

59 Piantoni, *Roma 1911*. See also A. Lancellotti, *Le Mostre Romane del Cinquantenario* (Rome, Ateneo, 1931); Comune di Roma, *Atti delle celebrazioni commemorative del 1911* (Rome, Comune di Roma, 1911).

60 D. Atkinson and D. Cosgrove, 'Urban rhetoric and embodied identities', *Annals of the Association of American Geographers*, 88:1 (1998) 28–49, especially pp. 29–31. On monuments in general see N. Johnson, 'Cast in stone: monuments, geography and nationalism', *Environment and Planning D: Society and Space*, 13 (1994) 51–66.

61 Kostof, *The Third Rome*, p. 57.

62 J. Dickie, 'La macchina da scrivere: the Victor Emmanuel monument in Rome and Italian nationalism', *Italianist*, 14 (1994) 261–85. See also P. Acciaresi, *Giuseppe Sacconi e l'opera sua massima: cronaca dei lavori del monumento nazionale del Vittorio Emanuele II* (Rome, Ateneo, 1911).

63 Kostof, *The Third Rome*, p. 57.

64 Dickie, 'La macchina da scrivere', p. 261.

65 M. Serio and G. Ruggeri (eds), *Il Vittoriano: materiali per una storia* (Rome, Palombi, 1986); Acciaresi, *Giuseppe Sacconi*.

66 M. Warner, *Monuments and Maidens: The Allegory of the Female Form* (London, Verso, 1985), p. 280.

67 P-L. Porzio, 'La forma Architettonica del Vittoriano nei disegni e nei modelli della fabbrica', in Serio and Ruggeri, *Il Vittoriano*, pp. 39–90.

68 On this see Atkinson and Cosgrove, 'Urban rhetoric and embodied identities', especially pp. 39–43.
69 Bosworth, 'The opening of the Victor Emmanuel monument', p. 79; Dickie, 'La macchina da scrivere', p. 261
70 Dickie, 'La macchina da scrivere', p. 261.
71 Atkinson and Cosgrove, 'Urban rhetoric and embodied identities', especially pp. 39–45.
72 E. Hobsbawm, 'Mass-producing traditions: Europe, 1870–1914', in E. Hobsbawm and T. Ranger (eds), The Invention of Tradition (Cambridge, Cambridge University Press, 1983), pp. 263–307, especially p. 267
73 Bosworth, 'The opening of the Victor Emmanuel monument', p. 85. Rail fares to Rome were subsidised by 75 per cent.
74 Ibid.
75 Notaro, Telling Imperial Histories, p. 22.
76 Rushworth, 'Architecture and art', p. 399.
77 D. Atkinson, Hitler's Grand Tour: The Triumphal Entrance to Fascist Rome, 1938, Royal Holloway, University of London, Department of Geography, Imperial Cities Project working paper No. 8 (1997), pp. 1–25.
78 Atkinson and Cosgrove, 'Urban rhetoric and embodied identities', especially pp. 34–45; F. Mastrigli, 'Roma pavesata', Capitoleum, 14 (1938) 219–34, especially p. 234. Figure 9 is a contemporary postcard.
79 On spectacle in the Fascist city see M. Isenghi, L'Italia in piazza: i luoghi della vita pubblica dal 1848 ai giorni nostri (Milan, Mondadori, 1994), especially pp. 310–30; D. Atkinson, 'Totalitarianism and the street in Fascist Rome', in N. Fyfe (ed.), Images of the Street: Planning, Identity and Control in Public Space (London, Routledge, 1998), pp. 13-30, especially pp. 24–7; M. Stone, 'Staging Fascism: the exhibition of the Fascist Revolution', Journal of Contemporary History, 28 (1993) 215–43.
80 Freud, 'Civilisation and its Discontents', p. 71.
81 A. Cederna, Mussolini Urbanistricà: lo sventramento di Roma negli anni del consenso (Bari, Laterza, 1979).
82 S. Kostof, 'The Emperor and the Duce: the planning of Piazzale Augusto Imperatore in Rome', in H. Millon and L. Nochlin (eds), Art and Architecture in the Service of Politics (London, MIT Press, 1980), pp. 270–325.
83 F. Scriba, 'Il mito di Roma: l'estetica e gli intellettuali negli anni del consenso: la Mostra della Romanità 1937/38', Quaderni di Storia, 41 (1995) 67–84; M. Rinaldi, 'Il volto effimero della città nell'età dell'impero e dell'autarchia', in Palazzo delle Esposizioni, La Capitale a Roma, città e arredo Urbano, 1870–1945 (Rome, Palazzo delle Esposizioni, 1991), pp. 118–29.
84 M. Fuller, 'Wherever you go, there you are: Fascist plans for the colonial city of Addis Ababa and the colonizing suburb of EUR '42', Journal of Contemporary History, 31 (1996) 397–418, especially pp. 408–14.
85 Bosworth, 'The opening of the Victor Emmanuel Monument', p. 78. Bosworth also notes that the pro-imperial lobby organisation, the Italian Colonial League, had its headquarters beneath the Vittoriano (p. 80).
86 M. Wyke, 'Screening Rome in the new Italy', in C. Edwards (ed.), Roman Presences: Receptions of Rome in European Culture, 1789–1945 (Cambridge, Cambridge University Press, 1999), pp. 188–204.

CHAPTER FOUR

Capitale du plaisir: the remaking of imperial Paris

Claire Hancock

Paris under the Second Empire was 'imperial' in a very different sense from contemporary London. While London was the mart of a huge empire, Paris was transformed into the main sphere of display of its imperial regime. The world was invited to witness the spectacle of the grandeur of Paris, making the city itself an object of consumption for wealthy visitors. Haussmann's reconstruction of the city was a conscious policy to make Paris a 'modern' city, up to the requirements of a modern economy. But Paris was not only opened up to capitalism and trade; it was also redesigned to glorify the imperial regime. As the landscape of the city was being reshaped, inroads were being made into what was felt by many citizens to be the irrepressible identity of Paris, the capital of the Revolution and therefore of the people. 'Imperial Paris' became a highly contested notion as those with conflicting political ideals fought for symbolic ownership of urban space and representation.

The development of the tourist trade produced new readings of the city as an object to be viewed and enjoyed. The British were foremost among the producers and consumers of these new readings which were found in guidebooks. Their Paris was shaped by the rivalry between the two imperial powers, with the French capital often constructed as a kind of inverted image of London. These representations of Paris from the outside influenced the ways in which its citizens came to understand the city; domestic and foreign authors conspired to elaborate a stereotypical characterisation of the city. It was felt by many that the urban policies of the imperial government were reinforcing these caricatures — that Paris was being remade for foreigners, and confiscated from its inhabitants.

A city remade

In 1864 A. de Césena, one of the chief propagandists of the Second Empire, suggested that 'a day will come when history will say about the capital of France, transformed as if by magic in less than a quarter of a century, "the Paris of Napoleon III" as it said "the Rome of Augustus"'.[1] The material transformation of Paris was indeed massive. However, this is one of the few instances in which Paris was compared directly with ancient Rome; Paris was much more commonly compared with Athens in contemporary discourse. Though these may seem to be just rhetorical devices, they reveal a deep-seated ambiguity about just how 'imperial' Paris wanted to appear. The analogy with Athens made reference to Paris's revolutionary past and also placed the city in European traditions of intellectual achievement and democracy, rather than in those of imperial authority and display. Strong claims were made about Paris's place in the intellectual and cultural world order. For de Césena, Paris was 'the brain of mankind',[2] and the collective work *Paris et les Parisiens au XIXe siècle* saw the universe as eagerly awaiting and copying Paris-manufactured ideas, books, plays, songs and fashions.[3] The ambiguity between different understandings of Paris could be read into the very landscape of the city. *Paris et les Parisiens* described the city's famed boulevards in these terms: 'it is this way that, on troubled days, rumbling riot and victorious revolution pass through; it is also the Capitoline way through which restored peace leads the triumph of emperors and kings'.[4] Victor Hugo, in his introduction to the 1867 *Paris-Guide*, chose to combine the characteristics of Athens and Rome with those of another historic city in his eulogy to his beloved city:

> Out of three mortal frames, Rome, Athens, Jerusalem, flew three ideas. From Rome Might, from Athens Art, from Jerusalem Freedom. The Great, the Beautiful, the True.
> They live on in Paris. Paris sums up these three cities: it has amalgamated them in its unity.[5]

In nineteenth-century Paris there was a broad consensus, ranging across the political spectrum, that the city could be regarded as a material embodiment of the French political sphere. Under the Second Republic (1848–51), the capital was an important focus of the debate between centralising and decentralising parties. Practical decision-making was taken from the local authorities and placed in the hands of a mayor who was a direct representative of the state, making it clear that local Parisian interests were subordinate to the more general national interest. However, under the Second Empire the city and its planning became even more bound up with the prestige of the state.

Haussmann, Préfet de la Seine from 1853 to 1870, undertook a restructuring of the capital on an unprecedented scale. New avenues were drawn through the central slums which had been revolutionary hotbeds. The artisan area of the Faubourg Saint Antoine was circled by a ring of boulevards. These changes sought to give a coherent, global plan to the city, and to link the different areas of the city into a general network of circulation. New water and sewerage systems were constructed, street lighting and paving were improved, and new squares and parks were created and opened to the public. Those peripheral areas which were within the walls of the city but legally separated by tax barriers were annexed to the capital in 1860.

It was impossible to make Paris a seaport, though this had been the ambition of nearly all regimes since the eighteenth century. Paris was unable to rival London in this respect, and French overseas imperial possessions did not directly produce significant changes in the city's economy, appearance or internal organisation. Rather, Parisian 'imperialism' referred to the authoritarian powers used to restructure the city, the personal involvement of the Emperor in drawing the new avenues, and the discretionary powers granted to Haussmann to expropriate and to borrow to rebuild.

Though the electorate of the Second Empire was predominantly rural, the regime saw itself as metropolitan. It did not try to minimise the leading role of the French capital in French history. Instead it asked the city to exchange its revolutionary glory for another role: to signify to the world progress, social harmony between classes, the greatness of arts and the triumph of industry and trade. The Rue de Rivoli, for instance, was not only a strategic thoroughfare against riot but was also a triumphal way to the future. Completed in 1855, it took visitors from the Louvre to the Great Exhibition on the Champs Elysées along a line of fine stone buildings, with lavishly lit arcades.

There has been much discussion of the extent to which 'Haussmannisation' fostered social segregation in Paris. The new type of *immeuble* was much more socially homogeneous than the buildings it replaced, and the general rise in rents drove some of the poor out of central Paris. However, as Gaillard has argued, strong contrasts remained between the new streets and the old back streets which were largely untouched.[6] Many artisan workers remained in districts which were close to their workplace, despite the increase in rents, and many traditional industries resisted pressures to force them out of the city. The very conditions of economic change, particularly the strong demand created by the boom in the building industry, encouraged craft and industry to remain close to the centre. The Second Empire had a public rhetoric of social inclusion and sought to promote its achievements to all classes. Thus, when French troops returned from the Italian campaign in 1859, the procession took place in the avenues of eastern Paris, the main working-class areas. Parisian crafts and industries were central features of the imperial exhibitions of 1855 and 1867.

Although the social consequences for Paris of the Second Empire Haussmannisation were more mixed than is often recognised, rebuilding did create a new symbolic landscape in the city. Housing was being renewed along new streets and along new principles. Not only did Haussmann deliberately favour expensive buildings and neglect working-class housing but the new *immeubles de rapport* were built at the same time as a shift in bourgeois attitudes which had formerly emphasised privacy, discretion and thrift. In the new Paris exterior ornamentation and rooms for reception made the bourgeois *appartements* more like aristocratic dwellings, and testified to a more extrovert lifestyle. In a similar way, whereas bourgeois tastes favoured closed urban forms in the first half of the century (closed squares, shopping arcades and private closets in cafés), with the ordinary street left to the working class, the Second Empire made the street clean, safe and ordered, allowing cafés and *grands magasins* to expand out onto it. In the perception of some contemporaries, the Second Empire was drawing people out of doors to take part in the vast pantomime of the imperial city. In 1860 E. de Goncourt, a literary figure of the time, noted in his diary that:

> Our Paris, the Paris where we were born, the Paris of the ways of 1830 to 1848, is disappearing. And it is not disappearing materially, but morally. Social life is undergoing a great evolution, just at its beginning. I see women, children, couples, families in this café. The inside is disappearing. Life is becoming public again. The club for the upper classes, the café for the lower, that is where society and the people are heading. It makes me feel, in this part of my feelings, like a traveller. I am foreign to what is coming, to what exists, as I am to those new boulevards, which speak no more of the world of Balzac, but of London, of some future Babylon. It is a shame to live in a time under construction: the soul feels uncomfortable, like a man in a brand-new house.[7]

The comparison with London emphasised the perceived foreignness of this 'great evolution', as well as the modernity of the new environment. In the light of late nineteenth and twentieth-century representations of the urban public space in the two cities it is somewhat ironic that the model of London was associated with the creation of a public domain of cafés and boulevards. In many ways, the imperial regime sought to modernise Paris in order to be seen to catch up with London. English visitors to the French capital in the early nineteenth century had easily dismissed the dirt and darkness of medieval streets. Writing on London in 1872, Taine expressed the common idea that 'certainly Napoleon III demolished and rebuilt Paris only because he had lived in London ...'.[8] While the political absolutism of the urban redevelopment strategy was clearly at odds with English ways of shaping the cityscape, specific elements of the new Paris made direct reference to admired features of London. Although attempts to create Parisian docks on a scale at all comparable with London's were predictably unsuccessful they were always inaugurated with much ceremony and feigned confidence. More successfully the drawing of large new streets provided with pavements, and the creation or replanning of the urban parks of the Bois de Boulogne, the Bois de Vincennes, the Parc Montsouris and the Parc des Buttes-Chaumont attempted to reproduce what was admired in London.

In T. J. Clark's analysis, Haussmannisation propagated a unified, singular image of Paris. This image was handed out to the inhabitants with precise instructions about how to view and understand it, through promenades, panoramas, exhibitions, official processions and urban events like the inauguration of the Boulevard de Sébastopol (Figure 10). Paris itself was being staged as a spectacle and could no longer be looked at naively.[9] Like contemporary London, Second Empire Paris was marked by self-celebratory displays, such as diora-

Figure 10   Inauguration of the Boulevard de Sébastopol, 5 April 1858

mas, panoramas and panstereoramas, which made claim to the universal status of the city. The Universal Exhibitions celebrated the technical and industrial achievements of the whole world, as well as staging each capital as a focus of modernity and progress. Most striking, however, was the setting up of the city itself as spectacle and object of consumption. The developing genre of the guidebook was instrumental in this 'commodification' of Paris. Tourism was one of the new 'industries' of the Second Empire, and guidebooks played a significant role in the literary production of the new Paris: 'in the later 1860s it seemed as if Haussmann had hardly a single friend, apart from the pamphleteers he paid and the editors of guidebooks, who are obliged to make the best of things'.[10] These early allies of Haussmann's urban policies helped to shape later ideas of the reconstructed city.

Paris for the tourist – and for the Parisian

Policies of self-promotion and attempts to control the image of cities were by no means unprecedented. For example, G. Labrot has fully documented this process in Rome during the sixteenth and seventeenth centuries. What he describes as 'astonishing manipulation' shifted from control of discourse about the Eternal City to a planning policy imposed on its urban fabric by the Popes: 'a passage from a purely linguistic grid of metaphors to one embodied in the material city'.[11] Guidebooks and other travel literature written for or by pilgrims played a major part in the shaping the representation of Rome and the ways in which its spatial structure was comprehended. This 'coercive image' of the city was used as a 'weapon' in the Roman clergy's fight against religious reform as well as against rival Italian cities such as Florence and Venice. [12]

The representation of Paris in travel books of the nineteenth century served similar political needs. A simplified and carefully groomed image of the city was constructed, from which elements of risk, mystery or degrading everyday detail were carefully excluded. For Rome the emphasis was on making pilgrims feel that they were in a familiar and clearly signposted environment which rightfully belonged to them as to every other Christian. In Paris there was a tension between a similar tendency to display a kind of culturally neutral and universally familiar space and an alternative which displayed the Parisian cityscape as deeply intertwined with Parisian identity, laden with specifically French values and reflecting the French character. Far from being the 'uninhabited world of monuments' described by R. Barthes as the standard fare of modern guidebooks, Paris was read as a landscape bearing deep marks of its national culture and its citizens.[13] The

British view of Paris was the one the French cared most about, as London was Paris's main competitor for the title of 'capital of Europe'. Additionally, the British were the largest national group of visitors throughout the century, and the increase in their number was only briefly set back by revolutionary events in 1830 and 1848–50.[14] The representation of Paris constructed during the nineteenth century was to a large extent inspired by British descriptions, which often wrote of the city as the diametric opposite of all that London was claimed to be.

Guidebooks recommended a number of routine performances to their reader to acquaint her or him with the city. The most important of these was to climb to a high point (Notre Dame, the Panthéon, the hills of Montmartre or the Père Lachaise) in order to enjoy the panorama. Later guidebooks, notably Galignani's *New Paris Guide for 1860* organised the geography of the city into a series of directed walks.[15] However, there were other devices which were used to impress on the reader that his or her guide was giving the keys to an understanding of the experience of Paris. One of these was that of the 'urban abstract', in which a particular site was marked out as highly symbolic of the whole Parisian experience, both unavoidable and compulsory for the tourist who wished to know the 'real' Paris. The Palais-Royal had played this role in the first decades of the century, but after Haussmannisation the boulevards took over. They were seen as revealing the essence of Parisian life and the Parisian character. Tourists were invited to join the crowd of *flâneurs* pacing the *trottoirs* amongst cafés and street entertainments, or to observe the moving panorama from the top of an omnibus.

This emblematic experience was one facet of the broader trope that guidebooks and travel literature were using to encapsulate Paris. Paris was the 'city of pleasure', to be contrasted with the 'city of business' across the channel. This contrast became such a commonplace that it was called upon casually, as though it were an unquestioned truth, as in this remark in Stanford's English guide to Paris: 'The omnibuses of Paris are far superior to those of London, not in speed, for London is a city of business, and Paris a city of pleasure, but in convenience, comfort, and economy.'[16] The *flâneur*, leisurely strolling along the boulevards of the 'city of pleasure', was a key element of this construction, and it became understood that '*flânerie*' was the exclusive preserve of Paris, impossible to reproduce properly in Regent Street, Unter den Linden or Nevski Prospect. From the late eighteenth century onwards British guides had observed that the Parisians were an out-of-door people, far less domestic than the English, spending much of their time in public places rather than cultivating the virtues of the home.

Significantly, English guidebooks to Second Empire Paris had a strong emphasis on the modern districts, where most wealthy visitors chose to stay, making brief excursions into older, more monumental areas of the city. Unlike later tourist literature, these works did not value a monument or an area on the basis of mere antiquity, and emphasised recent architectural achievements, the bright and sanitary new *quartiers*, and the new forms of modern everyday life. These guides reduced the city to a simplified geography of ancient and modern sights, leaving out all reference to areas which did not fit this compact and attractive image of a socially cohesive modern city wrapped around a historic core of monuments.

These English descriptions were echoed in many French guidebooks. While de Goncourt's bitter reflections on the changes taking place in Paris suggested that the characterisation of Parisians as an 'out-of-door' people was a misinterpretation of their deepest tendencies, authors of new guidebooks for the French public, such as Delvau, enthusiastically promoted this idea:

> To live at home, to think at home, eat and drink at home, to love at home, suffer at home, die at home seems boring and inconvenient to us. We need publicity, broad daylight, the street, the cabaret, the café, the restaurant, to testify favourably or unfavourably about ourselves, to chat, to be happy or unhappy, to satisfy the needs of our vanity or our mind, to laugh or to cry: we like to pose, to show off, to have a public, an audience, witnesses of our life. [17]

The extrovert life of the Parisians and the little dramas being played out in every café or street became part of the promotional policy of the French capital. English guidebooks, such as Galignani's, pointed to the exposure of the 'fair sex' in public places, unaccountably 'deemed perfectly respectable' by the French. What began as a prudish English critique of the unawareness on the part of gross Parisians of the need for female seclusion and, more generally, the lack of privacy in Parisian buildings and lives was transformed into a sales pitch for the city. This promotion of Paris as 'capitale du plaisir'[18] provoked some hostile reactions ('to believe that the idlers and high livers are all there is to Paris is to commit a gross mistake')[19], but most local authors eagerly accepted this identification of Paris with its boulevards, its cafés and its *flâneurs*. Texier's *Tableau de Paris* of 1853 defined the city as 'the classical land of cafés' and saw 'its boulevards and its strollers, container and content' as unique and inimitable possessions.[20] Similarly Conty's guide of 1863 dubbed Paris 'the city of pleasure and pleasures *par excellence*'.[21]

Writing on the construction of place identities 'amid the processes of globalisation and fragmentation' of the late twentieth century has suggested that 'part of the image of place is increasingly produced for actual or potential visitors' and that 'identities almost everywhere have to be produced partly out of the images constructed for tourists'.[22] Second Empire Paris seemed to be experiencing a very similar process of identity construction influenced from outside in the mid-nineteenth century. There have been various attempts to rehabilitate the seemingly frivolous and philistine figure of the tourist. Both Buzard and Urbain have depicted the tourist as a key figure in the understanding of modern cultural representations, and tourist rituals as processes whereby 'cultures recapitulate, express, exchange and valorise emblematic signs of their identity and their difference'.[23] James Duncan has described processes which protect tourists from a potentially destabilising 'cultural shock' by mimicking the 'authentic' and creating specific environments for tourists, who can thus proceed through their visit without having their values and certainties challenged.[24] Such processes may involve destructive or adulterating effects on the physical environments and cultural landscapes of places. The response of some contemporary commentators to the growth of tourism in Second Empire Paris suggests that these processes were contested and resisted.

The foreignness of New Paris

French texts about Paris usually wrote in unashamedly self-confident terms of the sustained fascination that the city exerted on foreigners. Yet there were deeper ambiguities in this relationship with the foreigner's gaze. French writings on the city often called upon the foreigner's view as a rhetorical device to underline some striking quality of the city, but were also often highly uneasy about the role of that view in reshaping both the physical landscape of the city and its interpretation. The areas of Paris that writers reacted against most strongly and describe as 'foreign' were the modern areas built on the northwestern fringe of the city and the newly opened thoroughfares. Texier thus addressed the stereotypical wealthy English visitor in these terms: 'For you, milord, Rivoli Square! ... Whether you like it or not, Paris has you among its vassals and subjects; it imitates your homeland most perfectly; but be not mistaken, it holds you, and is only trying to hide your chains!'[25]

According to Renaudin, writing in 1867, Parisian hospitality was such that 'there are no foreigners who may not feel themselves in Paris a little, and often completely, at home'.[26] But there is another side to this. Many suggested that Paris was dressing itself up in its party attire to seduce the foreigner. Paris was ceasing to be itself, and was becoming altered and adulterated by huge numbers of tourists and foreign residents. Desnoyers and Janin called the French capital 'the city of foreigners *par excellence*'[27] in 1846. This issue seemed to become even more pressing during the Second Empire. In 1867 the significantly-entitled *Paris, capitale du monde* described the invasion of the imperial city by the 'barbarian' hordes:

> Paris is not the capital of the eighty-nine départements any more, it is called the capital of the world! Indeed, there is no trace left of Parisian society, but Paris is home to the European upper crust, to which it owes its extravagant fashions, its amusements, its passion for splendour, and its incredible carelessness. ... Paris has a mission, it is the entertainer of Europe. ... It attracts the Barbarians, but the Barbarians overwhelm it day after day, by imposing their habits, pleasures and customs on it. ... What is to happen if this worldwide immigration continues? Paris will be an unheard-of jumble of all races, of all adventurers—a city of racing, gambling, dancing, perpetual parties, bacchanalia. No more people, just an anonymous, stateless crowd, without behaviour, without nationality, a crowd ready to submit to all, like the multitude which, in Rome and Byzantium, flowed massively, but meekly, around the palace of Caesar.[28]

Significantly these 'Barbarians' were wealthy tourists, who pushed up the cost of living, confiscating the city from its citizens, who were unable to compete economically. The whole reshaping of the city was interpreted as the result of the influence of foreigners. This view was common among writers, including those supportive of the regime and those who were opposed to it. For Claudin in his *Paris* of 1862, contemporaries were 'fortunate enough to live in an epoch of transformations' and those changes were 'most perceptible in Paris, the centre of railways, the universal station, and caravanserai of all parts of the globe'.[29] Claudin felt that the development of the railways had turned Paris into 'everybody's city', and 'the capital of Mexico-Walachia'.[30] The numerous new strangers had not, unlike their forebears, 'melted into Paris', but had undertaken to change it to suit their habits. Claudin suggested that the Emperor Napoleon III's 'wise policy' meant that 'this capital, which was for a while threatened with being able neither to house nor to feed the myriad foreigners crowding into its walls, is now up to welcoming this demanding crowd and offering suitable hospitality'.[31]

E. Pelletan in *La Nouvelle Babylone* of 1862 was much more critical of Haussmann's works, his 'craze for demolition and building'. 'Do you know what they said, to justify pulling down half of Paris? They said that the invention of steam made it the inn of Europe.'[32] 'As a result of the foreign invasion, there was such a crowd on the pavement that passers-by had to queue in the street as for a show. There was no option, in those circumstances, but to cut back and cut through the city, to give way to the flow of circulation'.[33] Pelletan suggested that the reconstruction of the city had been undertaken to relieve the government's 'national conscience':

> It decreed in its wisdom that Paris should display suitable hospitality; and instead of rotten slums, muddy streets, dirty shopfronts and darkened gables, it spread before the foreigner's eye long avenues with façades either new, freshly cleaned or painted white. What a good opinion he must derive from the inhabitants at the sight of such dwellings!'[34]

By 1875 Maxime Du Camp in his work on Paris was also recalling the ugliness and dirt of old Paris, but in his case to plead in favour of Haussmann's work. Though Du Camp sometimes disapproved of the influx of foreigners, which he saw as a corrupting influence, he also celebrated the transformation of the city, suggesting that:

> the larger, the airier, the more magnificent Paris, the more foreigners will be attracted to it, will stay there and bring in money which is a source of prosperity for the people. Some constructions which appear as luxurious madnesses repay a hundred times what they have cost, because they attract foreigners and keep them among us.[35]

English commentators both before and after the fall of the regime were also inclined to interpret the rebuilding of Paris from this perspective. Thus for W. B. Jerrold 'the Emperor has made a show capital as a speculation. All Europe contributes to the grandeur of the fashionable world of Paris.'[36] According to the anonymous journalist who wrote a *Diary of the Besieged Resident in Paris during the War* in the crisis of 1871:

> Paris is a city of pleasure—a cosmopolitan city; it has made its profit out of the follies and the vices of the world. Its prices are too high, its houses too large, its promenades and public places cost too much for it to be able to pay its own way as the sober, decent capital of a moderate-sized country, where there are few great fortunes. ... Paris is a house of cards.[37]

For many what seems to have been of primary importance was not whether this creation of a 'show capital' made economic sense, but its implications for urban identity. Foreigners would routinely describe the city of Paris as representative of the Parisian character. In their eyes the city provided the conjunction of a pleasant climate and a light-minded, gay, superficial people, who were prone to submit to authority and its abuses as long as they were entertained by grand ceremonies and flattered by architectural feats. Conversely, voices from a wide social range of inhabitants spoke of the confiscation of their capital by an international elite of high-livers, lured to Paris by the regime's advances. To Parisians it seemed that Napoleon III had used their city to engage the nation in a dialogue with 'all the peoples of the universe' except themselves. (See Figure 11.)

Despite London's incontrovertible economic and political supremacy, Paris is the city that has been remembered in Walter Benjamin's phrase as the 'capital of the nineteenth century.'[38] Paris went much further than London in making the city and its boulevards objects of desire and consumption, much in demand throughout Europe and North America. Paris was less a city of an industrial age than a marker of the beginning of the era of the tourist, the consumer and the idler. Contemporary depictions of Paris went beyond Benjamin's fixation on the semi-privatised, enclosed and socially selective space of the arcades in celebrating not so much commerce and 'commodity fetishism' directly as a wider image of an extrovert and popular city. The Paris of guidebooks and other urban commentaries of the time seems closer to David Harvey's account of the Second Empire city as the site of conflicting expressions of capitalism and of self-glorification of the regime.[39] In their different ways, both Harvey and Richard Sennett point to the ways in which Paris was a key space of political and

Figure 11 Souvenir of the Exposition Universelle of 1867. 'Answering the call of the Emperor Napoléon all the peoples of the universe hasten to Paris to take part in the Universal Exhibition at the great display of the arts of industry'

social conflict.[40] Even during the Second Empire there was a certain fascination and thrill in seeing a crowd whose revolutionary and violent credentials were unquestioned, tamed and exhibited as seemingly harmless street vendors or entertainers on the Champs Elysées.

Between 1851 and 1870 Paris was an 'imperial' city of a distinct kind: transformed not so much by its relationships with the wider world through trade or conquest as by the will and self-conscious direction of an emperor. And during this transformation many Parisians seem to have experienced a loss of their sense of ownership of the city. Arguably the developing modern city of the late nineteenth century was an alien and 'foreign' experience for all, but in Paris there was quite specific hostility to the creation of a city designed for consumption by foreigners. The 'whole world', invited in to attend carefully staged spectacles and imperial ceremonies embodied in the urban landscape, was felt to be a threatening and prying force; Paris was losing its soul to make an exhibition of itself.

The opposition to the regime did not dispute the central role of Paris, just the authoritarian appropriation of the capital to represent the imperial reign. Haussmannisation made inroads into the old, medieval areas of the centre of Paris, the scene of the fights of the Revolution, destroying the narrow streets where barricades had once been erected. But the Commune, which followed the fall of the Empire, proved that this physical restructuring of the capital had not succeeded in neutralising the aspirations of the people. However, after 1871 the Third Republic, far from changing the planning policies that had characterised the Second Empire, carried them further. A participant in the Commune and one of the starkest critics of the Second Empire, Jules Vallès, nevertheless praised the new open spaces and large boulevards of Haussmannised Paris as 'the Agora of our Athens',[41] places where classes could meet and interact, and thereby enact, so to speak, republican ideals. Such versatility and fluidity of the interpretation of the cityscape point to the importance of popular 'directions for use' of urban spaces, including those found in guidebooks and travel literature. A landscape planned for a new Rome could thus be handed back to Athens, an imperial city reverting to republican practices.

Notes

1 A. de Césena, *Le Nouveau Paris: guide de l'étranger* (Paris, Garnier, 1864), p. 1.
2 *Ibid.*, p. 704.
3 A. Dumas, T. Gautier *et al.*, *Paris et les Parisiens au XIXe siècle* (Paris, Morizot, 1856), p. iii.
4 *Ibid.*, p. 156.
5 L. Ulbach (ed.), *Paris-Guide* (Paris, Lacroix Verboeckhoven, 1867), p. xxxvi.
6 J. Gaillard, *Paris: la ville, 1851–70* (Paris, Champion, 1977).

7 E. de Goncourt, *Journal* (Paris, Pléiade, 1860), p. 327.
8 H. Taine, *Notes sur l'Angleterre* (Paris, Hachette, 1872), p. 17.
9 T. J. Clark, *The Painting of Modern Life: Paris in the Art of Manet and his Followers* (London, Thames & Hudson, 1984).
10 *Ibid.*, p. 41.
11 G. Labrot, *L'Image de Rome: une arme pour la Contre-Réforme, 1534–1677* (Seyssel, Champ Vallon, 1987), p. 136.
12 *Ibid.*
13 R. Barthes, 'Le Guide Bleu', in *Mythologies* (Paris, Seuil, 1957).
14 Estimates suggest that there were about 40,000 British visitors in 1856 and 60,000 in 1867. There was also a substantial 'colony' of British residents. See C. Leribault, *Les Anglais à Paris au XIXe siècle* (Paris, Musée Carnavalet, n.d.); P. Gerbod, 'Les touristes étrangers à Paris dans la première moitié du XIXe siècle', *Bulletin de la Société de l'Histoire de Paris et de l'Ile-de-France* (1983) 241–57; P. Gerbod, *Voyages au pays des mangeurs de grenouilles: la France vue par les Britanniques du XVIIIe siècle à nos jours* (Paris, Albin Michel, 1991).
15 A. & W. Galignani, *Galignani's New Paris Guide for 1860* (Paris, A. & W. Galignani, London, Simpkin Marshall, 1860).
16 E. Stanford, *Paris Guide* (London, Stanford, 1858), p. 50.
17 A. Delvau, *Les Plaisirs de Paris: guide pratique illustré* (Paris, Achille Faure, 1867), p. 64.
18 G. Claudin, *Paris* (Paris, Dentu, 1862), p. 172.
19 M. du Camp, *Paris: ses organes, ses fonctions et sa vie dans la seconde moitié du XIXe siècle* I (Paris, Hachette, 1869), pp. 14, 323–4.
20 E. Texier, *Tableau de Paris* (Paris, Paulin & Le Chevalier, 1852), pp. 356 and 29.
21 H. A. de Conty, *Paris en poche: guide pratique illustré de l'étranger dans Paris et ses environs* (Paris, Faure, 1863), p. 23.
22 J. Urry, *Consuming Places* (London, Routledge, 1995), p. 165.
23 J-D. Urbain, *L'Idiot du voyage: histoires de touristes* (Paris, Plon, 1991), p. 231; J. Buzard, *The Beaten Track: European Tourism, Literature and the Ways to Culture, 1800–1918* (Oxford, Clarendon Press, 1993).
24 J. S. Duncan, 'The social construction of unreality: an interactionist approach to the tourist's cognition of the environment', in D. Ley and M. S. Samuels (eds), *Humanistic Geography: Prospects and Problems* (London, Croom Helm, 1978).
25 Texier, *Tableau de Paris*, p. 52.
26 E. Renaudin, *Paris exposition ou Guide à Paris en 1867* (Paris, Delagrave, 1867), p. vi.
27 L. Desnoyers and J. Janin, *Les Étrangers à Paris* (Paris, Warée, 1846), p. v.
28 E. Texier and A. Kaempfen, *Paris, capitale du monde* (Paris, Hetzel, 1867), p. 9.
29 Claudin, *Paris*, pp. i–ii.
30 *Ibid*, p. 55.
31 *Ibid*, pp. 56, 64–5.
32 E. Pelletan, *La Nouvelle Babylone: lettres d'un provincial en tournée à Paris* (Paris, Pagnerre, 1862), p.15.
33 *Ibid.*, p. 20.
34 *Ibid.*, p. 60.
35 M. du Camp, *Paris: ses organes, ses fonctions et sa vie dans la seconde moitié du XIXe siècle* VI, (Paris, Hachette, 1875), p. 333.
36 W. B. Jerrold, *The Cockaynes in Paris* (London, Camden Hotten, 1871), p. 116.
37 *Diary of the Besieged Resident in Paris* (London, Hurst & Blackett, 1871), p. 359.
38 W. Benjamin, 'Paris, capitale du XIXe siècle' in *Essais* II (Paris, Denoël Gonthier, n.d.), pp. 37–53.
39 D. Harvey, *Consciousness and the Urban Experience: Studies in the History and Theory of Capitalist Urbanization*, (Oxford, Blackwell, 1985).
40 R. Sennett, *The Fall of Public Man* (London, Faber, 1977).
41 J. Vallès, *Le Tableau de Paris* (Paris, Français Réunis, (1880, reprinted 1971) p. 132.

CHAPTER FIVE

The Potemkin city:
tourist images of late imperial Vienna

Jill Steward

In 1913 the Vienna correspondent of the London *Times*, Wickham Steed, wrote, 'For forty years the Viennese have been studying how to draw a stream of foreign visitors to their city and for forty years have been astounded at their failure.'[1] Nevertheless, by the early twentieth century Vienna, capital of the Habsburg empire, was one of the most popular tourist centres in Central Europe. One reason for this was the city's function as the home of the emperor and the political and symbolic centre of the empire. The most visible signs of Vienna's imperial status were the royal residences and the monumental public buildings lying along the western section of the Ringstrasse, the wide boulevard encircling the inner city. The architect and critic Adolf Loos once commented, 'When I walk along the Ring I always get the feeling that a modern Potemkin has wanted to create, in the visitor to Vienna, the impression of a city exclusively inhabited by nobles.'[2] Loos compared the buildings of the Ringstrasse with the 'villages of cloth and cardboard' which General Potemkin, a favourite of Catherine the Great, had built to impress her when she visited an impoverished part of the Ukraine. The object of his sarcasm was not just the buildings themselves but the social, political and cultural world which they symbolised. The construction of the Ringstrasse in the late 1850s marked the beginning of the physical modernisation of the city, but by 1900 the social and political constitution of the empire appeared increasingly anachronistic.[3] Unlike the other great European empires, whose imperial status was based upon conquest and overseas colonialism, the Habsburg empire still looked back to feudal and dynastic principles. In the early twentieth century the Habsburg lands extended through the kingdom of Hungary and the empire of Austria – the latter stretching from the Alpine lands of the Tyrol, through Lower and Upper Austria and the Crown lands of Bohemia, to Polish Galicia, parts of northern Italy and the southern Slavic lands.

At the beginning of the early twentieth century all the qualities which contemporary tourist publicity now associates with Vienna, such as culture, gaiety and *gemütlich* charm, were already present as central elements in the city's touristic image. Guidebooks, souvenirs and the tourist publicity of the period show that the city's appeal to visitors lay as much in the splendours of its imperial past as in the modernity of its new facilities. This chapter examines the early days of the Viennese tourist industry and considers the role played by the city's imperial status in the development of its touristic image. The latter presented a parallel with the way in which the Habsburg dynasty came to be depicted in its own official 'mythology', a 'mythology' which found expression in the context of ritual celebrations that were tourist attractions in their own right. Both forms of representation helped to generate nostalgic images of the past which disguised the troubled nature of the present. One of the main causes of the empire's difficulties was the growth of nationalism in Central Europe in the second half of the nineteenth century, a phenomenon which called into question the political rationale of the empire. From abroad the empire was perceived as undeveloped and politically 'difficult', a source of disquiet in the political capitals of Western Europe. Even the Imperial Austrian Exhibition, held in London in 1906 to promote Austrian trade and industry, and regarded by contemporaries as a successful exercise in public relations, failed to change traditional perceptions of the 'backward' and 'uncivilised' nature of the greater part of the empire's dominions.[4]

Imperial Vienna and the emergence of a tourist culture

The largest part of Vienna's tourist traffic came from within the Austrian lands of the empire. Although Wickham Steed attributed the lack of foreign visitors to the city's lack of soul, a more pragmatic reason was Vienna's position, well to the east of the most important European tourist routes.[5] In the early twentieth century the number of foreign visitors still failed to match those of the other imperial tourist centres, Paris, London or Berlin. For example in 1913 there were around 100,000 visitors to the city from outside the empire, which was still only about a quarter of the number of non-French visitors to Paris.[6] Reinforced by hundreds of thousands of visitors from within the empire, the numbers were sufficiently large to make tourism an important element of the city's economy.

Although Vienna was a well established centre for eighteenth-century grand tourists, the city's role as a modern tourist centre did not begin until the International Exhibition of 1873. The exhibition provided an opportunity for the empire to maintain its claim to a place among the leading European powers, following military defeat two years earlier when the declaration of the German empire had spelt the end of Austrian hopes of political leadership in northern Europe. The exhibition was one of the earliest major foreign ventures of the British travel agent, Thomas Cook, but, despite bringing substantial numbers of visitors to the city, it turned out to be a financial disaster.[7] Bad publicity flowing from Vienna's inability to cope with the needs of its visitors helped to put off the foreign crowds, while domestic tourists were discouraged by an outbreak of cholera and a major stock exchange crash.

In Central Europe the steady, if uneven, spread of modernisation and economic development and the rapid extension of the railway system were important factors in the growth of tourism.[8] The 1873 exhibition provided an important stimulus to the provision of modern tourist facilities in Vienna so that, by the early 1880s, the city was able to accommodate steadily increasing numbers of tourists clutching their Baedekers. The appearance of tourist zones was indicated by the hotels, *pensions* and restaurants which sprang up around the main railway stations, between the Ringstrasse around the inner city and the Gürtel, which marked off the inner suburbs. The first tourist association was founded in 1882 and, in the following year, the Orient Express provided a luxurious and rapid link with the west.[9]

Vienna's imperial character was a central feature of the way visitors saw the city, irrespective of their place of origin or the purpose of their visit. The city was distinguished from the other regional capitals of the empire by its function as the residential seat of the emperor. The royal presence generated a glamour lacking elsewhere. This was evident in the way the tourist crowds gathered in the inner courtyard of the royal palace of the Hofburg to view the *Burgmusik*, the changing of the guard (Figure 12). Buildings and monuments symbolising the city's relationship with the Habsburg dynasty generated much of the touristic urban landscape. The imperial palaces, the imperial Vault, and even the Ringstrasse itself, were important tourist attractions. Begun in 1857, the Ringstrasse lay between the suburbs and the inner city, on the belt of open land which had been the site of the old fortifications. The emperor Josef II had made part of this land available for recreational purposes. The Ringstrasse project was the outcome of economic and population pressures on the inner city and the desire of the military for a means of deploying troops rapidly. Many of the open areas and buildings, such as the Votivkirche, which commemorated the emperor's escape from an assassin, the Hofburg, never fully completed, and the military parade ground of the Heldenplatz, were directly associated

Figure 12   Postcard of tourists watching the *Burgmusik*, the changing of the guard in the inner courtyard of the Hofburg, 1906

with the imperial family and constituted visible symbols of dynastic power.[10] As court space these areas competed with the areas occupied by the monumental public buildings of the Rathaus, the Museums and the University, which expressed the power and values of the municipal bourgeois elites who controlled the later phases of the Ring's construction.

Many of the sights listed in the tourist guidebooks were testaments to the efforts of the Habsburgs to instil dynastic loyalty into their subjects. The formal, baroque gardens of the summer palace of Schönbrunn had been open to the public since the 1820s and were popular with tourists and Viennese alike. By the 1880s they were easily accessible by *Stadtbahn*, the new city railway, or by electric tram. The Schönbrunn gardens were excellent examples of the way in which the baroque use of space was also a representation of the principles of absolutist power. From the folly of the Gloriette, the view out over the garden led the eye along the axial pathways of the garden and its alleyways to the city beyond. As Robert Rotenberg has remarked, these vistas seemed to extend out beyond the limits of the palace grounds through the outstretched city and to connect with various landmarks marking the central points of royal power.[11] This 'bird's eye' view of the city was routinely included among the mandatory tourist spectacles listed by guidebooks.

[81]

As tourism became well established literature aimed at tourists contributed to the social and spatial mapping out of tourist zones. Guidebooks and publicity material marked out specific places and spaces as tourist sights, incorporated verbal and visual images which reinforced particular ways of viewing the city and indicated the whereabouts of appropriate forms of leisure and entertainment. Visitors were told where their requirements could be met and which sights and spectacles were most worthy of attention. The most important of those within the tourist zones became recognised as commercial assets as visitors behaved in a way which was influenced by the standardising and normalising recommendations of their guidebooks.[12]

All the guidebooks to Vienna paid particular attention to the sites around the Ringstrasse associated with the high culture of art, music and drama. These were important attractions for Central European visitors, many of whom associated Vienna with bourgeois versions of the Grand Tour.[13] The Museums, the Opera House and the Burgtheater were cultural monuments in their own right and, illuminated by the new electric lighting, they contributed to the city's image as a major cultural centre. Vienna was seen both as the home of Mozart, Beethoven and Brahms and as the site of an aristocratic way of life in which the cultivation of art and music was central. Other spaces and sights important to tourists included the city parks, the *Stadtbahn* and the electric trams, still a novelty to some Central European visitors. Begun in the 1850s, the goal of the early phase of the tramway network had been to link central Vienna with the more distant areas of the city such as the Prater and the foothills of the Vienna Woods, where the upper middle class still spent the summers.[14] The old wine-growing villages of the Vienna Woods had been popular with the Viennese for weekend and evening outings since the end of the eighteenth century. This habit persisted, although by the end of the following century the inner suburbs extended out into the foothills and the largest of the remaining wine taverns were increasingly orientated towards tourism.[15]

On the other side of the city, the other main site of leisure and entertainment was the Prater. Opened to the public by Josef II in 1766, this open space contained lawns, paths, amusement and sporting facilities. It was much used for formally organised spectacles such as the Flower Corso and the workers' May Day parade, while the 1873 Exhibition Hall housed conferences and congresses. While in theory the Prater was open to all, in practice the social classes did not mix. Nets sealed off the grounds when musical and theatrical events took place, which were kept exclusive by the price of admission tickets.[16] Humbler visitors were catered for by the Volksprater, with its public houses, snack bars and amusement park. The latter was the site of one of the first cinemas, and its moving landscapes soon superseded those of the traditional dioramas and stereoscopes. The giant ferris wheel, built to commemorate Franz-Josef's Jubilee in 1898, rapidly became to Vienna what the Eiffel Tower was to Paris, an instantly recognisable symbol of the city.[17] An Olympic Arena, which opened in 1902, could hold 4,000 people and claimed to be the largest open air theatre in Europe. A popular success was an early version of a theme park, 'Venice in Vienna', which attracted 2 million visitors when it opened in 1895. Evoking another 'city of pleasure', a favourite honeymoon destination for the Viennese, 'Venice' also included a version of the Moulin Rouge.[18] The associations conjured up by the latter were no coincidence, since prostitution was also one of the attractions of the Prater.

A long-standing element in the city's traditional place image was the pleasure-loving reputation of its inhabitants, famous as an expression of the popular culture of the working people as well as the social life of its elites. The letters and reminiscences of grand-tourists and travellers such as Lady Wortley Montagu and Mrs Frances Trollope contributed to this picture.[19] Foreigners frequently commented on the way the authorities appeared to use the pleasure-loving disposition of the people to maintain their compliance.[20] The role played by the state in the construction of public amusements had been noted as early as 1814, when Vienna was host to the European diplomatic community during the Congress of Vienna. An observer remarked, 'That gaiety, that brilliancy, and those pleasures, were contrived more for political ends, than for the apparent purpose of rendering Vienna, for the time, the most attractive and agreeable capital in Europe.'[21] As the city's tourist culture developed, one of the features of the city's image which most appealed to visitors was that of the 'city of pleasure' and this became more prominent in its tourist publicity.

Guidebooks were an important influence on the way visitors came to experience a strange place. By the early twentieth century the appearance of illustrated guidebooks such as the *Wiener Cicerone* and Bermann's *Illustrierter Führer durch Wien* indicated the broadening of the tourist market.[22] Less austere than the famous Baedeker, they addressed a different public and used illustrations to identify the main sights so that there could be no mistakes of recognition. At the same time they encouraged visitors to see the city in a specific way, as they 'framed' the city's landscapes as aesthetic spectacles. By omitting certain areas and specifying certain itineraries, the guidebooks to Vienna helped to divert the visitor's attention from certain aspects of city life such as the prostitutes who frequented certain parts of the Gürtel and the homeless under the bridges of the new canals.[23]

One of the advantages which Vienna enjoyed over other large cities such as London was its geography. The compact old aristocratic core which lay at the heart of the main tourist zone was relatively undeveloped, apart from some luxury shops and hotels, and was insulated from social change by the parks and monuments of the Ringstrasse. Both the daily ritual of social display of the Corso promenade on the Kärtnerstrasse, and the *Fiaker* Ball of the carnival season, which had been reinvented as a commercial enterprise for tourists, reminded visitors of a happier social world and made it relatively easy for them to distance themselves from the aesthetic and social ugliness of modern urban life.[24] By the twentieth century tourists desired to escape from the unpleasant aspects of modern urban life but still wished to enjoy its comforts and conveniences. Unfortunately the very existence of tourists and the infrastructure required to service their needs contributed to the visible signs of modernity outside the tourist zones such as the new apartment houses, factories, and above all, the traffic which made it increasingly difficult to satisfy the tourists' desire for suitably picturesque urban landscapes. Corners of the city that remained unscathed, such as Beethoven's home in Heilingenstadt, rapidly acquired a new commercial value in the geography of Vienna's tourist culture. Typical of a certain style of vernacular architecture, the house was popular with artists and visitors alike as the embodiment of 'charming old Vienna'.[25] Ironically, the pressures of overcrowding and the development of the rural areas on the outskirts of the city helped to generate many of the evocative images of scenes around Vienna which were sold to tourists.

The tourist industry was an important source of income for the city's many painters and graphic artists, as well as for the commercial and amateur photographers who produced images for the postcard trade. Invented in Austria in 1869, by the early twentieth century postcards were in their Golden Age and were sold everywhere.[26] In Vienna the main sites of interest such as the Graben, parts of the Ringstrasse, and the inner city core, acquired new commercial significance as they, and their inhabitants, were endlessly represented. Popular images were constantly recycled, appearing first as water colours and then as postcards. Many images of the city's urban landscapes were reproduced in this form for tourists. Painted in the idealised Biedermeier style of Rudolf Alt, they minimalised the monumentality of the buildings and created a sense of intimacy with the street people.[27] The chestnut sellers, the gypsies, the exotic *Ostjuden* (Galician Jews) and the street musicians, all signs of the grinding poverty found in the city, seemed less threatening or alien when seen as decorative features of the urban landscape.

In 1873, at a time when much of Vienna outside the inner core was rapidly becoming a building site, one of the exhibits at the exhibition was a *tableau vivant*, an authentically peopled recreation of the old eighteenth-century city, which foreshadowed the subsequent commercial imaging of the city.[28] As the city's tourist zones became commercialised the everyday life of its streets and their inhabitants were turned into self-conscious spectacles for touristic consumption, often through the lens of the ubiquitous Kodak. All this worked to reinforce the stereotypical belief in the city's *gemütlich* charm, a kind of mental cosiness, and the quality which the local press ascribed to 'true' Viennese as opposed to 'foreigners'. Like the street signs for *alten Wiener Küche*, the concept evoked a time before the building of the Ringstrasse, of 'characters' in beerhouses, wine gardens and cafés in the old villages and summer resorts which were being swallowed up by the new suburbs. The alliance of *Gemütlichkeit* and nostalgia was also present in the *Wiener Cicerone*'s identification and depiction of Viennese types, a genre which was a popular subject of the documentary postcard (Figure 13). Drawing on a long tradition in Viennese literature, both nostalgic and satirical, the *Cicerone* lamented that such types were no longer as common as they used to be. The *Wiener Cicerone* included many photographs, some of which used actors (Figure 14). Posed as 'Viennese types' they were arranged as if on a stage so that the city behind them was turned into an extension of its own theatrical space.[29]

The empire and its problems

Included amongst the Viennese sights were the representatives of the empire's diverse populations. Foreign visitors to the city invariably reported on its ethnic variety. According to the 1890 census, 65.5 per cent of Vienna's inhabitants had been born outside the city.[30] This was particularly evident in the case of the Jews. Western visitors to the city used the term 'Orientals' to refer not only to the Muslims of the Balkans but also to the extensive Jewish populations found throughout the empire. Western visitors were reminded of Metternich's old aphorism, that the Orient began east of the Landstrasse, and continued to think of Vienna as located on the cultural boundary between the 'civilised' west and the 'uncivilised' east.[31] Foreign visitors were constantly struck by the conspicuously exotic and outlandish *Ostjuden*, marked out by their clothing and speech, as were the Hungarian gypsies, the Balkan Muslims and the Bohemian nursemaids.[32] It was this ethnic variety which gave such a distinctive character to the city's social, cultural and culinary life. For domestic visitors this aspect of

Haus-Hofmusikanten.
Wiener Typen.

Figure 13 Postcard of Viennese types: door-to-door street musicians, 1902

Viennese life brought into play numerous and opposing images of cultural identity which were bound up with class and with ethnic, linguistic and religious affiliation.

In the early twentieth century this situation was accentuated as it became increasingly evident that the main reason for the persistence of the empire was the survival of its ruling dynasty. The rapid growth of nationalism in Central Europe, particularly among the Bohemian Czechs, the Galician Poles and the southern Slavs, was a constant source of worry to the Austrian government. The growth of national and ethnic self-consciousness posed a particular problem for the empire, which possessed no clear or dominant image of its own cultural and national identity as such.[33] The official version of Habsburg 'mythology' represented the emperor as a kind of folk hero and the empire as a 'family of nations'. In Vienna this 'myth' received specific expression in the various celebratory rituals which punctuated the emperor's reign.[34] The architectural showpieces along the Ringstrasse, designed to create an imperial city worthy of the name, constituted an ideal *mise-en-scène* for state events intended to impress both foreign

Figure 14 'Greetings from Vienna', 1905. A highly constructed image in which the theatrical space of the figures is superimposed on to the backdrop of a photograph of the Freyjung

and domestic visitors. Particularly memorable was the silver wedding pageant of 1878, involving 10,000 participants dressed in the costumes of Habsburg Flanders. Designed and orchestrated by the history painter Hans Makart, it depicted the benign effects of Habsburg rule on art and industry. Tourist attractions in their own right, these imperial spectacles represented the emperor as the benevolent centre of a peacefully coexisting but heterogeneous collection of picturesque ethnic groups.

Unfortunately the image of a 'family of nations' was increasingly at odds with the reality of the situation as different ethnic groups asserted their claims to their own distinctive national, linguistic and cultural identities. On the streets of Vienna the rise in national consciousness gave many of the imperial city's tourist sights a new significance. Many of the monuments listed in the guidebooks, such as the statues of Goethe and Schiller, stood for German high culture and, although of interest to German-speaking tourists, to others they symbolised German dominance in cultural matters and the control which the city's German-speaking *haute bourgeoisie* exercised over the empire's educational and administrative systems.[35] For many visitors the city's imperial monuments represented an idea of empire which was perceived as increasingly irrelevant and antagonistic to their own concerns.

Displaying the city:
the Imperial Austrian Exhibition

By the early twentieth century tourism was beginning to make an important contribution to the Austrian economy as the Alpine and the sub-Alpine areas grew increasingly dependent on its commercial benefits. In Vienna the city's trade and tourist associations were well aware of the contribution which the industry made to the city's financial well-being and were eager to increase the number of foreign visitors. Exhibitions of all sorts were an established feature of modern urban life and, as the competition for tourists became more severe, a standard means of promoting trade and tourism.[36] Many of the European powers which participated in the big international exhibitions, such as Chicago (1893), Paris (1900) and St Louis (1904) put on displays which were orientated towards the justification of overseas colonialism and the demonstration of technological and racial superiority.[37] The Austrian 'family of nations', whose main rationale lay in the dynastic mission of the Habsburgs, fitted uneasily into this format. This only served to reinforce the empire's foreign image as a decaying presence within the complex system of European political and economic alliances. The problematic nature of the 'family' image was compounded by the increasing restiveness of the non-German nationalities, the Czechs, the Serbs and the other Slavic groups. International tensions failed to help the situation. In London the British government worried about German ambitions in the Balkans, while in Berlin the Kaiser fretted about the Prince of Wales's attempts to cultivate links between Great Britain and Austria, Germany's official ally. This led the Prince of Wales to pay a formal visit to Vienna in 1903 (including a trip round the Ringstrasse) and to have regular meetings with the emperor during his annual 'cure' at the Bohemian spa of Marienbad.

By the early twentieth century the relationship between tourism and publicity was recognised everywhere except in official Austria. Although the Austrian state provided very little financial support for their work, trade and tourist organisations were increasingly aware of the importance of publicity as a means of attracting foreign tourists. In 1906, when the exhibition impresarios Harold Hartley and Imre Kiralfy proposed a big Austrian trade exhibition, 'Austria in London', to be held at Earl's Court, Vienna's trade and tourist associations enthusiastically agreed to participate. The emperor supported the venture and the Austrian government agreed to contribute financially, although the bulk of the cost was to be borne by the exhibiting organisations.[38] London was a suitable choice for such an exhibition since many of the Austrian elite greatly admired the style and way of life of the English aristocracy and shared a mutual passion for hunting. The western provinces of Austria were popular with British tourists as increasing numbers visited their health resorts and began to abandon the beaten tourist tracks of Switzerland for the less heavily developed Tyrol.[39] However, the appeal of Vienna itself was still principally to the well-to-do visitor, often with personal or business connections. Benefiting from royal patronage, the proposed exhibition became the Imperial Austrian Exhibition. A large number of exhibits were directly related to tourism, one of the largest of which was a photographic journey through Austria staged by the Ministry of Railways.

The intention of J. R. Whiteley, the founder of the trade exhibitions at Earl's Court, was to give the British a 'living picture' of other nations. By this time trade exhibitions were a well established genre, many of them characterised by the construction of exotic and dream-like images. This effect was easier to achieve away from the homeland, when visitors were unable to compare the 'dream landscape' of the exhibition with the reality outside.[40] However, rather than drawing on the more unfamiliar and exotic aspects of imperial life, the Austrian exhibition focused on themes which were reassuringly familiar. Ethnic villages were common features of trade exhibitions, and one of the main exhibits at the Imperial Austrian Exhibition was a reconstruction of a Tyrolean village. This had become a well established feature of Austrian contributions to foreign trade exhibitions.[41] Using elements established as attractive and successful components of Alpine tourism, the vernacular style of the village and the display of the crafts and pastimes of its inhabitants emphasised the homely, rural values of a rapidly disappearing peasant world.

By contrast with this rural idyll, Vienna was represented as a cosmopolitan city of culture, luxurious and fashionable elegance and high-class shopping facilities: an image supported by the numerous exhibits of luxury goods, arts and crafts, and the presence of major art organisations, such as the newly formed Wiener Werkstätte, the Hagenbund and the Secession. The art journal *The Studio*, which took an interest in Austrian art, contributed a Special Summer Issue.[42] All the standard tourist sites of Vienna were represented in the display, including the Belvedere Palace, the Karl's Church, St Stephen's Church and the Franziskanerplatz. The 'life and customs of the common people, the social life of Vienna', included 'Vienna at work' in a bakery, a dairy and a sausage factory. The need for amusements and spectacles in trade exhibitions was provided for by 'authentic' Viennese attractions such as 'Vienna by night' and variety acts from the Prater. The effect of verisimilitude was strengthened by the presence of Bassett's Big Wheel. A whirl of social events for high society accompanied the exhibition, while visits from royalty provided photo opportunities. The strong relationship which already existed between the anglophile Austrian aristocracy and their English counterparts was undoubtedly reinforced by a party at the Savoy thrown by Arthur Krupp, the president of the committee, at which 700 guests were served by the Tyrolean villagers and allowed to choose their own wine. This dimension of the exhibition supported Vienna's traditional image as a 'city of pleasure' which was reinforced by the immense popularity of Franz Lehar's *Merry Widow* when it made its London début the following year.

By selecting the Tyrolean peasant as the representative of Austria's diverse ethnic groups the exhibition focused on an image known to be attractive to British tourists and one which firmly aligned the country with the familiar Alpine lands of the west rather than the alien, distant and undeveloped lands of the east. But even the favourable publicity received by the exhibition could not overcome the established Western view of the empire. This was not surprising, as political troubles had not been left behind. The handbook of the Bohemian section of the exhibition painted a vivid picture of Prague's tourist attractions but also set out Bohemia's claims to a separate historical and cultural identity.[43] An image from the *Illustrated London News* (1906), produced in its own studio, just after the close of the exhibition, vividly expressed the situation. Picturesque peasants posing as representatives of the empire's diverse ethnic communities were grouped in front of the familiar Alpine village.[44] The relatively sophisticated and modern city of Vienna was represented by three discreetly placed 'Civilised Gypsies', thus relegating the city to a location within an imaginary Bohemia.[45] The caption, 'A hard family to govern: the emperor Franz-Josef's motley empire – The extraordinary diversity of nationalities composing the Austrian-Hungarian empire', suggests that, for this section of the press at least, the associations evoked by the empire were still those of the 'uncivilised' borderlands and their unruly inhabitants.

The last days of the empire

As political power in Austria gradually began to shift away from Vienna and the Habsburg hereditary lands to the centres of the new political forces of nationalism located in the cities of Prague, Cracow, Zagreb and Lvov, Vienna's imperial role began to decline. By the early twentieth century the influence of nationalism was visible, not only on the social and political life of the empire, but also in the touristic behaviour of its inhabitants as Bohemian Czechs chose to holiday in the Slavic southern lands rather than in the German-speaking areas of the Tyrol and Lower Austria. In the imperial cities of Prague, Cracow and Budapest monuments of Czech, Polish and Magyar culture became increasingly important as tourist attractions.

For the jubilee of 1908 the Ringstrasse was turned into the setting for yet another pageant, in which the imagery of 'the family' and its history demonstrated the way in which the emperor's position was increasingly grounded in symbolism rather than effective power. Each successive epoch of Habsburg history was included, and each ethnic group was clad in its own national costume. The final touch was added at mid-day by the appearance of an obliging rainbow. Koloman Moser's 1908 jubilee postcard combined powerful images of the Gloriette and the palace of Schönbrunn with the head of the ageing emperor (Figure 15).

Despite the strength of Vienna's touristic image as an imperial city, the waning of the power on which its status depended, although still a source of glamour and spectacle, increasingly reminded observers that empires are subject to decay. The monumental buildings on the Ringstrasse, for all their splendour, seemed frozen in their historical fancy dress, epitomising the political stalemate which characterised

Figure 15   Koloman Moser's commemorative postcard for Franz-Josef's Diamond Jubilee, 1908

Austrian politics. On a wider front, events invariably reminded foreigners of the politically backward and troubled nature of the empire. Two years before the Austrian Imperial Exhibition, the London *Strand Magazine* had published an article on the East End of London focusing on Jewish immigrants from Eastern Europe. 'In Alien-land' referred to 'this foreign land which is in London but not of it'.[46] This was analogous to the way that Westerners invariably perceived similar immigrants on the streets of Vienna as symbols of the empire's political and cultural distinctiveness and its inherent alterity. For although the Austro-Hungarian empire was part of Europe, it retained its separateness, a legacy of former times. At the same time, the empire's decline evoked Western fears about the fragility of the boundary between the 'civilisation' which justified colonial imperialism and the 'barbarism' which it kept at bay.[47] In the year of the 1908 jubilee Austria annexed Bosnia and Herzegovina, an event which caused consternation in the Western press. In Britain the story in the *Illustrated London News* was copiously illustrated with pictures of wild scenery and brigand-like peasants displaying all the stereotypical features which the British press generally associated with the empire's least westernised territories.[48]

The end of the First World War saw the collapse of the empire. In the inter-war period, tourism became central to the economy of an Austria much reduced in size and shorn of its troublesome eastern dominions. For most tourists at the end of the twentieth century 'Vienna' still means Habsburg Vienna. To its foreign visitors the city presents a carefully constructed image, with the complex history of spaces such as the Heldenplatz carefully neutralised. The art of the Secession, deeply unattractive to visitors to the 1908 jubilee, has become the subject of intense marketing. The 'coffee house' culture view of turn-of-the-century Vienna presents the city's artists and intellectuals as the driving force behind a 'glorious explosion' of European modernism, ignoring the way in which Vienna, an intensely conservative and antisemitic city, was abandoned by many of its more innovative artists and intellectuals. In its publicity Vienna is still imperial Vienna, the city of waltzes and *Sachertorte*.[49] The tourist zones are still almost identical with those which existed before the First World War but now include the post-imperial spectacle provided by Turkish and Balkan immigrants in the *Naschmarkt*, alongside the consciously staged heritage displays of people in eighteenth-century dress in the area around the Hofburg and the other symbolic monuments of former imperial splendour.

Notes

1 H. Wickham Steed, *The Hapsburg Monarchy*, (fourth edition, London, Constable, 1919), p. 206.
2 Cited in B. Gravagnuolo, *Adolf Loos: Theory and Works* (London, Art Data, 1995), p. 54.
3 C. E. Schorske, 'The Ringstrasse, its critics and the birth of urban modernism', in C. Schorske, *Fin-de-siècle Vienna: Politics and Culture*, (New York, Knopf, 1980), pp. 24–115.
4 See L. Wolff, *Inventing Eastern Europe: The Map of Civilization on the Mind of the Enlightenment*, (Stanford CA, Stanford University Press, 1994).
5 Wickham Steed, *The Hapsburg Monarchy*, p. 206.
6 F. Baltarek, 'Fremdenverkehr und Sport', in *Das Zeitalter Kaiser Franz Josephs-Glanz und Elend, 1880–1916* II (Schloss Grafenegg, Niederösterreichische Landesmuseums, 1987), p. 167.
7 *Cook's Excursionist and International Tourist Advertiser* (London), April (1873), pp. 3–4. I am indebted to the Thomas Cook Archive for this information.
8 P. Jordan, 'Die Entwicklung der Fremdensverkehrsströme in Mitteleuropa 1910–90 als Ausdruck politischer und wirtschaftlicher Veränderungen', *Mittelungen der Österreichischen Geographischen Gesellschaft*, 132 (1990) 144–71.
9 E. H. Cookridge, *Orient Express: the Life and Times of the World's most Famous Train*, (London, Penguin, 1957), pp. 41–2.
10 C. E. Schorske, 'Museum in contested space: the sword, the sceptre and the Ring', *Jahrbuch der Kunsthistorischen Sammlungen in Wien*, 88 (1992) 11–20. E. Lichtenberg, *Vienna: Bridge between Cultures*, trans. D. Muhlgassser and C. Reisser (London, Belhaven, 1993), pp. 72–81.
11 R. Rotenberg, *Landscape and Power in Vienna*, (Baltimore, Johns Hopkins University Press, 1995), pp. 55–6.
12 See D. McCannell, *The Tourist: A New Theory of the Leisure Class* (New York, Schocken, 1976).
13 W. Kaschuba, 'German *Bürgerlichkeit* after 1800: culture as a symbolic practice', in J. Kocka and A. Mitchell (eds), *Bourgeois Society in Nineteenth Century Europe*, (Oxford, Berg, 1993).
14 P. Capuzzo, 'Transportation System and Urban Space, Vienna, 1865–1938', unpublished paper, third International Conference on Urban History, 'Cities in Eastern and Western Europe', Central European University, Budapest, 29–31 August (1996).
15 H. Gruber, *Red Vienna: Experiment in Working Class Culture, 1919–34*, (Oxford, Oxford University Press, 1991), pp. 116–19; R. Rotenberg, 'Viennese wine gardens and their magic', *East European Quarterly*, 4 (1984) 447– 60.
16 Rotenberg, *Landscape and Power*, pp. 80–2; U. Storch, *Das Pratermuseum* (Vienna, Museen der Stadt Wien, 1993); Gruber, *Red Vienna*, pp. 116–18.
17 R. Barthes, *The Eiffel Tower and other Mythologies*, trans. R. Howard (Berkeley CA and London, University of California Press, 1979). For the significance of the ferris wheel see also L. de Cauter, 'The panoramic ecstasy: on world exhibitions and the disintegration of experience', *Theory, Culture and Society*, 10 (1992) 1–23.
18 N. Rubey and P. Schoenwald (eds), *Venedig in Wien, Theater- und Vergnügsstadt der Jahrhundertwende*, (Vienna, Ueberreuter, 1996).
19 See M. Wortley Montagu, *Letters and Works*, ed. Lord Wharncliff, rev. W. Thomas (London, Bentley, 1837); F. Trollope, *Vienna and the Austrians, with some Account of a Journey through Swabia, Bavaria, the Tyrol, and the Salzburg*, (London, Bentley, 1838).
20 For an account of Vienna which renders it feminine by focusing on the visibility of the women of the 'burger class' and emphasising the political 'softness' of its men see V. Gayda, *Modern Austria: Her Social and Racial Problems, Italia Irridentia*, (London, Unwin, 1915), pp. 295–6.
21 Anon., *Austria and the Austrians*, (London, Colburn, 1837), p. 62.
22 See, for example, M. Bermann, *Illustrierter Führer durch Wien und Umgebungen*

(Vienna, Hartleben, 1908); W. Hollrigl, *Wiener Cicerone 1907. Illustrierter Führer durch Wien and Umgebungen, Vienna* (Vienna, Dorn, 1907); J. Meurer, *A Handy Illustrated Guide to Vienna and Environs* (Vienna and Leipzig, Hartleben, second edition, 1906).

23 On 'tours' and 'boundaries' see M. de Certeau, *The Practice of Everyday Life*, trans. S. Rendall (Berkeley CA, University of California Press, 1984), pp. 95–102.

24 I. Barea, *Vienna: Legend and Reality* (London, Pimlico, 1992), pp. 318–23. See D. Olsen, *The City as a Work of Art* (London and New Haven CT, Yale University Press, 1986), pp. 235–48, for a discussion of Vienna as a setting for *Selbstdarstellung* or presentation of the self.

25 R. Kassal-Mikula, 'Architecture from 1815–48', in R. Waissenberger (ed.), *Vienna in the Beiedermeier Era* (London, Alpine Fine Arts Collection (UK) 1986), pp. 151–3. See *Wiener Landschaften* (Vienna, Museen der Stadt Wien, 1993), and Rotenberg, 'Gardens of reform' in *Landscape and Power* pp. 148–87, for a discussion of attitudes to Vienna's urban landscape, its parks and gardens.

26 F. Czeike, 'Wiener Kunstpostkarten', *Wiener Geschichtsblätter*, 38:4 (1983) 167–9.

27 R. Paulin, 'The Beidermeier Anomaly: Cultural Conservatism and Technological Progress', in R. Robertson and E. Timms (eds), *The Enlightenment and its Aftermath* (Edinburgh, Edinburgh University Press, 1991), pp. 88–9.

28 Anon., *Art Journal*, July (1873), p. 217; P. Greenhalgh, *Ephemeral Vistas: The Expositions Universelles, Great Exhibitions and World Fairs, 1851–1939* (Manchester, Manchester University Press, 1988), p. 105.

29 For the role of theatre in Vienna see W. E. Yates, *Theatre in Vienna*, (Cambridge, Cambridge University Press, 1997).

30 E. Sagarra, 'Vienna and its population in the late nineteenth century: social and demographic change, 1870–1910', in G. J. Carr and E. Sagarra (eds), *Fin-de-siècle Vienna*, (Dublin, Trinity College, 1985), pp. 187–203.

31 L. Wolff, *Inventing Eastern Europe: The Map of Civilization on the Mind of the Enlightenment*, (Stanford CA, Stanford University Press, 1994).

32 See review of V. Tissot, *Vienne et la vie viennoise* (Paris, Dentu, 1878) in the article 'Vienna and Viennese life', *Blackwood's Magazine* May (1879) 603–24.

33 For a discussion of this view of the Empire see S. Wank, 'Some reflections on the Habsburg empire and its legacy in the nationalities question', *Austrian History Yearbook*, XXVIII (1997) 131–46.

34 C. Magris, *Der habsburgerische Mythos in der österreichischen Literatur* (Salzburg, Muller, 1966); J. Shedel, 'Emperor, Church and people: religion and dynastic loyalty during the Golden Jubilee of Franz Joseph', *Catholic History Review*, 9 (1990) 71-93; A. Wheatcroft, *The Habsburgs: Embodying Empire*, (London and New York, Viking, 1995), pp. 27–84.

35 For the political implications of cultural monuments see R. Berman, *Modern Culture and Critical Theory: Art, Politics and the Legacy of the Frankfurt School* (Madison WI, University of Wisconsin Press, 1989), p. 165.

36 For the role of tourism see, for example, P. Fritzsche, *Reading Berlin 1900* (Cambridge MA, Harvard University Press, 1996), pp. 66–72, and for trade exhibitions, see S. West, 'National desires and *regionale* realities in the Venice Biennale, 1895–1914', *Art History*, 18:3 (1995) 404–34, and D. Rowe, 'Georg Simmel and the Berlin Exhibition of 1896', *Urban History*, 22:2 (1995) 216–28.

37 Greenhalgh, *Ephemeral Vistas*, p. 105.

38 H. Hartley, *Eighty-eight not out: A Record of Happy Memories*, (London, Muller, 1939), pp. 147–54. State funding for organisations involved in foreign exhibitions was usually limited and often controversial, as in the 1904 St Louis exhibition. See J. Wiegenstein, *Artists in a Changing Environment: The Viennese Art World, 1860–1918* (Ann Arbor MI, University of Michigan Press, 1980), p. 313.

39 For the British relationship with the eastern Alps see A. Bürstmuller, 'Der Anteil britisher Bergsteiger an der Erschliessung der Ostalpen', in O. Hirsch (ed.), *Österreich und die angelsächsische Welt. Kulturebegnungen- und Vergleiche* (Vienna and Stuttgart, Braümuller, 1968), pp. 559–601.

40 See for example R. Rydell, *All the World's a Fair: Visions of Empire and the American International Expositions, 1876–1910* (Chicago, University of Chicago Press, 1984).
41 E. N. Kaufman, 'The architectural museum from World's Fair to restoration village', *Assemblage*, 9 (1989) 21–39.
42 C. Holmes (ed.), *The Art Revival in Austria* (London, Studio, 1906).
43 *Bohemian Section at the Austrian Exhibition, Earl's Court, London: A Guide to the Bohemian Section and the Kingdom of Bohemia: A Memento* (Prague, Wiesner, 1906). See also F. Lützow, *The Story of Prague*, (London, Dent, 1902).
44 *Illustrated London News*, 15 December 1906, p. 895.
45 M. Tyers, 'Beyond words: in search of Bohemia', *Romance Studies*, 25 (1995) 85–7. See also J. V. Polisensky, *Britain and Czechoslovakia*, (Prague, Orbis, 1968), pp. 64–5.
46 G. R. Sims, 'Off the track in London', *Strand Magazine*, 160:27 (1904) 472.
47 S. Arata, 'The occidental tourist: Dracula and the anxiety of reverse colonialism', *Victorian Studies*, 33:4 (1990) 621–45: P. Brantlinger, *Rule of Darkness: British Literature and Imperialism, 1830–1914*, (Ithaca NY, Cornell University Press, 1988).
48 *Illustrated London News*, 15 December 1906, p. 895.
49 See, for example, the publicity magazine *Vienna Scene*, (Vienna, Vienna Tourist Board, 1994/95), p. 20.

CHAPTER SIX

Imperial visions:
rebuilding the Bank of England, 1919–39

Iain Black

Architecture needs some ornament in its design and my prompting has always been to avoid the pedantry of the old forms which have lost all meaning to us, and at the other extreme, the senseless cubical blockings which pass for ornament in some modernist art. My ideal, instead, has been to breathe into it some living significance ... symbolism in a higher sense may be one source of magnetic energy to art and poetry. I might define its meaning in the words of Bacon as 'imagination above reason expressed by similitude, types, parables, visions and dreams'.

Sir Herbert Baker, 'Symbolism in Art'[1]

In the nineteenth century the City of London became the undisputed centre of a world trading system that, although always wider than the formal British empire, was nonetheless indelibly marked by that imperial space. As the monetary hub of empire, and as a focal point for commodity trade, the City functioned as the clearing house of the world economy, orchestrating trade and capital flows between Britain and its colonies and also between third countries whose trade never touched Britain's shores. Despite the continuing excavation of these economic and financial roles, we still know remarkably little about how the production and reproduction of the City's landscape were shaped by its place in the wider imperial project.[2] Yet the City was clearly identified in the public imagination as the heart of empire. Such imaginative geographies of empire were constituted through a particular representational space at the heart of the City and by a number of collective associations around key moments in imperial history. The symbolic site which framed the idea of the City as the heart of empire was Bank Junction, the public space where seven of the City's key commercial streets converge, surrounded by the monumental architecture of the Bank of England, the Royal Exchange and the Mansion House. This site, captured in Niels Lund's classic painting 'The heart of the empire' (1904), began to acquire the character of an imperial Roman forum in the 1840s, when the Royal Exchange was rebuilt by Sir William Tite, enclosing the space at the eastern end with a reoriented Exchange faced with a massive temple portico (Figure 16).[3]

Lund's painting plays a key role in Stephen Daniels's recent account of the changing roles of St Paul's Cathedral in visions of the City, nation and empire.[4] Discussing the symbolic exchange between God and Mammon offered by the visual relations between St Paul's and the commercial heart of the City, he suggests how the very title of Lund's painting 'alludes to contemporary geo-political theories of imperial destiny, situating London as 'the "heart" of the imperial organism'.[5] This imperial space at the heart of the City was energised at key moments of ceremony and spectacle. On the occasion of Queen Victoria's Diamond Jubilee in 1897 the royal party passed through the City after the service at St Paul's, Bank Junction decorated with festoons, garlands, drapes and evergreens. *The Times* noted that should the party be long delayed there was still much to observe: 'It is using no figure of speech to call this spot the heart of London, and of the Empire'.[6] In 1900 these City spaces saw a more spontaneous gathering as news of the relief of Mafeking led to a virtual suspension of trading on the stock exchange. Some 5,000 City workers waving flags and singing patriotic songs celebrated a symbolic moment in the history of British imperialism.[7]

Figure 16   A new imperial forum? The Bank of England and the Royal Exchange as engraved by F. Appel, *c.* 1860

[97]

The complexities of reading this particular representational space of empire have recently been confronted in sustained fashion by Jane Jacobs in her book *Edge of Empire*. Commenting upon Bank Junction as 'a symbolic site of a Britain made great by its global reach', she suggests that 'today it is an imperial space in a post-imperial age'.[8] Her account is directly concerned with the presence of the imperial past in recent debates over the redevelopment of Bank Junction and how the legacy of empire lives on as a particular constitutive force shaping the meaning and identity of the City in an uncertain post-imperial world. However, there are dangers in this kind of 'presentist' history. Indeed, both Daniels's and Jacobs's accounts of the landscape of the City as the heart of empire provide only a partial reading of the production and reproduction of the site. The continued emphasis on the particular townscape painted by Lund in 1904 has, in fact, obscured the specific and important ways in which individual elements *within* that townscape have stories to tell about the complex relations between City and empire. In this chapter, I want to revisit Bank Junction in the inter-war period and consider the rebuilding of the Bank of England by Sir Herbert Baker. In so doing I want to emphasise the importance of a *late* imperial context for the reproduction of the heart of the City, a context given scant attention by either Jacobs or Daniels.

The question of rebuilding the Bank of England was first actively considered during the First World War. The Bank's work had increased dramatically as the government continually added to the national debt to finance the war effort, and this increased pressure on space in Threadneedle Street greatly. On 16 November 1916 the court of directors, the bank's governing body, appointed a Committee on Building, which met from January to September 1917.[9] Ideas circulated and various plans were made, but the war made detailed consideration of the issues difficult, and the whole question was postponed until after the war. It was not until 1920 that the Bank returned to the problem in earnest, establishing a Special Rebuilding Committee on 13 May that year.[11] On 22 July the architect F. W. Troup was invited to assist the committee.[12] Troup, who had recently converted the former lunatic asylum of St Luke's Hospital in Old Street to house the Bank's new Printing Department, worked on designs for the new Bank between 1920 and 1921, producing a range of alternative schemes.[12] Despite his early involvement, though, Troup was not in fact appointed as Chief Architect for the rebuilding project. Minutes of the Rebuilding Committee of 23 March 1921 record that 'It was agreed that the Chairman should see Mr. Herbert Baker, FRIBA, on his return from India, and ask him whether he would be prepared to advise the Committee on the questions referred to in their Report'.[13] Baker was in India working on the design of New Delhi, and Jackson notes how 'while returning to Britain in 1921, he had received a telegram in Aden from Cecil Lubbock, the Deputy Governor of the Bank, asking him to call on his arrival'.[14] Thus the first link between Baker and the new project was established. The circumstances surrounding the choice of Baker to advise the committee were far from straightforward. It is possible that Troup, had he not been so weighed down with contracts, would have been offered the work in its entirety. Another name associated with the project in its initial stages was that of Sir Edwin Lutyens. According to Jackson, 'he had been promised the job by the Governor of the Bank, Lord Cunliffe, but Cunliffe had died before the project was decided upon. Lubbock, the new Deputy Governor, knew Baker and the commission went his way.'[15] Baker attended his first committee meeting on 14 April 1921 and was instructed to prepare a report which considered 'whether the reconstruction could be satisfactorily carried out with the general appearance and style of the [present] building being preserved'.[16]

By the 1920s Baker had a distinguished record as an architect in the service of empire. A friend of Cecil Rhodes, he developed close links with South Africa, building Government House and Union Buildings in Pretoria between 1905 and 1913. From 1912 he was closely involved with Lutyens in the designs for imperial Delhi and was responsible for the Secretariat buildings there. Assessing Baker's work at Delhi, Irving called it 'a major milestone in an imperial career that spanned thirty-five years in Africa and Asia. No architect of any era had done so much important work throughout the British Empire.'[17] Though perhaps best known for such colonial architectural projects, Baker also contributed substantially to the shaping of late imperial London, completing India House in 1925 and South Africa House in 1930. Working simultaneously in both the metropolitan heart of empire and the colonies, Baker was a leading figure in the circuit of architects and architecture which centred on late imperial London.[18] Together with Lutyens he embraced wholeheartedly the imperial dreams of Edwardian Britain – dreams which persisted well into the inter-war years. Baker's architecture, drawing substantially upon European classical traditions of imperial style, was clearly marked by the *folie de grandeur* of this late imperial age. Firmly believing that empire was a force for civilisation and order in the world, he argued that its architecture should 'give outward expression to Britain's national ideals and ... "turn them to shape and give them a local habitation and a name" throughout the Empire'.[19] This organic unity between the heart of empire and its dominions lay at the centre of Baker's imperial vision, classicism providing the language of spatial order in which the dream of empire could be written.

Once commissioned, Baker worked quickly to prepare his report, presenting it to the Rebuilding Committee on 6 July 1921. Subsequently known as Baker's 'First Report', this document is of crucial significance in considering Baker's approach to the problems of rebuilding. He worked within the following terms of reference established by the committee: to maximise accommodation on the site; to retain as much of the existing building as possible, especially the external walls, which were considered of immense historical and architectural importance as well as affording protection from the dangers and noise of the public streets; to design a building with the architectural dignity worthy to give expression to the pre-eminence of the Bank of England.[20] Baker himself acknowledged the crucial importance of retaining as much of the old building as possible, whilst recognising the Bank's need for space. He drew attention to the supreme skill and ingenuity of Soane in designing the existing building (see Figure 16), calling it his 'most famous masterpiece' and noting how 'his genius is especially distinguished ... by his varied and ingenious treatment of domical skylighted construction' which 'gives an exceptional sense to its architecture of dignity and fitness to the purpose of a Bank'.[21] Yet it was Soane's curtain wall that was to prove crucial for Baker in negotiating the competing pressures between conservation and development. These strong facades, reflecting the stature and importance of the Bank in the City, were widely admired in both professional and popular opinion. The final paragraph of his report captures precisely these complexities and is worth quoting at length:

> the preservation and incorporation in the new building of the old external wall, of the banking halls behind it and of many other old rooms of Sir John Soane's building, should go far to meet the reasonable conservative sentiment of the public, and would enable your Court, while not ignoring its obligations as Trustees of a precious national heirloom, to develop on its traditional site a new Bank which would be sufficiently large and efficiently planned to fulfil the new duties imposed upon it by the War; which without any necessary conflict of style, might record in its architecture for future generations the Bank's historical periods of growth during the two great wars of England's history and which might contain the elements of architectural dignity commensurate with the Bank's position and destiny in the City and the Empire.[22]

The ideas set out in this report clearly shaped the rebuilding of the Bank in all but a few details. However, before his plans were accepted the Rebuilding Committee sought Baker's opinion on an alternative scheme for an entirely new building on a cleared site, to be judged in comparison with his first scheme. It was clear that Baker's heart and, one suspects, that of the committee, were never behind this notion, though he carried out his task with customary thoroughness.[23] Baker was clearly uncomfortable about drawing upon an explicitly modern architecture on a site of such outstanding national importance. If the court were to completely sacrifice the old building, he asked, would it 'be prepared to make the still further sacrifice of architectural tradition and appropriate expression which might be involved by building in the modern manner of London buildings, in which the glass predominates over the wall surfaces?'[24] Indeed, Baker argued eloquently that, given the immense historical and cultural importance of the site and of Soane's building, no architect could conceivably operate as if he had a free hand. A new Bank of England, he claimed, presents 'a unique and highly privileged artistic problem in which the artist no less than his patrons should suppress the ambition of full self-expression'.[25] By retaining elements of the existing building the architect could acknowledge something of the greatness of Soane's achievement and also crystallise 'in one great work of art the spirit both of the past and of the present'.[26] Clearly, the Bank's directors agreed, and the plans submitted by Baker with his First Report were approved on 15 July 1922.

As this detailed reading of Baker's reports indicates, the rebuilding of the Bank required particular sensitivity to issues of conservation, historical continuity, public taste and opinion. In consequence the court decided to publish a plan and illustration, notifying its intentions on 25 July 1922. These were, in fact, very close to the final achieved design (see Figure 17). That the Bank, ostensibly a private institution, had felt the need to go public in this way was immediately picked up by *Country Life*:

> the issue to the Press of Mr. Herbert Baker's scheme for rebuilding is surely something of a portent ... it means that the Court of Directors, eminent people in the City of London, see that their business is also other people's business; that they are the trustees for the amenities of the heart of the Empire ... time was when the first notice of such a change in the aspect of the City would have been the rattling down of Soane's great wall ... for the Bank's directors have no statutory or customary duty to the public.[27]

Such accounts clearly indicated the importance of the rebuilding of the Bank in the public imagination. The Bank, as the empire's premier financial institution, symbolised in its very fabric the stability of the pound sterling throughout the wider imperial monetary space. Economic discourse which conflated the Bank, the City and the empire was frequently conjoined with questions of aesthetics and architectural style as the rebuilding plans were received and digested. *The Architects' Journal*, for example, noted how:

Figure 17 Herbert Baker's late imperial reconstruction of the Bank of England, 1938

The great architectural question of the moment [is] the proposed alteration to the Bank ... the 'Old Lady of Threadneedle Street' is so familiar [and] beloved a landmark that any proposal for any alteration is bound to cause a searching of hearts and an outburst of criticism. Soane's masterpiece is an integral part of the City; it is impossible to conceive the City without the Bank as the Bank without the City. Perhaps, without exaggeration, it may be said that it stands for far more than the City; that its low impressive walls of solid masonry symbolise the integrity of the British Empire.[28]

It was not long before critical voices were heard. Opposition to the nature of the planned rebuilding, if not to the need to rebuild *per se*, crystallised around the trustees of the Soane Museum. Eminent architects in their own right, as well as guardians of the spirit and purpose of Soane's work, the trustees – Aston Webb, Reginald Blomfield, Paul Waterhouse and Edwin Freshfield – wrote to *The Times* on 25 July 1923. The initial cause of their intervention was the revelation that the City Corporation was pressing the Bank to cede territory to allow the widening of both Prince's Street and Threadneedle Street. According to the trustees such concessions would have destroyed not only the domical banking halls but also the facades – the very embodiment of Soane's Bank. By this time it was becoming clear that much of Soane's interior would be lost in the reconstruction, an inevitable consequence of expanding accommodation on the site. But, to many, the facades were seen as inviolable. Webb and the other trustees also attacked

Baker's proposed portico on the Threadneedle Street front as 'meaningless', claiming that Soane had 'deliberately aimed at horizontality, and the introduction of this new feature is quite alien to the spirit of his design' (see Figure 17).[29] Baker, clearly stung by this attack, penned a reply in *The Times* two days later, claiming that the portico had two distinct functions: first, it would create valuable space above the entrance to compensate for the space sacrificed through the preservation of Soane's walls and halls; second, it had 'a higher meaning [forming] the architectural connexion between the old low facade and the new high building ... raised behind it'.[30] For Baker the architectural problem was maintaining the unity of the expanded building while preserving as much of Soane's work as possible. On 30 July the trustees published a brief rejoinder, again cautioning against making additions to the facades.[31] Further disquiet followed. A correspondent in the *Morning Post*, suggested that the Bank might consider building an extension on the vacant site of the old General Post Office, preserving the original building intact and establishing a private tube link between the sites for rapid communication! He continued, 'if the Bank is raised as suggested it will entirely dwarf the Royal Exchange and Mansion House and mar the pleasant surroundings of the centre of the City, the heart of the Empire'.[32]

Baker's plans were approved in November 1923 and his position as Chief Architect was finally confirmed with a written agreement on 16 April 1924; Troup had been confirmed as Supervising Architect on 25 February.[33] A contract with Holloways, builders of the new Bank, was signed in January 1925 and demolition began one month later.[34] With the general outlines in place Baker began to devote more and more time to the details of the scheme. Figure 18 shows the completed portico above the main entrance in Threadneedle Street. In a letter to Alexander, secretary to the Rebuilding Committee, Baker outlined his thinking about the pivotal role the portico was to play in the rebuilding scheme as a whole. Referring to the six figures intended for the Threadneedle Street entrance, he wrote:

this sculpture has been designed there primarily for the architectural reason of giving some visible gradated connection in the form of a buttress to the base of the superstructure which rises behind the existing front portico. I am anxious to keep the content or meaning of the sculpture subordinate to the expression of its architectural function. To think out the proper relation between the meaning and function I require the help of a sculptor to work with me. ... I want a man for this who is prepared to give deep thought to the matter and who is ready to hammer out a number of designs ... the young sculptor whom I have put to the test and have not found wanting is Charles Wheeler.[35]

Figure 18 The new Bank of England; the entrance front in Threadneedle Street, 1931, showing telamones and figure of the 'Old Lady' by Charles Wheeler

Wheeler, a protégé of Baker's, was to become intimately involved with the Bank's rebuilding project for over ten years.[36]

Another thread of empire was woven into the rebuilding of the Bank by the statuary needed to connect the Threadneedle Street portico with Soane's entrance front. In a letter to George Booth, one of the Bank's directors most closely involved in the rebuilding, Baker acknowledged that 'we shall before very long have to think out a scheme for sculpture. The necessities are the six figures of the front Porticoes ... I'll try to get some thoughts by drinking at the fountains of inspiration in Rome.'[37] Baker, in signalling his debt to the architecture of another great empire, underlined his commitment to designing the new Bank within a broadly imperial classical context.[38] Writing to Booth from Italy on 26 October 1929, Baker noted, 'Here are Wheeler and I redesigning the Bank! – in its sculpture. We have had some strenuous hard thinking days in Rome and Florence. The action has proved very right. Wheeler just wanted this insight into the higher realms at this time, to lift and widen his range of thought; and I too with him.'[39]

Wheeler was also required to model a new figure of the 'Old Lady', to be placed high on the pediment (see Figure 18).[40] Booth suggested that he should draw upon the existing design but bring it closer in style to the telamones (buttress figures) below.[41] Subsequently both Booth and Baker rejected Wheeler's suggestion of a child to be placed in the Old Lady's lap and approved a model with a building of four columns and pediment.[42] The 'new' Old Lady, as she was immediately dubbed by the press, was the first section of the new Threadneedle Street facade to be unveiled. On 22 October 1930 the *Daily Mail* carried a report on the unveiling subtitled 'awkward-looking sculpture'. It continued, 'Controversy has been aroused in the City by the sculpture representing the "Old Lady of Threadneedle Street" ... "Hideous" and "grotesque" are some of the descriptions ... the sculpture is that of a burly woman in loose draperies, seated in a very awkward-looking manner.'[43] Later that year the *Evening Standard* quoted Wheeler in defence of his work: 'my design represents the new spirit of the age, the spirit of reconstruction after the war. The Old Lady ... holds a model of the building that symbolises reconstruction.'[44]

The telamones were unveiled on 22 January 1931. Baker wrote to Booth later that day, remarking that 'they all function as beautiful buttresses and the left hand corner with the keys is nearly perfection; but some of the limbs are still big in the others and Wheeler will spend another week or so paring them down'.[45] Baker, who was leaving for India, concluded, 'I am finishing *en route* for Dover ... I go happily having seen the portico finished. I only hope the music won't be a terror to face! ... my wife sends her kind regards; and says she is proud that Baker now rises above Soane.'[46] In addition to their overtly architectural function, the sculptural details of the Threadneedle Street facade carried distinct symbolic references, as Wheeler himself noted. The four carved male figures 'are guardians of wealth', while the two female figures 'are bearers of wealth, holding as they do Cornucopiae'.[47] The centre keystone, between the two female figures, 'is carved with a double-warded key which was suggested by the lines from "Lycidas" – "Two massy keys he bore of metals twain. The golden opes, the iron shuts amain" – Sir Herbert Baker thinking that the Bank's duty of locking up and of releasing wealth was hereby suitably recorded.'[48] Press opinion was divided over the merit of the telamones. *The Times* noted how the figures, 'caryatid in form, though not in function, [are] perfectly related in scale'; indeed, 'the subtleties of composition which Mr. Wheeler has contrived within the strict convention of the six figures cannot be too much admired'.[49] By contrast, the *Daily Mail* struck a more populist note in a leader entitled 'The Bank's giants':

> Ordinary people with ordinary ideas about art had a shock yesterday when the sheets were removed from the giant stone figures which form part of the decorative scheme of the new Bank of England ... Gazing up from the pavement before the Royal Exchange yesterday a crowd of City people stared in amazement at the figures – four male and two female ... Three of the males are completely nude, and the way in which the sculptor, Mr. Charles Wheeler, has treated them made scores of people ejaculate: 'Epstein!' They wanted to know whether anybody had ever seen men with such enormous muscles and such thick legs ... The two female figures pleased everybody better, though *their* legs, too, came in for a lot of adverse comment.[50]

Figure 19 shows in detail the designs for the bronze doors at the Threadneedle Street entrance. The designs here were largely those of Charles Wheeler, though as always he worked in close co-operation with Baker. Shortly after their unveiling Wheeler wrote to Alexander explaining the symbolic qualities of his designs, and revealing the clear sense that both Wheeler and Baker had of the Bank's place in an imperial world economy. This was no simple mapping of the Bank into the formal geography of the British empire, for the designs revealed a relationship between the Bank, the City and the world economy which was mediated through a wider empire of money. Referring to the main doors, Wheeler noted how:

> the left hand flap stands for the foundation of the Bank and the right hand one for the rebuilding. Each bears a Latin inscription to this effect, spaced around a lion's head. The lions' heads are surmounted by Caducae. The foundation Cadeceus is topped by an Argosy, which was a chief vehicle of the distribution of wealth in the days of William III, while the rebuild-

Figure 19 The new bronze entrance doors of the Bank of England,
Threadneedle Street, 1931

ing Caduceus has, instead, the hand of Zeus grasping the lightning which symbolises the electrical force (i.e. cables etc.) which is the means of conducting business now used by bankers. The slower communication is suggested by the soft lines of the wings of the left hand Caduceus and the quicker by the straight lines of the right hand wings. The constellations of 'Ursa Major' and 'The Southern Cross' stand for both sides of the world, meaning the Bank's operations are world-wide, and the 'Pole Star' at the top left-hand corner is the lode star of the old navigators. To suggest water for the ship, and air for the ether-waves, dolphins and swallows embellish the respective Caducae staves.[51]

The idea of centrality was a major structuring principle of the design. The Bank, as guardian of the pound sterling, was placed at the centre of an imperial space economy tied together by the circulation of sterling. As the empire's pre-eminent financial institution it concentrated the power of a world currency in a specific place while simultaneously legitimating its circulation across wide areas of the globe. The time–space compression forged by the changing communications technologies shaping this imperial monetary space was also symbolised. Finally, these designs firmly recognised the strong historical continuities between the Bank in the 1690s and its place in the world in the early twentieth century. Confidence in the place of the Bank in the imperial and world economy, as a historical fact as well as a contemporary geographical reality, was neatly captured in the configuration wrought by Wheeler. Such themes were carried through in the decoration of the two side doors flanking the main entrance. Wheeler notes how these are 'decorated with features of lions guarding mounds of money, with the English charge from the "Royal Arms", as well as with the Caducus and the head of Medusa made into grilles'.[52]

The use of such direct references to both royal and imperial authority was not uncontested, however. A letter in *The Builder* complained about the use of the '"Three lions passant gardant" of the royal shield of England' on the left-hand door.[53] The author continued, 'The Bank of England is an ordinary joint-stock banking concern, its shares being held privately in this country ... it is not a national possession ... certainly it is not royal in any way whatsoever. Can you tell me what is the reason for its assuming the arms which have hitherto belonged solely to His Majesty the King?'[54] The concerns expressed here pointed to the dangers of using symbolic associations to express identity in architecture. While Baker may have held strong views about the place of the Bank in the national life, as embodying something distinctively English in its very fabric, it was clear that this view was considered highly problematic by observers. When taken with his well known penchant for the wider imperial project, by combining references to

King, state, nation and empire in his commissions for sculptural detail on the Bank's facades, Baker was knowingly treading a fine line between projecting an image he thought appropriate to the Bank and attracting strong critical reaction. This critical response caused the Rebuilding Committee to write to Baker seeking clarification about the use of the royal arms. Baker indicated that he did not consider the 'three lions passant gardant' to be trespassing on the royal arms, as, in not using the royal crest or shield, they were merely to be considered symbols of English nationality, not as orthodox heraldry. Though undoubtedly a partial view of Baker's symbolic frame of reference, it seemed to convince the Bank's directors and the matter was closed.[55]

Baker's achieved design received its share of serious architectural criticism.[56] Much of it focused, inevitably, on the perceived mismatch between Soane's strong Roman work embodied in his surviving curtain wall and Baker's altogether lighter and more eclectic classicism above. Nowhere was this contrast more evident than at Tivoli corner, at the junction between Princes Street and Lothbury (see Figure 17, far left). The corner took its name from the temple of Vesta at Tivoli, which had provided the model for Soane's design. In Soane's Bank the rounded portico was set off by a highly original low pediment and pilaster combination, behind which there was nothing but sky. With the addition of Baker's new structure the pediment was removed, leaving only the series of urns standing upon Soane's portico, out of context and rendered devoid of meaning. C. H. Reilly, a prolific writer on bank architecture in the 1920s and 1930s, was emphatic in his criticism of Baker here. Writing in *The Banker*, he claimed, 'I would have liked to have praised the new form of this famous corner but I cannot ... it is now but an approach, an over-elaborate step, to a commonplace little cupola above a low dome which itself is but a subsidiary feature to the cliffs of the great hotel rising behind'.[57] The cupola was topped by a bronze figure of Ariel by Wheeler, 'pleasant enough in itself', according to Reilly, but 'totally out of character ... with the strictly Soane columns'.[58]

In the 1920s and 1930s the City of London, especially the 'forum' between the Bank, the Royal Exchange and the Mansion House, was identified strongly in the public imagination as the 'heart of empire'. This was as much to do with the City's role as the monetary hub of empire, of course, as with any overt architectural display. Indeed, when compared with the recently rebuilt Whitehall quarter in Westminster, full of the pomp and circumstance of a pre-war belief in British imperial supremacy, many of the City's spaces were a far more muted affair.[59] The reasons for this are manifold. The City had always been essentially a private landscape of capital. Even a major institution like the Bank of

England had no formal public status until its nationalisation in 1946. The pattern of landholding was complex and fragmented, which, coupled with the irregularity of its medieval street plan and building plots, meant that organic accretion of buildings and styles predominated over any attempt at conscious planning. Rebuilding of the central financial district in the mid-Victorian decades did indeed introduce a palatial classical style for the many new joint-stock banks and insurance companies being established in the capital.[60] But this was largely a series of private responses to both practical and symbolic needs, drawing on the classical language of architecture without any conscious attempt to reflect the City's place and purpose in the empire.[61] It was precisely this nineteenth-century townscape that was captured by Lund.

The rebuilding of the Bank of England was different. Together with other major rebuilding projects around it in the 1920s and 1930s, such as Edwin Lutyens's design for the Midland Bank in Poultry and Edwin Cooper's National Provincial Bank in Princes Street, its design was explicitly constituted within a series of imaginative geographies of empire. Baker, designing within a consciously imperial classical tradition, left inscriptions of empire on all aspects of the Bank's rebuilding, from the general plan to the smallest details of sculptural and allegorical work on the facades and interiors. There were certain ironies in this, of course. Baker, in giving architectural expression to the new Bank, was working within an imperial vision drawn from the Pax Britannica, the gold–sterling standard and the unquestioned imperial supremacy of the long nineteenth-century.[62] Between the 1870s and 1914 the Bank had indeed been at the apex of a world system focused on the City as the centre of an imperial world economy. Until the First World War the pound sterling did function unquestionably as *the* world currency, with the Bank as its guarantor. The war, however, shattered the nineteenth-century liberal world order where the happy coincidence of unregulated multilateral trade flows, British imperial expansion and the global circulation of sterling had focused control of the world economy in London. The Bank, naturally, had grown accustomed to acting on a world stage.[63] But the world had changed. By the sterling crisis of 1931 it was becoming clear, to those who wished to look, that the natural as opposed to symbolic centre of the world economy was now New York, and that the dollar was now the top currency.[64] Baker's design for the new Bank of England, like his work with Lutyens in imperial Delhi, can therefore be best described as *late imperial*. In both examples the circumstances surrounding their conception had radically changed by the time of their completion. Baker designed the new Bank as a building 'commensurate with the Bank's position and destiny in the City and the Empire', yet the nature of the world economy which shaped the Bank's external role had, by the 1930s, fundamentally changed. The final touches to the new Bank were made in the years of the Second World War, a conflict which changed the British empire as much as the First World War had changed the nineteenth-century liberal world economy. And yet the legacies of empire live on. As a prominent and enduring feature of the late imperial rebuilding of the City of London, Baker's Bank of England continues to make a distinctive contribution to the post-imperial landscape of London.[65]

Notes

This chapter arises from work on a wider project entitled 'Rebuilding "The Heart of the Empire": Financial Headquarters in the City of London, 1919–39', funded by the Nuffield Foundation. I would like to thank the Foundation for its generous support. I would also like to thank the staff of the Bank of England Archive, London, for their kind and helpful advice in connection with this project. I am also very grateful to David Gilbert and Felix Driver for their helpful comments on a draft of the chapter.

1 H. Baker, 'Symbolism in Art', paper read to the Royal Institution of Great Britain, (London, Royal Institution of Great Britain, 1933).
2 On economic and financial aspects of the City/empire nexus see, for example, G. Ingham, *Capitalism Divided? The City and Industry in British Social Development* (London, Macmillan, 1984); P. J. Cain and A. G. Hopkins, *British Imperialism: Innovation and Expansion, 1688–1914* (London, Longman, 1993); P. J. Cain and A. G. Hopkins, *British Imperialism: Crisis and Deconstruction, 1914–90* (London, Longman, 1993). For a recent, if brief, commentary on the difficulties of interpreting the influence of empire on the City's landscape see F. Driver and D. Gilbert, 'Heart of empire? Landscape, space and performance in imperial London', *Environment and Planning D: Society and Space*, 16 (1998) 11–28.
3 J. Summerson, 'The Victorian rebuilding of the City of London', *London Journal*, 3 (1977) 165, notes how the Royal Exchange, 'in combination with the Bank of England to the north and the Mansion House to the south-west, made up a scene that had, and still has, something of the character of a forum'.
4 S. Daniels, 'The Prince of Wales and the shadow of St Paul's', in S. Daniels, *Fields of Vision: Landscape Imagery and National Identity in England and the United States* (Cambridge, Polity Press, 1993), pp. 11–42.
5 *Ibid.*, p. 31.
6 Quoted in D. Kynaston, *The City of London II, Golden Years, 1890–1914* (London, Chatto & Windus, 1995), p. 162.
7 *Ibid.*, p. 208.
8 J. M. Jacobs, *Edge of Empire: Postcolonialism and the City* (London, Routledge, 1996), p. 38.
9 Bank of England Archives, London (hereafter B. of E.), E28/131, Final Report of the Committee on Rebuilding, 12 March 1941.
10 *Ibid.*
11 *Ibid.*
12 N. Jackson, *F. W. Troup, Architect, 1859–1941* (London, Building Centre Trust, 1985).
13 B. of E., E28/127, Rebuilding Committee Minutes, 23 March 1921.
14 Jackson, *F. W. Troup*, p. 55.
15 *Ibid.*
16 B. of E., E28/127, Rebuilding Committee Minutes, 14 April 1921.
17 R. G. Irving, *Indian Summer: Lutyens, Baker, and Imperial Delhi* (New Haven CT, Yale University Press, 1981), pp. 275–6.
18 The notion of circuits of architecture and architects within the empire has been

raised recently, in a different context, by Mark Crinson. See M. Crinson, *Empire Building: Orientalism and Victorian Architecture* (London, Routledge, 1996).

19 Quoted in Irving, *Indian Summer*, p. 278.
20 B. of E., E28/129, Baker's First Report, 6 July 1921, p. 1.
21 *Ibid.*, pp. 1–2. For more details on Soane's work at the Bank see J. Summerson, 'The evolution of Soane's Bank Stock Office in the Bank of England', in J. Summerson, *The Unromantic Castle and other Essays* (London, Thames & Hudson, 1990); N. Pevsner, *A History of Building Types* (London, Thames & Hudson, 1976).
22 B. of E., E28/129, Baker's First Report, 6 July 1921, pp. 6–7.
23 See H. Baker, *Architecture and Personalities* (London, Country Life, 1944).
24 B. of E., E28/129, Baker's Second Report, 12 December 1921, p. 2
25 *Ibid.*, p. 6.
26 *Ibid.*, p. 6.
27 'The public and modern buildings', *Country Life*, 29 July 1922.
28 'The question of the Bank of England', *The Architects' Journal*, LVI (1922) 173–4.
29 'The Bank of England: Soane's design in danger', *The Times*, 25 July 1923.
30 'The Bank of England: answer to the Soane trustees', *The Times*, 27 July 1923.
31 'The Bank of England', *The Times*, 30 July 1923.
32 'Proposed addition to the Bank', *Morning Post*, 10 August 1923.
33 B. of E., E28/131, Final Report of the Committee on Rebuilding, 12 March 1941.
34 *Ibid.*
35 B. of E., ADM 30/57, Head Office Rebuilding: Sculpture, Letter from Herbert Baker to A. O. Alexander, 22 November 1927.
36 Wheeler worked on numerous projects with Baker. On his election as an ARA the *Daily Telegraph* (23 January 1934) noted, 'among Mr. Wheeler's work are carvings on the rebuilt Bank of England, South Africa House and India House in London, and on Rhodes House at Oxford, Winchester College War Memorial cloisters and the Indian Memorial at Neuve Chapelle. His bust of "the Infant Christ" was purchased for the nation by the Chantrey bequest in 1924.'
37 B. of E., ADM 30/57, Head Office Rebuilding: Sculpture, Letter from Herbert Baker to George Booth, 2 May 1925.
38 See 'Baker, Sir Herbert (1862-1946)', in J. Fleming, H. Honour and N. Pevsner, *The Penguin Dictionary of Architecture* (fourth edition, London, Penguin, 1991), p. 30, where his style is described as being 'as imperially classical as Lutyens' but much weaker, less original, and less disciplined'.
39 B. of E., ADM 30/57, Head Office Rebuilding: Sculpture, Letter from Herbert Baker to George Booth, 26 October 1929.
40 The phrase 'Old Lady of Threadneedle Street' is thought to derive from a cartoon by James Gillray entitled 'Political ravishment: or the Old Lady of Threadneedle Street in danger'. See W. Marston Acres, *The Bank of England from Within, 1694–1900* (London, Oxford University Press, 1931), I, p. 283.
41 B. of E., ADM 30/57, Head Office Rebuilding: Sculpture, Note on sculpture by Herbert Baker, 10 June 1929.
42 *Ibid.*, Note on sculpture by Herbert Baker, 30 November 1929.
43 'The City's new "Old Lady": awkward-looking sculpture', *Daily Mail*, 22 October 1930.
44 'The new "Old Lady" defended: Bank sculptor on his interpretation of spirit of 1930', *Evening Standard*, November 1930, B. of E., E5/2.
45 B. of E., ADM 30/57, Head Office Rebuilding: Sculpture, Letter from Herbert Baker to George Booth, 22 January 1931.
46 *Ibid.*
47 B. of E., ADM 30/57, Head Office Rebuilding: Sculpture, Note by Charles Wheeler, 'Description of bronze doors and stone sculptures on Threadneedle Street portico', 12 February 1931.
48 *Ibid.* 'Lycidas' was a poem by Milton, written in 1637 and considered one of the finest elegies in the English language. See M. Drabble (ed.), *The Oxford Companion to English Literature* (Oxford, Oxford University Press, 1985) p. 595.

49 'Bank of England sculptures: Mr Wheeler's figures on the new pavilion', *The Times*, 2 March 1931. Though in function the telamones drew inspiration from Roman architecture, their achieved design by Wheeler was more suggestive of Teutonic than of strictly classical influences; see C. H. Reilly, 'The emergence of the new Bank of England', *The Banker*, 17, 18 (1931) 98.

50 'The Bank's giants: "unveiling" by workmen', *Daily Mail*, 3 March 1931.

51 B. of E., ADM 30/57, Head Office Rebuilding: Sculpture, Note by Charles Wheeler 'Description of bronze doors and stone sculptures on Threadneedle Street portico', 12 February 1931.

52 *Ibid.*

53 'Correspondence. The Bank of England', *The Builder*, 31 July 1931.

54 *Ibid.*

55 B. of E., ADM 30/57, Head Office Rebuilding: Sculpture, Letter from Herbert Baker to A. O. Alexander, 28 August 1931.

56 See J. Booker, *Temples of Mammon: The Architecture of Banking* (Edinburgh, Edinburgh University Press, 1990), p. 237.

57 C. H. Reilly, 'The Tivoli corner of the Bank of England – then and now', *The Banker*, 43, 44 (1937) 198.

58 *Ibid.* Drabble, *Oxford Companion*, p. 40, notes how the figure of Ariel refers to the 'airy spirit in Shakespeare's *The Tempest*, whom Prospero has released from bondage under the "damn'd witch Sycorax" and employs as executor of his magical schemes'.

59 See M. H. Port, *Imperial London: Civil Government Building in London, 1851–1915* (New Haven CT, Yale University Press, 1995).

60 See D. J. Keene, 'The financial district of the City of London: continuity and change, 1300–1871', in H. Diederiks and D. Reeder (eds), *Cities of Finance* (Amsterdam, Royal Netherlands Academy of Arts and Sciences, 1996) pp. 279–302.

61 See I. S. Black, 'Symbolic capital: the London & Westminster Bank headquarters, 1836–38', *Landscape Research*, 21:1 (1996) 55–72.

62 See Ingham, *Capitalism Divided?*, pp. 96–127.

63 P. L. Cottrell, 'The Bank of England in its international setting, 1918–1972', in R. Roberts and D. Kynaston (eds), *The Bank of England: Money, Power and Influence, 1694–1994* (Oxford, Clarendon Press, 1995) pp. 83–139.

64 Ingham, *Capitalism Divided?*, p. 200, notes how 'given the world depression, the City retreated into the security of the empire in which it found a ready-made banking network in which the use of sterling had a political basis'.

65 Jacobs's account of post-imperial conflicts over the architecture and symbolism of Bank Junction does not consider the late imperial reconstruction of the Bank, referring simply to 'Soane's Bank of England'. See Jacobs, *Edge of Empire*, p. 46.

PART II

Imperial display

CHAPTER SEVEN

Staging the imperial city:
The Pageant of London, 1911

Deborah S. Ryan

The imagination thrills at the thought of it – a great series of London Pageants, a vivid reproduction of historical scenes which will not only bring home to the citizens of London the historic greatness of their city, but will serve to shew in striking manner the important part it occupies as the centre of a world-wide Empire. Such a series of Pageants will form a fitting culmination to the many recent representations of scenes from the history of other ancient English cities. The aim will be not merely to provide a pictorial and dramatic display which will please the eye without leaving any lasting impression, but to stimulate thought and imagination, and to demonstrate and remind us of the closeness of the associations which link the overseas dominions to the centre of British Imperial rule.[1]

In 1911 the Pageant of London was staged at the Festival of Empire and Imperial Exhibition at Crystal Palace. As the *Official Guide* suggested, it was a spectacular event. The pageant comprised four parts, staged over three days by 15,000 volunteers in over forty scenes. It told the story of London 'from the dawn of British history' to the meeting of the allied sovereigns in London in 1814 and the founding of the overseas dominions. The entertainments concluded with an elaborate 'Masque Imperial' that was 'An Allegory of the Advantages of Empire'.[2]

In this chapter I consider the ways in which the urban ceremony and display of the Pageant of London depicted the capital as an imperial city, paying particular regard to the uses of landscape and space in the pageant performance. Despite such public display, however, pageants were not simply state propaganda. Like exhibitions and other forms of spectacular entertainment, it was the element of participation and the opportunities that pageants gave their performers to make their own entertainment that was crucial to their success. A diary/scrapbook compiled by a young woman who performed in the Pageant of London vividly illustrates the personal investments and meanings that performers gained from pageants, which often subverted their organisers' educational and imperial intentions.

Twentieth-century pageants

The twentieth-century historical pageant was by no means a new phenomenon. In fact, the Pageant of London was the latest in a series of spectacular civic historical pageants, staged outdoors, which told the history of geographical places. A new meaning was given to the word 'pageant' in 1905 when Louis Napoleon Parker (1852–1944), dramatist and composer, produced his elaborate outdoor play at Sherborne to commemorate the twelve-hundredth anniversary of the town's foundation.[3] Indeed, in the early twentieth century a wave of 'pageantitis' was reported to be sweeping Britain.[4] The Sherborne pageant was quickly imitated by others in different towns as a means of raising money for charity and celebrating anniversaries.[5] Pageants spread to the United States and remained popular until the Second World War.

Despite the contagion of pageantitis there has been little study of this uniquely twentieth-century form of popular entertainment.[6] At the height of their popularity, pageants were thought to be of important educational value, instilling in participants and audiences alike a love of region, nation and empire. Pageants were very popular events, but despite their popularity, or perhaps indeed because of it, they were rarely thought of as works of art.[7] Pageants need to be understood in the context of other spectacular forms of popular entertainment in the early twentieth century — the spectacle plays of Imre Kiralfy[8] and Max Reinhardt, 'toga plays',[9] exhibitions[10] and the cinema epics of D. W. Griffith and Cecil B. De Mille — which all relied on large casts and the participation of the masses.

Twentieth-century historical pageants told the history of the place in which they were staged, from ancient times to more or less the present day. They were dependent upon the idea of an 'authentic' place with a history that could be told through its landscape and were usually held outdoors, at the site of most significant historical interest in the town. The audience remained seated in one place and looked upon a single arena which was usually constructed as an amphitheatre to give classical connotations to the spectacular performance. Most pageants contained little in the way of spoken words and depended instead on music (often specially composed for the event), dancing and spectacular staging. The pageanteers were mostly volunteers from the local community and it was thought important that people should transgress the roles they held in real life: for example, a blacksmith might appear as a king; the lord of the manor as a serf. Thus pageants involved all members of the community in the telling of the public history of a place.

This public history was also a lesson in imperial geography. Most British pageants had an imperial finale depicting the town in question as a mother figure surrounded by the daughter towns named after it in the colonies and dominions.[11] What made the Pageant of London distinct from those pageants staged in provincial towns was its emphasis on the imperial city throughout. It depicted not only the 'romance and importance' of London's civic development but also 'its position as the seat of national Government and the heart of the British Empire'.[12] Thus the Pageant of London was an immensely popular form of imperial propaganda and entertainment. Furthermore, as I show later, it owed much to the imperial vision of Frank Lascelles, known in the popular press as 'the man who staged the Empire', who made a career as a pageant master both 'at home' and abroad in the colonies and dominions.

The Festival of Empire

The Pageant of London was part of a wider series of events and exhibitionary practices which focused on empire and drew on the same kinds of spectacular language and conventions. Its host, the Festival of Empire and Imperial Exhibition, was just one of a rash of patriotic exhibitions, including the Coronation Exhibition at Imre Kiralfy's White City, and other events which celebrated the crowning of the King and Emperor George V. As a souvenir brochure of the festival declared:

> The Festival of Empire at the Crystal Palace this summer means, in a phrase, a Social Gathering of the British Family ... the primary object which the organisers have in view is the firmer welding of those invisible bonds which hold together the greatest empire the world has ever known ... Men and women who left the old roof years ago to found new homes and forge new links of empire across the seas will gather together under the family tree to renew past associations and to relate to the old people at home the wonders of those new-found lands that lie beyond the seas ... each of our great Dominions... are sending over their children in thousands to join in this great 'family gathering'.[13]

The domestic metaphor of the empire as one big family headed by the King and Queen, with Britain, and particularly the south-east of England, as its home was not only part of the reinvention of the royal family but was also frequently invoked and acted out in exhibitions and pageants. For example, the 1924 British Empire Exhibition at Wembley was described in its *Official Guide* as a 'Family Party of the British Empire'.[14]

Pageants and exhibitions were also concerned with imperial trade

[119]

and industry. For example, the publicity material surrounding the Festival of Empire emphasised the stability of the industrial and administrative aspects of the British empire. The *Official Guide* was keen to stress the importance of the empire to the public, particularly its produce and contribution to industry. It sought 'to demonstrate to the somewhat casual, often times unobservant British public the real significance of our great self-governing Dominions, to make us familiar with their products, their ever-increasing resources, their illimitable possibilities'.[15] At a time when there were doubts among politicians about the future of the empire, exhibitions and pageants stressed the resources of the colonies and dominions and put them on display.[16]

The Festival of Empire utilised the vast area of the Crystal Palace and its grounds, which were, as one of the souvenir publications declared, 'an ideal place for a striking display of our commercial supremacy'. The choice of the Crystal Palace as the venue for the Festival of Empire helped shape the meaning of the events (although it must be remembered that the Crystal Palace was originally erected in Hyde Park and was moved to Sydenham later). Nonetheless, with the resonances of 1851 in mind, the organisers described the venue as 'almost historical'. Moreover, although the emphasis of the festival was on London as *the* imperial city at the heart of empire, the siting of the Crystal Palace on the outskirts of the city, in the suburbs, at the juncture between country and city, was also important, as 'there on the sun-lit slopes of Sydenham Hill, with the rolling downs of Surrey stretching away into the grey distance, Briton will meet Briton'.[17] This imperial suburb was a place where city met country, where spectators could be reminded not just of London's administrative role but also of the countryside of the south-east, which stood for an idealised rural England.[18] Furthermore, many of the imperial citizens who frequented and participated in exhibitions and pageants were drawn from the suburbs.

Imperial exhibitions and pageants often sought to reconstruct the far-flung outposts of the empire. For example, the Festival of Empire contained a display of 'our Dominions beyond the Seas' which were represented by three-quarter-size replicas of their parliament buildings, in which examples of the productive and industrial wealth of the different dependencies were exhibited alongside 'lifelike' tableaux illustrating the most important scenes connected with their development. This was the world-as-exhibition, or rather empire-as-exhibition, on a grand scale.[19] This setting out of the physical places of empire as spaces which could be traversed was shared by pageants which used similar techniques to mount realistic displays.

Thus in exhibitions and pageants visitors and pageanteers were able

[120]

to journey through the empire. The Festival of Empire's 'All Red Tour' (see Figure 20) was a mile-and-a-half trip by electric railway through the overseas dominions. 'Realistic scenery, colonial life and activity,' it was claimed, were 'accurately represented and illustrated by native men and women, living animals, etc.' Passengers took in views of colonised industries, local scenery and 'native' life as they travelled between each parliament building, where they could see exhibits.[20] On each train guides explained details and objects of interest en route. The tour started in Newfoundland and ended in South Africa, via Canada, Jamaica, Malaya, India, Australia and New Zealand. Therefore visitors to the exhibition were to an extent pageanteers: they were touring the empire, performing the role of travellers, witnessing imperial progress and learning how to be part of the British empire and how the empire was part of them. Hence the souvenir booklet declared:

> Without doubt this is the most magnificent educational spectacle ever seen in London. The Empire, with its manifold characteristic and infinite resources, is presented on a scale of realistic exactitude never before attempted. Not only is shown an accurate representation of the physical features of the Dominions beyond the Seas, but visitors are able to see the empire at work, and thus to realise something of the enormous productive wealth of each Dominion.[21]

Thus the festival, like the Pageant of London, was more than just a productive display of the empire. It also sought to stress the historical and even emotional ties of the lands and peoples of the empire. Whilst the citizens of the empire from the colonies and dominions were welcomed to the festival, those living 'at home' were taught the proud history of the empire and, through the Pageant of London, the 'Empire City'. This, it was hoped, would helped foster a sense of the tradition of empire and individuals' relations to it, as citizens. It was in this setting that the Pageant of London was performed.

The Pageant of London

The Pageant of London ground, fifty acres in extent, was situated on the north side of the Crystal Palace. By the grandstand (see Figure 21) designed by Sir Aston Webb (architect of several important imperial landmarks in London) on the lines of an old Greek amphitheatre, there was a replica of 'Old London'. Across the lake in the pageant ground a replica of the old London Bridge was erected, and to the right and left stretched other scale models of 'Old London', including the Tower of London, old St Paul's, Westminster Abbey and Ludgate Hill.

With a cast of 15,000 volunteers, the Pageant of London was a spec-

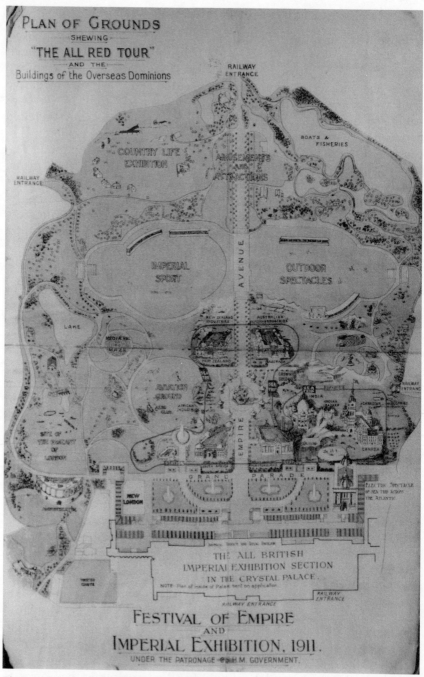

Figure 20 Plan of grounds showing the 'All Red Tour' and the buildings of the overseas dominions, Festival of Empire and Imperial Exhibition, Crystal Palace, Sydenham, 1911

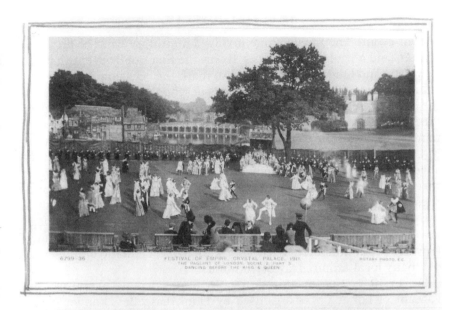

FESTIVAL OF EMPIRE, CRYSTAL PALACE, 1911.
THE PAGEANT OF LONDON. SCENE 2, PART 3.
DANCING BEFORE THE KING & QUEEN

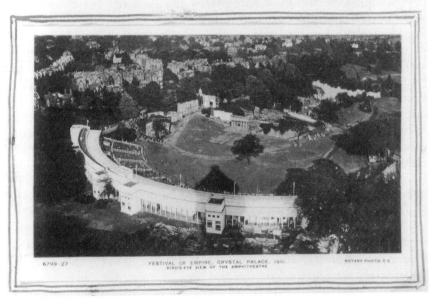

FESTIVAL OF EMPIRE, CRYSTAL PALACE, 1911.
BIRD'S-EYE VIEW OF THE AMPHITHEATRE

128

tacular event. The music alone involved a military band of fifty performers and a choir of 400 voices. It was the first public event that the new King and Queen attended, and to mark the occasion they held an enormous party to entertain thousands of schoolchildren from all over the country, described by an observer as the 'greatest Royal tea-party in the history of the world'. Here the children were educated and entertained by the historical scenes of the great dominions from the Pageant of London. The performers from the earlier scenes of British history appeared as 'shades', 'with long, flowing, transparent, grey veils over their historical costumes of all ages, and as our scenes of the new countries went on, these shades of the past drifted through'.[22] Others in the early twentieth century also sought to educate children in the ideals of empire through such forms of entertainment. For example, Baden Powell's Scout Jamborees harnessed similar spectacular techniques, as did many local Empire Day celebrations.[23]

An event of this magnitude required considerable planning. The Pageant of London was organised by Frank Lascelles, known in the popular press as 'the man who staged the Empire'. For twenty-five years Lascelles staged pageants in Britain and the empire which took the idea of the imperial city as their major theme. Even Lascelles's pageants that celebrated provincial towns, such as that in Oxford in 1907, always contained an imperial finale. Furthermore, his second pageant in 1908 celebrated the tercentenary of Canada in Quebec. Two years later he was Master of the Pageantry at the celebration of the opening of the Union Parliament of South Africa, Cape Town, 1910. He followed the 1911 Pageant of London with another imperial extravaganza: the coronation durbar at Calcutta in 1912, in which over 300,000 indigenous peoples and troops participated. In 1924 Lascelles organised the Bristol pageant (subtitled 'Cradle of the Empire'). As well as being staged on its home ground, which was referred to in publicity material as the most imperial of British cities, the Bristol pageant was also staged at the British Empire Exhibition, Wembley. Later in the exhibition Lascelles staged one of his most magnificent events: the Pageant of Empire.

Lascelles started working on the idea of an historical pageant of London in 1907 whilst his Oxford pageant was taking place. At first he envisaged that the pageant would take place in Regents Park.[24] By late December 1907 Lascelles had set up an office for the London pageant at the Savoy Hotel,[25] and it was planned to hold the pageant the following summer. In February 1908, however, it was decided to postpone the pageant until the summer the following year, for several reasons. First, the King did not want anything to distract attention from the Franco-British Exhibition which was to take place in 1908. Second,

Knightsbridge Gardens would be available as a venue in 1909. And, finally, following the success of the Oxford Historical Pageant, Lascelles had been asked by the Canadian government to organise a pageant as part of the celebrations of the tercentenary of Canada at Quebec, in front of the King and Queen, in autumn 1908 and needed to go in advance to make preparations.[26]

The postponement of the Pageant of London to 1909 also gave the Historical Committee of the London Pageant time to organise a series of lectures on London history to educate potential pageanteers.[27] They approached the University of London Extension Board about the possibility of arranging a series of historical lectures in the metropolitan boroughs to 'interest the citizens of London in its history ... so as to utilise the Pageant for the highest educational and civic purposes'. Such lectures would, the committee hoped, demonstrate 'the important and striking part which London has paid in the history of the nation' and would create a historical background to give 'vividness and reality to the scenes of the Pageant alike for those who take part in them as actors and to the general public as spectators'. It was intended that the lectures would deal with the broad features of the historical events of the scenes that would be included in the pageant. A meeting was held at the Mansion House to discuss how such a lecture series might be organised, to which the chairman of the London County Council and the mayors of all the metropolitan and suburban boroughs were invited. The meeting itself included a short lecture on 'The Place of London in History' by the geographer Halford Mackinder (who was also a member of the Senate of London University and Director of the London School of Economics).[28] As a promoter of imperial unity through educational schemes Mackinder would have been sympathetic to the aims of the Pageant of London. Indeed, at exactly that time Mackinder was developing a series of lantern slide lectures for the colonies under the auspices of the Colonial Office Visual Instruction Committee, one of which depicted a journey from London, the imperial city, to the empire.[29] In his address to the assorted worthies at the Mansion House meeting Mackinder urged 'the importance of enlarging and vivifying the interest of Londoners in the history of their city in its relation to the history of the nation'. He strongly asserted that the history of London was distinct from that of other European cities: not only was it the seat of rule but 'London may be likened to a personality taking part in the clash and balance of forces and personalities which have gone to make the history of the empire and the history of the world.'[30]

Despite the interest that the idea of a Pageant of London aroused, in January 1909 Lascelles decided to put it off until 1910.[31] During 1909 the pageant became part of the proposed Festival of Empire and Imperial Exhibition at Crystal Palace, thus acquiring official government backing.[32] By 1909 the Earl of Plymouth was involved with the organisation of the pageant, and his influence helped to gain official support. Following the death of the King, the Festival of Empire, Imperial Exhibition and Pageant of London were postponed once more until 1911 and refocused as a celebration of the coronation of George V. This rescheduling suited Lascelles who was busy in 1909 organising the Bath Historical Pageant, and in 1910 was organising pageants in South Africa.

By the time the organisation of the Pageant of London really got under way in 1909 Lascelles was therefore very experienced in pageant organisation. He developed a style and content that were distinct from those of his rival, Parker, which used considerably larger casts. The writer Arthur Mee commented on Lascelles's distinctive use of landscape and space:

> Frank Lascelles must think of life as one stupendous spectacle; he must see it down the avenues of time like a vast unfolding of picture after picture, an unfolding with a machine-like precision in which every little part and every little thing moves subject to control, and he wields his powers like a great magician, with Nature as his instrument, and Space as his stage.[33]

Lascelles believed that pageants should be concerned with the 'dramatic movement of masses' rather than with 'spoken dialogue, which is often tedious in the open air'.[34] He consequently made much use of the movement of masses of people in processions and dance, often in blocs of colour influenced by his practice as a painter.

The Pageant of London was certainly a complex and ambitious undertaking. It told the 'history of the empire's heart' in over forty scenes organised in four roughly chronological parts, with the performance spread over three days.[35] It aimed 'to show forth the gradual growth and development of the English people as shown in the history of this, the Empire City. Step by step we watch it on its upward way as the cycle of the first three parts of the pageant unfolds it before our eyes.'[36] Many of the scenes took liberties with the actual places where events happened. Moreover, with static scenery, the members of the audience had to use their imagination to change historical periods and continents. The Crystal Palace's lake, for example, took on a number of different geographical identities.

Lascelles based each scene on an actual historical event and used well known historians and writers in their reproduction. As well as scenes depicting the history of London as a capital city, there were scenes which showed London as the starting place for journeys of exploration which resulted in the acquisition of foreign territory. Thus Part One started with 'The Dawn of British History' and a scene of 'primitive' London, followed by Roman London and the Triumph of Carausius (written by Lascelles's frequent collaborator, Charles Oman), King Alfred, the Danish invasion, the Norman Conquest, and ended with the investiture of the first Prince of Wales, concluding with a tournament at Smithfield to represent 'days of chivalry'. The pageant continued in Part Two with the Canterbury pilgrims and went, via a scene of 'The Passing of Mediaevalism' and scenes of 'Merrie England', to the knighting of Drake. These visions of Tudor England, which were very popular in the late nineteenth and early twentieth centuries, provided alternative imperial models to that of the Roman empire, avoiding any suggestion of the inevitability of decline and fall.[37] Part Three of the pageant started with 'Trade with the Indies' in the seventeenth century, followed by the presentation of Princess Pocahontas to the court, the execution of Charles I and the Restoration, finishing with the end of the 'Great War' (i.e. the Napoleonic Wars) and the meeting of the allied sovereigns in London in 1814.

The Pageant of London's most explicitly imperial message came in its fourth and final part. This was a 'Masque Imperial' staging landmarks in the history of the 'mother country' as well as those of the dominions (see Figure 22). The Masque Imperial was written by Francis Hartman Markoe, a recent Oxford University graduate. Markoe had previously collaborated with Lascelles on the Oxford pageant, writing 'The Masque of the Mediaeval Curriculum', a modern attempt at a morality play. The Masque Imperial symbolised the growth of the empire – 'the toil and self-sacrifices of the early pioneers and the worthiness of Britannia to be the Mother of such men and women'.[38] The masque started with the discovery of Newfoundland and went on to include, for example, the imperial assemblage at Delhi and the proclamation of Queen Victoria as Empress of India in 1877, a relatively recent historical event.[39] Many of the scenes included exotic animals such as elephants, camels, zebus, llamas and asses from the Zoological Congress housed in the grounds of the Crystal Palace. The Masque Imperial concluded with an 'Allegory of the Advantages of Empire' which gave the flavour of a morality play to the pageant. It featured a host of allegorical figures: the 'Genius of the World'; the 'Voice of the World'; various 'Queen Needs', including the 'Queen Need of Knowledge'; 'Britannia' accompanied by spirits of her meadows, forests, lakes, mists and mountains (to name but a few out of many); the 'Queen of Wisdom'; and, finally, figures representing the colonies, performed by pageanteers from the countries concerned. The finale

Figure 22   The Masque of Empire, Pageant of London, 1911

showed the gathering of the overseas dominions around the mother country. This scene, versions of which Lascelles used repeatedly in his pageants, both domesticated and feminised empire by depicting Britain as the mother and the dominions as her daughters, invoking imperial ideals of home and family.

Pageanteers, performance and pleasure

Despite its focus on London as an imperial city, the Pageant of London also relied upon a strong sense of local identities which were suburban rather than imperial or even metropolitan. Fifteen thousand volunteers were recruited by borough, with each borough taking responsibility for a specific scene. In keeping with egalitarian pageant ideals, the organisers intended the pageant to include 'men and women of all sorts and conditions, from Peers and Peeresses down to Clerks and Artisans'.[40] This raises the questions of why these men and women chose to volunteer and what pleasure they expected to gain from their experience as performers in the Pageant of London.

The diary of Miss M. P. Noel, honorary secretary of the Kensington committee, throws some light on the experience of the pageanteers and their reasons for volunteering. Miss Noel was a young unmarried woman from Kensington who shared a house with a female friend. Miss Noel was clearly of some social and financial standing to be able to afford to spend the whole summer as a volunteer performer and to be given the position of honorary secretary. Her diary records her personal triumphs and frustrations, pageant gossip and the follies and foibles of her fellow pageanteers. The diary is illustrated by drawings, photographs (some taken by herself, some cut out from souvenir programmes), ephemera such as tickets and passes, and press cuttings.

The diary gives a fascinating insight into Miss Noel's own role in the pageant and records the complex preparations, tensions and rivalries behind the event. She was responsible for the decoration of the Kensington pageant car (also known as a 'cabriolet'). The pageant car seems to have been adapted from an old one which had a gilt ram on it which she had great problems removing. The central figure on the car was one of the Queens of Need in her costume with 'a sceptre of bulrushes & sitting in a coracle'.[41] Her responsibility for the pageant car was a constant source of worry to her, involving many trials and tribulations:

> [I] looked at the Kensington car in despair. After some time we got a man to heave the ram off & we removed the paper flowers. Mrs Colquhoun & Mr Napper turned up, laden with material & flowers, very confident, & rather patronising to us. We didn't care, we knew we couldn't do anything & that we had nothing to do it with nohow & that probably the car, a huge thing, would never be done at all. We twisted string aimlessly & inseriously [sic] about & people laughed at us. Then we both began to get very cross & sat down at opposite ends at a dead standstill. Croydon just then flew into a violent rage & saved the situation. I went off to a very argumentative committee in the Royal Box at ten, & came back to find things, to my horror, precisely where I had left them & people laughing at us. But then the miracle began. Helpers turned up, vast bundles of greenery & rushes arrived, & the car began to [take] shape exactly as I wanted it to come. I got the Mills & Miss Barlow to work on the cabriolet & simply laboured.[42]

Despite all the trouble it caused her, she was clearly proud of the responsible position she held in relation to the car. She recorded the following conversation in her diary:

> 'Who is responsible for this car?'
> 'I am responsible for this car.'
> 'Yes, but the horses must be got in. Where is the *man* in charge of this car?'
> '*I* am responsible.'
> Then even he laughed and said I was plucky or something.[43]

Eventually all her hard work paid off and the Kensington car won a prize: 'We were pleased, too pleased. I am not inclined to think, for I wish we hadn't gone around chortling & showing the thing to everyone like a couple of children.'[44]

Miss Noel was officially responsible for 'The Knighting of Drake', which formed part of the scene depicting 'The Spacious Days of Queen

Elizabeth'. However, it is clear from her diary that she took part in several other scenes in the pageant, including the Mediaeval and Georgian ones, as well as the masque, making her own costumes. She contributed her own ideas to her various scenes which she jealously guarded: 'Took grapes & onions into Merrie England, not so successful as they promised to be ... Miss de Lorey danced & waved madly about in Spacious Days. I wish people would not always copy our inventions.'[45]

Much of Miss Noel's diary is taken up with her view of her fellow pageanteers. Her opinion of other women pageanteers was tied up with suburban rivalries, as is evident from this entry: 'Oh yes ... George Prince of Wales told us that someone asked who we were and if we were Woolwich people and the answer was "Oh no, they're ladies!" Poor Woolwich!'[46] Moreover, the opportunity of mixing with genuine aristocrats was part of the thrill of taking part for Miss Noel. However, she also resented the fact that the titled women were given the more aristocratic pageant roles, in contradiction of the usual pageant ideal where pageanteers assumed roles that were the reverse of their own position in society.

Despite some of her reservations about casting, as her diary progresses Miss Noel increasingly identifies her fellow performers by the names of their roles, rather than their 'real' names. This steady blurring of reality and fiction for the pageanteers was commented upon in a report in the *Daily Mail*:

> There is a reality and a lack of self-consciousness in it that is extraordinarily convincing. These people are not acting; they are living ... Some of them ... seem to be adopting, almost unconsciously, through their constant habit of harking back three centuries of an evening, the stately port and easy dignity of their London forebears nine generations back.[47]

The pageant clearly offered its performers possibilities of escapism and fantasy. It is clear from Miss Noel's diary that pageanteers made their own meanings from the pageants and their own entertainment. The *Daily Mail* commented that 'there is no mistaking the pleasure that they have in it themselves'. Pageanteers volunteered for their own reasons. The report also suggests that part of the attraction may have been to escape from modern-day life:

> There is something very charming in the idea of all those good folk of Lewisham and Forest Hill and other parts of London coming, in their old-world costumes after a day, perhaps, of riding in motor-omnibuses and sitting on office stools, to live in the evening through the scenes of the old London that has gone.[48]

Miss Noel's reasons, it would seem, were social ones. Despite all the tensions and rivalries she described, she clearly valued the sociability and friendships that the pageant offered. In particular, she relished the opportunity to meet eligible young men (she conducted a major flirtation with 'George Prince of Wales'). She also enjoyed doing things that young Kensington ladies should not, like travelling to Crystal Palace on the 6.45 a.m. workmen's train.[49]

Nowhere in the diary does Miss Noel talk about the pageant developing in her a sense of civic pride or citizenship, imperial or otherwise, despite the best intentions of those who promoted pageants as educational propaganda, and she clearly loathed Lascelles. Despite this, towards the end of the diary she expresses a sense that she had written a history of the pageant which had become public property:

> For many things yet remain to be chronicled of which one may wish for a souvenir, & many things there be which may not be chronicled, even in the German tongue, because forsooth this book has attained too much fame to remain an entirely private affair as I have wished. Therefore will readers note that as far as possible I have suppressed all personal impressions & stuck to facts, & such impressions as there are, be mainly dictated by perversity. And I don't care what Freda says, it's my book & I'll write what I like in it & show it to whoever I choose to honour.[50]

Conclusion: staging the imperial city

The Pageant of London depicted London as an 'imperial city' in a number of ways. First, as the landscape for a performance, it established London as the heart of empire, the place to which inhabitants from the colonies and dominions came to be 'at home'. Second, it reinforced London's role as the administrative and political centre of empire, by drawing on its metropolitan structures and colonial offices to recruit pageanteers. Third, those same pageanteers were educated in London's history as the city at the empire's heart, in the major events of the city and the role that the city played in the acquisition of overseas territories. Finally, it was hoped that this education would instil in pageanteers and audience alike a sense of citizenship of London, the imperial city, and of the British empire in general, and invoke local, national and imperial pride. Much of the pageant's performance was down to the guiding vision of Frank Lascelles's organisation. According to Margaret Baxter, a participant in the Pageant of London, Lascelles's genius was that he presented empire as a

> LIVING story before the eyes and mind of youth and adult alike, and upon the millions of onlookers was imprinted the history of the British Empire, in a way which no mere Exhibition could convey, fostering in a

unforgettable manner the knowledge of, the pride and faith in our great vast overseas heritage.[51]

The Pageant of London was thus a 'living panorama' of empire.

However, if the performers in imperial propaganda such as the Pageant of London were able to subvert its meaning for its own ends then so too were the spectators. A humorous account in a newspaper cutting in Miss Noel's diary of 'Uncle Tweedle' taking his nephew 'Tony' and his friend 'Wall' to the Festival of Empire and Pageant of London gives some idea of how it may have been consumed. For all the high imperial ideals of the exhibition organisers, the account of their trip is focused on the pleasures to be had from the exhibition's pleasure grounds. Thus the All Red Route is notable mainly for the fun they had when they threw pieces of chocolate at the tea planters. Furthermore, some of the audiences of the Pageant of London were not that well behaved, either: Miss Noel complained of the audience of one performance: 'Bad day, 8,400 police and family with a very low average of manners.'[52]

Although some may have subverted the pageant's message for their own ends, it clearly did have the patriotic and educational impact its organisers intended on others. For example, in Uncle Tweedle's account of the Festival of Empire it is only the pageant whose imperial message comes across:

> Imposing processions ... [teach] boys more about the past, artistically, historically, and personally, than miles of museums and tons of schoolbooks. Magnificent conceptions of the great episodes of history; centuries sweep before one's eyes with multi-coloured realism. A living epic of the ages ... a gorgeous spectacle ... surely the biggest piece of theatrical performance ever attempted in any age whatever. Historic. Event of National Importance.[53]

The value of a Lascelles pageant was, for many commentators such as Arthur Mee, greater than that of the printed word. Mee declared, 'Though we have books, we have them in excess, and the value of the pageant, in such directing hands as those of Frank Lascelles, is that it picks out great events for us, makes them alive again, and impresses them upon the mind.'[54]

The possibilities of spectacle in conveying powerful ideas were not lost on those who had different aims from Lascelles. For example, on 17 June 1911 48,000 women from twenty-eight women's organisations marched in the Women's Coronation Procession with floats, banners, music and historical costumes, rivalling the official coronation procession. This was 'the most spectacular, the largest and most triumphant, the most harmonious and representative of all the demonstrations in the campaign'.[55] This seven-mile-long procession subverted the spectacles of popular entertainment, such as the Pageant of London. As Lisa Tickner suggests, the procession 'reached the limit of public spectacle not just as a political device, but as a practical possibility'.[56] The suffragettes never organised in this way or on such a scale again. However, other political organisations, from both the left and the right, used the pageant form for their own ends.[57]

Pageants were, like exhibitions, an effective means of educating the public in imperial ideals. Despite official government involvement pageants should not, however, be seen merely as imperial propaganda, even if some intended them to be so. The success of pageants was dependent upon the goodwill and enthusiasm of the pageanteers, who, as Miss Noel's diary shows, subverted the meaning of the pageant to their own personal ends. The diary also indicates that pageanteers were often more concerned with local identities and rivalries than with national and imperial identities. The former concerns would also be uppermost in the minds of those in the audience, a substantial number of whom consisted of friends and relatives of the vast number of pageanteers required for spectacular productions.

Notes

1 *Festival of Empire: The Pageant of London* (second edition, uncorrected proof, 1910), p. 15.
2 *Festival of Empire: The Pageant of London, May to October, 1911: Pageant Programme*, parts I–IV, (London, Bemrose, 1911).
3 L. N. Parker, *Several of my Lives*, (London, Chapman & Hall, 1928), pp. 277–303.
4 'Some impressions of the pageant: preparations', *Oxford Magazine*, 17 October 1907, p. 9.
5 R. Withington, *English Pageantry: An Historical Outline*, II (Cambridge, Cambridge University Press, 1918), pp. 228–9.
6 See, however, *ibid.*; D. Glassberg, *American Civic Pageantry: The Uses of Tradition in the Early Twentieth Century*, (Chapel Hill NC, University of North Carolina Press, 1990).
7 M. Kelly, 'Pageants', in H. Downs (ed.), *Theatre and Stage: An Encyclopaedic Guide to the Performance of all Amateur Dramatic, Operatic, and Theatrical Work*, (Westport CT, Greenwood Press, 1978), p. 693.
8 B. E. Gregory, 'The Spectacle Plays and Exhibitions of Imre Kiralfy, 1887–1914' Ph.D. dissertation, University of Manchester, 1988.
9 D. Mayer, *Playing out the Empire*, (Oxford, Oxford University Press, 1994).
10 See, for example, P. Greenhalgh, *Ephemeral Vistas: The Expositions Universelles, Great Exhibitions and World Fairs, 1851–1939*, (Manchester, Manchester University Press, 1988).
11 Parker, *Several of my Lives*, p. 294.
12 *Pageant of London* (1910), p. 17.
13 *Souvenir of Royal Visit to the Festival of Empire, Imperial Exhibition and Pageant of London Crystal Palace, Coronation Year 1911*, (London, Bemrose, 1911), p. 5.
14 M. Grant Cook & F. Fox, *The British Empire Exhibition, 1924: Official Guide*, (London, Bemrose, 1924), pp. 9–10. For further discussion of the 'domestication' of empire and home see M. Bell, '"The Pestilence that walketh in darkness": imperial

health, gender and images of South Africa c. 1880–1910', *Transactions of the Institute of British Geographers*. New Series, 18 (1993); D. S. Ryan, 'The *Daily Mail* Ideal Home Exhibition and Suburban Modernity, 1908–51', Ph.D. dissertation, University of East London, 1995; D. Gilbert and D. S. Ryan, 'The Empire in the Suburbs' (Imperial Cities Project working paper, Department of Geography, Royal Holloway, University of London, 1996).

15 Quoted in J. M. MacKenzie, *Propaganda and Empire*, (Manchester, Manchester University Press, 1985), p. 106.
16 Greenhalgh, *Ephemeral Vistas*.
17 *Souvenir of Royal Visit*, p. 6.
18 R. Colls and P. Dodd, *Englishness: Politics and Culture, 1880–1920*, (London, Croom Helm, 1986).
19 T. Mitchell, 'The world as exhibition', *Society for Comparative Study of Society and History*, 31:2 (1989) 217–36.
20 *Festival of Empire Crystal Palace 1911: Official Guide to the All Red Route*, 1911.
21 *Souvenir of Royal Visit*, p. 6.
22 M. Baxter, 'An imperial triumph', in Earl of Darnley (ed.), *Frank Lascelles: Our Modern Orpheus*, (London, Oxford University Press, 1932), p. 49.
23 See T. Jeal, *Baden Powell* (London, Pimlico, 1991), p. 511; P. Horn, 'English elementary education and the growth of the imperial ideal, 1880–1914', in J. A. Mangan (ed.) *'Benefits Bestowed'? Education and British Imperialism* (Manchester, Manchester University Press, 1988), pp. 39–55; D. S. Ryan, 'Imperial Suburbs: Empire Day, 1896–1958' (Imperial Cities Project working paper, Department of Geography, Royal Holloway, University of London, 1997).
24 Bodleian Library, Oxford, G.A.Oxon.c.164, Letter from Frank Lascelles to Falconer Madan, in Oxford Historical Pageant, *H. Personal*, 9 December 1907, p. 103.
25 *Ibid.*, 17 December 1907, p. 108.
26 *Ibid.*, Ms note by Falconer Madan in Oxford Historical Pageant, p. 121.
27 *Ibid.*, Ms note by Falconer Madan in Oxford Historical Pageant, p. 121.
28 *Ibid.*, Letter from R. D. Roberts, Registrar of the Board for the Extension of University Teaching, University of London, May 1908, no page number.
29 See J. R. Ryan, 'Visualising imperial geography: Halford Mackinder and the Colonial Office Visual Instruction Committee', *Ecumene*, 1:2 (1944) 157–76; *Picturing Empire: Photography and the Visualisation of the British Empire* (London, Reaktion, 1997).
30 *Festival of Empire: The Pageant of London* (1910), p. 20.
31 Bodleian Library, Oxford, G.A.Oxon.c.164, Ms note by Falconer Madan added to letter from Clarendon, Kilmorey, Kintore, William Bull, Harry E. Brittain, Honorary Secretaries to the London Pageant, in Oxford Historical Pageant, *H. Personal*, 30 December 1907, no page number.
32 See London University: British Library of Political & Economic Science, Coll Misc. 459, 'Minutes of the Festival of Empire Committee, 1909-10'.
33 Arthur Mee, 'Down the avenues of time' in Darnley, *Modern Orpheus*.
34 *Festival of Empire: The Pageant of London* (1910), pp. 18–19.
35 J. Holt, 'Threads of empire', *Daily Mail* 18 May 1911, p. 10.
36 *Pageant of London Programme*, part I, p. ix.
37 Colls and Dodd, *Englishness*.
38 *Souvenir of Royal Visit*, p. 9.
39 See *Festival of Empire: Souvenir of the Pageant of London*, 1911.
40 W. T. Stead, 'Our modern Orpheus', in Darnley, *Modern Orpheus*.
41 National Art Library, Victoria & Albert Museum, London, 86.HH.16, M. P. Noel, 'Scrapbook containing material relating to the Pageant of London which was given as part of the Festival of Empire, 1911', entry of 8 July 1911.
42 *Ibid.*, 15 July 1911.
43 *Ibid.*, 15 July 1911.
44 *Ibid.*, 15 July 1911.
45 *Ibid.*, 10 July 1911.

46 *Ibid.*, 7 July 1911.
47 *Daily Mail*, 7 August 1911.
48 *Ibid.*
49 Noel, 'Scrapbook', 15 July 1911.
50 *Ibid.*, 'Epilogue'.
51 Baxter 'Imperial triumph', p. 50.
52 Noel, 'Scrapbook', 13 July 1911.
53 *Ibid.*
54 Mee, 'Avenues of time', p. 35.
55 L. Tickner, *The Spectacle of Women: Imagery of the Suffrage Campaign, 1907–14* (London, Chatto & Windus, 1989), p. 122.
56 Ibid.
57 S. Nicholson, 'Theatrical Pageants in the Second World War', *Theatre Research International*, 18:3 (1993) 186-96; M. Wallis, 'Pageantry and the Popular Front: ideological production in the thirties', *New Theatre Quarterly*, 10:38 (1994) 132–56.

CHAPTER EIGHT

'Capital of the Colonies': real and imagined boundaries between metropole and empire in 1920s Marseilles

Yaël Simpson Fletcher

The 1922 National Colonial Exposition in Marseilles included a West African tower three times the height of the original in Timbuctu, an enormous Indochinese palace based on the temple of Angkor Wat, and a Near Eastern compound crowded with minarets, domes and courtyards (see Figures 23–4). Together these buildings were designed to materialise the cultural heterogeneity of the French empire. These inflated simulations of indigenous architecture, with their 'vertiginous and phony exactitude' (to borrow a term from Jean Baudrillard), provided a backdrop for the performances of colonial actors.[1] African families from Mauritania, Senegal, the Ivory Coast and French Sudan engaged in the everyday activities of village life. Bedouin chiefs camped in a courtyard, Indochinese artisans displayed their wares, North African merchants plied their trade in markets and colonial troops formed a guard of honour in each exhibition hall.[2] From the top of the red earthen African tower, reinforced by unseen iron girders, visitors brought up by lift could gain a panoramic view not only of the 36 hectare exposition but also of the surrounding city, the Mediterranean coastline and the distant hills.[3] These concentric spaces provided both points of contact and lines of separation for residents of the empire, of Marseilles and of other regions in France.

In recent years scholars in many fields have considered various aspects of the cultural geography of colonialism. In one approach, international expositions are conceived as relocated representations of Asia, Africa or the Americas for display to Europeans and Americans.[4] Herman Lebovics, for example, has portrayed the 1931 International Colonial Exposition in Paris as a symbolic space placing the empire firmly within the boundaries of French culture.[5] Another approach has focused on the imagery and experience of travel between the cultural spaces of the metropole and the colonies. The literary scholars Mary Louise Pratt, Ali Behdad and others have considered European trav-

Figure 23   The West African Tower at the 1922 exposition in Marseilles

ellers in colonial Africa and Asia, while the historians Antoinette Burton, Laura Tabili and Tyler Stovall have examined the experience of people from the colonies visiting, labouring or performing military service in the metropole.[6] Timothy Mitchell and Zeynep Çelik have productively combined both approaches in their analyses of Arab and Turkish accounts of visits to nineteenth-century European expositions.[7]

This chapter attempts to draw together the insights of the new postcolonial studies and of urban social history. Rather than focusing simply on the imagery of an exposition, or on the movements of people across imperial spaces, it investigates questions related to the location of the 1922 Colonial Exposition in Marseilles, a city intimately connected with the French empire. Situated on the Mediterranean coast, Marseilles functioned as a double gateway; it sent French soldiers, administrators and settlers to the colonies, and brought the colonies, in the form of people and products, to the metropole. The 1922 exposition, designed to celebrate the dominance of this metropolitan port city in the empire, instead highlighted the liminality of Marseilles, exposing the fragility of the imperial divide between metropole and colonies.

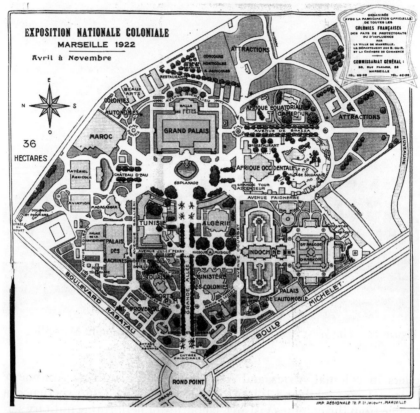

Figure 24 Plan of the 1922 exposition in Marseilles

More specifically, this chapter considers how the 1922 Colonial Exposition was defined simultaneously as a work site, as a living space and as a political arena for different kinds of French colonial subjects. The first section discusses the ways in which the organisers, visitors and local residents viewed the exposition and its relation to the surrounding city. The second focuses on the struggles of colonial workers in Marseilles, both on and off the exposition grounds. The third explores the use of colonial soldiers to represent the bonds between nation and empire. The final section examines the range of interactions between Marseilles residents and colonial subjects in the exposition.

Marseilles, Colonial Exposition site

The Marseilles chamber of commerce, a powerful force in the city, took the lead in promoting Marseilles as a site of colonial expositions. After the success of the 1906 Colonial Exposition the organisers immediately began discussing the idea of a Marseilles-sponsored decennial update, so to speak, on the French empire. By 1913 plans were well under-way for an exposition in Marseilles scheduled for 1916. The onset of war in 1914 brought other concerns to the fore. Yet plans for a colonial exposition eventually acquired a new national political and cultural significance, leading some legislators to propose holding an exposition of all allied colonies in Paris, rather than an exposition of only French colonies in Marseilles. But the original organisers mounted a sharp defence of their plans, arguing that the 1922 National Colonial Exposition in Marseilles 'would represent a date in history not only for their ancient city, but above all a time for the whole Nation, saved in its entirety, joyously to affirm her rebirth, her resurrection'.[8] Claiming imperial significance for Marseilles, superseding even that of Paris, the organisers of the 1922 exposition portrayed the port city as the lynchpin of the administration and development of the French empire. Countless exhibits, speeches and articles reiterated this theme.[9] Marseilles' business and political elite envisaged the city as the 'definitive colonial metropolis'.[10] This positioning of the city as an intermediary between the empire and the metropole provided a naturalising logic for the location of the exposition. One journalist even evoked the image of the city as a 'radiant' hostess at a ball, presenting the colonies, like debutantes, to metropolitan France.[11]

The location of the exposition near the heart of Marseilles expressed this idea in spatial terms (see Figure 25). A visitor from Paris had to enter the city in order to tour the simulated French empire, in a journey that paralleled that of a metropolitan traveller departing by ship from Marseilles to North Africa or Indochina. The usual point of arrival in Marseilles was the Saint-Charles railway station, the southern terminus of the route from Paris. It was then a short distance to the main avenue, the famous Rue Canebière, which led to the historic harbour, the Vieux Port. The steamship docks adjoined a working-class neighbourhood which housed many immigrants just to the north of the Vieux Port. A visitor to the exposition would take a taxi or a tram down the Canebière and then take an avenue south-east about three kilometres through shopping, business and residential districts to the Parc du Prado, the location of the exposition. The city's supposed climatic and geographical similarity not only to the southern Mediterranean coast but also to Central and West Africa sustained the illusion of travel.[12] It seemed that Marseilles was 'a blessed site for a colonial exposition. Here, no element, whether object or person, was deracinated'.[13] This implied not only that colonial products 'naturally'

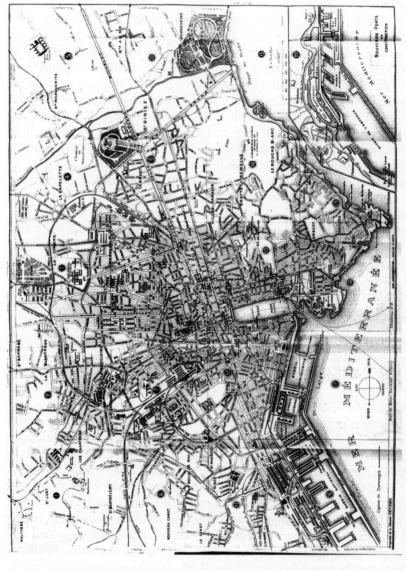

Figure 25 Plan of the city of Marseilles, 1922. The exhibition site is towards the top right-hand corner of the map, in the south-east of the town

accrued to Marseilles, but also that colonial people belonged in the city.

A Marseilles geographer, writing in 1922, characterised the wartime procession of troops from the French and British colonies along the Canebière as 'a sort of living ethnographic museum'.[14] One official directly compared the exposition with this avenue on which 'the entire world passes. ... The city, which is always celebrating this exposition, has prepared, organised, constructed and opened another ... the grand Colonial Exposition.'[15] Timothy Mitchell has discussed the prevalence of an exhibitionary logic in which 'the world [was] organized and grasped as though it were an exhibition'.[16] Taking this concept of the 'world-as-exposition' a step further, in Marseilles a seamless urban spectacle seemed to erase the distinction between the informal scenes of the city and the formal tableaux of the exposition. But in both places this exhibitionary complex created a division between spectators and performers which worked to obscure the socio-economic embeddedness of each in the other's world. Thus the construction of the Canebière as a permanent 'exposition' of the world transformed the colonial soldiers, seamen and industrial workers present in Marseilles into exotic figures on display. It rendered invisible their participation in the modern urban economy of a twentieth-century port. Similarly, the promoters of the exposition envisaged 'authentic' exhibits of indigenous daily life which rigorously excluded any Western objects, even if commonly used in the colonies.[17]

Indeed, officials deliberately sited the 1922 exposition so that 'one would not see the domes of Angkor or the Moroccan minarets silhouetted against a block of flats or competing with the chimney of a factory'.[18] As the architecture demonstrated, the exhibits drew on the same underlying colonialist 'phantasmatics' – the exotic Orient, primitive Africa, mysterious Islam – as other European expositions.[19] Yet commentators detected a new veracity in the structures and peopling of this exposition. Hanoi Street, for example, was planned to be 'not one bit like those papier-mâché streets of previous expositions, but rather a genuine street, with real houses in which the artisans would truly live'.[20] In the shops a visitor could 'surprise all sorts of workers absorbed by their daily occupations'.[21] The Tunisian section was represented as totally 'genuine', with streets 'full of character, of mystery and of shadow', a market so authentic that 'one could positively believe it to be in Tunis' and even a muezzin calling out the hours for Muslim prayer.[22] A British journalist observed that, near the West African tower, 'natives lead their ordinary, everyday life in rough tents, and perform their daily rites in a special little pavilion, set apart for their use as a Mosque, perfectly unconscious of the why and wherefore of their temporary transfer to a foreign shore'.[23] This reference to the obliviousness of the 'natives' not only to their surroundings but also to their role in the exposition constituted an essential element in the argument for authenticity. Any self-consciousness would have transformed the West Africans into actors of skill and intelligence, and revealed the exposition as a constructed and partial spectacle.

The physical barriers surrounding the exposition emphasised the separation of this apparently ordered and controlled simulacrum of the empire from the rest of the city. The exposition functioned as a retreat, a site of relaxation, fantasy and pleasure:

> When one is tired of wandering round, there can be nothing more pleasant than to sit awhile in the Moorish Café and sip the excellent coffee whilst listening to the eccentric sound of the Arab musician's one-chord instrument. Though trams and taxis run along the Parade close by – emblems of the busy industrial Marseilles – within the closed area of the exhibition reigns but the languid spirit of the Orient, with its seductive charm and fascination.[24]

In contrast, another visitor, a local seamstress originally from Corsica, found herself upon entering the exposition 'seized by a whirlwind of music, of colours'. She immediately regretted the absence of her husband, a sailor 'who, having travelled around the world, would have known what to show [her] and would have explained all'. Instead she chose a direction at random and wandered along, recognising Algerian oranges from her childhood in Corsica, admiring Tunisian artisans, passing from 'the spiced odours of *brochettes* to the refreshing perfumes of pineapples and coconuts', finally to 'arrive in Asia'. Senses overloaded by 'all these colours, music, smells, dust, movement, all these others', the young woman travelled home by taxi, a tranquil and luxurious refuge.[25] For her, as for many others, it was not so much the organisation as the confusion of scenes that proved so fascinating.

Indeed, the caption of a two-page spread in a special issue of *L'Illustration* read: 'the veiled Algerian women mingle with European visitors, and the high African tower dominates the Indochinese gateway'. The drawing portrayed well dressed European men, women and children of different classes, three fully veiled women with stylish footwear and parasols, Indochinese women and men, easily identifiable by their long dark tunics and close-fitting caps or broad-brimmed straw hats, a European woman in a rickshaw, and a black man in a hat, tunic-style jacket, trousers and elegant shoes.[26] The last of these is an ambiguous figure, apparently a Caribbean or African visitor to the exposition; beyond its walls he could have easily become part of the Marseilles urban spectacle. The mingling of people in this illustration resonated with descriptions of the cosmopolitan Canebière.

The contradictory nature of the conception of the Exposition as an authentic distillation of colonial experience was evident in the journalistic coverage of the French President's visit. The President, Alexandre Millerand, capped his month-long tour of French North Africa with a three-hour visit to the Colonial Exposition in Marseilles three weeks after its opening. One reporter described the President's reception in Marseilles on 6 May as impressive enough, though 'not as splendid or picturesque as those of the last weeks, when, under the Moroccan sky', he was saluted by red-cloaked tribal chiefs.[27] Nevertheless, as noted by another reporter, Millerand's tour of the exposition on 7 May 'recalled in the most lively, intelligent, picturesque manner all that he had been able to see and retain of his long and studious voyage'.[28] The writer René Benjamin, however, punctured the illusion of veracity with gentle mockery. He exposed the 'fever of last-minute preparations' for the President's visit, with the Commissioner General of the exposition, Adrien Artaud, rushing around 'in a rickshaw, going with all the speed of two Annamite legs, from north to south and from east to west'. When the day of Millerand's visit arrived, Benjamin reported on some of what the presidential party did not observe behind the scenes: recently arrived West Africans quarantined in the infirmary; the same ten Annamite guards who had saluted Millerand at the entrance of the palace of Angkor running around to the exit in order to salute him there; and 'beautiful Marseillaises in Tunisian dress' staffing the small exhibit hall of Tunis.[29]

Millerand's visit also provided an opportunity for political commentary and action. An editorial in a regional newspaper complained that there had been many more foreign than French waiters staffing the banquet for the President held at the exposition. With nationalist fervour it called for the investigation, in particular, of allegedly hostile German (boche) waiters, who could possibly have been prepared to attack Millerand.[30] At an anti-war meeting timed to coincide with the President's visit to the exposition, speakers criticised the mayor of Marseilles as well as President Millerand before an audience of 800. A communist orator concluded the meeting with 'a tirade against the Colonial Exposition, which [he said] symbolised all the thievery, all the murders, all the plundering, [that took place] in the name of civilisation'.[31] Such criticisms, however, seemed to have had little impact on the exposition's public appeal. It attracted over 2 million visitors in the six months between April and November 1922.[32]

Colonial workers

Visitors to the Colonial Exposition were not the only outsiders to arrive in Marseilles during the course of 1922. A continuous influx of immigrants augmented the city's large Italian community, and clandestine migrants from Spain and Morocco joined the numerous Berber workers from Algeria in the work placement camps, dockyards and industries of Marseilles.[33] African and Indochinese seamen could always be seen around the port district, mingling with Armenian, Greek, Russian and Syrian refugees. While the onset of war in 1914 had halted all plans for an exposition, it did bring to the mass of French people a direct experience of empire, so to speak, as hundreds of thousands of colonial conscripts came to serve in metropolitan France. Many arrived in Marseilles, substantially influencing the character of the city. The colonialist writer Charles Régismanset dramatically evoked this period: 'Suddenly, on the docks of Marseilles, the liveliest, most colourful of French cities, one could see going about soldiers and workers from all our colonies, North Africa, West Africa, Madagascar, Tahiti, Somalia, even Indochina. This Babel-like procession certainly constituted the greatest colonial event since the beginning of the century, a veritable reverse crusade.'[34] It is worth noting Régismanset's curious choice of words. 'Babel-like' (babelique) suggested a riot of difference rather than an orderly manifestation of the French imperial mission, whether assimilation or association. 'Crusade' also had strong connotations other than that of a simple rallying of the faithful for action; it could also mean an invasion, which would have placed Marseilles on the front line.

In the immediate post-war years many colonial workers were repatriated, but the recognition of the extent of French military losses soon led to renewed demand for immigrant and colonial labour. In this confusing situation, demobilisation brought returning Marseilles veterans into conflict with immigrant and colonial workers. Tension ran particularly high among the maritime work force based in Marseilles.[35] The years 1920 and 1921 saw protests by white French seamen against the employment of 'native' or 'coloured' seamen on ships belonging to Marseilles-based firms.[36] During the same period West African and Malagasy seamen formed their own union to defend their interests.[37] It is not surprising, therefore, that when the organisers of the Colonial Exposition resumed building plans they gave instructions that, 'despite the abundance of foreign workers in Marseilles, ... French labour [meaning white French citizens] should be employed as far as possible'.[38] One exception to this arrangement was a small group of skilled workers from the colonies. These 'two hundred Annamites, one hundred Moroccans, as well as Senegalese, Mauritanians, Tunisians [and] Algerians' were brought over for specific tasks which European workers could not perform, such as mosaic cutting and intricate carving.[39] They followed the instructions of French architects and designers such as a M. Salgé, described by the Commissioner of Arts as 'this proper Provençal become Indochinese'.[40] Intended as praise, this comment also indicated the French denial of the possibility of indigenous creative leadership, despite evident appreciation of the colonial workers' manual dexterity.

A typical account of the building of the exposition portrayed it as the work of a harmonious and industrious work force, 3,000 strong: 'Marseillais and colonial workers laboured with the same passion to do well so that the artistic marvels of our ancient empire would live again under our sky'.[41] There were, however, labour conflicts. One reporter described how the Annamite workers, the so-called 'French of Asia', arrived at the exposition site demanding the same eight-hour day enjoyed by metropolitan French workers since 1919. The architect in charge admitted the workers' 'right' to labour only eight hours but threatened to send back anyone who exercised the right.[42] Collective protest may have been suppressed, but individual Indochinese workers continued to argue with the authorities over wages, labour requirements and dates of return to Hanoi. Given the opportunity, workers like Phan Van Duoc, a custodian of temporary living quarters on the exposition site, expressed their resistance through negligence and absence. He apparently allowed his compatriots to use the kitchen and bathing facilities of these quarters, much to the displeasure of the European residents. Duoc was fired and (presumably) repatriated to Vietnam, though not before he had attempted to gain employment on a ship bound for Indochina.[43] The French administrators found the few colonial white-collar employees particularly difficult to deal with. For example, the assistant director of the Indochinese section, M. Pauher, harassed the draftsman Phan Hieu Kinh and two others who had moved into Marseilles into giving up their on-site room (used for storage and occasional stayovers). Clearly the idea that these Indochinese men were moving about freely in (mostly) European living quarters, as well as having a life outside the walls of the exposition, was deeply troubling. Kinh had to wait six months for a compensatory wage increase, and ten months later refused to return to Hanoi as scheduled.[44] In challenging discriminatory treatment, such workers undermined the presumption that colonial subjects on the exposition site should be treated as if they were still in colonial Indochina rather than in metropolitan France.

Colonial soldiers

The undoubted contribution of colonial soldiers and workers to the Allied victory had an important impact on the character of the 1922 Colonial Exposition. Planners broadened the focus of the exhibits from merely overseas commerce and development to include the importance of colonial manpower to the metropole itself.[45] Ceremonies and speeches celebrated the bravery and loyalty of colonial soldiers.[46] Cambodian and Annamite soldiers, Senegalese and Moroccan riflemen, Algerian cavalry and Tunisian royal guardsmen, many wearing medals for heroism in the war, greeted official visitors, participated in the many parades and processions, staffed the exhibits, and policed the indigenous population living inside the exposition's walls.[47] But they were also exhibits themselves – as representatives of this or that type of colonial soldier, living in 'typical' housing – the Algerian cavalry in Bedouin tents, for example, and the Indochinese militia in cabins surrounded by a bamboo palisade.[48] The dominance of this exhibitionary mode for the colonial troops was made very clear by the contrast with the Syrian and Lebanese militia and camel corps members who acted as guides in the section on the Levant. This section consisted of exhibit rooms sponsored by the Marseilles chamber of commerce. The displays recounted the history and extent of French interest in this eastern Mediterranean region, even though Syria and Lebanon were recent mandates rather than colonies. Commentators on the Exposition noted visitors' surprise on 'seeing soldiers like ours, men resembling those here at home [rather than] soldiers black like Nubians or bronzed like the Indochinese!' Moreover, they spoke fluent French.[49] Clearly, for many French the term 'overseas' denoted a rather simplistic caricature of 'racial' and cultural difference.

Officials frequently compared the service of the soldiers at the exposition to their service during the war. But this time, those united by the violence of battle came together in celebration, human signifiers of the *paix française*, the civilised peace supposedly brought everywhere by French rule.[50] Régismanset portrayed the presence of two Annamite riflemen in the Algerian palace as emblematic, commenting, 'Ancient Annam pays a visit to ancient Islam! ... [a] joyful symbol of the powerful bloc constituted by all our overseas possessions under the care of the same motherland'.[51] This positive conception of 'ancient Islam' was an important feature of the 1922 exposition. There was a functioning mosque accessible only to the faithful, and the exposition directors sponsored a major celebration for the observance of the birth of Mohammed.[52] The event gathered together all the Muslims of the exposition, including Algerians, Sudanese, Mauritanians and Syrians.

This primarily religious ceremony also provided (according to the Commissioner for Morocco) an opportunity for the Muslims 'to declare their recognition of and devotion to France as guardian, civiliser, and protector'.[53] Although these festivities were closed to ordinary visitors, officials and journalists were present. Most newspaper reports about the event adopted a self-congratulatory tone which took for granted the closing tribute of a Tunisian lieutenant, addressed to Adrien Artaud, the Commissioner General of the exposition: 'Long live France, protector of Islam!'[54]

Yet Marseilles had no mosque outside the walls of the exposition, and no French observers expressed any concern that Muslim workers lacked an official place to worship. By contrast, in Paris the construction of a substantial mosque reflected a growing attentiveness on the part of the French authorities to regions with high concentrations of North Africans.[55] This official involvement in religious affairs was directly linked with an increase in the control and surveillance of Muslims in France. In Marseilles, however, the socialist municipality continued to ignore both the religious needs of resident North Africans and the advantages to the state in fulfilling such needs. Indeed, the restriction of Islam to the grounds of the exposition was crucial in the city's quest to maintain a metropolitan French identity.

A civilising mission?

For the directors, the exposure of indigenous peoples to a benevolent France was part of the purpose of the exposition. This objective was expressed most clearly by Emile Thomas: 'The natives who have returned to their homes will affirm better still all that they have seen, felt, tried. If they have been for us friends over these past seven months, they will become over there the most eloquent missionaries of French civilisation.'[56] But this statement begged the question of exactly what kind of contact the 'natives' who acted as living exhibits actually had with French civilisation. Its inherent contradictions were perhaps most apparent with those groups brought from Central and West Africa as '"samples," like the great tree trunks on the ground', in the words of the colonial administrator of Guinea. Indeed, he found 'most interesting' the 'several blacks of the forest, who had just arrived with their fetishes', who not only did not speak French but had no language in common with the other Africans at the exposition.[57] For these others, French civilisation consisted of gawking crowds taking photographs, crowds for whom African men learned to pose 'just as we do'.[58] But the unequal encounter was also resisted: 'The women showed us only their backs. They refused all appeals: the missionaries in front of me spoke their language; they responded without turning round.'[59] Living in public, these African women took what action they could to maintain their privacy.

For women who were performers the situation was different. They had living quarters, along with various other non-military personnel, in a section of the exposition closed to the public. Indeed, the exposition directors actively tried to prevent any contact between these women and women from another centre for display and recreation in Marseilles, the red light district:

> The native women, particularly the Annamite women, sometimes receive in the evening visits from untrustworthy French or foreign women who seek, it seems, on apparently banal pretexts (to drink a glass of grenadine, for example), to entice them out of their quarters and perhaps also off the path of virtue. These native women would not know how or would not dare to escape such solicitations. ... They should be able to appeal for help from the native assistants who have the experience and authority to rid them of undesirable visitors, if so required.[60]

In response, the administrator of the Indochinese section installed armed guards at the entrance to the cantonment. Their task was 'to forbid access to the section to all women without exception, unless they carried a permit, and to all non-resident natives'.[61] While no doubt providing security for the women, this action also took the initiative for action out of their hands, severely limiting their freedom.

The young women, some still girls, of the corps of the royal Cambodian ballet attracted the particular attention of visitors to the exposition. Their performances evoked not only universal praise but also orientalist fantasies of the Cambodian past. Dramatically lit and elaborately costumed, the dancers performed on the monumental steps of the Indochinese palace. The journalist Ludovic Naudeau described them as 'sparkling ghosts of an inscrutable past, a time when ... the voluptuous *apsaras* held out their golden arms to the Brahmanic gods, similar to those who undulated before us, in that beautiful Provençal night'.[62] An article in the satirical journal *Le Bavard* made much of the erotic connotations, reporting an admittedly false account which claimed that the Cambodian dancers were carrying 'an illness, alas! already too well known'. The article then recounted a baroquely worded retraction, and reported that the dancers, indeed, lived honourably. Nevertheless, it commented, they 'have contributed a good deal to conferring on the Colonial Exposition of Marseilles the mysterious power which attracts the most sceptical and fascinates the most blasé'.[63] One of their elderly admirers, the Marquis de Beauvoir, was allowed to visit the young women. After gaining the permission of their guardian and the director of the Indochinese section, he even took them to his country estate for an afternoon.[64] The various types of regulated interactions between performers, visitors and Marseilles residents only highlighted the degree of control exerted by officials within the walls of the exposition.

In a different sort of controlled, 'civilising' contact, officially sponsored delegations from the colonies came to France to visit the exposition and take part in edifying tours of French industry and agriculture. Colonial administrators carefully selected twenty-four West African chiefs to stop in Marseilles en route to Paris for the 14 July celebrations.[65] In Marseilles they stayed 'in tents in familiar surroundings', thus becoming themselves participants/actors in the exposition.[66] A group of Indochinese notables whose presence was required for ceremonies involving high officials of the French government lived for weeks in those 'authentic' quarters on the Rue de Hanoi. For example, the Minister of Colonies Albert Sarraut visited the Indochinese section as part of the inauguration of the Colonial Exposition on 16 April. A former Governor General of Indochina, Sarraut decorated Indochinese soldiers and was thanked for his achievements by 'Tonkinese workers, Annamite merchants and Cochin-Chinese notables'.[67] The current Governor General, Maurice Long, visited on 22 July, and received compliments for his work in Indochina by one of the notables, speaking, as noted by the reporter, in 'excellent French'.[68]

These demonstrations of loyalty were an important part of the imperialist message of the exposition. But, for the colonial delegations themselves, such activities inside the walls of the exposition were hardly their main purpose. In an account of his experiences there, the Vietnamese intellectual and journalist Pham Quynh dismissed the participation of Indochinese delegates in receptions and ceremonies as simply a fulfilment of the need for richly dressed 'notables' to give a touch of the exotic. He complained that they were not even notified about the different congresses held in conjunction with the exposition, in which 'only speakers from the metropole held forth gravely on questions about which they were most often ignorant'. He advised the Indochinese delegates to the 1931 exposition in Paris to consider themselves tourists, observers of the spectacle of French life.[69] Pham Quynh waxed eloquent on the charms of Paris, the locus of French civilisation. Ironically, despite his contempt for the Colonial Exposition with its 'papier-mâché' Angkor Wat, Pham Quynh's panegyric to French culture ended up fulfilling Emile Thomas's hope for the missionary function of returning colonial subjects.

Excluded from these civilised heights was Marseilles, which Pham Quynh dismissed as a port 'containing a population much more cosmopolitan than French'.[70] Indeed, the arrival of HM Khai Dinh, the emperor of Annam, on 21 June 1922, transformed Marseilles into a site for the open display of Vietnamese nationalist sentiment. While a mainstream journalist commented on the 'contained emotion' of the Annamite riflemen upon seeing their emperor, a radical nationalist living in Marseilles, Phan Chau Trinh, took the opportunity to publish a manifesto ridiculing Khai Dinh's pretensions to modern democratic government.[71] Indeed, the police, concerned about the possibility of 'criminal acts' directed against the emperor, placed certain Vietnamese involved with the 1922 Colonial Exposition, including the journalist Pham Quynh and the draughtsman Phan Hieu Kinh, under special surveillance.[72]

Conclusion

Even before the 1922 National Colonial Exposition, Marseilles was itself represented as a kind of spectacle, its diverse population drawn from many parts of the world. As the subaltern presence increased, forming what the Jamaican writer Claude McKay called 'a great gang of black and brown humanity', it became more of a specifically colonial spectacle, exposing the illusory nature of the division between metropole and empire so neatly laid out in the exhibit halls of the exposition.[73] But, for the colonial workers of the exposition, the simulation of empire with its inequitable labour laws was all too real. Colonial soldiers and dignitaries performed the same acts expressing loyalty to the French as in their home colonies, but in the exposition they also had to carry the weight of being living symbols of the beneficence of the French empire, just as the presumed unity of the Muslims present was seen to symbolise French religious tolerance. The sharply defined space of the exposition was both separate from and part of the surrounding city, communicating a message about the centrality of the empire for Marseilles, and the centrality of Marseilles for the empire. Yet the easy movement of imperial subjects into, within and across the spaces of the city conveyed another message.

The Catholic conservative George Valois called Marseilles 'a colonial city, ... [like] a capital of the French colonial empire'.[74] But the city's undoubted economic significance was not so readily translated into cultural capital. Rather, the identification of Marseilles with the colonies became a handicap, virtually disqualifying the city as a representative of French civilisation. For many observers, the increasingly visible presence of colonial peoples in Marseilles cast doubt on the metropolitan French identity of the city. This process was best exemplified in a passage penned in 1924 by the reporter Albert Londres:

as for the people who suppose that there is no longer a colonial exposition in Marseilles, I will not go so far as to blame them, but I do pity them. Do you want to see Algeria, Morocco, Tunisia? Give me your arm. I will guide you along the Rue des Chapeliers: here are the shacks [*gourbis*], the wogs [*bicots*] and the women [*moukère*].

Not only did Londres denigrate the North Africans living on this Marseilles street; he also expressed contempt for the Colonial Exposition itself, in effect challenging the official celebratory vision of a proud city displaying a glorious empire. Characterising the smells, sights and customs on the Rue des Chapeliers as utterly alien, Londres suggested that one could just as well be in the ghetto of Oran (in Algeria).[75] Thus the 1922 Colonial Exposition provided contemporaries with yet another instance of Marseilles's supposed alterity, and offers us more evidence of the elusive and imagined nature of boundaries between metropole and empire.

Notes

I am grateful to the Camargo Foundation, the American Association of University Women Educational Foundation and the Emory University Graduate School of Arts and Sciences for support for the research and writing of the project from which this chapter is drawn. My thanks to Alice Conklin, Felix Driver, Ian Christopher Fletcher and David Gilbert for their comments and suggestions.

1 Baudrillard uses the term to describe the method of the television documentary: see Jean Baudrillard, *Simulacra and Simulation*, trans. Sheila Faria Glaser (Ann Arbor MI, University of Michigan Press, 1994), p. 28.
2 Cf. Ludovic Naudeau, 'L'Exposition coloniale de Marseille', *L' Illustration*, 21 October 1922, p. 388; Adrien Artaud, *Rapport général: Exposition nationale coloniale de Marseille 16 avril – 19 novembre 1922* (Marseilles, Commissariat Général, 1924), p. 140.
3 Emile Ripert, 'Promenade à travers l'Exposition coloniale de Marseille', *Les Annales*, 16 July 1922.
4 Cf. Patrick Boulanger, 'Des danseuses cambodgiennes aux cavaliers algériens, visions d'empire', in Pascal Blanchard, Stéphane Blanchoin, Nicolas Bancel, Gilles Boëtsch and Hubert Gerbeau (eds), *L'Autre et nous: 'scènes et types'* (Paris, ACHAC and SYROS, 1995), pp. 167–70; Sylviane Leprun, *Le Théâtre des colonies: scénographie, acteurs et discours de l'imaginaire dans les expositions 1855–1937* (Paris, Harmattan, 1986); Catherine Hodeir, Michel Perre and Sylviane Leprun, 'Les expositions coloniales: discours et images', in Nicolas Bancel, Pascal Blanchard and Laurent Gervereau (eds), *Images et colonies: iconographie et propagande coloniale sur l'Afrique française de 1880 à 1962* (Paris, BDIC-ACHAC, 1995), pp. 129-39; Alan Trachtenberg, 'White City', in *The Incorporation of America: Culture and Society in the Gilded Age* (New York, Hill & Wang, 1982), pp. 208–34; Thomas G. August, *The Selling of the Empire: British and French Propaganda, 1890–1940* (Westport CT, 1982).
5 Herman Lebovics, 'The seductions of the picturesque and the irresistible magic of art', in *True France: The Wars over Cultural Identity, 1900–45* (Ithaca NY, Cornell University Press, 1992), pp. 51–98.
6 Mary Louise Pratt, *Imperial Eyes: Travel Writing and Transculturation* (London, Routledge, 1992); Ali Behdad, *Belated Travelers: Orientalism in the Age of Colonial Dissolution* (Durham NC, Duke University Press, 1994); Antoinette Burton,

'Making a spectacle of empire: Indian travellers in *fin-de-siècle* London', *History Workshop Journal* 42 (1996) 127–46; Laura Tabili, *'We ask for British Justice': Workers and Racial Difference in late Imperial Britain* (Ithaca NY, Cornell University Press, 1994); Tyler Stovall, 'Colour-blind France? Colonial workers during the First World War', *Race & Class* 35:2 (1993) 35–55.

7 Timothy Mitchell, 'Orientalism and the exhibitionary order', in Nicholas B. Dirks (ed.), *Colonialism and Culture* (Ann Arbor MI, University of Michigan Press, 1992), pp. 289–317; Zeynep Çelik, *Displaying the Orient: Architecture of Islam at Nineteenth-Century World's Fairs* (Berkeley CA, University of California Press, 1992).

8 Charles Régismanset, *L'Exposition nationale coloniale de Marseille, 1922* (Paris, Françaises Réunies, 1921), p. 34.

9 Cf. Régismanset, *L'Exposition nationale coloniale*, p. 29; Jacques Léotard, 'Marseilles et les colonies', *Guide officiel: l'Exposition nationale coloniale de Marseille 1922*, ed. Adrien Artaud (Marseille, Société du 'Petit Marseillais', 1922), p. 9.

10 Louis Bonnaud, 'L'Exposition nationale coloniale: ses origines – ses buts – son organisation', *1922 l'Exposition nationale coloniale de Marseille décrit par ses auteurs*, (Marseille, Commissariat Général de l'Exposition, 1922), p. 28.

11 Ludovic Naudeau, 'L'Exposition coloniale de Marseille', p. 398.

12 Cf. *Boston Evening Transcript*, 4 October 1922; Régismanset, *L'Exposition nationale coloniale*, pp. 24–5.

13 Charles Régismanset, *Huit jours à l'Exposition coloniale de Marseille* (Paris, Cres, 1922), p. 78.

14 Jacques Léotard, *Le Port de Marseille* (Paris, Dunod, 1922), p. 158.

15 Citation from A. Bréal article in *Le Petit Journal*, 25 May 1922, 'L'étonnante Marseille', *Le Sémaphore de Marseille*, 28 May 1922. Cf. Alvan Sanborn, 'Marseilles has a Colonial Exposition', *Boston Evening Transcript*, 6 September 1922; Albert Detaille, *Les Noyaux de cerises: une enfance marseillaise* (Marseilles, Detaille, 1978), p. 128.

16 Mitchell, 'Orientalism and the exhibitionary order', p. 296.

17 Cf. Catherine Hodeir, 'Être "indigène" aux expositions? Paris 1931 et Paris 1937', in Blanchard et al., *L'Autre et nous*, pp. 157–62; Çelik, *Displaying the Orient*, p. 93.

18 August Giry, 'Le parc de l'exposition: ses origines – ses transformations – son avenir', *1922 l'Exposition … décrit par ses auteurs*, p. 37.

19 Çelik, *Displaying the Orient*, pp. 61, 181; Panivong Norindr, 'Representing Indochina: the French colonial fantasmatic and the *Exposition coloniale de Paris*', *French Cultural Studies*, 6 (1995) 35–60.

20 Régismanset, *L'Exposition nationale coloniale*, p. 50.

21 Naudeau, 'L'Exposition coloniale de Marseille', p. 377.

22 *Ibid.*, p. 392; Geoffroy Saint-Hilaire, 'La Tunisie', *1922 l'Exposition … décrit par ses auteurs*, p. 169. See also Régismanset, *Huit jours à l'Exposition coloniale*, p. 56.

23 W. Beldimano, 'The Colonial Exhibition at Marseilles', *Graphic*, 8 July 1922.

24 *Ibid.*

25 Michèle Castelli, *Rue Château-Payan: Marie de Lola II* (Paris, Editions Universitaires, 1984), p. 23. This book is a memoir of Castelli's grandmother, Marie Amadei-Baldini.

26 Sabattier, 'La Rue annamite à l'Exposition coloniale de Marseille', *L'Illustration*, 27 May 1922, pp. 504-5.

27 *Le Journal des débats politiques et littéraires*, 8 May 1922.

28 *Le Matin*, 8 May 1922.

29 René Benjamin, 'Une promenade à travers l'Exposition coloniale', *L'Illustration*, 27 May 1922, p. 502.

30 *L'Ami du peuple*, 30 May 1922, newspaper cutting in Archives nationales de la France, Paris (hereafter AN), F/7/12976.

31 AN, F/7/12976, Special Commissioner report No. 1861, Marseilles, 8 May 1922.

32 Adrien Artaud, *Rapport général*, p. 493. My thanks to Laurent Morando for this reference.

33 There is no record of the numbers of indigenous civilians arriving from Algeria because before 1925, as residents of one of the three Algerian *départements*, they

were entitled to free movement between the colony and the metropole. Nevertheless, the number of North African workers living in Marseilles in the 1920s has been estimated to have fluctuated between 10,000 and 15,000: see Marie-Françoise Attard-Maraninchi and Emile Temime, *Migrance: histoire des migrations à Marseille*, III, *Le Cosmopolitisme de l'entre-deux-guerres, 1919–45* (Aix-en-Provence, Edisud, 1990), p. 39. The police reported over 100 Moroccans arriving each month between May and July 1922. *Archives départementales des Bouches-du-Rhône*, Marseilles (hereafter AD), 1M/1770, Special Commissioner, Service for the Control of Ports and Railways, Marseilles, to Prefect, Bouches-du-Rhône (hereafter BdR), 18, 22, 23, 24, 31 May, 5, 22, 26, 27 June, 3 July 1922.

34 Régismanset, *L'Exposition nationale coloniale*, p. 76.

35 AD, 1M/1834, Special Commissioner report Nos. 2138, Marseilles, 20 April 1920; 4674, Marseilles, 12 October 1920; 4864, Marseilles, 24 October 1920.

36 AD, 1M/1834, Special Commissioner report Nos. 1070, Marseilles, 18 February 1920; 1898, Marseilles, 26 March 1920; 1044, Marseilles, 17 February 1920; cutting 'Le chômage des marins', 30 October 1920; AD, 1M/1835, Central Commissioner, Marseilles Police, to Prefect, BdR, 21 October 1921; telegram, Director, Maritime Inscription, to Transmar, Paris (copy to Prefect, BdR), 24 October 1921; General Secretary, Union of Commercial Seamen and Fishermen, Marseilles Section, to Prefect, BdR, 5 November 1921.

37 AD, 1M/1834, Statutes of the Professional Union of West African Seamen in Marseilles, March 1920. AD, 1M/1778, Special Commissioner to Prefect, BdR, No. 1863, 22 June 1922.

38 Artaud, *Rapport général*, p. 30.

39 *Le Sémaphore de Marseille*, 12 April 1922; J. de la Nézière, 'Les artisans et les industries d'art indigène', *1922 l'Exposition ... décrit par ses auteurs*, p. 218.

40 José Silbert, 'Les beaux-arts', *1922 l'Exposition ... décrit par ses auteurs*, p. 51.

41 A. Detaille, 'Quand Marseille, métropole coloniale, fêtait son exposition, 1922', *Le Revue Marseille*, 81 (1970) 30.

42 René Benjamin, 'Une promenade à travers l'Exposition coloniale', p. 506.

43 *Archives nationales de la France, Centre des Archives d'Outre-mer*, Aix-en-Provence (hereafter CAOM), FOM/767/1657, Pauher to Guesde, 28 September, 10 October 1921; Pauher to Director of Personnel, Messageries Maritimes, 30 August 1921.

44 CAOM, FOM/767/1657, Pauher to Nguyen Van Dan and Phan Van Kinh, 6 August 1921; Pauher to Guesde, 7 January 1922; Kinh to Pauher, 8 September 1922; Guesde to Kinh, 16 September 1922; Pauher to Guesde, 21 September 1922.

45 Régismanset, *L'Exposition nationale coloniale*, pp. 6–7.

46 Cf. speeches by Interior Minister Adrien Artaud and President Millerand on 7 May 1922, *Le Petit Journal*, 8 May 1922; *Le Journal des Débats*, 9 May 1922.

47 Cf. *Le Matin*, 17 April 1922; *Sémaphore de Marseille*, 12 April 1922; CAOM, FOM/759/1632, Chief Resident, Indochinese section, to Commander of Arms, 11 May 1922.

48 P. Guesde, 'L'Indochine', *1922 l'Exposition ... décrit par ses auteurs*, p. 95.

49 Commissaire Adjoint Belandou, 'Les intérêts français en Syrie et dans le Liban', *1922 l'Exposition ... décrit par ses auteurs*, p. 206; cf. Artaud, *Rapport général*, p. 271.

50 Cf. Belandou, 'Les intérêts français', *1922 l'Exposition ... décrit par ses auteurs*, p. 209.

51 Régismanset, *Huit jours à l'Exposition coloniale*, pp. 98–9.

52 *Le Petit Marseillais*, 7 November 1922.

53 A. Terrier, 'Maroc', *1922 Exposition ... décrit par ses auteurs*, p. 201.

54 *Le Petit Marseillais*, 8 November 1922. By the 1920s most colonial administrators recognised the political advantages of tolerating or even encouraging Islamic religious practice, and the potential for religious suppression to ignite revolt. Alain Ruscio, *Le Credo de l'homme blanc* (Paris, Editions Complexe, 1995), pp. 288–95.

55 Neil MacMaster, *Colonial Migrants and Racism: Algerians in France, 1900–62* (London, Macmillan, 1997), p. 105.

56 *Le Petit Marseillais*, 21 Nov. 1922.
57 Benjamin, 'Une promenade à travers l'Exposition', p. 507.
58 F. Ronserail, 'Les photographes, les noirs soudanais et l'Islam', *Le Petit Marseillais*, 27 October 1922, p. 4.
59 Benjamin, 'Une promenade à travers l'Exposition', p. 507.
60 CAOM, FOM/759/1632, [illegible name] to M. Dauffes, Principal Inspector, undated note.
61 *Ibid.*, Chief Resident, Indochinese section, to Commander of Arms, 11 May 1922.
62 Ludovic Naudeau, 'L'Exposition colonial de Marseille', p. 378.
63 'Les danseuses cambodgiennes', *Le Bavard*, 21 October 1922.
64 Albert Detaille, *Les Noyaux de cerises*, p. 148.
65 CAOM, AP/520, Governor General of French West Africa to Minister of Colonies, April 1922.
66 *The Times* (London), 5 July 1922.
67 Artaud, *Rapport général*, p. 406.
68 'M. Maurice Long à l'Exposition de Marseille', *Le Journal des débats*, 23 July 1922.
69 Pham Quynh, 'Souvenirs d'Exposition coloniale', *Nam-Phong*, 162 (1931) 49–52. My thanks to Chris Goscha for this reference.
70 *Ibid.*, p. 51.
71 *Le Matin*, 22 June 1922; Ngo Van, *Viêt-nam, 1920–1945: révolution et contre-révolution sous la domination coloniale* (Paris, L'Insomniaque, 1995), p. 40.
72 CAOM, 3 SLOTFOM/125, Guesde report, 13 April 1922; Jolin to Guesde, 29 April 1922.
73 Claude McKay, *A Long Way from Home* (San Diego CA, Harcourt Brace, 1937, reprinted 1970), p. 277.
74 George Valois, 'Marseilles, porte de l'Orient', *L'Action française*, 23 October 1922.
75 Albert Londres, *Marseille: porte du sud* (Paris, Arléa, 1927, reprinted 1992), p. 319.

CHAPTER NINE

Commemorating empire in twentieth-century Seville

Anthony Gristwood

My aim in this chapter is to explore some issues concerning social memory, commemoration, and the social construction of contemporary identities in the urban arena. By examining the production and iconography of two exhibitionary events in twentieth-century Seville, I want to illuminate the complex connections between debates about the location of Spanish culture, definitions of 'Spanishness' and the recasting of the legacy of Spanish imperialism. As a key site within Spanish national mythology and imperial history, Seville has been closely bound up with the construction of narratives of state and empire formation. What impact has imperialism had on the spaces and urban experiences of inhabitants in the erstwhile administrative and trading centre of the Spanish imperium? Attempts to regenerate and re-imagine urban space have opened up tensions within the imaginary category 'Spanish'. More specifically, in their selective appropriation of history and their reconfiguration of urban space, the 1929 Iberoamerican Fair and the 1992 World's Fair raise questions about the location of the city within wider articulations of national and imperial space. As an imperial centre, Seville was a significant node in the economic networks of empire, and the city was also implicated in the scripting of those wider spaces culturally. Promotional strategies designed to re-imagine and regenerate cities are familiar economic and political phenomena, positioning sites within imaginary cultural systems of space; this 'repackaging', however, also has consequences for the reconstruction of mythologies of the nation and imperial progress.[1]

Following Patrick Wright, we may understand the past as a 'cultural presence', appropriated for contemporary 'self-understandings' for a variety of purposes by different groups.[2] While the resultant cultural landscapes can be seen as 'fields constitutive of identity ascription',[3] sanctioned pasts are malleable and contested.[4] The expositions of 1929 and 1992 both represent moments of crisis for Spain as a post-imperial state; and both are part of struggles to grapple with the condition of modernity and the consequences of modernisation. If, as Massey argues, place identities need to be understood in a relational sense as both contingent and dynamic, then cities, too, are places struggling to reinvent themselves anew, 'spaces of desire' – terms of reference for the construction of new identities.[5]

Seville has played a variety of roles within the developing nation state and imperium. A Visigothic, then Moorish, city, Seville's vigorous and cosmopolitan urbanity was purged after the Christian Reconquista (Reconquest). Its Sephardic Jewish inhabitants, who had coexisted peacefully with Arab, Berber and Christian inhabitants, were ghettoised, persecuted and eventually expelled from Spain entirely under the racist ideology of *limpieza de sangre* (purity of blood). With the 'discovery' of the New World, Seville became the privileged holder of the trading monopoly with the Americas, and although this epoch of wealth and political influence ended when the monopoly passed to Cadiz, it left a material legacy in the form of the city, exemplified by the symbolic concentration of the power of Church, commerce and state in the architectural conjunction of cathedral, royal palace and *la lonja* (mercantile exchange) in the heart of the old city.

Integrating national space: representing Spain in 1929

As the host of the 1929 Iberoamerican Fair, Seville acted as symbolic carrier of Spain's classical heritage. The organisers declared the nearby ruins (the Roman city of Italica and its amphitheatre) a national monument.[6] According to myth, Seville itself had been founded by Hercules on the edge of the known world (hence the phrase 'Non plus ultra'). In one of the exhibition posters, the confining chains of the Pillars of Hercules have been broken by the lion of Hispania, which, along with the feminised cities of Seville and Barcelona, gazes out towards the New World. The architecture of the fair itself was praised for its sense of enduring solidity and its adherence to classical forms evoking ancient Athens or Rome.[7] Moreover, the design of the surrounding gardens included facsimile and actual fragments of ancient sculpture and architecture.

The Iberoamerican Fair simultaneously tapped a vein of nostalgia for past splendours embodied in the monuments and relics of an imperial and maritime past, and reflected a regenerationist urge to improve the infrastructure, industry and housing stock of the city. One contemporary account characterised its aims in the following terms:

> to promote the study and treatment of problems of communication, commerce, and finance; and, in general, the moral and material ques-

tions of mutual interest to the Iberian Peninsula and the American countries ... [and to] ... strengthen even more the bonds that already exist between Spain, Portugal and the Americas.[8]

Originally envisaged as a reaffirmation of Spain's international status after the loss in 1898 of the Philippines and Cuba (the last of Spain's imperial possessions in the New World), the fair was eventually held during the dictatorship of Primo de Rivera, when ideas of pan-Hispanism and the integrity of the nation state of Spain were increasingly prevalent. In reconstructing the mythology of the foundation of the nation state of Spain in terms of a specifically Western modernity and imperialism, the fair highlights the tensions within the category 'Spanish' between notions of purity and hybridity, reflected in the representation of Spain's Moorish past and the representational strategies adopted by Latin American participants. The representation of 'New World-as-exhibition' and 'Nation-state-as-exhibition' emerged at a time of centralisation in Spanish political administration and the homogenisation of national space and time, in the face of Catalan nationalism and Andalusian regionalism. These conflicting ideas of identity were to be played out in the spaces of the host city.

In the fair, national and imperial times and spaces were centred around the concept of *la madre patria* (the Motherland), associated with an ideology of shared culture, and especially the Spanish language itself. The written word and the printed book were given a dedicated section in the fair: exhibits included the tracing of the genealogy of Spanish in reconstructions of medieval scriptoria and codices, displaying Iberian, Visigothic, Arabic and Hebrew texts, Christian and Hebrew presses from the fifteenth century, and its global expansion – printing under Philip II in the Low Countries and in early modern Mexico, Chile and the Philippines. The Iberoamerican Press pavilion offered daily national newspapers for sale, with Spanish regional gazettes and the 'foremost' American periodicals arranged by country.[9] The Municipal Newspaper Archive (Hemeroteca) of Madrid was invited to contribute a newspaper exhibit, the 'exact expression of a glorious past'.[10] Together these elements comprised a narrative of the diffusion of the written word which was explicitly linked with the expansion of Spanish political and cultural power. Moreover, as a living archive of the national, regional and Latin American press, the exhibition reinforced the idea of imagined communities at these different scales, and thus of the interconnection of regional, national and, indeed, international spaces.

The Iberoamerican Fair formed part of the Universal Spanish Exposition of 1929, which was held jointly with Barcelona. The combined exposition programme characterised the fair as a means to build closer ties between the nations of America and Spain, 'already united by the shared ties of race and of language', and also to promote 'great commercial exchange with these countries'.[11] Although art, history and commerce were intended to be the three fundamental themes of the fair, the commercial came a very poor third in the case of Seville's contribution. Within the category of arts, moreover, modern and industrial arts were regarded as 'less important' than the exhibition of 'retrospective' art, arranged both generically and regionally.[12] A nostalgic heritage was evoked through this 'retrospective' art, which 'with its historical teachings, in Spanish folklore [was] brilliantly represented in an exposition which has to include costumes, typical buildings and manual crafts ... in a city which in its monuments registers the influences of various civilisations'.[13]

Above all, the history represented at the fair was that of Spanish colonisation in America, displayed through 'panoramas, in plans and maps, engravings, documents', popularised by 'historical authorities and scenographic artists' as a 'revindication which has raised up the name and the prestige of old Spain'. The organisers intended the fair to 'inculcate to ... new ... Hispano-American thought the admiration and the respect which are due to the nation which gave them life, freedom and civilisation'.[14] Hispanic-American links were characterised as those of a racial family, with Hispania the mother figure of the Spanish state. Thus the inscription at the main entrance to the Iberoamerican fairground, quoted from the Nicaraguan poet Ruben Darío, read:

> Illustrious bountiful races
> Fertile blood of Spain
> Brotherly spirits
> Brilliant souls
> Hail!

The image of Hispania was repeatedly deployed in the iconography of the fairground architecture and art. Outside the entrance, under three arches, a statue remains of Hispania, resembling images of Queen Isabel (whose Avenue leads away into the fairground), at whose side is the imperial lion conferring ownership on the western hemisphere of the globe. Flanking her are two other allegorical female figures. As Marina Warner notes, the female body operates in such a context as the literal embodiment of the state, as a container or vessel, inscribed with the text of desired meanings.[15]

The Fountain of Hispanicity in the southern section of the fair, adjacent to the Plaza de los Conquistadores, portrayed Hispania atop the prow of a caravel (symbol of the voyage of 'discovery') between two figures representing the river Guadalquivir and the river Plate (of the Old and New Worlds). Woman-as-figurehead appears again on the cover of the Exposición General Española guide, although here the two ships are fronted by female figures representing Barcelona (on the left) and Seville (on the right), who is distinguished by her mantilla (hair comb) and a tiny globe held in her palm. Both cities' coats of arms are displayed below, above two doves: the realities of 'discovery' and imperial power are idealised in soft, feminised terms of peaceful co-operation, which is extended to include the two Spanish cities' relationship within Spain – they share her sheltering cloak.

The Art Deco design of one of the main publicity posters for the Iberoamerican Fair has Hispania standing in the centrepiece of the fairground, the Plaza de España, surrounded by female figures representing the Latin American countries, some depicted in pre-Columbian dress, presenting gifts of produce and crafts to the 'Motherland', under a streamer of their flags. This set of relationships had their devotional aspect: above the entrance to the Mexican pavilion was inscribed 'Through my Race spoke the Spirit', and written across an inner doorway was an invocation dedicated to Spain: '"Mother Spain: because in my lands you fired the sun of your culture and in my soul the holy torch of your spirit, now my lands and my heart have flourished". Mexico.'

In one early proposal, the Iberoamerican Exposition was envisaged as a project to 'unite the two hemispheres, to one common dedicated aim of "work", under the protection [of] and with the support of the motherland (*la madre patria*) of "Spain"'.[16] In this scheme, the name of the city was literally to be inscribed on the landscape of project and city: 'Seville is the initiator of the project, so it is just that her initial "S" forms the base and point of departure [of the plan].' The initial would have formed the 'gyratory centre', or pivot of the exposition, and from this apex of a triangular site the shapes of the pavilions themselves would outline the spelling of the city name. At the two ends of the central S were to be 'two great domes' representing the Old and New Worlds, to be decorated with friezes and reliefs depicting countries' natural products and customs, at the centre of which would stand a 'statue of Seville crowning the nations'. Connecting galleries would be united in the heart of the S by the pavilion of the royal house, whose minaret would 'signify that under its [i.e. the royal family's] protection, and with its support, are exalted, achieved and carried out the highest aspirations of the *patria* and in their representation those of her daughters the Spanish provinces', including the eight Andalusian provinces. The minaret was to have provided a panoptic view of the whole fair layout, a paternalistic vision of national and international unity under the Spanish Crown, and also a self-conscious promotion of Seville's name across Spain and Latin America. The whole was to have been entered through a triumphal arch, which would 'serve as a monument to Columbus', depicting 'a brilliant page in the history of Spain'.

Although these grandiose designs were never constructed, the eventual layout of the fair exhibited a similar imagined geography. The fairground was set in the midst of the Parque María Luisa, designed and landscaped by the French landscape gardener Jean-Claude Forestier, itself an exercise in 'bio-imperialism'; the pavilions were constructed between two main avenues, the central one being the Avenue de la Raza (Avenue of the Race). Other streets and intersections were named after Reconquista figures such as El Cid, Queen Isabel, and notable *conquistadores* and explorers (Cortés, Pizarro, Elcano, Magellan). The fairground itself was broadly divided into two sections, linked by an amusement zone. There were two architectural showpieces in the northern half, the Plaza de España and the Plaza de América.

The Plaza de España (see Figure 26), designed by the Sevillano architect Aníbal González, forms a hemispherical arena which constructed national space and time (or, to adapt Anne McClintock's terminology, panoptic time and anachronistic space) by representing the nation state of Spain in relation to its 'Others'.[17] Its architecture is eclectic and historicist, drawing on Mudéjar, Renaissance and baroque elements: indeed, all styles which influenced Seville appear to have been repre-

Figure 26   Postcard drawing of the Plaza de España, *c*. 1926

sented. This promotion of a hybrid 'regional' style is reinforced by the flanking towers' recapitulation of the Giralda, or bell tower, of Seville's cathedral. Under the arches of the colonnade are an integrated set of representations of national space and time: ceramic friezes depict key historical moments from each province, arrayed in alphabetical order from left to right across the semicircular plaza. Of the forty-eight scenes, which were chosen by the provincial authorities, twenty-six at least relate directly to the Reconquista, or to 'national unity' under the monarchs of Castile, whilst a further eight select moments from the Peninsular War, or scenes of 'discovery' in the New World by Columbus and others. At least two-thirds of the scenes thus clearly recapitulate the national foundation myth of modern Spain, in which political unity and stability were wrought under Castilian control, nurtured by expansion in the New World, and maintained in struggle against the 'Other', represented by vanquished Moors and French invaders. The construction of a national identity of unified Spain is directly linked with the Reconquista and, by extension, to the conquest and settlement of Latin America. These discourses of purification, race, religious affiliation and national space sit uneasily with the hybridity of architectural forms; indeed, they are not easily reconciled with the medium of the scenes themselves, which draw upon elements of Arabic and Moorish techniques of ornamentation (such as the use of polychromatic ceramics) in the expression of regional tradition.

Underneath these ceramic friezes were placed tiled maps of each province, showing borders, settlements, and river and road networks in relation to their neighbours, emphasising provincial boundaries and inter- and intra-provincial links between urban centres. Above, city pennants, historical flags, such as those of the Catholic monarchs, and provincial banners were flown. Provincial authorities also supplied promotional material which was housed in the ceramic shelving either side of each frieze, enabling further touristic consumption of each province.[18] Territorial unity was also expressed by repeated columnar escutcheons, red and yellow tiles (after the Spanish flag) and tiled castle and lion symbols inlaid into the floor of the plaza (symbolising the unification of Castile and León). The inner and outer sections of the plaza were connected by four bridges, dedicated to Castile, Aragón, Navarre and León, unifying the whole. The plaza effectively represents an itinerary around Spain, as a nation state, in which provinces are smoothly connected together in space and time to form the imagined community of national space (while inside the Plaza de España building, there was a large-scale relief map of Spain). As the venue for the inauguration of the fair (9 May 1929) the plaza became the *mise-en-scène* for historical and folkloric pageants which blended regional costumes and dances with narratives of national history and political power. Contemporary Moroccans were costumed as Moors,[19] and there were military parades before the royal family and dictator.[20]

Purity versus hybridity: representing the exotic

The construction of national space and time at the fair was augmented by representations of Spain's overseas colonies, both past and present.[21] Here the exhibition may be conceived as an 'epistemological space' in which the exotic was enframed within the familiar space of the city. By the staging of cultural and racial difference, as Derek Gregory suggests, 'aesthetic appreciation was transformed into political ontology. The colonial order of things was detached and distanced from its concrete particularities, glossed as a harmonious visual composition, and its more disturbing pathologies were erased.'[22] Difference was represented in terms of leisure, pleasure and consumption, a strategy which both effaces those differences and 'wraps' exotic cultures within the everyday, thereby detaching such exhibits from their contexts, 'contributing to the erosion of historical memory'.[23]

The two remaining colonial possessions, the Moroccan protectorate and Spanish Guinea, were both represented in adjacent pavilions at the end of the Avenue of the Race, where the northern sector of the fairground abutted the amusement zone. Indeed, the Moroccan contingent was itself split between the pavilion proper and the pavilion of the Moorish Quarter (Barrio Moro), located in the amusement zone itself.[24] The Moroccan pavilion was designed by a Spanish architect, in Islamic style, complete with minaret; the decoration combined domestic architectural techniques, whitewash and tilework. Exterior ornamentation evoked the sacred: at the corners of the original design were to have been domes and a minaret reproduced from actual mosques, whilst the ensemble was simultaneously 'in its direction, proportions and decorations in the most pure local style' and surrounded by vegetation appropriate to the country of origin. The architect writes that 'we believe that though a building will be achieved which will pass for exotic in Seville, it will encapsulate very well the atmosphere, light and tradition of the Sevillan pueblo', again, wrapping the exotic in the local whilst adhering to the conceit of authenticity.[25] The interior, a large patio surrounded by commercial galleries, included 'Moroccan bazaars' and 'a café, constructed in typically Moorish style'. The Moorish Quarter was built as 'a typical street' of Tetuán with authentic workshops and stalls in which indigenous artisans were paid to produce jewellery, metalwork and other artefacts.[26]

The Gulf of Guinea pavilion, housing the 'colonial and native popu-

[162]

lation', was also designed (by a Spaniard) to simulate indigenous style and materials, using wooden frames and grass roofing, decorated with 'primitive' art (see Figure 27). The main building was surrounded by four tribal 'houses' and a kiosk for coffee and cocoa.[27] The inhabitants of these 'houses', brought especially from Guinea, were objectified as spectacle, performing tribal dances and ceremonies. The quest for authenticity extended even to local fauna. One poignant memo states that a chimpanzee sent from Fernando Po, accompanied by a military guard, 'has died in its cage' en route.[28] At the time of a royal visit shortly after the fair opened, the Guinean pavilion, still unfinished, juxtaposed 'a group of gorillas' and 'two nude Pamúes [indigenous tribespeople]'. Inside, the 'natives of the mainland and islands ... performed their typical dances, accompanied by primitive instruments'; after this spectacle, the royal couple were given 'parcels of Bubu chocolate' as gifts.[29]

The strategies of self-representation employed in their own pavilions by the Latin American ex-colonies exhibited a variety of positions along a continuum between pure indigenism and Hispanism, often in hybridised combinations of elements of the pre-Columbian and colonial past, an approach which worked against the dominant discourse of purity in the representation of Spain as a nation state.[30] Some opted for an architecture that derived purely from the colonial heritage. For example, Uruguay's permanent pavilion, avowedly constructed with

Figure 27 Postcard view of the Spanish Guinea pavilion at the Iberoamerican Fair of 1929

the aim of '[constituting] in Seville a perennial reminder of the friend-ship of Uruguay toward Spain', was erected in a pure Hispanic style.[31]

In contrast, the Mexican pavilion was designed with an exterior recalling Toltec geometries, frescoes and figurative sculpture, and included the emblem of Mexico, a stylised Quetzalcoatl, or eagle, with a serpent, as the centrepiece of the frieze above the main entrance to the building.[32] The pair of seated figures at the top of the front facade were copies of the Toltec sculptures at Chichén Itzá (the Chacmool). Coloration was muted to yellow and red in order 'to avoid a strong con-trast with the buildings of Seville'; the Mexican legation wrote about the architectural design competition in terms of 'the love which we the Mexicans feel for everything which is connected with Mother Spain', and looked forward to the Mexican contribution being the 'most grand and significant ... amongst the peoples of the Hispanic race'.[33] Furthermore, it was claimed that 'Her art ... her customs, her names, are fundamentally Spanish and uniquely Sevillano. Mexicans will find themselves at home in Seville ... Our popular fiestas are yours.' Even so, the Mexican pavilion's design embodied indigenism rather than hybridity. Likewise, the Guatemalan pavilion reproduced in stylised blue and white ceramic the steles of classical Mayan civili-sation: but this architecture fulfilled a basically instrumental function – the 'propagation of Guatemalan coffee ... reputed as one of those of best quality in the whole world'.[34]

The Peruvian pavilion was constructed 'after official buildings in Peru', reproducing Inca dry-stone masonry at basement and ground level, including sculptural details, doorways and supporting statuary; the interior included a cloister employing the same style. Its contents, in addition to the usual maps of territory, communications and statis-tics, included sections on 'aboriginal Peruvian' and modern textile industries. The arts were divided into 'ancient Peruvian art', from the Inca and pre-Inca eras, including plans and drawings of monumental Inca architecture from a variety of sites, musical and literary works 'related to the history of Spain and America', and works which 'glorify Spain', along with 'typical [indigenous] Peruvian music'.[35]

The Colombian pavilion also combined pre-Hispanic and colonial motifs. Its overall shape recalled that of a colonial baroque church, with two flanking towers; the decoration, however, evoked pre-Columbian forms: in the guardian figures flanking the main doorway, accompanying coiled serpents, and the geometrically carved half-columns and crouched Indian archers carved in the frieze above the back entrance, as well as in the patterns of the tiled frieze along the roof line. According to the plans of this pavilion, the site included tobacco and coffee kiosks: the former's interior wall was to be decorated with the words 'Colombian tobaccos and Spanish paper: the ideal combination for cigarettes' above a container of free samples, a commercial affirmation of hybridity.[36] The coffee kiosk was designed as a large geometrical face, complete with somewhat macabre smile (the mouth formed a counter where samples of coffee could be tasted, while the eyes formed windows to the coffee lounge). Chile, meanwhile, was represented by a pavilion envisaged as 'a surprising artistic fusion of the Spanish and the native, harmonised in a succession of rising storeys',[37] constituting 'without doubt, a lovely homage offered to Mother Spain'.[38] The project was also described as a 'reason for pride for all the Iberoamerican race', evoking the 'characteristics attributed to the formidable Spaniards of the *conquista* and the valiant native elements [of the country]'.[39]

The Iberoamerican Fair closed during the Great Depression, leaving the city deeply indebted well into the period of Franco's regime. Its final days spanned the collapse of de Rivera's dictatorship, the monarchy, and the rise of the ill-fated Republic – a period of political and social upheaval culminating in civil war and the subsequent decades of repression and cultural isolation under Francoism.

Recasting the imperial: Expo '92

Following Franco's death (in 1975) and the transition to a democratic, quasi-federal state through the 1980s, the year 1992 was greeted in Spain as an *annus mirabilis*, a symbolic landmark in the country's emergence from economic and cultural isolation under the dictatorship. Madrid became the European cultural capital, the Olympic Games were held in Barcelona, whilst Seville was once again the location of a Universal Exposition. The political significance of Expo '92 was conceived in a variety of ways. First, as a commemoration of the quincentenary of the 'discovery' of the New World by Columbus in 1492, a historic moment that was portrayed in solely Spanish terms; second, as a celebration of Spain's renaissance after Franco, culturally and socially, and in particular as an evocation of Spain's desire for closer integration into the European Union; third, as an instrumental marker of ten years' national political power of the Partido Socialista Obrero Español (PSOE) and of its leader, Felipe González. Both Expo and the other 'Fiestas de '92' were appropriated for the credit of the PSOE. Deputy Prime Minister Alfonso Guerra, for example, affirmed at a party meeting in Seville that Expo had been a 'socialist act', and that the 'public socialist effort [was] admired around the world'; for González, whilst Expo had been the work of all Spaniards, it had been due to 'some more than others'.[40] The PSOE had won the general election of 1982 on a platform which included EEC entry and above all the 'definitive modernisation' of Spain, under the motto *Cambio* (Change). Part of this modernisation process was reflected in the designation of the Expo site as a space for future high-technology research and development, designed to transform Andalusia into a 'California in Europe'.[41]

As Penelope Harvey notes, the organisers of the Universal Exposition had to negotiate a complex, highly charged cultural politics, reflected in the often ironic and reflexive strategies of self-representation employed by participants – a consequence of both post-colonial sensibilities and the need to relocate 'Spanish' identity within a quasi-federal state.[42] First, and most obviously, the commemoration of the 'Discovery' was in itself highly problematic. In 1982 the General Assembly of the Bureau International de Expositions had assigned 1992 as a provisional date for the organisation of a joint commemoration between Chicago and Seville – a century after the World's Columbian Exposition in Chicago.[43] However, the controversy over the memorialisation of 'Discovery' was a major factor in the cancellation of this part of the event, in the wake of a confrontation between the Democrat mayor of Chicago and the Republican state governor.[44] The proposal itself quickly generated controversy over the provenance of 'discovery' itself – Iceland and Denmark countered with the claims of Leif Eriksson, whilst the Irish recalled the legend of St Brendan's voyage west.[45] Within the 'Columbian' camp, nearby Huelva asserted its alternative claim over Seville to have been the point of departure for the first voyage of Columbus.

The legacy of the Spanish empire was recast by Expo '92 in two senses: first, as a narrative of imperial history in which 'discovery' was re-imagined in terms of technological progress and the modernist project of knowledge gathering; second, in terms of contemporary multiculturalism, with the city of Seville itself as an intercultural 'bridge' or 'meeting place'. Early promotional literature articulated these aims in the following terms:

> Expo '92 will not be about the Discovery of America as such, but rather about discoveries in a generic sense, not just geographical discovery but also about all those achievements which opened up new horizons in all areas of human endeavour; about man's past as a discoverer and also about the challenges of the future ... Expo '92 promises to be one long fiesta, a celebration of liberty, solidarity and harmony among the peoples of the world.[46]

The dominant narrative of the past presented at Expo '92 was history as West-authored grand narrative. This revisioning of history and its representation within an event which was arguably the apotheosis of capitalist conspicuous consumption, as Leslie observes, overwrites conflictual histories and historiographies with an officially endorsed selective history: 'The ruling power ... flexes its musculature, mobilising spectacular and boastful resources to impose a certain reading on history' in a process which 'seeks to efface unwholesome traces of a past that will not pass away'. National grandeur is promoted, 'patriotism [becomes] a marketable commodity ... moulded into commemorative object. It becomes a saleable historical event as souvenir, substituting for memory'.[47] A critical response to this process of selection, effacement and myth-making requires us to 'untwine the several strands of history and to preserve the plurality of historical interpretation'.[48] Indeed, there *were* alternative memorialisations within the dominant regime of representation: for example, the Mexican pavilion's stated aims, according to a spokesperson, were to show that 'our history is quite enough previous to the arrival of Columbus ... [we] had our own history, and we aim to show the whole of that historical process of our country'. Moreover, the entrance to the pavilion was marked by the symbol of a giant cross, ostensibly to signify both the 'cultural crossroads' that Mexico 'has been for the length of its history' and to counter the Castilian Spanish spelling of the country's name with a J, asserting instead the X of Mexican Spanish.[49] Amongst the Middle Eastern countries, the Saudi Arabian pavilion presented each visitor with a complementary copy of a magazine discussing the contribution of medieval Arab explorers, geographers and natural philosophers to 'Discovery'.[50] Indeed, those elements which directly celebrated the quincentenary itself were relatively isolated at the southern end of the site (the Pavilion of the Fifteenth Century, the Cartuja monastery, Port of the Indies). The Pavilion of Discoveries (in the form of a globe captured within a Cartesian grid), constructed as the intended thematic centrepiece of the fair, was gutted by fire shortly before the inauguration (see Figure 28). This event, along with the sinking on its launch of the facsimile of Elcano's ship, left something of a lacuna in the commemorative theme.[51] The Cartesian grid did, however, permeate publicity images: the gridded globe is integral to the official logo, and was reproduced on the site furniture, tickets and postcard imagery.

Expo '92 was staged on the waste ground of La Cartuja, a quasi-island created by modification of the river course, and linked to the old city by a narrow strip of land; the entire area was landscaped, replanted and covered by an astonishingly wide range of architectural forms and state-of-the-art telecommunications infrastructure. In addition to offering an opportunity for speculative development, the site had its

Figure 28 The ill-fated Pavilion of Discoveries (architect, Javier Feduchi) at Expo '92.

symbolic resonances: it had been from Seville that the caravels had set sail, and the monastery on the island (from which it takes its name) was reputed to have been used as a refuge by Columbus himself and to have held his entombed body before its transfer to Santo Domingo. The layout of the site pavilions, as a space of representation, recentred Spain symbolically and ideologically in space and time. Two distinct narratives were consumed by the visitor traversing the site. First, from the southern gate, one followed a temporal narrative of modernity as progress, by tracing the Camino de Descubrimientos (Route of Discoveries), passing the Pavilion of the Fifteenth Century and the Pavilion of Navigation through to the Plaza del Futuro with its technopolis of the future. Simultaneously, one traversed space by travelling through a simulacrum of the world in the inner segment of the site (Avenida de Europa, Plaza de Américas, and so on), a journey which could be commemorated by the stamping of a facsimile passport.[52] Within this alternative cosmology the Spanish pavilion (the largest on the site) was centrally located at the hub of several axes: to the west was the Avenida de Europa, comprising the pavilions of the EU countries; to the east it looked out over the arc of the Spanish autonomous regions' pavilions on the far shore of an artificial lake; and, on its northern shore, towards the Latin American galleries (Plaza de Américas). The Spanish pavilion was, furthermore, the culmination of constructed narratives of history, both the 'Route of the Future' and the 'Route of Discoveries'.[53] The landscape embodied what Ian Gibson has described as the new democracy's 'obsession with making up for lost time, a determination to figure prominently on the map of the contemporary world'; the history of Spain and of empire were reduced to legitimating myths, and the 'plurality of historical interpretation' was lost.[54]

Contemporary disquiet with the Spanish imperial heritage led quickly to condemnation of the proposed commemoration by Cuba, which decried the presence at the fair of the United Nations Organisation and was backed by Eastern Bloc and Third World countries, implementing an economic blockade against Spain; Cuba and Ghana combined to attack the 'commemoration of the slave trade'.[55] On the opening day of the fair an international demonstration under the slogan 'We unmask '92' was broken up in the old city,[56] whilst another tried to block access to the fair, as 'a manifestation of revulsion against Expo and its consequences of neocolonialism, slavery and waste'.[57] The political coalition Izquierda Unida (United Left) decided to boycott the inauguration, announcing that 'a Universal Exhibition at the end of the twentieth century was not desirable ... it seems to us excessively pretentious to hold one in Andalusia'.[58] Amerindians participating in the inauguration of the US pavilion criticised its content and cultural stance. A Cheyenne chief and 'Miss Indian America' enacted a ritual in which the water and earth of the building were blessed; afterwards the latter condemned those responsible for the US pavilion for having exploited the ritual as a 'circus spectacle ... without consideration for their historical reality'. No tribal group representatives were invited onto the official rostrum during the opening ceremony. The pavilion was also condemned for having 'done nothing to show the true cultural heritage of the Indians'.[59]

Alternative commemorations highlighted the ambivalence of the commemoration of the quincentenary and its consequences. An abstract sculpture by the Basque artist, Eduardo Chillida, had already been commissioned by the exposition commissary of Seville and the Sepharad Foundation in answer to requests in 1981 for the Inquisition's persecution of Sephardic Jewry to be memorialised. Under discussion by successive municipal administrations, the work was not unveiled until a decade later as part of the 'celebrations' of 1992, initiating a whole programme of activities by the commissary and Jewish organisations.[60] The sculpture, which the artist intended as a utopian call for the 'Jewish, Arab and Christian peoples to join hands', occupies a marginal space on the eastern bank of the Guadalquivir next to the Queen Isabel bridge.[61] It is unacknowledged, untitled and graffiti-daubed, but represents the absolute antithesis of the sculpture dominating the entrance to the 1929 fairground, that of a rampant Cid, 'scourge of the Moor', symbol of racial and cultural purification.

Conclusion

The 1929 Iberoamerican Fair and Expo '92 reconfigured the meanings of empire at two distinct post-imperial moments in Spanish history, and the cultural politics of these commemorative events was irreducibly bound up with that of Seville itself as a pivotal site in national self-imagination. The identities of places are in a constant state of becoming, and the struggle to remake the spaces of the city manifests structures of power, characterised by Jane Jacobs as 'the discursive and representational constitution of symbolic space, the differentials of cultural capital, the struggle of visions to materialise or be resisted'.[62] Narratives of imperial and national history are deeply implicated in the production and consumption of urban spaces; as the case of Seville shows, meaning is constituted in the complex interchange between the representation, use and material form of these spaces.

The focus on two particular moments, two events impacting powerfully on the urban landscape, illustrates how the material construction of imaginative geographies of nation and empire is realised at specific sites, exposing tensions within the articulation of identities of place and people. As Allan Pred observes, such singular events trigger a shock of recognition, illuminating general processes operating on a variety of temporal and spatial scales.[63] It would be wrong, however, to confine our attention to the visible landscape. I have argued that the archive of unrealised schemes and the politics surrounding them may be as eloquent as the built form itself; these absences also convey important messages about contradictory and painful aspects of identity. I have also emphasised the ways in which these meanings are constructed and enacted in performance, both ceremonial and mundane.

This account of two exhibitionary events in twentieth-century Seville has revealed a nation state struggling with the implications of contradictory projects of modernity and imperialism for its identity. If the Iberoamerican Fair reinforced nostalgia for imperial greatness and national unity, Expo '92 distanced itself from the imperial past, recasting 'Spanishness' as cosmopolitan efficiency in a globalised world.[64] In 1929 Seville was scripted as a museum-piece of quintessential Spanishness, frozen in time on the periphery of an increasingly isolated state.[65] After Franco, Spain found itself seeking to break with the past while at the same time commemorating its heritage: Seville was one of the most significant sites for such paradoxical negotiations of empire and modernity.

[170]

Notes

1 For discussion of contemporary place promotion, see G. Kearns & C. Philo (eds), *Selling Places: The City as Cultural Capital, Past and Present* (Oxford, Pergamon, 1993); J. R. Gold & S. V. Ward (eds), *Place Promotion: The Use of Publicity and Marketing to Sell Towns and Regions* (Chichester, Wiley, 1994); T. Hall, '(Re)placing the city: cultural relocation and the city as centre', in S. Westwood & J. Williams (eds), *Imagining Cities: Scripts, Signs, Memory* (London, Routledge, 1997), pp. 202–18.

2 P. Wright, *On Living in an Old Country: The National Past in Contemporary Britain* (London, Verso, 1985), p. 3.

3 K. Anderson & F. Gale (eds), *Inventing Places: Studies in Cultural Geography* (Longman-Cheshire, Melbourne, 1992), p. 3.

4 For a detailed analysis of these processes see G. Kearns, 'The city as spectacle: Paris and the bicentenary of the French revolution', in Kearns & Philo, *Selling Places*, pp. 49–98.

5 D. Massey, *Space, Place and Gender* (Cambridge, Polity Press, 1994), pp. 146-56. See also J. M. Jacobs, *Edge of Empire: Postcolonialism and the City* (London, Routledge, 1996).

6 A. Braojos Garrido, *La imágen aérea de la Sevilla de Alfonso XIII* (Seville, Ayuntamiento de Sevilla, 1992). The site was associated with three emperors (Trajan, Hadrian and Theodosius).

7 J. M. Salaverría, *Sevilla y el Andalucismo* (Barcelona, Gustavo Gili, 1929), pp. 142–7.

8 C. Marcial, *Two International Expositions in Spain: Sevilla Exposition; Barcelona Exposition* (USA, International Telephone & Telegraph Corporation, 1929), no pagination.

9 *La Exposición Ibero-americana: Sección del Libro,* (Seville, 1929), pp. 16–23.

10 *Memoria publicada con motivo de la presentación en la Exposición Iberoamericana de Sevilla de algunas de las publicaciones hispanoamericanas que se conservan actualmente en la Hemeroteca* (Madrid, Municipal Imprenta, 1929), p. 5.

11 *Exposición General Española 1929* (Seville, 1929), p. 3.

12 *Ibid.,* p. 5.

13 *Ibid.,* pp. 5–7.

14 *Ibid.,* p. 7.

15 M. Warner, *Monuments and Maidens: The Allegory of the Female Form* (London, Weidenfeld & Nicolson, 1985).

16 Archivo Municipal, Seville, Documentación de la Fería Iberoamericana (hereafter DIBA), C118/3, undated, unsigned manuscript, 'Memoria descriptiva del anteproyecto para la Exposición Hispano-americana en Sevilla' (no pagination). This entry for the original architects' design competition for the fair in 1911 was presented anonymously under the title 'Adelante! Que llevas al César': see E. Rodríguez Bernal, *Historia de la Exposición Ibero-americana de Sevilla de 1929* (Seville, Ayuntamiento de Sevilla, 1994), pp. 152–3.

17 A. McClintock, *Imperial Leather: Race, Gender and Sexuality in the Colonial Contest* (London, Routledge, 1996).

18 A letter from the Executive Committee to the Chief of the Sección del Libro of the fair of 11 April 1929 suggests that the ceramic shelves flanking the benches should house literature referring to 'historical episodes' of the provinces and also to books of 'famous signatures' (DIBA, Sección del Libro, C85/3).

19 '"Moors" of the Moroccan pavilion who ... add a picturesque note,' wrote a contributor to *Blanco y Negro*, 1982 (12 May 1929) n.p. These Moroccan participants simultaneously played the historical role of vanquished Moors and represented one of Spain's last colonised peoples (those of the Spanish Moroccan protectorate).

20 Pictures of the opening ceremony were distributed quickly around Spain by air mail to the national press, and occupied several pages of the coverage of the inauguration by *Blanco y Negro*, a Madrid-based publication intended for an elite or middle-class metropolitan readership, distributed as a supplement of the conservative newspaper *ABC*. Pavilions of 'Electricity' and of 'the Telegraph' at the fair further enhanced

notions of the unification of national space.

21 Also represented at the fair was the Portuguese colony of Macao, in a pavilion of 'intricate Chinese form', replete with dragon and lion decorations (DIBA, C92/1, architectural drawing).

22 D. Gregory, 'Geography, Eurocentrism and the Empire of Theory', keynote address at the International Group for the Study of Representations in Geography colloquium, Royal Holloway, University of London, September 1996, pp. 15–21.

23 E. Leslie, 'Wrapping the Reichstag: revisioning German history', *Radical Philosophy*, 77 (1996) 6–16 (quote from p. 12); H. Lebovics, *True France: The Wars over Cultural Identity, 1900–45* (Ithaca NY, Cornell University Press, 1992), pp. 51–97; T. Mitchell, *Colonising Egypt* (Cambridge, Cambridge University Press, 1988).

24 DIBA, C118/3; see R. Rydell, *All the World's a Fair: Visions of Empire at American International Expositions, 1876–1916* (Chicago, University of Chicago Press, 1985), and T. Benedict, *The Anthropology of World's Fairs: San Francisco's Panama Pacific International Exposition of 1915* (Berkeley CA, Scolar Press, 1983) for comment on the relationship between the colonised and the 'amusements' in the world's fair genre.

25 DIBA, C92/3, 'Memoria', 31 January, 1928.

26 *Ibid.*, Letter from the Director of the Escuela de Artes e Industrías Indígenas de Tetuán, 17 November, 1928.

27 The tribes to be housed were listed as the 'Bubis, Pamúes, Coviscos, Annobon', their houses as *galeras*, denoting sites of spectacular display of objects. DIBA, C92/2, 'Golfo de Guinea: Proyecto de Pabellón Colonial y Poblado Indígena para la Exposición Ibero-americana. Pliego de Condiciones Complementarias; Pliego de Condiciones Facultativas: Memoria', 14 May 1927.

28 *Ibid.*, Memo, 4 January, 1929.

29 *El Liberal*, 12 May 1929, p. 1.

30 S. Assassin, *Séville: l'Exposition ibéro-américaine, 1929–30* (Paris, Institut Français d'Architecture/Norma, 1992).

31 DIBA, C89/3, Letter from the Spanish legation in Montevideo to the Comissario Regio de la EIA, 21 January 1927.

32 DIBA, C90/2, 'Pabellón de Mexico, planos'.

33 DIBA, C90/1, Letter from the Mexican legation in Madrid, 'Mexico en la Exposición Ibero-americana de Sevilla', undated, received by the Secretaría General, EIA, 17 May, 1926.

34 DIBA, C89/2, *Diario de Centro America*, 18 December 1928, cutting.

35 DIBA, C89/1, 'Programa para la concurrencia del Perú a la Exposición Iberoamericana de Sevilla', 20 January 1926. In addition, a cage was built at the end of the Avenue of Peru to house two llamas (Memo, 20 September 1929).

36 DIBA, C88/4, 'Pabellón de Colombia: planos; Pabellón de Café suave de Colombia: planos', March 1929.

37 DIBA, C88/1, cutting, *La Nación*, 9 January 1928.

38 *Ibid.*, 11 November 1927.

39 DIBA, C88/1, Letter from the Chilean legation in Madrid to Cruz Conde, Comissario Regio and Civil Governor of Seville, undated.

40 *El País*, 25 May 1992.

41 M. Castells & P. Hall (eds), *Andalucía: innovación tecnológia y desarrollo económico* (Madrid, Espasa-Calpe, 1992); M. Castells & P. Hall (eds), *Technopoles of the World: The Making of Twenty-first Century Industrial Complexes* (London, Routledge, 1994).

42 P. Harvey, *Hybrids of Modernity* (London, Routledge, 1996).

43 Sociedad Estatal Exposición Universal, *Expo '92 Sevilla: arquitectura y diseño* (Milan, Sevilla 92 / Electa, 1992), p. 23.

44 A. Urrutia Núñez, 'Chicago 1893 – Sevilla 1992: la Exposición Universal Colombina del siglo XX sobre la era de los descubrimientos', in *Anuario del Departamento de Historia y Teoría del Arte*, V (Madrid, Universidad Autónoma de Madrid, 1993), p. 164.

45 UN General Assembly discussion, *ABC*, 27 September 1986, p. 35.
46 Sociedad Estatal Exposición Universal Sevilla 1992, *Spain's Universal Exhibition, Seville, 1992: Discover It*, (Madrid, Artes Gráficas, 1989), no pagination.
47 Leslie, 'Wrapping the Reichstag', p. 11.
48 G. Finlayson, 'Naming, myth and history: Berlin after the Wall', *Radical Philosophy*, 74 (1995) 5–16 (quote from p. 14).
49 *Diario 16*, 9 April 1992, p. 8. Compare the stance of the Mexican presence at the 1929 event.
50 P. Lunde, 'The Middle East and the Age of Discovery', *Aramco World*, 43:3 (1992).
51 Its lost contents (including facsimile Renaissance and Enlightenment 'laboratories') were replaced by a film, *Eureka: the passion for discovery*, a 'recreation of the most important events in the history of discovery', in 'homage to the discovering passion of man'; *Diario 16*, 7 April 1992, p. 5.
52 See Harvey, *Hybrids of Modernity*, pp. 156–7, for an account of the consumption of such 'empty signifiers'.
53 Some attention was paid to the diversity of contemporary Spain, with Autonomous Communities' pavilions, whose design and contents were regionally controlled, and the designation of the first two days of the fair as 'Days of Honour' celebrations for the Basque Country (Euskadi) and Catalonia (Catalunya), 21 and 22 April respectively. (See *Diario 16, Crónica de la Expo*, 21 April 1992, p. vi; *Diario 16, Crónica*, 22 April, 1992, p. vi). There was nevertheless regionalist dissent, for example concerning the lack of Andalusian representation in the leadership of Expo (*Diario 16, Crónica*, 24 September 1992). The Partido Socialista Mallorquina, a Balearic separatist party, characterised the event as a celebration of the 'brutal colonisation ... imposition by force of a culture, customs and religion and economic despoliation' by Castile of Majorca, dissolving 'the sovereignty of our people' (P. Sampol i Mas, 'Els Cossiers i l'Expo '92', in P. Sampol i Mas & S. Serra i Busquets, *En defensa d'arquest país* (Palma, PSM Nacionalistes de Mallorca, 1993), pp. 47-8.
54 I. Gibson, *Fire in the Blood: The New Spain* (London, Faber, 1992), p. 5; Finlayson, 'Naming, myth and history', p. 14.
55 *ABC*, 27 September 1986, p. 35: 'Alianza Popular la condena del bloqueo cubano a la Expo '92'. Nevertheless, a Cuban pavilion was constructed, and visited by Castro himself on the country's national day (*Diario 16*, 12 April 1992, p. 8).
56 *Diario 16*, 20 April 1992, p. 5.
57 *Ibid.*, 21 April 1992, p. 5; *Diario 16*, 22 April 1992, p. 8.
58 *Ibid.*, 9 April, 1992, p. 7.
59 *Diario 16, Crónica*, 21 April 1992, p. 23.
60 *Ibid.*, 4 April, 1992, p. 5.
61 Eduardo Chillida, in *Diario 16, Crónica*, 4 April 1992, p. 5.
62 J. M. Jacobs, 'The battle of Bank Junction: the contested iconography of capital', in S. Corbridge, N. Thrift & R. Martin (eds), *Money, Power and Space* (Oxford, Blackwell, 1994), pp. 361–2.
63 A. Pred, *Recognizing European Modernities: A Montage of the Present* (London, Routledge, 1995).
64 D. Franklin, 'Mitteleuropa on the Med.', *Economist*, 25 April 1992, pp. 5–24.
65 This was a regime of representation reinforced by Franco's dictatorship: after the Nationalist victory in the Civil War, Franco visited Seville and wrote in the Golden Book of the Archive of the Indies, 'before the relics of one empire, with the promise of another'. See I. Gibson, *En busca de José Antonio* (Barcelona, Planeta, 1980), p. 36.

CHAPTER TEN

Portable iron structures and uncertain colonial spaces at the Sydenham Crystal Palace

Andrew Hassam

In Melbourne today one can still see examples of the portable iron housing imported during the heady years of the 1850s gold rush. Whole streets of iron houses were erected by speculators to house the massive increase in the population of Melbourne which, according to a contemporary report, leapt from 23,000 to 80,000 between 1851 and 1852.[1] In South Melbourne a complete row of iron houses still stood 100 years later, and in the early 1980s the sole remaining cottage was acquired and restored by the National Trust. Still portable today, two other iron houses from the early 1850s, one a Bellhouse house, have been moved to the site from elsewhere in Melbourne.[2]

Such a combination of durability and portability points to an uncertainty in the nature of iron structures. On the one hand, the houses were much like tents, only a little more sophisticated; you bought them in one place and erected them in another. Like tents, iron houses were at the mercy of the elements; they leaked in the rain, and became ovens in the sun. Iron was not the best material out of which to build a house, and as William Howitt wrote at the time: 'They will prove admirable houses – for the doctors.'[3] Unlike tents, on the other hand, iron houses were durable. They were prefabricated, but were not necessarily intended to be temporary, and their portability and their propensity to leak should not be seen as denying them a degree of permanence. Corio Villa, manufactured by Charles Young & Co. of Edinburgh and shipped out in 1855, is a substantial and richly decorated building that still stands in Geelong, overlooking the wharf onto which it was unloaded.[4]

Iron houses, therefore, were spatially ambivalent: they combined the portability of a tent with the durability of a more traditional house. They were unlike modern prefabricated structures (and the term 'prefabrication' belongs to the twentieth century) in that they were designed to be dismantled and moved to another site as required. In this sense, they were like the migrants they housed, capable of remaining on one site or moving on as circumstances dictated. This combination of what were seen as conflicting cultural values produced an uncertain, ironic response. Alfred Joy, who arrived in Melbourne in September 1853, called his iron house Oxford Lodge. It is possible he was perfectly serious about this; he came from Oxford and may have wanted his house to remind him of his English home. Yet the idea of calling his two-room house a lodge when it shared the characteristics of a tin shed is either pretentious or ironic. Joy was not someone to take himself too seriously, and the day after buying the land for his house in North Melbourne he noted in his diary: 'Shouldered my pick & shovel & turned the first sod on my estate.'[5] In employing the discourse of landownership ironically, Joy shows himself uneasy about his own relationship to the land.

In *The Lie of the Land*, Paul Carter poses the question:

> Is it not odd that ours, the most nomadic and migratory of cultures, should found its polity, its psychology, its ethics and even its poetics on the antithesis of movement: on the rhetoric of foundations, continuity, genealogy, stasis? Is it not decidedly odd that a culture intent on global colonization should persistently associate movement with the unstable, the unreliable, the wanton and the primitive?[6]

Carter draws attention to the paradoxical connection between the mobility of Western culture and its determination to privilege dwelling over travelling: 'If we were grounded,' he says, 'the cultural opposition between movement and stasis would disappear.'[7] Carter lives predominantly in Australia and most of his work employs Australian examples. Yet Carter's primary engagement is with European thought and, unlike other post-colonial theorists, from whom he pointedly distances himself, Carter uses comparisons between Europe and Australia not so much to define a colonial condition as to examine the continuity between European and colonial uncertainties.

Carter's comments about the cultural tension between movement and stasis therefore prompt us to examine colonial culture not as something distinct from the metropolitan culture but as a culture sharing the spatial uncertainties of Britain. In a narrow sense, portable housing can be seen as a colonial phenomenon and read in terms of a distinctly colonial spatiality. Governor Phillip brought with him a wooden house on the First Fleet, and from the 1820s John Manning, a London carpenter and builder, established a specialised business supplying wooden houses to intending migrants:

> Gentlemen emigrating to the New Settlement, Swan River, on the Western Coast of Australia, will find a great advantage in having a comfort-

able Dwelling that can be erected in a few hours after landing, with windows, glazed doors, and locks, bolts, and the whole painted in a good and secure manner, carefully packed and delivered at the Docks, consisting of two, three, four, or more roomed Houses, made to any plan that may be proposed; likewise Houses of a cheaper description for labouring men, mechanics, etc. etc.[8]

From 1836, John Manning supplied houses to the new colony of South Australia, and Governor La Trobe's Cottage, erected in Melbourne in 1839, was also a Manning house.[9]

Yet a discussion of any peculiarly colonial spatiality also needs to bear in mind that the fantasy of colonial settlement, evidenced in Manning's advertisement through the establishment of 'a comfortable Dwelling that can be erected a few hours after landing, with windows, glazed doors, and locks, bolts' was a British fantasy. It was middle-class: security was needed to protect middle-class property and middle-class privacy. And it was also imperial: it regarded the spaces to be settled as homogeneous, effacing prior occupation and a diversity of climate and terrain. The fantasy of settlement was, in Carter's terms, a fantasy of grounding by which movement and the transgression of space were defined as aberrant.

Yet, if we take this view, that the fantasy of settlement was British, middle-class and imperial, then it is equally important to identify and examine ambivalent spaces within Britain. As Carter implies, Britain as much as Australia lacked stability; to accept the migrant view of Britain as essentially 'grounded' is to be complicit with imperial ideology. And, as Jane Jacobs has recently shown, the preservation of binary classifications such as core and periphery continues to produce ambivalent territories in a post-imperial, post-colonial London.[10] The argument that I am interested in examining, therefore, is that spatial uncertainty, produced out of a tension between such cultural opposites as movement and stasis, or portability and permanence, is not distinctly colonial, and that it was a pervasive aspect of late nineteenth-century Britain. In short, I want to try to destabilise the image of the metropolitan centre by locating within it the uncertainty migrants found in colonial space.

Paxton's Great Exhibition building of 1851 as panopticon

The Great Exhibition of 1851 provided a focus for portable iron houses, and for portable iron structures generally. The Great Exhibition was primarily a showcase for British industrial manufacturing, but there were also over seventy model buildings on display, among them a number of portable iron houses. There was even a model of one of the houses now owned by the National Trust of Victoria, a cast-iron house manufactured 'for emigrants' by E. T. Bellhouse & Co. of Manchester. Manufacturers like Bellhouse were already manufacturing a range of iron buildings, and the title of a pamphlet published by Young & Co. in the mid-1850s gives an indication of the range of structures on offer: *Illustrations of Iron Structures for Home and Abroad, consisting of Stores, Dwelling-houses, Markets, Arcades, Railway Stations, and Roofing, etc etc.*[11]

Of course, the most celebrated portable iron structure was the 1851 exhibition building itself, which not only won the medal for the category of 'Civil engineering, architecture and building contrivances', but also won the supreme prize, the Great Medal.[12] Here, the naming of the building as the Crystal Palace by Douglas Jerrold in *Punch*, even as it was under construction, ingeniously diverted attention away from the building's utility while at the same time directing attention to one of the building materials, glass. Critics, on the other hand, emphasised the functionality of the building, and John Ruskin, unable to find any moral purpose in its design, described it as 'a greenhouse larger than ever greenhouse was built before'.[13] Paxton's Great Exhibition building quite clearly owed a great deal to the horticultural glasshouse. Paxton himself had developed many of the features of the exhibition building at Chatsworth, where he had been head gardener since 1826. As John Hix puts it: 'The Crystal Palace was a direct descendant of the botanical glasshouse and represented the horticultural advances of the nineteenth century in its form and function .'[14]

Twentieth-century cultural historians have tried to understand the social significance of this escalating use of glass in the second half of the nineteenth century, which was permitted by changes in glass production technology (which made good-quality sheet glass available) and the abolition of the tax on glass in 1845. Tony Bennett, in *The Birth of the Museum*, places Paxton's glass exhibition building in the context of concerns about the adequate surveillance of large numbers of working people in public spaces. Bennett lists three general principles that he argues came together in the 1851 Great Exhibition building, the last of which is 'the provision of elevated vantage points in the form of galleries which, in allowing the public to watch over itself, incorporated a principle of self-surveillance and hence self-regulation into museum architecture'.[15] He concludes: 'In thus allowing the public to double as both the subject and object of a controlling look, the museum embodied what had been, for Bentham, a major aim of panopticism – the democratic aspiration of a society rendered transparent to its own controlling gaze.' In stressing the opening up of the interior of the building

[177]

to the regulating eye of the spectator, Bennett might have noted that on average there were also 350–400 police officers stationed inside the building.[16] Nonetheless, he establishes a case for self-surveillance and self-regulation, and uninhibited views were part of the architectural brief for the building: internal walls were to be omitted, 'allowing the eye to range at liberty, and to appreciate the extent and the vista'.[17]

Yet, while Bennett links glass and visibility, he does not pursue the link between iron and portability. Bennett places the exhibition building in the context of other glass and iron constructions: 'The architectural sources which fuelled the development of nineteenth-century exhibitionary institutions are many and various: shopping arcades, railway stations, conservatories, market halls and department stores to name but a few.'[18] His list is remarkably similar to the list of portable structures in Young & Co.'s catalogue of *Iron Structures for Home and Abroad*, but Bennett emphasises the size of such structures rather than their portability. A full analysis must also take account of structures that can be both static and yet infinitely portable.

The 'Brompton boilers' and the engineer as architect

The profits from the Great Exhibition were used by the Royal Commissioners to buy a number of estates in Kensington and to establish on them a whole array of imperial institutions dedicated to 'Science and Art'. Prince Albert took a particular interest in the rehousing of the Marlborough House art collection and in 1855, with the need for a building urgent, the Royal Commissioners turned to the engineers Charles Young & Co. They took just four days to produce plans for a temporary iron museum.[19] Unlike the Great Exhibition building, however, with its huge acreage of glass, the iron museum was clad in corrugated iron. The restricted glazing was an attempt to avoid the extremes of temperature experienced in Paxton's building, but it did not help the blank external appearance of the structure, which was so ridiculed that it was painted like a canvas marquee in green and white stripes;[20] as the building had three galleries of the same span placed side by side, the journal *The Builder* soon coined the nickname 'the Brompton boilers'.[21]

Again, the choice of name reflects the uncertain nature of portable iron structures: both Alfred Joy, in his choice of Oxford Lodge for his house in Melbourne, and *The Builder*, in its choice of 'the Brompton boilers' for the South Kensington Museum, undermined the pretension of such structures. The nickname 'Brompton boilers' drew attention to what the term 'Crystal Palace' sought to avoid: portable iron buildings owed more to the engineer than to the architect. As William Howitt noted of the iron houses in Melbourne, 'These ... look like huge caravans, the roofs being arched like them; or like great steam-engine boilers, or gasometers.'[22] In Melbourne parlance, portable iron structures were termed 'iron pots'.[23]

The large public iron buildings of the middle years of the nineteenth century were feats of industrial engineering. Paxton's 1851 Great Exhibition building was constructed by the engineering contractors Fox Henderson & Co., and its iron components were precision-engineered in the Midlands before being brought by rail to London and riveted together in Hyde Park. As Dickens put it: 'The proposed edifice could be constructed at Birmingham, at Dudley, and at Thames Bank, "brought home" to Hyde Park ready-made, and put up like a bedstead.'[24] The same engineers who built the iron buildings were building Britain's ever expanding railway system. Charles Fox was involved in constructing the 'sheds' (or roofs) of Paddington and Birmingham New Street stations. Young & Co.'s exhibit at the Great Exhibition was a set of four simultaneous-acting level-crossing gates, and it is likely that the company also supplied some of the portable iron railway stations still standing in Brazil.

Portable iron structures can therefore be seen as just one aspect of a culture that was redefining space through industrial technology; owing more to the engineer than the architect, here were buildings that travelled. At least 4 million people visited the Great Exhibition,[25] an unprecedented movement of the British population, and it was fitting that the largest building in Europe should have shared the same technology as the trains that brought them to see it. It was fitting too that the building was designed to come down as fast as it went up, and, following a vote in Parliament on 30 April 1852 ordering its removal, the building was quickly dismantled and carried away.

The Sydenham Crystal Palace as horticultural hothouse

In June 1854 the Great Exhibition building opened as the Sydenham Crystal Palace on the top of Sydenham Hill, to the south-east of London. The Hyde Park building had been modified in a number of ways to suit the new site. The ground floor area was reduced, but because of an increase in the height of the building its actual volume was increased by 50 per cent and the glass surface nearly doubled in area. This prompted Ruskin, who again failed to see any architectural merit in the building, to call it 'a cucumber frame between two chimneys'.[26] Paxton's horticultural background can certainly be seen in his landscaping of the 200 acres that stretched away to the east. The land nearest the building was terraced in the Italian style, with symmetrical fountains and a grand central walk stretching away down the hill. Lower down, however, the

English parkland style was adopted, with walks winding through groups of trees and an irregularly shaped lake, dotted with islands occupied by full-size plaster models of various dinosaurs.

In its relocation from Hyde Park the Crystal Palace at Sydenham had gained two transepts and two wings, and was no longer primarily an exhibition hall of industrial technology. The display of art and architecture which dominated at least half the nave area was designed to provide the visitor with 'in practical fashion, an idea of the successive stages of civilisation which have from time to time arisen in the world, have changed or sunk into decadence, have been violently overthrown, or have passed away, by the aggression of barbarians, or the no less degrading agency of sensual and enervating luxury'.[27] The warning against sensual luxury should perhaps be read against the removal of the penises from the male statuary and the riveting into place of fig leaves just one month before the opening day. But, in grander terms, the representation of previous civilisations was integrated into a self-congratulatory narrative that seemed to lead inexorably from the earliest civilisations to Victorian Britain. Britain became not just one of many civilisations but the natural point towards which all 'the successive stages of civilisation' pointed. The Crystal Palace therefore helped produce an image of Britain of which the building could become a symbol. As Henry Pilcher, a bank manager visiting from New South Wales in 1866, implicitly admitted in his diary, the Crystal Palace had in fact become Britain: 'No one has seen England unless he has been to the Crystal Palace.'[28]

In calling the Sydenham Crystal Palace 'a cucumber frame between two chimneys' Ruskin was correctly noting its debt to horticultural architecture, but he was wrong in at least one fundamental respect. Unlike either the Hyde Park building or a cucumber frame, the Sydenham Crystal Palace was heated, as of course a winter garden needed to be. Here Paxton again drew on his experience at Chatsworth, installing a low-pressure hot water system like that he had used for his horticultural glasshouses.[29] The Sydenham Crystal Palace, therefore, was more of a hothouse than either a greenhouse or a cucumber frame, and the creation of an artificial environment allowed Paxton to grow plants and trees inside the building as well as outside.

Paxton installed an additional boiler at the north end of the building to allow him to display hothouse exotics and, in particular, the palms that he bought in 1854 on the closure of Loddiges' nursery at Hackney.[30] The Hackney Botanic Nursery was started in 1771 by the German gardener, Conrad Loddiges, and it developed into a complex of steam-heated hothouses, among them a palm house, complete with artificial rain and said to have been the largest in the world.[31] John Hix has argued that the engineering of an artificial climate was directly related to the nineteenth-century romanticism of the far-away place: 'it evoked the idyllic milieu of the New World and recently developed tropical lands, in contrast to the cold and unpleasant climate of northern Europe and the British Isles'.[32] Hix cites a description of Richard Turner's Regent's Park Winter Gardens (1846) given in Knight's *Cyclopaedia of London* (1851),

> a veritable fairy land transplanted into the heart of London, an actual garden of delight, realising all our ideal. From the keen frosty air outside, and the floweriness aspect of universal nature, one steps into an atmosphere balmy and delicious ... The most exquisite odours are wafted to and fro with every movement of the glass doors. Birds singing in the branches ... make you again and again pause to ask, is this winter? Is this England?[33]

In some hothouses additional features were combined with the plants: Loddiges' had its artificial rain, and at Chatsworth in the 1840s small tropical birds were introduced.[34]

Paxton apparently had no real interest in having birds in his 1851 Great Exhibition building, though a group of sparrows seems to have colonised the building during construction and there was a rumour that the organisers feared resident sparrows might defile Queen Victoria herself at the official opening.[35] Some robins that made the new Sydenham building their home in 1854 were quickly eradicated,[36] but Henry Pilcher found birds flying about in 1866, a feature that heightened the visitor's sense of escape to another place:

> Different portions of the Crystal Palace abound in plants and trees brought from all parts of the World and placed in different parts of the building, in temperatures suitable for them, it has even the Australian gum growing within its walls, handsome creepers & vines are growing up the interior uprights of the building and many birds flying about loose, if a visitor could for a moment forget where he was, he would wonder what place of bliss he had got into.[37]

Of course, to the extent that this 'place of bliss' mimicked the far-away places of empire, it reminded Australians uncannily of their other, southern home. The artificial climate of the hothouse, reversing outdoors and indoors, produced an exotic climate that was paradoxically familiar to the visiting Australian. When Australians went to the Royal Botanic Gardens at Kew they picked out the Australian trees and plants growing in the Temperate House: 'Here I greeted the Australian plants with delight, they looked homelike and friendly. When I came to the wattles in blossom, of which there was a great variety, quite a lump came into my throat.'[38] In escaping the climate of the colonies, the visitor from Australia suddenly felt at home in the artificial climate of the metropolitan hothouse; and had Joseph Paxton's plans for a Crystal Sanatorium ever been realised, who knows but that Pilcher, a consumptive bank manager from New South Wales, might have found himself being treated in London in an Australian climate among Australian birds and botanical specimens.

Metropolitan Aborigines

The Sydenham Crystal Palace had other exhibits to catch the Australian eye. Richard Teece, a twenty-eight-year-old insurance clerk from New South Wales, found Aborigines in the Crystal Palace: 'We were somewhat amused at seeing a number of photographs of Queensland blacks under the heading of exhibits from South Australia, & a little mortified to learn that Melbourne was the whole of Australia.'[39] The photographs of Aborigines were most probably exhibited by Richard Daintree, a man who, as Agent General for Queensland from 1872 to 1876, worked tirelessly to promote Queensland as a migrant destination.[40] He was far more successful at mounting effective exhibitions than his counterparts from the other Australian colonies, even if, judging from Teece's comments, his efforts at the Crystal Palace had become appropriated by South Australia.

For Australian visitors to the Sydenham Crystal Palace the sense of being at home indoors must have become even more uncanny when they came to the south transept. Here was housed the Ethnological and Natural History Department, and its displays brought together animals, plants and human figures from various areas of the globe. The routes suggested by the guidebook were intended to achieve the maximum effect from this integration of different types of exhibit: 'Continuing along the path, we pass a glass-case containing a selection of North American birds, and beyond this we arrive at a group of North American Red Indians engaged in a war-dance, and surrounded by trees and shrubs indigenous to North America.'[41] In this way the visitors could wander around the less civilised regions, marvelling at the inhabitants of the New World and the Old World before arriving, if they followed the route taken by the guidebook, in Australia. The effect may be judged by Henry Pilcher's description of the Natural History Department:

> it is that portion of the building which is set apart for the groupings of men animals and plants, these are so arranged, as nearly as possible, so that the men, animals, and plants, of the various climes to which they severally belong may be exhibited separately together, keeping each climate's productions separate. Life-sized plaster of Paris (or some compo-

sition perhaps wax I do not know) figures of the men women & children, of the various aboriginal tribes of all new countries, are here shown, and the figures are also coloured to represent faithfully the colour of the different races, Australia has her share of representation, our natives by comparison rank very low in the scale of civilization, the figures are all faithfully executed and very life like, some are placed in the attitude of inflicting a death blow upon an enemy, and look so natural, that to come upon one of these groups suddenly is apt to startle anyone.[42]

Like his guidebook, Henry Pilcher emphasised the novel manner in which the specimens were displayed. In grouping together humans, animals and plants, the intention was to imitate different environments, to recreate the connections between botany, zoology and ethnology that were not possible at Kew Gardens, London Zoo or the British Museum. But, of course, this way of exhibiting natural history was also intended to allow visitors to experience these environments as discrete places rather than simply as exhibits; there was a deliberate policy to eschew the glass cabinet for, according to the guidebook, 'picturesque groupings.'[43] Such a division of the internal space of the building is behind Pilcher's apparent surprise at seeing aboriginal figures while wandering between the trees and the stuffed animals.

This experience was made possible by the glasshouse and the heated, artificial environment that permitted exotic plants, fish and birds to survive in Europe. Hence the clear connection between the display of ethnological figures at Sydenham and John Claudius Loudon's vision back in 1817 of the future development of the hothouse, 'when such artificial climates will not only be stocked with appropriate birds, fishes and harmless animals, but with examples of the human species from the different countries imitated, habited in their particular costumes and who may serve as gardeners or curators of the different productions'.[44] Despite its mid-Victorian intention to educate the general public, the south transept of the Sydenham Crystal Palace evokes Loudon's romantic vision, the creation in London of the authentic inhabited tropical forest.

Of course, by the 1850s the romanticism had waned, the image of the tropical forest had darkened and it was now inhabited by savages who were not so benign as Loudon's indigenous curators. In practical terms, aborigines resisted being 'civilised' and did not assimilate in the way envisaged by the British; understandably, Aborigines felt that living in their own way on their own land was preferable. Elsewhere in the empire the indigenous peoples did not come up to expectations; rebellions in India in 1857 and in Jamaica in 1865 suggested to the British that others could reach only a certain level of civilisation. In scientific terms, this was rationalised in terms of race. Indigenous people were no longer viewed as variants of a common species, and the humanitarianism that had been shown in the anti-slavery movement gave way to a construction of black Africans, Native Americans, Maoris or Aborigines as innately different, as races apart, incapable of improvement to the level of the British.

There was apparently nothing in Henry Pilcher's Anglo-Australian way of looking at the world that made him question this. The Crystal Palace confirmed the heights that British civilisation had reached, the broadening gap between the British and the colonised of the empire, and the necessary disappearance of Aborigines as the lowest race on earth that such a narrative entailed. Indeed, the very notion of progress depended on the belief that some had not progressed, that there were people in the world who were backward and whose backwardness would ensure that they died out. If the Crystal Palace, that fairy palace of light, celebrated the dizzy heights that a technologically and culturally progressive civilisation could reach, the illusion was built on aboriginality constructed as the antithesis of civilisation. Empire could be justified by theories of racial superiority, and the success of the narrative of progress that underpinned the Crystal Palace was built on the necessary construction of a racial hierarchy, at the bottom of which were those primitive and savage Aborigines whom Australians saw exhibited.

Metropolitan tropical forests

With the sweeping away of savagery came the creation of new imperial spaces. The 'penetration' and opening up of the tropical forest was one of the major projects of British imperialism, both literally, in terms of economic exploitation, and metaphorically, in terms of christianising the Dark Continent's dark inhabitants. All was to be made transparent to the 'controlling gaze' that Bennett identified in the design of the Great Exhibition building; just as the presence of curators in museums had gradually been replaced by display cards and guidebooks, so indigenous people were no longer to be necessary to a European understanding of imperial spaces. However, in the hothouse context, Bennett's controlling gaze does not produce 'self-surveillance and hence self-regulation'; it is not democratic in impulse and the viewer does not 'double as both the subject and object of a controlling look'. Visitors to the Great Exhibition looked down not only onto the exhibits but onto other visitors. But the Crystal Palace gallery was also a direct descendant of the gallery in the botanical hothouse, which functioned as a watering platform and a vantage point from which to view the plants. An engraving of the Kew palm house in the *Illustrated London News* of 1852

(Figure 29) shows visitors 'transported into a tropical forest', wandering along shaded walks among 'the vegetable Titans', while above, on the gallery, others look down not on the people below but on the profusion of the forest. The text accompanying the engraving invites the visitor to

Figure 29 The Great Palm House, Kew Gardens. *Illustrated London News*, 7 August 1852

enjoy a 'bird's eye' view from the gallery, but it is a view of the gardens outside, not of other members of the general public.[45]

Anne McClintock, among many, has pointed out that the achievement of mastery over the new spaces of empire was cast in gendered terms. This was because much of the work was carried out by European men and because imperial ideology was patriarchal.[46] Yet this clearing away of the concealed spaces, this 'penetration' of space, required a feminine space that resisted. If, as Paul Carter argues, the cultural opposition between movement and stasis would disappear once we were grounded, then oppositions between concealment and visibility, feminine and masculine, or between Aborigine and European, would also disappear once imperial ideology had completed its work. But of course imperial ideology, bound up as it was with the economic strength of an industrialised Britain, did not aim for the eradication of difference, it aimed to control far-away peoples and places. For such power to be maintained, tension between the oppositions had also to be maintained. The stability and the clearing of the ground inherent in the myth of settlement can – indeed, must – never be achieved. Complete mastery would be the end of mastery.

It was in the tropical forest of the botanical hothouse that some of these tensions were articulated in the metropolis. The hothouse, in the manner of its construction, enacted a tension between mobility and stability. But it also enacted the tension between concealed and open spaces; for, unlike in the self-surveying 1851 Great Exhibition building, it was possible, and perhaps desirable, for the visitor to the botanical hothouse to get a little lost among the trees. A comparison of the interiors of the Hyde Park and Sydenham Crystal Palaces shows that, although the vista remained, the Sydenham building had many areas screened by the plants, trees, creepers and vines (see Figure 30). If the assertion of cultural authority depended on a landscape that resisted the all-encompassing imperial gaze, then what was being imitated in Sydenham, as in the hothouse, was a 'feminine' Nature based on dark and wild recesses. In the same way that dinosaurs lurked among the trees of the parkland, inside, among the botanical specimens, were examples of human prehistory. Indigenous people were the proof of Social Darwinism, a construct of the British middle classes; bourgeois imperial culture demanded a Nature full of concealed spaces in which lurked lower and historically prior forms of humanity. By inserting ethnological figures into the forest the Sydenham Crystal Palace was merely allowing the visitor to re-enact the interplay of concealment and vision on which imperial mastery depended. Through industrial technology it was creating in the metropolis the necessary fantasy of imperial space.

Figure 30 Interior of the Crystal Palace, Sydenham. From Henry Russell Hitchcock, *Early Victorian Architecture in Britain* (New Haven CT, Yale University Press, 1954)

Boomerangs in Bethnal Green

Despite the fears of the organisers of the Great Exhibition, the gathering of large numbers of working people in London in 1851 did not result in social unrest. And working people having apparently proved they were not 'wanton', in Carter's sense, and could behave as responsible citizens, a number of prominent men looked at ways of sustaining the exhibition's educative project by establishing a museum for working people in the East End. Several schemes were discussed but nothing materialised until 1865, when it was suggested that the Brompton boilers, due to be dismantled and removed from South Kensington, might be re-erected in the East End. A site was found in Bethnal Green on Poor Land previously rented to butchers, and the following year, 1866, the Brompton boilers were dismantled ready for their removal to Bethnal Green.[47] The Bethnal Green Museum opened in 1872 with a combination of the Wallace art collection and two popular science collections: 'One was devoted to Food (explaining the chemical constituents of foodstuffs, and teaching good dietary principles), the other to Animal Products (a mix of natural history and industry, showing what useful things could be made of fur, feathers, bones etc.).'[48] Both of these were transferred with the museum from South Kensington, where they had been intended to educate the working classes in health and household management.[49] The museum also temporarily acquired the Lane Fox collection of ethnological artefacts in the middle of 1874, the collection comprising, with the exception of a small number of skulls, mainly weaponry and miscellaneous implements.

The choice of Bethnal Green was not entirely arbitrary. Bethnal Green was an area of working-class radicalism and the exhibition was to be an experiment in the educative use of anthropology. George Stocking has argued that the Great Exhibition stimulated new ways of thinking about human sociocultural evolution, quoting William Whewell, Master of Trinity College, Cambridge, in 1852: 'by annihilating the space which separates different nations, we produce a spectacle in which is also annihilated the time which separates one stage of a nation's progress from another'.[50] This annihilation of time and space also affected Lane Fox, and the objects in his collection were displayed sequentially and by type, so that, for example, throwing-sticks and boomerangs were so arranged as to suggest an evolutionary gradation from straight to curved shapes: 'the whole of the Australian weapons can be traced by their connecting links with the simple stick, such as might have been used by an ape or an elephant before mankind appeared upon this earth, and I have arranged them so as to show this connection on the screens'.[51]

Boomerangs might instruct the working classes of Bethnal Green in three ways. First, the evolution of material culture was demonstrated to be fundamentally conservative; the arrangement of artefacts was designed to show evolution as a succession of small, slow and inevitable stages, a model that could be used to justify the existing social order. Second, the model of evolution suggested by the sequential arrangement of artefacts could be applied to racial as much as to social progress. In a lecture given before the Anthropological Institute at the Bethnal Green Museum in July 1874 Lane Fox pointed out that not only did the implements of 'existing savages' show no sign of having degraded from a more complex cultural form, aboriginal wooden implements, being constructed on the grain of the wood, also demonstrated that Aborigines were the 'lowest amongst the existing races of the world'.[52] Lastly, the collection was arranged so that it could be easily comprehended by the working-class mind, a mind, as Lane Fox inferred in his lecture, not dissimilar to that of the savage.[53] In sum, the boomerangs in the Lane Fox collection were used simultaneously to constitute and demarcate both race and class.

But visitors to Bethnal Green might have seen other boomerangs on display carrying a slightly different message. In a letter to the Colonial Secretary in Brisbane dated 13 November 1874 Richard Daintree, the Agent General for Queensland, wrote: 'the complete series of photographs exhibited at Vienna [the 1873 exhibition] has been sent to the Brisbane Museum, another is now available for the Bethnal Green Museum in the East of London, and a fair collection is already placed at the Crystal Palace'.[54] Many of Daintree's photographs were of geological formations and agricultural life, reflecting his earlier employment as a geologist in Victoria and later in northern Queensland. However, he also photographed Aborigines, and the 'photographs of Queensland blacks' seen by Richard Teece at Sydenham in May 1875, if not Daintree's own, were almost certainly part of the collection to which Daintree refers in his letter of November the previous year. A photograph of Daintree's Queensland annexe for the 1872 International Exhibition at South Kensington (Figure 31) shows two enlarged photographic prints of Aboriginal men, holding discreetly positioned weapons in place of fig leaves, looking down on a bust of Queen Victoria, while between the prints is a display of 'native weapons'. The Queensland display at the 1876 Centennial Exhibition in Philadelphia included similar prints of Aboriginal men, in line with the displays of the other colonies: 'the Australians considered Aboriginal weapons and implements significant elements in the presentation'.[55] It is probable, therefore, that Daintree's Bethnal Green display included some prints of Aborigines and similar Aboriginal artefacts, and, like Lane Fox's display, Daintree's photographs and artefacts were intended to instruct. But the immediate political and economic aim of Daintree's work as Agent General was to promote migration to Queensland, and

Figure 31 The Queensland Annexe at the London International Exhibition, 1872

in this his display at Bethnal Green differs from that of Lane Fox. While Lane Fox intended that East Enders should know and remain in their place, Daintree intended them to move, preferably to Queensland. Indeed, at the time migration was argued to be a necessity for the racial health of the working-class areas of the metropolis. The colonial context highlighted yet again a mobility that the metropolitan context attempted to deny; less a case of demarcation than of embarkation.

The Brompton boilers having been moved to the East End of London so that the working classes might be kept in their place, the re-erected iron structure was encased in architectural brick as though it was feared the Bethnal Green Museum might also go walkabout. The brickwork may have been intended to give the museum extra rigidity, but it made the building look more like a railway station than anything else. Yet to the extent that, as Hitchcock has argued, railway stations combined the relative permanence of masonry with the contrasting impermanence of their iron and glass train sheds,[56] the addition of a brick shell to the Brompton boilers heightened the tension between stasis and mobility. In this sense the museum embodies the tension between the Aboriginal displays of Lane Fox and those of Daintree, the tension between remaining in place and migration.

Even the railings outside the Bethnal Green Museum articulated opposing messages. On the one hand they demarcated space and people, marking an inside of rational recreation opposed to the illicit pleasures of darkest London outside; the Bethnal Green Museum, like the Sydenham Crystal Palace, the People's Palace in the Mile End Road and the People's Palace in Glasgow, was intended to instil civic virtues in a potentially unstable working-class population. On the other hand, the railings erected outside the museum had been uprooted by a crowd demonstrating in favour of parliamentary reform in Hyde Park in 1866,[57] as witnessed by Henry Pilcher only twelve days before his encounter with the Aborigines at Sydenham: 'the mob rushed the gates, broke them down, pulled up the iron palisading, attacked and sadly maltreated hundreds of policemen, tore up many young trees in the Park, very much injured the flower beds, and did all the damage it was possible for an uncontrolled ruffianly mob to perpetrate'.[58] Both the Brompton boilers and the Hyde Park railings were displaced in 1866, and while they have remained where they were re-erected, side by side in Bethnal Green, there is a degree of situational irony in their conjunction that draws attention to the instability of boundaries in nineteenth-century Britain. And in a broader sense, like the portable iron houses owned by the National Trust in Melbourne, they are testimony to the uncertain spaces of the British empire itself.

Notes

1 William Howitt, *Land, Labour and Gold, or, Two Years in Victoria* (Kilmore, Vict., Lowden, 1855, reprinted 1972), p. 157.
2 'Portable houses … What are they?', *Trust News*, 10:7 (1983) 12.
3 Howitt, *Land, Labour and Gold*, p. 159.
4 Gilbert Herbert, 'A cast-iron solution', *Architectural Review*, 153 (1973) 367–73.
5 Alfred Joy, Diary 1853, Australian National Maritime Museum, Sydney, 19 October.
6 Paul Carter, *The Lie of the Land* (London, Faber, 1996), pp. 2–3.
7 *Ibid.*, p. 3.
8 John Archer, *The Great Australian Dream: The History of the Australian House* (Sydney, Harper Collins, 1996), pp. 46–50.
9 *Ibid.*, pp. 25, 46–50; 'Portable houses', 12.
10 Jane M. Jacobs, *Edge of Empire: Postcolonialism and the City* (London, Routledge, 1996).
11 Herbert, 'A cast-iron solution', p. 373.
12 John McKean, *Crystal Palace: Joseph Paxton and Charles Fox* (London, Phaidon Press, 1994), p. 41.
13 John Ruskin, *The Stones of Venice*, I (London, Dent, n.d.), p. 361.
14 John Hix, *The Glasshouse* (London, Phaidon Press, 1996), p. 175.
15 Tony Bennett, *The Birth of the Museum: History, Theory, Politics* (London, Routledge, 1995), p.101
16 *Great Exhibition of the Works of Industry of all Nations, 1851: Official Descriptive*

and Illustrated Catalogue, I (London, Spicer, 1851), p. xlv.
17 McKean, Crystal Palace, p. 12.
18 Bennett, The Birth of the Museum, p. 101.
19 This paragraph draws on several sources: John Physick, The Victoria and Albert Museum: The History of its Building (Oxford, Phaidon Press, 1982), pp. 19–24; Survey of London XXXVIII, The Museums Area of South Kensington and Westminster, (London, Athlone Press, 1975), pp. 98-9; Hix, The Glasshouse, pp. 138-9; Herbert, 'A cast-iron solution', p. 378; the building may have been designed by the civil engineer, William Dredge (The Museums Area of South Kensington, p. 98).
20 The Museums Area of South Kensington, p. 98.
21 Physick, The Victoria & Albert Museum, p. 25.
22 Howitt, Land, Labour and Gold, pp. 158–9.
23 J. M. Freeland, Architecture in Australia: A History (Melbourne, Cheshire, 1968), p. 113.
24 Charles Dickens, 'The private history of the palace of glass', Household Words: A Weekly Journal, 18 January 1851, p. 386.
25 McKean, Crystal Palace, p. 60.
26 Ibid., p. 49.
27 Quoted in Patrick Beaver, The Crystal Palace: A Portrait of Victorian Enterprise (Chichester, Phillimore, 1986), p. 84.
28 Henry Incledon Pilcher, Diary 1866, Australian National Maritime Museum, Sydney, 4 August.
29 George F. Chadwick, The Works of Sir Joseph Paxton, 1803–65 (London, Architectural Press, 1961), p. 148.
30 Ibid., p. 148; the north transept was destroyed by fire on 30 December 1866.
31 Hix, The Glasshouse, pp. 36–7
32 Ibid., p. 42.
33 Ibid., p. 141.
34 Ibid., p. 88.
35 McKean, Crystal Palace, p. 29.
36 Tom Carter, The Victorian Garden (London, Bracken, 1988), p. 134.
37 Pilcher, Diary, 4 August 1866.
38 Margaret Tripp, Letters 1872–73, La Trobe Collection, State Library of Victoria MS 11539, 23 April 1872.
39 Richard Teece, Diary 1875, National Library of Australia MS 5354, 29 May.
40 Peter Quartermaine, 'International exhibitions and emigration: the photographic enterprise of Richard Daintree, Agent General for Queensland, 1872–76', Journal of Australian Studies, 13 (1983) 40–55.
41 Samuel Phillips, Guide to the Crystal Palace and Park (London, Bradbury, 1854), p. 105.
42 Pilcher, Diary, 4 August 1866.
43 Phillips, Guide to the Crystal Palace, p. 16.
44 Hix, The Glasshouse, pp. 42–4.
45 Illustrated London News, 7 August 1852, pp. 97–8.
46 Anne McClintock, Imperial Leather: Race, Gender and Sexuality in the Colonial Contest (London, Routledge, 1995).
47 The establishment of the Bethnal Green Museum is dealt with in Physick, The Victoria & Albert Museum, pp. 144–5.
48 Anthony Burton, Bethnal Green Museum of Childhood (London, Victoria and Albert Museum, 1986), p. 44.
49 The Museums Area of South Kensington, p. 99.
50 George W. Stocking, Jr, Victorian Anthropology (New York, Free Press, 1987), p. 6.
51 A. Lane Fox, 'On the principles of classification adopted in the arrangement of his anthropological collection, now exhibited in the Bethnal Green Museum', Journal of the Anthropological Institute, 4 (1875) 302.
52 Ibid., p. 301.
53 Bennett, The Birth of the Museum, p. 201.

54 Quoted in Quartermaine, 'International exhibitions', p. 50; I depend on this excellent article for much of my information regarding Daintree as a photographer.
55 Marc Rothenburg and Peter Hoffenberg, 'Australia at the 1876 exhibition in Philadelphia', *Historical Records of Australian Science*, 8:2 (1990) 58.
56 Henry Russell Hitchcock, *Early Victorian Architecture in Britain*, I (1954; London, Trewin Copplestone, 1972), p. 493.
57 Physick, *The Victoria & Albert Museum*, p. 146.
58 Pilcher, Diary, 23 July 1866.

CHAPTER ELEVEN

'The scenery of the torrid zone': imagined travels and the culture of exotics in nineteenth-century British gardens

Rebecca Preston

The introduction of a new hardy tree or shrub, or the acclimating of one hitherto supposed too tender for the open air, may ... be considered one of the most patriotic of gardening efforts.

John Claudius Loudon, 1826[1]

The theory and practice of gardening through the nineteenth century were marked not just by the extraordinary pace of change but also by the sheer tenacity of the idea that the introduction of foreign plant material on to British soil, and more precisely British domestic soil, was the ultimate horticultural expression of patriotic endeavour. With an almost missionary zeal professional and amateur gardeners set about transplanting and cultivating plants from across the globe. What Lucille Brockway has called 'botanical imperialism' was not a new phenomenon, as horticulture had benefited from foreign introductions from at least the Middle-Ages.[2] But the availability and quality of 'new' plants vastly increased as the European empires expanded. Commercial horticulture developed rapidly in the period after the end of the Napoleonic Wars, funded by private individuals, the state and the nursery trade. Countless exotic plants were successfully imported from overseas, many of which required glazed protection in their new temperate climate. Initially exotics were displayed in imitation tropical landscapes under glass – spectacular glasshouses filled with fully grown exotics which were open to the public as nurserymen's showrooms. On visiting one of London's largest horticultural emporia in 1829, Jacob Rinz was breathtaken:

The first garden I visited was that of Messrs Loddiges, and never shall I forget the sensation produced in me by this establishment. I cannot describe the raptures I experienced on seeing that immense Palm House ... I fancied myself in the Brazils; and especially at that moment when Mr. L. had the kindness to produce ... a shower of artificial rain.[3]

[194]

Such conservatories provided polite entertainment where gardening as a scientific pastime was rapidly popularised among those who were to acquire conservatories for their private consumption. With experience, horticulturalists found they could also recreate the scenery of the tropics or 'torrid zone' out of doors.

Environmental determinism was the primary criterion for the classification of plants as exotic. However, although exotics properly emanated from the tropics, a plant might be deemed such purely on its appearance. Species with strange or 'prehistoric' characteristics were prized as exotic, regardless of their actual geographical or climatic requirements. They were suggestive of foreign landscapes in much the same fashion as true exotics. The cultivation of all 'exotics' in British soil helped frame the unknown world in a familiar context, and their culture in the home landscape allowed a personal as well as a national understanding of far-away places. This offered a very private form of imperial display which quietly expanded the horizons of its audience and allowed for a form of imaginative travel beyond, yet framed by, the realm of home. The Other landscapes suggested by exotics and their arrangement within the garden were arguably as important in shaping the imaginative geographies of British imperialism as exploration and travel abroad.

Horticulture, like natural history, developed in an *ad hoc* fashion, seeking, collecting, cataloguing and improving specimens for British consumption. Combining a civilising bent with absolute faith in the idea of technological progress, the culture of exotics as explained in the gardening press was intent on adapting alien stock to British conditions. Interest in acclimatisation was not confined to horticulture. The general subject was of great interest in nineteenth-century Europe, and the acclimatisation of animals and people, as well as plants, was widely reported.[4] Moreover, as Michael Osborne shows, 'when the notion spread to Britain [from France] ... gentlemen breeders led the way, appropriating the subject to their own concerns, seeking out unchanging ornamental plants for the garden and animals for the hunt'.[5] Edward Said's interest in 'the function of space, geography and location' is primarily literary, but we can extend his reading of *Mansfield Park* to more material forms of cultural imperialism. The Park, he says, 'is located by Austen at the centre of an arc of interests and concerns spanning the hemisphere, two major seas, and four continents'. Further, 'She sees clearly that to hold and rule Mansfield Park is to hold and rule an imperial estate in close, not to say inevitable, association with it.'[6] John MacKenzie argues that 'gentleman geologists formed mental connections between private estates and imperial possessions and developed a "taxonomic acquisitiveness" from their ambition to survey not only every colony but also all unexplored areas of the globe'.[7] What Said describes as 'the importance of an empire to the situation at home'[8] was not confined to the estates of gentlefolk; mental connections were also formed in the smallest of gardens, through pots and window boxes and Wardian cases, 'open[ing] up a broad expanse of domestic imperialist culture without which Britain's subsequent acquisition of territory would not have been possible'.[9]

Love of gardening was seen as evidence of a highly civilised, economically buoyant and patriotic society. 'Horticulture,' wrote the *Gardener's Magazine*, 'as a means of subsistence, is one of the first arts attempted by man on emerging from barbarism; and landscape gardening, as an act of design, is one of the latest inventions for the display of wealth and taste in ages of luxury and refinement.'[10] It had 'diffused itself through all ranks of society, [to] become the favourite recreation of the merchant, of the private gentleman, and the man of letters'.[11] Unlike so many other fashionable amusements gardening was a rational, health-giving and patriotic exercise enjoyed by men and women alike; gardeners were performing a national duty, for the 'taste thus excited by the zeal of amateurs has naturally rendered the introduction of rare plants an important object of commerce'.[12] Very different writers have argued that 'a wide variety of non-governmental agencies discovered that imperial patriotism was also [financially] profitable ... as well as immensely popular':[13] 'Patriotism, for this [commercial] social class as for so many other Britons, paid.'[14] Thus amateur horticulture was promoted as both a patriotic duty and a domestic pleasure. Practically and ideologically the garden was central to private understandings of the empire and of the wider world as a site of imperial potential.

An inexpensive periodical for amateurs, *Floral World*, provided an effective channel for the popular expression of these ideas. In 1859 it celebrated the range and scope of the suburban garden:

> O polar frost, and O torrid sunshine! O bright orient and O mysterious occident, your delicatest darlings here blossom side by side ... for the garden is a living microcosm of the world, a living map of climes and seasons, a gathering of all things curious and useful and beautiful, from 'the cedar that is in Lebanon, to the hyssop that groweth on the wall.'[15]

William Robinson, whose life's work was devoted to the naturalisation of hardy plants from around the globe, acknowledged the role of the garden in constructing ideas about the world when he noted that although 'it is given to few to see many of these sweet plants in their native lands ... those who love our gardens may enjoy many of them about us, not merely in drawings or descriptions, but the living, breathing things themselves'.[16] The creation of one's own garden, planted with fashionable but individually chosen specimen evergreens, tropical climbers and Cape heaths, brought together an idiosyncratic selection of empire spoils which symbolised the riches procured for the benefit of the homeland. Robinson's recommendation that 'in such [domestic] plantations one might have in the back parts "secret" colonies of lovely things which it might not be well to show in the front of the border'[17] suggests a private understanding of what he called 'the great garden of the world itself.'[13] This was 'a world of delightful plant beauty that we might make happy around us ... which we should [otherwise] have little chance of seeing'.[19] Here, at the farthest reaches of the garden, voyages of exploration were made; strange plants remained hidden in thickets until extravagant flowers or fruit gave them away.

The search for plants for British gardens was not confined to the British empire proper, although formal imperialism certainly facilitated their extraction and transplantation. The mainstay of British and Continental European botanical imperialism in the nineteenth century was the Americas. As gardening was held to signify advanced civilisation, plant hunters frequently looked to the lands of other empires for wild and cultivated specimens. While advanced civilisations were respected for their horticultural and agricultural skills, 'primitive' countries were described as having plants in an aboriginal stage of development. This was most fully expressed by Darwin in *The Origin of Species* but was a view that underpinned much horticultural writing of the period:

> If it has taken centuries or thousands of years to improve or modify most of our plants up to their present standard of usefulness to man, we can understand how it is that neither Australia, the Cape of Good Hope, nor any other region inhabited by quite uncivilised man, has afforded us a single plant worth culture. It is not that these countries, so rich in species, do not by a strange chance possess the aboriginal stocks of any useful plants, but that the native plants have not been improved by continued selection up to a standard of perfection comparable with that given to plants in countries anciently civilised.[20]

In Darwin's book uncivilised lands offered up weeds. But weeds were useful precisely because they illustrated the gulf between the primitive plants of the New World and those selected by 'anciently civilised' lands. The beautiful plants of Africa, for example, were held to originate chiefly from Algeria, Morocco, Egypt and, occasionally, the Cape. As James Ryan has argued for imperial photography, 'landscape views were the counterpart to the representation of ethnographic types': 'Images of vegetative pandemonium ... signified not only the rich potential of the land, but also the absence of indigenous industry and labour.'[21] Contemporary commentary extended this ethnographic model to a nation's propensity for gardening. 'In fact,' said Shirley Hibberd in *Rustic Adornments for Homes of Taste* (1856), 'none but the most sordid and abandoned [of nations] are utterly without a garden, or the best substitute that can be had for one'.[22] Finally, 'we are told upon excellent authority', by *The Book of Gardening* in 1900, 'that it is only among the most brutal and degraded races of savages that gardening is unknown'.[23]

Conversely, 'civilised' non-European nations were applauded for their horticultural skills but derided for their taste. In an extract from the journal of his voyage to Canton, published in the *Gardener's Magazine* of 1827, 'to collect the double Camellias &c.', gardener James Main noted that 'on the first view of the coast of China the stranger concludes that the inhabitants are a nation of gardeners' and, 'stepping on shore', that the land was 'well-cultivated'. What it merited in cultivation, however, the Chinese landscape lacked in taste in equal measure, for 'nothing presents itself but a little world of insignificant intricacy'.[24] 'In short,' he continued, 'except for the beauty and rarity of the plants, the visitor finds nothing interesting in their style of gardening: no scope of ornamental disposition; no rational design; the whole being an incongruous combination of unnatural association.'[25] After several pages of diatribe against 'this display of vitiated taste' the journal conceded that, 'it must be owned that no nation possesses a greater number of vegetable blessings, nor have any people on earth turned such to more account ... [Their plants have added] to the wealth, the sanative luxury, and dietetic comfort, of half the world.'[26] Similar charges of 'insignificant intricacy' were often levelled against other European horticultural styles, particularly those of France and Italy. 'Formal' design – rigorously trained ornamental plants, 'ridiculously fantastic trellis work'[27] and geometric planting – was held as the antithesis of the English garden ideal, and thus of the free and liberal conduct of its government and populace, for most of the century.

The oriental gardens cultivated in Europe, then, were not likely to represent in verisimilitude the domestic landscapes of China or Japan. Instead, an oriental garden might be suggested by a combination of exotic plants and architectural details. Shirley Hibberd, for example included 'Summer houses in the Chinese style' in *Rustic Adornments*. To complete their 'fantastic and pleasing effect', he recommended, they contain 'gaily disposed exotics ... [such as] rose, jasminum, or clematis'.[28] These were appropriate plants for a Chinese structure in England, being hardy and popular climbers of temperate Asian origin. Such details, however, were calculated to produce a fantastic effect rather than any sense of 'authenticity'. 'Exotic', 'Moorish', 'oriental', 'torrid', and 'tropical' were largely interchangeable terms, all suggesting something Other (see Figure 32). John Claudius Loudon, for example, described how 'a Chinese conservatory, filled and surrounded with Chinese plants, may very easily and very naturally be executed. A glazed Mosque, Pyramid, or Pagoda, containing palms, &c., might give a pretty good idea of the scenery of the torrid zone. To design such things, only requires a little knowledge of the botanist and the traveller.'[29] Jane Loudon's *Ladies' Magazine of Gardening* for 1841 was more pragmatic in its treatment of exotic embellishments for the flower garden of a 'suburban villa'. It suggested how an 'enclosed space may be laid with asphalte, or paved with Alhambra mosaic tiles, which are warranted to resist frost, and which may be obtained at Singer's manufactory on the Surrey side of Vauxhall Bridge'.[30]

Scenery deemed exotic was not confined to that emanating from the non-European world. Southern Europe was frequently exoticised in much the same fashion as the East. In 1829 the *Gardener's Magazine* recommended that 'exotic scenery may be expressed or represented in gardening, where local or other circumstances are favourable. Italian may consist of suitable structures, trellises, etc., furnished with vines, portable orange, lemon, pomegranate, olive, and myrtle trees.'[31] Sixty years later *The English Flower Garden* suggested that the plants of Southern Europe and Southern Africa could conjure their home landscapes at one and the same time: 'the geraniums in the cottage window bring us the spicy fragrance of the South African hills; the lavender bush of the sunny hills of Provence where it is at home.'[32] Mary Louise Pratt has shown how, from the late eighteenth century, 'one by one, the planet's life forms were to be drawn out of the tangled threads of their life surroundings and rewoven into European based patterns of global

Figure 32 A parrot house or vinery in the Moorish style. From Shirley Hibberd, *Rustic Adornments for Homes of Taste* (London, 1856)

[199]

unity and order'. Further, 'the eye that held the system could familiarize ("naturalize") new sites/sights immediately upon contact, by incorporating them into the language of the system. The differences of distance factored themselves out of the picture: with respect to mimosas, Greece could be the same as Venezuela, West Africa, or Japan.'[33] Thus the act of planting the exotic in the garden immediately tempered any outlandishness it called to mind.

Descriptions of exotic plants tended to occasion rather more flights of fancy in the British press than did those of temperate zone species and, as so frequently in cases of orientalism, the East and its material culture were charged with lascivious and frequently feminised sexuality. In his 1831 'observation' of the shrub *Brugmansia suaveolens*, a *Gardener's Magazine* correspondent noted that one of his party 'was so affected by the sight, that, throwing himself onto a spacious armchair, he felt moved to quote Virgil'. The correspondent himself was only marginally less ecstatic, noting that 'the delicate whiteness of its large pendulous bells, contrasted with its ample green foliage, and as viewed in the imperfect illumination of candlelight, made a grand and exhilarating spectacle, one that to us seemed Orientally luxurious'. A native of the Americas, *Brugmansia*, or Datura, after its Indian name, was a known hallucinogen; even its scent intoxicated. Thus we may assume 'the fragrance of the blooms that pervaded the conservatory' that night lulled the party into forgetting they had never left Bury St Edmunds and had been transported instead to the oriental luxury of some Brazilian forest, or other imagined torrid zone.[34]

Much has been written on the psychosexual resonance of flowers in the garden, being particularly concerned with representations of the luxuriant forms of exotic species, hanging heavily near the open window at dusk.[35] Contemporary representations of this nature were often conveyed through the medium of verse; the forms of flowers ambiguously traced onto the page. A larger sense of eroticised danger was felt at the time to issue from scent – heady or malodorous humours – that were all the more powerful for their invisibility. Perfume, then, perhaps more than form, conjured other worlds and drifting across the threshold made tangibly domestic boundaries elastic, transporting its subject elsewhere in space and time. A common feature of garden writing, both in the nineteenth century and before, was the notion that history was carried through plants and gardens into the present. Mental travelling, or Mesmerism, reached almost epic proportions in the popular imagination from the middle of the nineteenth century.[36] These ideas coloured many aspects of contemporary cultural life, especially literature. Charles Dickens, for example, describes a window around which 'were clusters of jessamine and honeysuckle, that crept over the casement, and filled the place with their delicious perfume'. After an 'uncommonly sultry' day Oliver Twist drifts into sleep, and the boundaries between inside and outside, present and past, reality and dream, become increasingly confused. 'Although our senses of touch and sight be for the time dead,' says the narrator, 'yet our sleeping thoughts, and the visionary scenes that pass before us, will be influenced ... by the mere silent presence of some external object.'[37] Scent, the most evocative of the senses, is bound closely to memory. William Robinson was quite certain that 'the fragrant bushes of our gardens may entwine for us, apart from their gift of beauty, living associations and beautiful thoughts for ever famous in human story.'[38]

Perhaps the institution most significant in rendering exotic gardening accessible to the public was the Crystal Palace. Initially its influence was restricted to the staging of horticultural shows and the interest which it encouraged in glass structures. However, apart from the existing trees enclosed by the temporary exhibition building, almost the only horticultural exhibits were mechanical. (As opposed to botanical exhibits, which were well represented.) But, after its removal to the South London suburbs, the now permanent palace was established as a winter garden where geographically discrete spaces were devoted to plant cultivation. For instance, 'at the tropical end of the nave [were] the specimens of rice, and other tropical grasses, and Papyrus';[39] 'Date palms were imported direct from Egypt, and of a size to give a character to the Egyptian antiquities with which they were associated.'[40] Inspired by their experiences there, amateur gardeners began to acquire their own 'crystal palaces on a domestic scale'.[41]

Those villa dwellers without a substantial glasshouse but nevertheless keen to explore tropical landscapes without encountering the teeming millions at flower shows and public parks could pass their time in the common practice of visiting the 'open houses' of the landed elite out of season. At Dangstein, the Sussex seat of the wealthy Nevill family, the vast collection of glasshouses was open to the public for six days of the week in the 1860s. Here were cultivated 'economically important as well as beautiful plants ... Peruvian wax palm grew alongside cotton plants, tea and coffee trees, sugar cane, as well as mangoes, guavas and bananas.'[42] The walls of the fern house were 'all encrusted with shells from the East Indies and on the back wall are the letters L.D.N. 1872 in white coral upon red'. Thus the public as well as the Nevill family circle were offered a particular window onto the world, one which very much reflected Lord Nevill's activities overseas. Visitors might wander aimlessly 'from America into India through a glass door ... into Bombay in the rains'[43] while pondering the very considered aims of Lord Nevill, whose presence, like his initials, marked all four corners of his miniature empire. Darwin made botanising expeditions to Dangstein and Lady Nevill exchanged plants with Kew.

It was at Kew, of course, that landscapes had first been designed with the economic importance of plants in mind. Its role in demonstrating the effects of climate upon the British constitution was also important in contructing an imaginative geography of empire. In his *Wanderings through the Conservatories at Kew* of 1857, Philip Henry Gosse deliberately contrasted the oppressively exotic interior of the Palm House with the clement air of its English host: 'a door, and a length of a couple of yards, conducts us from the temperate to the torrid zone. Without was a pleasant, genial, English summer day, within is the damp and oppressive heat of Hindostan. Into what noble society are we now introduced?'[44]

If even the small fashionable garden encouraged a sort of global consciousness it did not preclude foraging for plants closer to home: in reality only a minority of men and women ventured abroad in their searches and many remained in their gardens to botanise. Instead the same 'spirit of adventure [which] brings to light botanical resources'[45] abroad was present at home, for most 'herborizers were as happy in the countryside of Scotland or southern France as they were in the Amazon or Southern Africa'.[46] In 1861 one amateur gardener complained to his magazine of the few opportunities for botanising: 'after the hours of business in a great town, it is impossible to make frequent journeys to the country to gather specimens for the herbarium'. The editor must have comforted not a few of his readers in his reply: 'There is no more agreeable or more instructive method of studying botany than by growing annual plants ... [which] is far more superior for all who desire full and accurate knowledge to all possible collection of wild specimens, no matter how many countries and climates may be laid under tribute.'[47]

By the non-agricultural classes rural landscapes in Britain were considered in similar fashion to uncharted territories abroad; for many prosperous men and women this was the nearest they would get to seeing plants in their natural habitat, gardens being resolutely domesticated places. The countryside, like its unscientific, ill educated and unruly populace, was considered wild and in need of rational, systematic order to catalogue its natural history. Philanthropists took it upon themselves to educate the rural poor; 'tourists' offering social commentary, such as William Cobbett and the Loudons, studied both the poor and methods of improving their domestic environment; naturalists studied the local flora and fauna. Unlike in foreign lands, the need to categorise the flora and fauna of Britain was felt to be more pressing owing to the perceived encroachment upon the uncultivated landscape by increasingly mechanised agricultural practices. Further, the expansion of the towns and suburbs – the habitat of many middle-class naturalists – was also identified as squeezing the wildness out of the countryside.

However, contemporary anecdotes reveal attitudes to nature and its documentation which were somewhat less missionary than those expressed in the horticultural and botanical press. One naturalist described herself in 1836 as 'moss mad';[48] twenty years later another recalled how she had 'ransacked' the beach at Ramsgate during a family holiday and pressed the plants under her mattress.[49] If amateurs did not necessarily engage with their hobby in the scientific manner proposed by prominent naturalists and botanists, they enjoyed the collecting all the same. Very soon, many writers were urging caution against the 'collecting expedition'. In his *Fern Garden* of 1896 Shirley Hibberd complained that 'the passion for fern collecting has in many instances been carried to ridiculous excess'.[50] Hibberd berated such 'collecting expeditions', dismissing them alongside 'the picnicking, archaeologico-exploring, and holiday perambulating that may be associated with this sport'.[51] But Hibberd had encouraged the collecting of such 'hardy exotics' as ferns, and in the 1860s had recommended their cultivation with foreign sorts in a domestic greenhouse such as his own (see Figure 33).[52] Not surprisingly, amateurs ignored conservationists' warnings, and continued to enjoy the *idea* of the collecting expedition with scant regard for botanical excellence. Even those who travelled abroad in their excursions could treat their hobby light-heartedly. Writing home from Ireland early in the century, this English tourist shows just how lightly his survey of colonial botany was undertaken:

Monkstown 10 August 1805

Dear Madam,
 No sooner had I left Dublin than I began to botanize, three beautiful plants did I pick up ... To be sure I didn't know whether they were thistles or mosses, but I was sure they were peculiar to Ireland for I had never seen 'em before, and so I was ... bringing them to you but Ben promised indeed we'll find the same weeds under any cliff in England and so I disposed of my collection at prime cost.

Yours, R.D.[53]

The majority of amateur botanists never ventured into imperial lands, and practised their hobby on local field trips or at home in the garden. Thus the amateur might continue to botanise for 'weeds' near home while also cultivating the new and beautiful varieties collected from overseas by more experienced plant collectors: both activities famil-

Figure 33   A greenhouse of hardy 'exotics' in a north London suburb, 1866.
Floral World, January 1866

iarised imperial notions of discovery, settlement and civilisation, completing them by cultivating their subjects in a domestic landscape.

It was to the cultivation of the northern hemisphere's flora that attempts at verisimilitude were reserved. Almost without exception, and from their earliest introduction, horticultural writing organised the plants of the temperate zone into naturalistic landscapes suggestive of their indigenous environments. And, as William Robinson hoped, 'It is also very probable that we shall, as various regions of the northern world are opened up, introduce to cultivation other fine wild species, and get precious races from them.'[54] Jane Loudon explained how to form

> what the landscape-gardeners call scenes. ... There might be an American ground, formed in some shaded hollow, and planted with rhododendrons, azaleas, and kalmias ... In another part of the pleasure-grounds there might be some Alpine scenery, with pines and firs, and particularly larches, interspersed with a few birch trees, planted on dry sandy soil, on hilly ground. ... In short, there are no limits to the numerous and beautiful scenes that might be laid out by a woman of cultivated mind, who possessed fancy and taste, combined with a very slight knowledge of trees.[55]

Beautiful scenes offering views of hardy plants could also be conjured more immediately, they did not necessarily require the luxury of extensive grounds. In the Domestic Notices of the *Gardener's Magazine* Miss Kent, author of *Flora Domestica* and a teacher of botany, was described as living 'in the very heart of London, between Paternoster Row and St Paul's, yet she has a thriving garden of pots on top of her house; not of sickly geraniums but of pretty little hardy natives'. On the same page Mr Sweet's lectures were also advertised, with an accompanying editorial passage claiming that if all those 'who possess a house, and a plot in the way of a garden, in the neighbourhood of London ... were to take six mixed lessons of botany and culture ... they would find themselves ... within the pale of a new world'.[56] On his retirement in 1861, Sweet's success was attributed to his having 'understood the geographical history [of plants]' as well as his 'master[y] of hybridization'. He urged amateurs to 'treat [plants] as Nature treats them at home'.[57]

However worldly were the grounds she cultivated, Jane Loudon's prospect remained essentially domestic. 'What a difference it makes,' she wrote, 'in the pleasure we have in returning home, if we have something that we know has been improving in our absence!' Further, she 'regard[ed] the trees and shrubs we have planted, and the scenes we have laid out, with almost parental fondness'.[58] All garden writers, however, concurred that the gardens immediately adjoining the house should be evidently domestic and in no way wild.

> We must, [said an amateur] adapt our gardens, that at least which enjoins the house, to the building, and make them a part of it, appropriate ... we must engraft upon our own romantic harshnesses something that will accord better with the equipment of the interior of our residences, something like furniture and ornament, and not leap from our windows into jungles, and steppes, and wildernesses, where the lion and panther would be more at home than the 'lady with her silken sheen'.[59]

The flower garden withdrew from the wilder outskirts of the garden, however small and, near the house, was a perfectly domestic and civilised place.

All sorts of gardening were then thought appropriate activity for women, for 'a genuine love for flowers promotes the love of home'.[60] The keeping of a good garden, like the upkeep of the interior, was evidence of an upright household. This was just as true of the 'middling sort' as of the poor household. In 1860 *Floral World* cited the 'increase and prosper' of floricultural societies as 'evidence of the healthiness of domestic life in England', because 'societies for the encouragement of horticulture are by their very nature civilising.' It added significantly that 'gardening makes men domestic.'[61] But for all that men and women probably shared the gardening according to personal preference or the custom of their class, the culture of flowering exotics was singled out in print as a particularly suitable occupation for women and girls. 'Nurture of exotics,' commented *The Gentleman's Magazine* as early as 1801, 'not only belongs more particularly to the female province, on account of its being an elegant home amusement, but because of there being much delicate work, essential to the welfare of the plants'.[62]

In her study of curry and cookery books in Victorian England Susan Zlotnick documents the process of naturalising a foreign item until it is fully incorporated into native material culture. The incorporation of foreign foodstuffs into English cookery was akin to the incorporation of foreign plants into English gardens: both acts could 'naturalise' the end product, which was usually considered more refined and cultivated. Zlotnick traces 'the "good" Victorian woman's moral agency and figurative power to domesticate the foreign ... through cookbooks and curry recipes'.[63] Through this process of hybridity and incorporation, she says, and 'by virtue of their own domesticity, Victorian women could neutralize the Other by naturalizing the products of foreign lands'.[64] Although it is doubtful that any Other was ever completely neutralised from foreign items within this period, largely owing to the thrills potentially induced by their consumption, Zlotnick is surely right in her concluding remark that 'Indian curry belongs to the Victorian interior as much as tea and crumpets'.[65] We can draw parallels with countless foreign plants incorporated into the Victorian exterior, many of which have since been subsumed into the so-called 'English' garden. But her premise that curry's 'belonging points to ways in which the Victorians understood India to be theirs' does not explain the quantities of plants 'belonging' to the Victorian garden with origins outside the British empire. Nor does it help us to understand why some belonged, like tea and camellias, even as their consumption continued to be exoticised. Rather, exotic introductions reflected a fascination with the general difference of places 'abroad' regardless of whether they belonged to the mother country. Deborah Ryan has argued that 'many people experienced the Empire through the cooking and consumption of imported foodstuffs',[66] and it is reasonable to suppose that empire goods were generally more familiar to consumers than entirely foreign items. But a familiar plant – or foodstuff – is not necessarily a naturalised one. Thus, as Ryan reminds us, the 'latent English taste for the spiced and half foreign which was a driving motive of imperialism'[67] ensured that foreign material culture was subsumed into its new home without altogether losing its original flavour. Exotics should not predominate in the kitchen or the garden. Rather, a member of 'the town-dwelling middle class ... might blend with the beauties of his own land some of the more striking productions of tropical regions'.[68]

In the last third of the nineteenth century it became common for horticultural writers to praise British flora over exotic introductions. One hoped that 'many a garden will have its raised bank devoted to these simple children of our native wilds, whose traditional histories sanctify them in our memory as associates in many of the greatest scenes of our history'.[69] Further, the 'interesting, literary, and domestic associations [of native species] ... will rival successfully the showy borders where exotics have their proper home'.[70] In the closing decades of the century, examples of Old English gardens began to appear, in print and on the ground, and even Shakespearean gardens complete with contemporary flora were created. Although most gardeners did not go to such lengths, many were influenced by the quantities of literature published advocating the 'old-fashioned' approach to garden design and planting. That this was a new form of the old appears to have mattered little. Perhaps it offered relief from increasingly scientised horticultural practice, perhaps it offered simplicity and familiarity after years of unstinted saturation by the 'new'. Perhaps a little less certainty in the strength of British imperial identity led to uncertainty as to the nature of the English garden. Whatever the reasons for this redefinition – and it may be that all these factors played their part – gardeners increasingly preferring native or *native-looking* flora to the exotic. In Barbara Campbell's *Garden of a Commuter's Wife* of 1911 'the thrill of oriental suggestion that the lily and iris tribes always bring with them' was tempered: 'In an old-fashioned garden such as mine, this result must be by suggestion only; for if it is allowed to dominate, it becomes incongruous, and would wholly denationalise the garden.'[71]

From the isolated collections and single specimen exotics favoured in the first part of the century to their naturalisation or domestication with indigenous flora in the latter, we can trace the gradual and uneven process of how foreign plants were accommodated in British gardens. Continuing a pattern discernible from the earliest moments of horticulture, the first part of the nineteenth century saw gardens and their printed representations in which 'foreignness' or Otherness was prized. Rare and strange-looking plants were labelled and laid out in gardens as objects of wonder. Later, as the number of plants increased (and correspondingly prices decreased), and when exotics no longer appeared quite so magnificently primitive, came the call for the assimilation of those plants hardy enough for the temperate zone and the removal of all those that could survive only under glass. 'It is reasonable to suppose,' wrote Robinson, 'that some of ... these lovely flowers that tumble into our lap, as it were, from the woods and hills of Western China, Japan, and California ... would take care of themselves, if trusted to likely spots, with us.'[72] Naturalisation also occurred accidentally. Even very soon after introduction, a previously exotic plant could become so familiar that it bred freely and without comment. After a few more years it could be subsumed with innumerable others of foreign extraction into that ever dubious category 'the English garden'. The naturalisation of exotics was not a rejection of botanical imperialism; it was its logical culmination. Exotics were naturalised alongside native varieties, with the result that they became indistinguishable. British science had trained them to be hardy and useful. But if the imperial project had now been rendered invisible in the garden itself, its success continued to be celebrated in pictorial representations. In spite of their exotic names, rhododendrons and other imported species had become such an established a feature of the landscape as to appear utterly native. Accompanied by that favourite imperial figure, the gentleman explorer, illustrations of naturalised exotics left the reader in no doubt of their origins, ensuring that something of their exotic association would remain (see Figure 34).

However large or small one's garden, then, the few plants it contained called up images and associations far beyond what their present form might suggest. As one writer rather elaborately noted, 'our chief pleasures, and many of our pains, arise out of associations', so that, 'though we cannot have the mountain dells, and creeping thorns, and purple knolls of wild thyme, we may have emblems of them in our little mural paradise'.[73] Cultivating exotics in British gardens was a way of familiarising unknown tropical landscapes which, for most people, would remain otherwise distant, hazy places palpable only through travellers' representations. In this way stay-at-home domestic types could travel imaginatively in foreign landscapes simply by walking in their gardens. Indeed, it may have been that tending one's own plantation of foreign species at home was a kind of surrogacy for more adventurous designs abroad. Although expatriates did return with seeds and stories which fuelled the passion for exotic gardening, their travels were never a prerequisite for the culture of exotics at home. Many of Britain's exotic gardeners never left its shores. Instead they explored the landscapes in miniature displayed in the spectacular conservatories that were such a feature of Victorian urban life. And so although most were unable 'to plan a garden on such a scale ... the idea of such an arrangement [could] be carried out in a small plot of a hundred feet square',[74] without its makers ever having to leave home, because, as Robert Louis Stephenson noted, 'inside the garden we can construct a country of our own'.[75]

Figure 34   Hardy rhododendrons naturalised in an English garden. From William Robinson, *The English Flower Garden* (seventh edition, London, 1899)

Notes

1 *Gardener's Magazine*, 1 (1826) 5. This was the first edition of the first periodical dedicated to the improvement of British horticulture, published from 1826 until Loudon's death in 1843.
2 L. Brockway, *Science and Colonial Expansion: The Role of the British Royal Botanic Gardens*, (New York, Academic Press, 1979), p. 168.
3 *Gardener's Magazine*, 5 (1829) 379.
4 M. A. Osborne, *Nature, the Exotic, and the Science of French Colonialism*, (Bloomington and Indianapolis IN, Indiana University Press, 1994); M. A. Osborne, 'Climates of opinion: acclimatization in nineteenth-century France and England', *Victorian Studies*, 35:2 (1991) 135–59.
5 Osborne, 'Climates of opinion', p. 137.
6 E. Said, *Culture and Imperialism*, (1993; London, Vintage, 1994 edition), pp. 101, 104.
7 J. M. MacKenzie (ed.), 'Introduction', *Imperialism and the Natural World*, (Manchester and New York, Manchester University Press, 1990), p. 9.
8 Said, *Culture*, p. 106.
9 *Ibid.*, p. 114.
10 *Gardener's Magazine*, 1 (1826) 1.

11 *Ibid.*, p. 57.
12 *Ibid.*, p. 55.
13 J. M. MacKenzie, *Propaganda and Empire*, (Manchester, Manchester University Press, 1984), p. 3.
14 L. Colley, *Britons: Forging the Nation, 1707–1837* (New Haven CT and London, Yale University Press, 1992), p. 302.
15 *Floral World*, 2 (1859) 198.
16 W. Robinson, *The English Flower Garden*, (London, Murray, 1883; 1889 edition), p. 292.
17 *Ibid.*, p. viii.
18 *Ibid.*, p. 155.
19 *Ibid.*
20 C. Darwin, *The Origin of Species*, (1859; London, Penguin Books, 1985 edition), pp. 95–6.
21 J. R. Ryan, 'Imperial landscapes: photography, geography and British overseas exploration, 1858–72', in M. Bell, R. Butlin and M. Heffernan, (eds), *Geography and Imperialism, 1820–1940* (Manchester and New York, Manchester University Press, 1995), pp. 62–3.
22 S. Hibberd, *Rustic Adornments for Homes of Taste*, (1856; London, Century Hutchinson, 1987 edition), p. 328.
23 W. Drury, *The Book of Gardening*, (London, 1900), p. 2.
24 *Gardener's Magazine*, 2 (1827) 135–6.
25 *Ibid.*, p. 137.
26 *Ibid.*, p. 140.
27 *Ibid.*, p. 136.
28 Hibberd, *Rustic Adornments*, pp. 496–7.
29 *Gardener's Magazine*, 5 (1829) 266.
30 *Ladies' Magazine of Gardening*, 1 (1841) 3–4.
31 *Gardener's Magazine*, 5 (1829) 266.
32 Robinson, *English Flower Garden*, p. 292.
33 M. L. Pratt, *Imperial Eyes: Travel Writing and Transculturation*, (London, Routledge, 1992; 1995 edition), p. 31.
34 *Gardener's Magazine*, 7 (1831) 37.
35 See, for example, Susan P. Casteras, *Images of Victorian Womanhood in English Art*, (Cranbury NJ and London, Associated University Presses, 1987), pp. 40 and pp. 58–9.
36 A. Owen, *The Darkened Room: Women, Power and Spirituality in Late Victorian England*, (London, Virago, 1989); R. Cooter, 'The history of mesmerism in Britain: poverty and promise', in Heinz Schott (ed.), *Franz Anton Mesmer und die Geschichte des Mesmerismus* (Stuttgart, Steiner, 1985), pp. 153–62.
37 Quoted in J. Sutherland, *Is Heathcliff a Murderer? Puzzles in Nineteenth Century Fiction*, (Oxford and New York, World's Classics, Oxford University Press, 1996), pp. 36–7.
38 Robinson, *English Flower Garden*, p. 292.
39 *Floral World*, 2 (1859) 76.
40 *The Gardener*, (1867), quoted in T. Carter, *The Victorian Garden* (London, Bell & Hyman, 1984), p. 136.
41 *National Magazine*, 1 (1851) 206.
42 J. Morgan and A. Richards, *A Paradise out of a Common Field: The Pleasures and Plenty of the Victorian Garden* (New York, Harper & Row, 1990), pp. 192–3.
43 *Journal of Horticulture*, (1872), quoted in Morgan and Richards, *Paradise*, p. 76.
44 P. H. Gosse, *Wanderings through the Conservatories at Kew*, (London, 1857), p. 44.
45 *Floral World*, 6 (1863) 235.
46 Pratt, *Imperial Eyes*, p. 35.
47 *Floral World*, 4 (1861) 43.
48 Quoted in A. B. Shteir, *Cultivating Women, Cultivating Science: Flora's Daughters and Botany in England, 1760–1860*, (Baltimore MD and London, Johns Hopkins University Press, 1996), p. 182.

49 *Ibid.*, p. 217.
50 *Floral World*, 8 (1865) 12.
51 *Ibid.*, p. 146.
52 *Floral World*, 9 (1866) 1.
53 Minet Library, London, IV/4, 173, Graham-Polhill Papers.
54 Robinson, *English Flower Garden*, p. 334.
55 J. Loudon, *Practical Instructions in Gardening for Ladies*, (1840; London, Smith, 1844 edition), p. 340.
56 *Gardener's Magazine*, 6 (1830) 487.
57 *Floral World*, 4 (1861) 11–12.
58 Loudon, *Practical Instructions*, p. 341.
59 *Gardener's Magazine*, 4 (1828) 89.
60 *Journal of Horticulture*, (1872), quoted in Carter, *Victorian Garden*, p. 181.
61 *Floral World*, 3 (1860) 89–90.
62 Quoted in Shteir, *Cultivating Women*, p. 35.
63 S. Zlotnick, 'Domesticating imperialism: curry and cookbooks in Victorian England', *Frontiers: a Journal of Women's Studies*, 16:2/3 (1995) 52.
64 *Ibid.*, p. 53.
65 *Ibid.*, p. 64.
66 D. S. Ryan, 'The *Daily Mail* Ideal Home Exhibition and Suburban Modernity, 1908–51', (unpublished Ph.D. thesis, University of East London, 1995), p. 199.
67 J. Morris quoted in Ryan, 'The Ideal Home Exhibition', p.188.
68 Hibberd, *Rustic Adornments*, p. 153.
69 *Ibid.*, p. 413.
70 *Ibid.*, p. 414.
71 Quoted in D. Kellaway, (ed.), *Women Gardeners*, (London, Virago, 1995), p. 68.
72 Robinson, *English Flower Garden*, p. 98.
73 Hibberd, *Rustic Adornments*, p. 427.
74 *Ibid.*, p. 338.
75 R. L. Stevenson, *Essays of Travel*, (London, Chatto & Windus, 1918), p. 187.

PART III

Imperial identities

CHAPTER TWELVE

'The Second City of the Empire':
Glasgow – imperial municipality

John M. MacKenzie

In 1899 J. K. McDowell wrote an excited preface for his book *The People's History of Glasgow*. In it he urged that the history of the city should be taught in schools and colleges in order to impart the lessons of ambition, useful industry, self-reliance, corporate endeavour and individual effort. All of these would demonstrate how Glasgow had become, and could remain, 'the first municipality in the world and the second city of the British Empire'.[1] 'I belang tae Glesca and Glesca belangs tae me' was clearly more than a drunken perception of the music hall artist Will Fyfe: it represented an overweening pride of place, a place that was 'goin' roun' and roun'', not just because of the power of the whisky but also because of its truly global perceptions.

McDowell's apparently outrageous claim as to 'the first municipality in the world' referred to the extent and depth of Glasgow's municipal socialism, partially learned from Birmingham and Manchester, but arguably taken further than anywhere else. Indeed, although Glasgow lacked a single towering figure like Joseph Chamberlain, some at least of its measures of municipal socialism antedated his.[2] McDowell's 'Second City of the Empire' was merely the repetition of a sort of mantra of pride in place and achievement which elite Glaswegians clung to and successfully disseminated among the other classes for more than a century. The phrase has been identified as first used in relation to the city as early as 1825.[3] It continued in use until the inter-war years of the twentieth century, even when decline and contraction had clearly robbed the city of such a status, if indeed it ever had it.

In 1946 C. A. Oakley published a history of the city which was to become a best-seller.[4] Its title was *The Second City*, a truncated reference that everyone was expected to understand immediately. Oakley claimed that Glasgow had achieved that coveted position in 1800 and retained it until at least 1914, fighting off all the efforts of Birmingham, Sydney, Montreal, Toronto or Calcutta to take it over. Even Liverpool was a competitor.[5] This competition for the accolade of second position reveals something of the nature of imperial power, that citizens sought to quantify fractions of share. From the early nineteenth century to the mid-twentieth this desire to compete and categorise seems to have been a vital component of pride in civic growth and success.

Alhough population was often used as the principal, and in some respects most dubious, criterion, this municipal claim could also be based on the degree of economic integration into the imperial enterprise. Indeed, few cities were as closely connected with imperial commerce as Glasgow, both in historical contexts and, particularly, in terms of the mature empire economy of the later nineteenth century. Phrases used in more modern times, 'Workshop of the Empire' or 'Engineer Extraordinary to the British Empire', perfectly encapsulated that relationship.[6] But such a union of fortunes is a hostage to the loss of one of the partners. In the twentieth century Glasgow was to be a major victim of the transformation of the imperial economy and the processes of decolonisation. The disintegration of empire and the loss of markets which were sentimentally, if not fiscally, protected produced the collapse of the city's industrial base. Sometimes this has been expressed in terms of over-specialisation, but it was not so much a narrow range of products that was the problem. From the eighteenth century onwards, the Glasgow economy was strikingly diversified. Rather, it was specialisation in imperial markets.

Yet this problem was not new. The striking thing about Glasgow's economic and spatial history is the extent to which it repeatedly renewed itself as the geographical orientation and the economic relations of empire were transformed. We now know that Glasgow's fortunes were on the up well before the Act of Union of 1707.[7] In the seventeenth century a small and relatively insignificant burgh, albeit graced by a great cathedral and a university, had risen to be the second city of Scotland. Its trading relations with Ireland, France and the Low Countries were well established.[8] Towards the end of that century it was already developing a notable transatlantic trade.[9] After the Act of Union, however, it took off. Glasgow's extraordinary command of the tobacco trade, greater than that of any other port in Britain, provided it with a really significant entrepôt role in respect of much of Europe.[10]

If the loss of the Thirteen Colonies, and with them the protection of the Navigation Acts, destroyed that entrepôt status, it did little to check the continuing burgeoning of the city. Its economic resilience was based on the continuation of its role as a producer of goods required in the planters' stores of America and the Caribbean. Radical colonial politics did little to change conservative settler tastes and trading loyalties. Moreover, its extensive connections with the West Indies developed further. It had taken up a commanding position in the production of plantation machinery, particularly in relation to sugar. It dominated the manufacture of sugar crushing, boiling and refining machinery, to the tune of no less than 80 per cent of world production.[11] In any case, its merchants soon developed connections not only with the West Indies but also with India and the Far East, despite, in the case of the latter two, the East India Company monopoly. Inevitably, these trades spawned mercantile pressure groups.[12] From the 1790s Glasgow became a major city of cotton production, first in luxury and then in coarse wares.

By this time the river had been canalised and dredged to such an extent that the former salmon stream could receive larger imperial, ocean-going vessels right into the heart of the city. Coal and iron deposits were within the city boundaries or near by, readily accessed by the canal trade. Iron foundries became increasingly important, and by 1860 heavy engineering and shipbuilding had taken over as the staple of Glasgow's imperial relationship. Imperial shipping lines were founded in the city, even if some of them subsequently moved their headquarters to Liverpool or London. Shipyards maintained close relations with these lines. At any given moment, vessels for deep-sea companies, as well as river and lake navigation throughout the world, could be found on their stocks.

With each of these transformations the city was rebuilt. In the medieval and early modern burgh the population lived cheek by jowl, servicing the city's ecclesiastical foundations, conducting trade and developing the city's status as a major centre of communications. The cathedral and its related institutions, including the university, were up the hill, the productive and commercial centre down the slope nearer the river. Tobacco changed these closely knit spatial relationships. It rapidly differentiated Glasgow's citizenry, particularly in helping to create a new commercial and professional elite. They moved out of the heart of the burgh into the first of the many new towns, the merchant city, in the 1760s. Once cotton was supreme, this area was increasingly colonised for commercial and, in some cases, industrial use. In the 1820s the middle class fled once more, to the drumlins of the Blythswood estate.[13] In the age of heavy engineering they were to flee yet farther west. A similar process occurred on the southern bank of the river, where the attempts at creating elegant Georgian suburbs failed as they were overwhelmed by industrial and commercial units, some of them large-scale. The working classes congregated in extensions of the old town, at the major canal ports like Port Dundas, but they also spread west and east, in the former case generally close to the river banks, providing ready access to work in iron foundries, docks and shipyards.

Through these processes, as has often been suggested, Glasgow had become a sort of combination of Manchester and Liverpool, a major industrial city and also a great port and shipbuilding centre. Its river was in effect a ship canal. The narrowness of the river ensured that the city grew as a great circle and not as a crescent, as in Liverpool. Rivers, canals, topography, historic layout as well as the legal and cultural bases of tenement building also ensured that these repeated overlayings and overlappings of imperial economic change took place within an extraordinarily tight compass, providing the city with one of the most pronounced population densities in Europe. This was of course a recipe for social deprivation, epidemics and high mortality on a massive scale, leading Glasgow to be described in the 1860s as possessing the greatest health and social problems, very much connected with its built environment, in the United Kingdom. Despite all the speculative efforts of private builders, building regulations, the City Improvement Trust and other aspects of municipal socialism, housing problems induced William Bolitho to publish a pamphlet in 1924 with a title offering a fresh twist to the city's imperial shibboleth, *The Cancer of Empire*.[14] The Second City thus developed a thoroughly unhealthy reputation, in which it yielded first place to none.

Glasgow indeed never seemed to do anything by halves. Between 1755 and 1821 it was the fastest-growing city in Western Europe, with a fourfold increase. Between 1801 and 1911 the population grew tenfold, a melting pot of peoples, with the grandest of architecture and the poorest of housing standards. By that time Glasgow far outranked all other Scottish cities in population or economic significance. It also had a less stable population. If in 1700 the obvious comparator was Edinburgh, by the second half of the nineteenth century the comparisons had become international. C. A. Oakley suggested that Glasgow was the sixth city of Europe.[15] The fascination with such figures surely stemmed from the fact that Glasgow had outgrown its immediate geographical context. From being just another Scottish royal burgh in the seventeenth century it had become a city of global significance.

This combination of growth and grandeur with poverty and social degradation created an imperial self-image which combined healthy pride and strength with social weakness, if not terminal illness. The remedy for the latter by the turn of the twentieth century was municipal socialism on a major scale, a quasi-social imperialism which fused its status as leading municipality and Second City. Such municipal socialism spread from the usual concern with water and gas supply to public health provisions (from hospitals to laundries, sewage and

refuse disposal), markets, lighting, veterinary and bacteriological services, civic reconstruction, building regulations (probably the tightest
in the country) and public transport. Such a convergence inevitably
underpinned all the city's spatial, social and cultural relations.

This necessary summary of the economic and social background is
familiar. But, surprisingly, the imperial dimensions of the social and
cultural history of the city have remained largely hidden. In the recent
historiography of Glasgow the British empire is everywhere, yet curiously nowhere. The indexes of the first two volumes of the new history
of the city contain barely any references to empire.[16] The close imperial economic connections are universally acknowledged, as they have
traditionally been in all works about the city. Implicitly, such economic relationships were fundamental to its class formations. Yet
nowhere are they carried through into interpretations of the character
of the built environment, urban society or cultural life.[17] Such silences
are not unique to Glasgow. It is intriguing to notice that Tony Lane's
Lawrence & Wishart history of Liverpool actually dropped the word
'empire' from its title when it was reissued.[18] Sean Damer's companion
volume also eschews imperialism throughout its analysis of the working-class history of the city.[19]

This silence is perhaps related to the dominance of class in Glasgow's radical social history, a desire to distance socialism from imperialism that would not be recognised by the early leaders and members
of socialist movements in the city. The history of the People's Palace,
built on Glasgow Green in the 1890s, neatly reflects this. Displays
which linked the working class with the regiments which recruited in
the city and were involved in imperial campaigns were removed in the
1980s for a more 'politically correct' people's history. A new radicalism, however, requires the globalising of the local, rendering redundant
such efforts to decontaminate social history.[20]

The most striking silence is in respect of slavery. Devine's book on
the Glasgow tobacco lords contains only two oblique references to
slaves or slavery.[21] The first two volumes of the new history contain
none at all. Yet the great merchants of the city, in their commercial
relations with the American colonies and the West Indies, and in their
ownership of plantations, were inevitably involved in both slave trading and ownership. Paintings and newspaper advertisements for run-
aways indicate the presence of slaves in the city. The controversy over
the retention or abolition of slavery was fought out between the city's
own pressure groups.[22] As in all major ports, a small population of
blacks was present from the eighteenth century, added to by Indian
sailors who came ashore in the nineteenth and early twentieth centuries. The latter often became itinerant pedlars, only later shopkeep-

ers and restaurateurs.[23] But the influence of empire on the social and cultural life of the city went deeper than the appearance of black faces in the streets.

It is now a commonplace that imperialism should be analysed in centripetal as well as centrifugal terms, that imperial influences should be seen as reflexive, not just as the radiating outwards of supposedly moral and material influences.[24] Jane Jacobs has recently redefined core and periphery in local terms, in which imperial relationships, encounters between first and fourth worlds, are re-constructed in spatial forms that are contiguous rather than globally separated.[25] The politics of imperial identity and power are thus reconfigured in adjacent space. Analyses of Glasgow's class differentiation similarly need to adopt the spatial, social and cultural perspectives of internal colonialism.

Glasgow was indeed just like the fast-growing cities of empire. Despite its older medieval and ecclesiastical origins, it was essentially a city of migrant workers, drawn in by the booming needs of the imperial economy. For much of the nineteenth century more than 50 per cent of the population were not born in the city. Glasgow's status as a rapidly developing industrial city and port, with growing employment opportunities, made it a magnet for both elective and forced migration. Poor harvests and near famine conditions brought Highlanders and other Scots to the city in the eighteenth century. In the 1810s and 1820s it absorbed many victims from the Clearances and in the 1840s and 1850s the destitute of the Irish potato famine. In 1831 there were already 35,000 people of Irish birth in the city. At the height of the famine Glasgow received as many as 8,000 Irish immigrants per week. Antisemitic persecutions and the suppression of national movements also brought in Jews and Poles. A considerable Italian community developed in the years before the First World War, followed later by Chinese, South Asians and Afro-Caribbeans.[26]

These migrant waves repeatedly colonised the poorest of housing, while the more settled working class moved out into the new areas of tenement blocks which stretched inland or along the banks of the river. As we have seen, the elite and middle classes of the city also moved outwards from the centre. This was a familiar pattern of city growth, but the spatial relations of class in Glasgow took distinctive forms. The exceptional tightness of the city's structure ensured that the classes often lived closer to each other than in other cities. The conventional east–west division is evident to a certain extent, but the classes lay in bands rising from the river. West of the decaying old city, working-class housing stretched along the banks of the river, north and south. Middle-class housing lay in a belt beyond this, enjoying the amenities of parks and higher land on the drumlins. Further working-class housing, as in Maryhill or Port Dundas, was often to be found beyond it. This spatial banding offered the middle classes valuable opportunities to colonise the working classes. Middle-class churches had 'missions' in the dockland areas. Efforts were made to convert immigrants, as in the Church of Scotland's Inland Mission to the Jews. Schools, Mechanics' Institutes (the first one in the country was founded in the city in 1823) and improving societies helped these processes. Youth organisations like the Foundry Boys' Religious Society (1867) and the Boys' Brigade (1883) followed similar patterns of working-class membership and lower middle or middle-class leadership. It is a surprising fact, and still open to some speculation, that Glasgow in the nineteenth century was largely free of really serious crime, such as murder, and, despite its cheap labour force and evidence of deprivation, had a more quiescent labour force and working class than many other cities. The city's structure, social organisation and building forms may have offered opportunities for social calming and the public architecture of social surveillance.[27]

Another factor seems to have been the strong sense of community which undoubtedly developed in the nineteenth century. In his study of imagined communities Benedict Anderson concentrates on nations, dynasties and cultural and linguistic groups.[28] But we surely need more analysis of cities as imagined communities. In the twentieth century, an Asian immigrant described himself as well content with Glasgow as his city state.[29] Indeed, it is just such a sense of a city state which runs through many of the nineteenth-century sources. Glasgow seemed to be in Scotland, but not wholly of Scotland. Its river was indeed a highway to empire, with the first stop North America, a notion which still informs some of the cultural life of the city.[30] Its role as a great social melting pot seemed to lend further opportunity for a distinctive sense of community. The city which is constantly renewing itself may well be a city which searches more assiduously for a distinct identity.

There were inevitably tensions among the immigrant communities and there is substantial evidence to suggest that each new group was feared, often discriminated against, and frequently made the butt of the humour of perceived racial differences. Highlanders, Irish and Jews all suffered such anxieties and taunts. Each gathered together into social and cultural groupings in churches, synagogues and societies, though they were never wholly ghettoised. Highland associations existed from the early eighteenth century (the first founded in 1727, to promote education among the immigrants to the city) and developed rapidly in the nineteenth. Highlanders, even if they were increasingly city-bred deracinated Highlanders, came to dominate the police force, a martial race policy in miniature. Similarly, the so-called Highland regiments, like the Highland Light Infantry, recruited most of their troops in the city. The Scottish soldier was less the representative of a Highland, pastoral, martial community than of endemically unemployed urban migrant workers. By the end of the century Catholics and Jews were also being recruited into the tartan, pipe-playing ranks. By that time Catholics and Protestants had established their 'uneasy peace', which from the 1870s found expression in the rivalry of the 'old firm', Rangers and Celtic.[31]

The dependence of these communities upon the imperial relationship was constantly visible in their everyday lives. The river, which was repeatedly used as an icon of the city, acted as a repeated reminder of connections with the wider world. Moreover, the middle and working classes seem to have shared a fascination with the Clyde, a river which in its upper reaches was polluted, smoking, alive with industry, shipping and employment but which downstream became a place of resorts, recreation and physical beauty, accessed by the very steamers that had made the city famous.[32] The grand homes of the elite, the holiday homes of the middle classes, the day trips of the working classes and, by the end of the nineteenth century, the annual week's holiday were all facilitated by the multifarious steamer services. The city exerted its power over the contrasting stretches of the river, its islands and sea lochs. Equally, in repeatedly extending its boundaries, in 1846, 1891 and 1912, often along the river banks, the city extended its own imperial rule over neighbouring burghs.

The river provided daily reminders of the greater empire beyond. The relations of Glasgow merchants and manufacturers with the empire had been apparent from the eighteenth century, as the business of the chamber of commerce and of pressure groups made apparent.[33] But, with the canalisation of the river, such connections became powerfully visible to all. From the mid-nineteenth century to the mid-twentieth, with some alarming cyclical fluctuations, the work of the shipyards was closely related to the imperial shipping lines, many of which were founded in or had close relations with the city. The builders Tod & McGregor produced the first economic screw steamship for deep-sea passenger trades, the *City of Glasgow*, in 1850. It was the proud boast of Connell's that for more than fifty years they were never without a vessel for the British India Steam Navigation Company on their stocks.[34] The Cunard, Anchor, Donaldson, City and Henderson lines all maintained loyalties to Clyde builders, as did Canadian-founded companies like Allan & Beaver. The Irrawaddy Flotilla Company, owned by P. & A. Henderson of Glasgow, had all its vessels built upon the Clyde.[35] These lines also sailed from the city, maintaining particularly close connections with Canada, India and Burma. Anchor Line vessels continued to carry freight and passengers from Yorkhill Quay, close to the city centre, to India until as recently as the late 1950s.

Countless other manufacturers developed a powerful iconography of empire in advertising and packaging their goods. These included products as diverse as the iron artefacts and structures of the city's many foundries, notably Walter Macfarlane's Saracen Works, and beverages such as Camp coffee and Tennent's India Pale Ale, favourites in the Indian empire. One of the city's heroes, Thomas Lipton, who opened his first grocery in 1871, created a notable instance of vertical integration in his ownership of Ceylon plantations, the processing of the leaf, and the packaging and sale of tea from the 1890s. His advertisements, with their slogan 'Direct from the tea garden to the tea pot', never failed to carry elephants, workers, scenery and shipping as part of their imperial imagery. Lipton owned one rubber and five tea estates, purchased in 1890, and he brought three Sinhalese servants to Britain, surely a conscious imitation of Queen Victoria's fascination with Indians. A committed Glaswegian of Protestant Irish origins, poor boy made good, his popular following was powerfully illustrated by the crowds lining the streets for his funeral in 1931. The fortune made in Ceylon and elsewhere was left largely to Glasgow charities.[36]

The companies that made up the North British Locomotive Company (amalgamated in 1903) built locomotives for the entire empire, a connection proudly displayed in their histories.[37] More than half their production went to the empire: their engines could be found on the railways of North and South America, Egypt, the Sudan, East, Central and South Africa, India, Ceylon, Malaya and Australasia, among other imperial territories. The entire community of Springburn was caught up in locomotive production in some way or another, and the shipment of the engines was a highly visible affair. During the history of these firms almost 30,000 locomotives were hauled out of the works through the streets of the city, by teams of Clydesdale horses, traction engines, and later by heavy diesel tractors, often before admiring crowds, to the 175 ton heavy lift crane at Stobcross Quay to be exported to the Empire or elsewhere (see Figure 35). In a Colonial Week in 1950 the company exhibited an engine for export to India in George Square. Even at that late date it was symbolic of the centrality of heavy industry, exporting and the empire (or former empire) in the city's life, displayed in what had become the most central square of the city. The sculptor George Wyllie's remarkable straw locomotive, hanging incongruously from this surviving crane, produced a real emotional response among Glaswegians.[38] In the end Wyllie symbolically burnt it.

Figure 35   A North British locomotive on its way to the Clyde for export to the Peiping Liaoning Railway in China, 1931

If the imperial economy was strikingly apparent, what of that other major area of visibility, the city's built environment? Some have seen the grid as the expression of imperial order, straight intersecting lines contrasting with the curves of nature and the concentric circles of much indigenous building around the world. Certainly Glasgow transformed itself from the curving streets of the medieval and early modern town into a city of successive grids. If the grid was essentially a product of the Enlightenment, its fashionable longevity over nearly two centuries came from the interaction of the model towns of home and the empire. Such imperial places were celebrated in street names such as Virginia, Havannah, Jamaica, Tobago and West Nile. In the Necropolis and the Southern Necropolis the city created burial grounds with monuments and statuary appropriate to its imperial status.[39]

But the city's architecture was more important in revealing a sense of global rather than local or national references. It was *sui generis*, illustrating an eclecticism which was quite unlike contemporary styles elsewhere in Britain. It resisted English influences, particularly the Gothic, and consciously sought to relate itself to a wider world.

Alexander Thomson, who was active between the 1840s and the 1870s, illustrates this well.[40] He had a brother who was a missionary in Africa and a brother-in-law in the army in India, imperial connections that must have been replicated among many members of the Glasgow middle class. Whether influenced by these connections or not, he was interested in the fundamentals of world architecture (including the African hut) and exhibited a distinct fascination with orientalism. He blended classical forms with striking Egyptian and Hindu elements, for example in his St Vincent Street and Queen's Cross churches, the latter destroyed by bombing in the Second World War.[41] Other examples of orientalism abound in the city, as do various cultural referents to Egypt and Greece, Rome and Venice. Sometimes such eclecticism was combined with highly innovative building techniques. Steel frame construction appeared in Glasgow almost contemporaneously with its use in Chicago. The city's banks and shipping headquarters, like those in St Vincent Place, were heavy with the symbolism of navigation and worldwide power. The enormously lavish City Chambers, built 1882–90, were designed to display the city's imperial wealth and significance, with many of the Classical and Renaissance features that became characteristic of the city's architecture in the later nineteenth century. The remarkable flowering of the arts in that period, in the Art Nouveau movement of Mackintosh and his associates or the paintings of the Glasgow Boys, also sought these wider connections, in this case in Vienna, North Africa or Japan.[42]

Of all the grand projects of municipal socialism, none evinced more excitement than the tapping of Loch Katrine in the Trossachs as the city's water supply. Opened in 1859 by Queen Victoria, this engineering and hydrological feat was celebrated as a triumph of Roman dimensions, a coming-of-age for the imperial city.[43] The connections with Scottish myth were obvious, with Rob Roy, Sir Walter Scott and the 'Lady of the Lake'. The natural world, in the shape of pure water from striking scenic surroundings, was brought to the centre of the city to banish the epidemics of waterborne diseases which had caused high mortality in recent years. The triumph was celebrated in a suitably gushing manner in the Scottish Gothic Stewart Memorial fountain of 1871–72 in a prominent position in Kelvingrove Park. That park also contains the vastly craggy statue of William Thomson, Lord Kelvin, professor of physics at the university for several decades, whose work on electromagnetism and electricity was placed at the service of the empire through the development of the telegraph and submarine cables.[44] Glasgow scientists were also responsible for the cyanide process which made the extraction of gold from the low-grade ores of the Rand possible.

Statuary was indeed one of the most prominent ways of celebrating empire in the city. The statues of imperial heroes like Colin Campbell, Lord Clyde, of Indian Mutiny fame, and David Livingstone are still prominently displayed, while the grandiloquent equestrian statue of Lord Roberts of Kandahar, displaying all his successes in India, the North West Frontier, Burma and South Africa, erected during the First World War, occupies the prime site at the front of Park Circus, facing the university. Through this bombastic display of imperial militarism, little 'Bobs', only remotely connected with Glasgow, becomes a giant symbol of the city's imperial connections. Perhaps the grandest piece of statuary is the Doulton fountain on Glasgow Green, erected there in 1890. This vast piece of Carrara stoneware terracotta has sculptures representing Canada, India, South Africa and Australia in its quadrants, with statues of Scottish, English and Welsh soldiers and a sailor above, with Queen Victoria inevitably surmounting all. Water was delivered through grand imperial lion masks.

This fountain had been designed and constructed for the Glasgow Exhibition of 1888, and indeed the cosmopolitanism of the city was neatly demonstrated in its penchant for exhibitions. No other British city outside London had such a successful series of major shows as those of 1888, 1901, 1911 and 1938, all powerfully emphasising the imperial connections of the city. Yet these exhibitions were only the most prominent of the many industrial, improving and didactic displays held in the city. The latter included industrial exhibitions in 1847, 1865, 1886–87 and 1890–91. They were all devoted to setting the industries and manufactures of the city in their wider global and imperial context while also displaying the products of other cultures, thereby improving and educating the working classes. These were the avowed aims of the 1865 show, held in the Trongate in association with the Glasgow Central Working Men's Club and Institute to promote 'the Social, Mental, and Moral Welfare and Recreation of the Industrial Classes'.[45] The Glasgow Industrial Exhibition at Burnbank, 1886–87, contained an Indian street with well stocked shops, together with exhibits by a number of Indian and Canadian companies, while the East End Exhibition of 1890–91 was specifically designed to bring some of the joys of the 1888 exhibition into working-class areas.[46] In the twentieth century there was a Civic and Empire Week in 1931 and a Century of Progress Exhibition in 1935, both of which stressed Glasgow's combination of municipal socialism, dominance in merchant and naval shipping, and imperial economic relations.[47] Colonial Weeks were held in other years, including one as late as 1950, already mentioned.

But it was the four great exhibitions which caught the imagination of the public and the attention of the press, publishers, companies and institutions in the city.[48] The first three were held in Kelvingrove Park, laid out on the banks of the Kelvin in the 1850s, supposedly to a design by Sir Joseph Paxton. The 1938 exhibition was at Bellahouston Park, south of the river, using Rangers' Ibrox home as its stadium. Although these exhibitions have been much studied, the manner in which they related imperialism to a Glaswegian and Scottish identity has been much less noticed. Each of them was indeed principally concerned with negotiating the identities of Glasgow, Scotland and the empire. Their supposed 'internationalism' was often satisfied by a few European exhibitors, but generally empire and Scottishness predominated. If the 1888 exhibition was a riot of orientalism, with its principal buildings known as 'Baghdad by the Kelvin', it also consciously sought to rival and exceed the recent exhibitions in London (the Colonial and Indian of 1886), Edinburgh (1886) and Manchester (1887), not only in the rather dubious game of number of admissions but also in the scale and grandeur of its exhibits and above all in its assertion of a distinct cultural identity. An Indian bazaar, with many Indian artisans and products for sale, competed with Canadian, Ceylonese and Burmese courts, but all these and other displays were related to Glasgow's position in invention, shipping and manufacture, as well as to Scottish history.[49] As is well known, the mixing of modernity with so-called native villages and also traditional towns from the host culture was common in exhibitions. This has usually been constructed as intending to draw powerful contrasts between enlightened new and benighted old, industrial and pre-industrial, contemporary civilisation and its absence in either geographically or chronologically distinct spaces.[50]

But a different approach is possible. Each of the Glasgow exhibitions was concerned to explore Scottishness in relation to the art and industry of the exhibition. It was not a remote Scottishness, uninformed and unreformed by modernity, but a Scottishness that gave a distinct meaning to Glasgow's industry and place in the modern world. Inevitably, these exhibitions accorded pride of place to the heavy industries of Glasgow, to the pioneering technology that had made the city globally significant. Thus in 1888 not only was there a magnificent assemblage of ship models, there were also models of engines, notably of the recently developed quadruple expansion engine, and of ships' accommodation. Walter Macfarlane's Saracen Iron Foundry, exporting throughout the empire, had a grandly orientalist display. But the emphasis on the Scottish past, particularly the realistic mock-up of the medieval bishop's palace, demolished more than 100 years earlier, on the archaeology and antiquarian concerns of Scotland, on the colossal statues of Burns and Scott, was intended to emphasise a distinctive historical and cultural identity which helped to explain not only the particular character of Glasgow but also its technical and imperial success. The profits of the exhibition were to fund a School of Art, a Museum and Art Gallery, a Scottish response to the South Kensington ambitions of 1851 and 1862.[51] The painting by Sir John Lavery (another Glaswegian of Irish extraction) of Queen Victoria opening the exhibition depicts a municipal imperial durbar, civic and mercantile power assembled around the Queen seated on a canopied throne. The city state becomes a miniature empire. The exhibition also promoted Scotland as a destination for tourism, as a romantic and sublime landscape worthy to be visited in association with the exhibition.

This counterpoint between Scottishness, imperialism and modernity, also between city, river and landscape, runs through all the succeeding exhibitions. The 1901 exhibition in some respects marked the bringing to fruition of the ambitions of 1888. The new Art Gallery, an outrageously eclectic red sandstone creation, now stood as the centrepiece of the exhibition. Once more, there were strongly orientalist elements: the city's business was represented in four huge 'triumph of navigation' sculptures; the ship models were joined by a magnificent display of the Glasgow locomotives that ruled the rails of the empire. Those cultural icons Burns and Scott, prominent in stone in 1888, reappeared in soap. Imperial territories predominated, and the whole event had a more didactic and idealistic feel to it than the private London equivalents of the day. It proclaimed itself the largest exhibition ever held in Britain, and once again brought together exhibits from many colonies, including the recently conquered Rhodesia. The Indian Theatre and the Japanese pavilion were notable features, as was yet another bazaar with wood, ivory, precious stone and metal wares 'from the skilled hands of Hindu mechanics', organised by the Indian firms of Framju Bhumgaro & Ardeshir and Byramjir.[52] The profits of the exhibition were contributed to the art purchase fund of the new galleries.

The 1911 exhibition was specifically designed to promote the Scottish cultural renaissance, which had already had its manifestations around the imperial world in the founding of Caledonian Societies, the holding of Highland Games and the erection of statues of Burns (several in Australia, for example). The very name of the exhibition, the Scottish Exhibition of National History, Art and Industry, made this clear. It laid considerable emphasis on the Scottish past, on celebrating the memory of distinguished Scotsmen and on Scotland's contribution to the world, while its profits were to found a chair of Scottish History and Literature at Glasgow University. Lord Kelvin's Atlantic cables were celebrated, as was the contribution of Scots to Canada. The Auld Toun and the Highland clachan, emphasising respectively Lowland

and Gaelic culture, coexisted with the latest technology like the cinematograph and aviation. The Scottish Aeronautical Society and the Scottish National Antarctic Expedition both had prominent displays. Shipping companies, engineering achievements and modern developments in nautical instrumentation, Glasgow's distinctive contribution to the world, were all emphasised in dominant displays. An innovation was a display on forestry, a major development of the empire in the period, and one to which Scots had made a particular contribution. Historical pageants, often a feature of the great exhibitions, concentrated on Wallace, Bruce, Mary Queen of Scots, Charles Edward Stuart and the inevitable Burns and Scott.

The traditional emphasis on Glasgow's industries was repeated, and it is perhaps not surprising that there were pilgrimages of Scottish Americans as well as parties of New Zealanders to the exhibition. Interestingly, Scottish art was given considerable prominence. The 1911 exhibition emphasised yet again that Glasgow's cultural amalgam of Scottishness enabled it to make its own major contribution to the economy of empire. The imperial city state, its own imagined community, connected itself with a variety of local, national and international economic and cultural constituencies.[53] Indeed, it was sometimes said to be a sort of Scottish Venice. La Serenissima it was not, but the claim underlined the notion of a great trading city state, connector of East and West, dependent on water for its livelihood.

The 1938 exhibition, the last imperial exhibition in the British sequence, once more had a Highland clachan as a cultural centrepiece. This clachan was surely meant to symbolise a historically distinctive genius, reasonably appropriate for a city positioned very close to the geological Highland line and with a major Highland community in its midst, which could be reconstituted for the modern world. For this idyllic vision of a rural past was displayed within a dramatically modernist architectural context (see Figure 36). Unlike Wembley's failure to promote any contemporary style, the 1938 buildings were uniformly and dramatically Art Deco, and by a Glasgow firm of architects. It illustrated a 'new model Scotland in built form', engineering and architecture dedicated to both national romanticism and imperial renewal, an abiding theme of the new media of the 1930s, film and the radio. The exhibition was consciously designed to raise Scottish industry out of the 1930s depression and to fit with the economic ethos of the Empire Marketing Board and the Ottawa agreements. It featured the displays of forty colonies and many local and national companies. Yet again, regeneration was portrayed as the inevitable consequence of linking Scottish genius with imperial markets.

As Glasgow and the empire declined, and as Europe seemed an

Figure 36 Tait's tower at the 1938 Glasgow Empire Exhibition rising above the funfair

increasingly dangerous place, the imperial rhetoric was enhanced. The exhibition was described as representing for a summer the 'Metropolis of Empire', Scotland's 'call to the uttermost ends of the earth', 'in the widest sense a University of Empire', an empire described as a 'Federation for Peace, for Progress and for Prosperity'.[54] The contribution of Scots was celebrated in a remarkable article by the historian J. D. Mackie, and Scotsmen were described as holding the highest offices of state throughout the empire.[55] Glasgow, the 'sea-born city and gateway of the Empire', the progressive city of municipal socialism, had contributed Scots who 'in the far-flung outposts of the Empire. ... never lose their identity. First and last they are Scotsmen, bound by ties of race and blood, by traditions and customs which, while their outward forms may change with the passing of the centuries, their inward and spiritual significance remain rooted in the heart.'[56] The Church of Scotland even dared to have a mural of the failed Darien scheme of the 1690s, which had helped to precipitate the Union of 1707, in its pavilion. David Livingstone, almost inevitably, was given pride of place in the Scottish pavilion, and Scotland's own position in another empire was stressed in an exhibit on the Roman Antonine Wall. Featured commodities included cotton, tea and rubber, and Glasgow was described as manufacturing no fewer than 2,000 commodities for export to an empire vastly larger than itself. As if to prove the point, the special connection between Glasgow and Burma was prominent.[57]

The number of visitors to the exhibitions ranged from 5,748,379 for 1888, close to London's 1886 figure, to 11.5 million for 1901, 9.37 million in 1911 and 12.6 million in 1938.[58] Only the 1938 exhibition made a loss, the others contributing notably to the causes for which they were organised. They entered the folklore of the city and certainly contributed to the sense of a wider global identity which was confirmed by the city's relationship with empire. The 1938 event also indicates just how enduring the imperial vision was, a continuation of late nineteenth-century ideas up to the Second World War which is closely related not only to the imperial content of the cinema and juvenile literature in the period but also to a powerfully imperial strand in Scottish nationalism.[59]

This same negotiation of the city's imperial identity can be found in many other cultural manifestations which also spanned a long chronological period, though we need a good deal of further research on them. It can be found, I strongly suspect, in the city's dominant Liberal Unionism and therefore liberal imperialism, and in the strength of its Conservatism after the Second World War. It can also be discovered in the many societies devoted to imperial issues, including those of women – for example, the Glasgow Ladies' Colonial Association and the Glasgow Ladies' Association for the Advancement of Female Education in India.[60] We need more research into the connections between the city's businessmen and missionary societies – for example, Sir William Mackinnon's evangelical ambitions in the 1870s and 1880, and the role of Lord Overtoun and others in funding the Free Church missions in Central Africa.[61] David Livingstone was of course appropriated by the city, at least by virtue of his education at the Andersonian Institution and his friendship with James 'Paraffin' Young. The paradigm and paragon of Smilesian self-help, he was given the freedom of the city and an honorary degree of the university.[62] Judged by the number of biographies published, his heroic imperial status was stressed in church, Sunday school, youth organisation and schools until the 1950s.

Many of these concerns came together with the founding of the Royal Scottish Geographical Society in 1884–85 and the survival of the society as a major cultural and intellectual force until modern times. It is true that the main initiative for its establishment came from Edinburgh, but the Glasgow branch was an important one in terms of membership and the connections with the shipping, evangelical and business communities.[63] The first ten years of its existence were very much bound up with Africa, almost inevitably the continent of the moment, given the publicity surrounding the partition. Early lecturers to the society stressed the Scottish contribution to and particular aptitude in connection with that continent, and significant contributions were made to the funding of the Emin Pasha relief expedition. Only later was Africa overtaken by the fascination with Antarctic exploration. Scotland's own independently funded national expedition set out in 1898 and was prominently featured in the 1911 Glasgow exhibition. We need a good deal more research specifically into the Glasgow branch of the RSGS, as well as into many other societies, not to mention cultural manifestations like panoramas, the music hall, pantomimes and other theatrical events. What, for example, was the Glasgow audience's reaction to Sir Henry Irving's debut in *The Indian Revolt, or, the Relief of Lucknow* in 1860?[64]

In relentlessly pursuing the shibboleth of 'Second City of the Empire' and other extravagant claims, the Glasgow elite was surely in the business of negotiating a distinct municipal identity, a means whereby a complex and potentially explosive ethnic mix could manufacture, or have manufactured for it, an imagined community which defined itself in relation to Scotland, England, the United Kingdom and the empire. Whether it meant much to the most deprived ends of the community, those packed together around the staggering number of shebeens and brothels of the old town near the High Street, or later in the notorious single ends of the tenement slums, must remain a matter of conjecture. Yet even they may have had relatives in the empire or may have seen the dominions as some kind of Shangri-la. Certainly, for the rest the evidence tentatively suggests that there was a culture of pride and consolation, in which work and emigration, religion and education, rational recreation and culture could be connected with a distinct contribution to a global enterprise.

Scots have long required a larger entity to which they could cleave in order to create an identity separate from that of their dominant neighbour.[65] Before the Union, and for the Jacobites up to 1746, the Auld Alliance with France performed that function. To a certain extent, it was also fulfilled by Scottish trading relations with Scandinavia and the Low Countries, as well as by the exploits of mercenary Scots soldiers in Russia and elsewhere. But, from the enthusiastic response to the opportunities of empire in the eighteenth century, Scots saw the 'British' empire as their ideal world stage. Scottishness was thus complemented by a wider British imperial identification.

In these ways Scots were able to globalise their sense of imagined community. Not for nothing did Sir Walter Scott refer to India as 'the Corn Chest for Scotland, where we poor gentry must send our youngest sons as we send our black cattle to the South'. The enterprising, clannish and thrusting Scot became a byword throughout the empire, much commented upon by imperial writers and travellers.[66]

Moreover, if the administration, law and institutions of empire were usually English in origin, the Scots spread their religion, social ethic, civic powers, educational traditions, aspects of their culture, and their technical and natural history interests around the empire.[67] The number of Scots in India, in colonial governorships or in technical, botanical and forestry services always seems to have exceeded the proportion that might be expected from the relative size of their population in the United Kingdom. The same search for a larger identity continues with the modern nationalist/internationalist cry (albeit strongly contested in Scottish nationalism) of 'Scotland and Europe', neatly replacing 'Scotland and the empire'.

When J. A. Froude visited Sandhurst, near Ballarat, in the Australian colony of Victoria in early 1885 its Scots mayor told him 'We want more Scots. Give us Scots. Give us the whole population of Glasgow.'[68] It is an awesome thought, particularly taken in conjunction with a recent estimate that there are some 10 million descendants of Glaswegians in the Commonwealth.[69] Given the capacity of Glasgow repeatedly to renew itself, it was unlikely that the mayor would get his wish, but his cry encapsulates a significant point about the city. Just as Scots negotiated their identity in relation to the worldwide connections of empire, so too did Glasgow see its destiny as surpassing the purely local concerns of Scotland or even the United Kingdom. The 'Second City of the Empire' idea was something more than a statistical point. It represented a relationship that was fundamental to its notion of a city state, a global pride in economic and social connections capable of welding its disparate population into a specifically civic and imperial identity. More than an empty boast, it was the embodiment of whole sets of ethnic, class and cultural relations.

Notes

I am particularly indebted to Jack Davis and his staff at the History and Glasgow Room of the Mitchell Library in Glasgow for much help in tracking down materials relating to the relationship between the city and the empire.

1 J. K. McDowell, *The People's History of Glasgow* (Glasgow, Hay Nisbet, 1899), preface, quoted in David Daiches, *Glasgow* (London, Deutsch, 1977), p. 191.

2 W. Hamish Fraser and Irene Maver, 'Tackling the problems' in W. Hamish Fraser and Irene Maver (eds), *Glasgow, II, 1830–1912* (Manchester, Manchester University Press, 1996), p. 433.

3 T. M. Devine and Gordon Jackson (eds), *Glasgow, I, Beginnings to 1830* (Manchester, Manchester University Press, 1995), introduction, p. 10.

4 C. A. Oakley, *The Second City* (London and Glasgow, Blackie, 1946).

5 Tony Lane, *Liverpool: Gateway of Empire* (London, Lawrence & Wishart, 1987), p. 77.

6 Michael S. Moss and John R. Hulme, *Workshop of the British Empire: Engineering and Shipbuilding in the West of Scotland* (London, Heinemann, 1977).

7 James McGrath, 'The medieval and early modern burgh', and Gordon Jackson,

'Glasgow in transition, *c.* 1660 to *c.* 1740', in Devine and Jackson, *Glasgow*, pp. 17–105.

8 See some of the contributions to T. C. Smout (ed.), *Scotland and Europe, 1200–1850* (Edinburgh, John Donald, 1986) and T. C. Smout (ed.), *Scotland and the Sea* (Edinburgh, John Donald, 1992). See also Christopher Smout, 'The culture of migration: Scots as Europeans, 1500–1800', *History Workshop Journal*, 40 (1995), pp. 108–17.

9 Jackson, 'Glasgow in transition', p. 72.

10 T. M. Devine, 'The golden age of tobacco', in Devine and Jackson, *Glasgow*, pp. 139–83.

11 Moss and Hulme, *Workshop of the British Empire*, p. 1.

12 The Glasgow West India Association and the Glasgow East India Association were two of the most notable.

13 Andrew Gibb, *Glasgow: The Making of a City* (London, Croom Helm, 1983) offers the most useful description of the growth of the city. For the Blythswood estate see pp. 95–100.

14 William Bolitho, *The Cancer of Empire* (London, Putnam, 1924).

15 Oakley, *Second City*, p. v.

16 There are none in volume I and six in volume II.

17 The second volume of the Manchester Glasgow history contains nothing on the theatre, parks, museums, exhibitions, statuary, street furniture, shows, art collections, the press, holidays or other aspects of the city's cultural life. Material on churches, societies and associations is also rather restricted. References to sport, architecture and the city's layout can be found in W. Hamish Fraser, 'The working class', and James Schmiechen, 'Glasgow of the imagination: architecture, townscape and society', in Fraser and Maver, *Glasgow*, pp. 300–51 and 486–518, although on the latter's showing the city's imagination was pretty restricted. Oakley, *Second City*; Daiches, *Glasgow*; Maurice Lindsay, *Portrait of Glasgow* (London, Robert Hale, 1972); and Jack House, *The Heart of Glasgow* (London, Hutchinson, 1972), are all superior in this regard.

18 *Liverpool: Gateway of Empire* became *Liverpool: City of the Sea* (London, Lawrence & Wishart, 1990).

19 Sean Damer, *Glasgow: Going For a Song* (London, Lawrence & Wishart, 1990).

20 Some of these ideas are developed in Felix Driver and Raphael Samuel, 'Rethinking the idea of place', editorial, and Doreen Massey, 'Places and their pasts', *History Workshop Journal*, 39 (1995), pp. v–vi, 182–92.

21 T. M. Devine, *The Tobacco Lords: A Study of the Tobacco Merchants of Glasgow and their Trading Activities* c. 1740–90 (1975; Edinburgh, Edinburgh University Press, 1990) pp. 59, 62.

22 The Glasgow West India Association fought for the retention of slavery, but there was also a powerful branch of the Anti-Slavery Committe (Records of the Glasgow West India Association, 1807–1969, the Mitchell Library, Glasgow). The papers of the Glasgow Emancipation Society and various other abolitionist material can also be found in the Mitchell Library. See also the interesting references to Glasgow in J. R. Oldfield, *Popular Politics and British Anti-slavery: The Mobilisation of Public Opinion against the Slave Trade, 1787–1807* (Manchester, Manchester University Press, 1995).

23 Mary Edward, *Who Belongs to Glasgow? 200 Years of Migration* (Glasgow City Libraries, 1993), pp. 120–34.

24 John M. MacKenzie, *Propaganda and Empire: The Manipulation of British Public Opinion, 1880–1960* (Manchester, Manchester University Press, 1984). See also my chapters in the forthcoming (1999) *Oxford History of the British Empire*, Andrew Porter (ed.), *The Nineteenth Century*, and Judith Brown and W. Roger Louis (eds), *The Twentieth Century*.

25 Jane M. Jacobs, *Edge of Empire: Postcolonialism and the City* (London and New York, Routledge, 1996).

26 For population figures see Gibb, *Glasgow*; Devine and Jackson (eds), *Glasgow*; Fraser

and Maver (eds), *Glasgow, passim*. Edward, *Who Belongs to Glasgow?*, provides a useful introduction to immigrant communities, another theme largely absent from the Manchester histories.

27 Schmiechen, 'Glasgow of the imagination', offers some suggestions for the notion of architectural social calming: Fraser and Maver, *Glasgow*, pp. 92–3. These could perhaps be developed further along the lines of Tony Bennett's Foucauldian analysis in *The Birth of the Museum: History, Theory, Politics* (London, Routledge, 1995).

28 Benedict Anderson, *Imagined Communities* (London, Verso, 1991).

29 Edward, *Who Belongs to Glasgow?*, p. 133.

30 See, for example, Tom Cox, 'West End pearls', *Guardian*, G2, 16 January 1998, pp. 12–13, on the distinctive character and considerable success of popular music in the city. This was described as stemming from the international character of the city and its 'port mentality': 'The next stop is America.'

31 Oakley, *Second City*, pp. 165–8.

32 By 1825 there were already fifty-three steam pleasure craft and passenger steamers on the Clyde. The number grew considerably later in the century. Gordon Jackson and Charles Munn, 'Trade, commerce and finance' in Fraser and Maver, *Glasgow*, pp. 58–60.

33 Microfilms of the papers of the Glasgow Chamber of Commerce, the West India Association and the East India Association, Minutes and Correspondence, 1812–14 and 1829–47, are in the Mitchell Library.

34 Moss and Hulme, *Workshop of the British Empire*, p. 1.

35 Captain H. J. Chubb and C. L. D. Duckworth, *The Irrawaddy Flotilla Company, 1865–1950*, (London, National Maritime Museum, 1973).

36 Sir Thomas J. Lipton, Bt, *Leaves from the Lipton Logs* (London, Hutchinson, 1931), pp. 174–80; Oakley, *Second City*, pp. 224–5; Bob Crampsey, *The King's Grocer: The Life of Sir Thomas Lipton* (Glasgow City Libraries, 1995).

37 *The History of the North British Locomotive Company Ltd* (privately printed, Glasgow, North British Locomotive Company, 1953). For the significance of locomotive building to the community of Springburn and the people of Glasgow see Murdoch Nicolson and Mark O'Neill, *Glasgow: Locomotive Builder to the World* (Glasgow, Polygon, 1987).

38 Nicolson and O'Neill, *Glasgow: Locomotive Builder*, frontispiece and p. 3; personal reminiscence and interview with Wyllie, 1990.

39 Charlotte Hutt (ed.), *City of the Dead: The Story of Glasgow's Southern Necropolis* (Glasgow City Libraries, 1996), contains information on many significant figures buried in the Southern Necropolis, including Lipton and Robert Paterson, the inventor of Camp coffee.

40 Ronald McFadzean, *The Life and Work of Alexander Thomson* (London, Routledge, 1979); for Thomson's imperial family connections see pp. 18, 186.

41 For the churches, see McFadzean, *Life and Work*, pp. 98–101, 158–61 and *passim*; see also Miles Glendinning, Ranald MacInnes and Aonghus MacKechnie, *A History of Scottish Architecture* (Edinburgh, Edinburgh University Press, 1996), chapter 6; Andor Gomme and David Walker, *Architecture of Glasgow* (London, Lund Humphries, 1968), chapter 6.

42 Robert Macleod, *Charles Rennie Mackintosh, Architect and Artist* (London, Harper Collins, 1968); Pamela Robertson (ed.), *Charles Rennie Mackintosh: The Architectural Papers* (Wendlebury, White Cockade, 1990); Roger Billcliffe, *The Glasgow Boys* (London, Murray, 1985). Much detailed information on buildings, parks, statues and fountains can be found in Elizabeth Williamson, Anne Riches and Malcolm Higgs, *The Buildings of Scotland: Glasgow* (London, Penguin, 1990).

43 It was described as 'worthy of the Roman Empire' in the 'Civic and Empire Week Programme', Glasgow, 29 May to 6 June 1931, p. 27.

44 Crosbie Smith and M. Norton Wise, *Energy and Empire: A Biographical Study of Lord Kelvin* (Cambridge, Cambridge University Press, 1989).

45 'Glasgow, East End Industrial Exhibition of Manufactures, Science and Art, December 1890–21 April 1891: Official Catalogue', 1891.

46 'Glasgow, Industrial Exhibition Catalogue', 1865; 'Review of the Glasgow Industrial Exhibition at Burnbank, 1886–87'.

47 'Civic and Empire Week Programme', 1931; 'Century of Progress Exhibition, 6-18 May 1935, Kelvin Hall', official handbook and programme.

48 Perilla Kinchin and Juliet Kinchin, *Glasgow's Great Exhibitions, 1888, 1901, 1911, 1938, 1988* (Wendlebury, White Cockade, 1988).

49 Albums of cuttings, Glasgow Exhibition, 1888, Mitchell Library, Glasgow.

50 MacKenzie, *Propaganda and Empire*, chapter 4; Paul Greenhalgh, *Ephemeral Vistas: the Expositions Universelles, Great Exhibitions and World's Fairs, 1851–1939* (Manchester, Manchester University Press, 1988), chapter 4; Burton Benedict, *The Anthropology of World's Fairs: San Francisco's Panama Pacific International Exposition of 1915* (London and Berkeley CA, Scolar Press, 1983).

51 Kinchin and Kinchin, *Great Exhibitions*, p. 19.

52 'Glasgow International Exhibition, 1901: The Official Guide', p. 27; see also 'Glasgow International Exhibition, 1901: The Official Catalogue' and albums of official cards, agendas and photographs in the Mitchell Library collection.

53 'Official Catalogue, Scottish Exhibition, Glasgow, 1911'.

54 *The Glasgow Herald, Empire Exhibition, Special Number*, Thursday 28 April 1938, p. 37; G. F. Maine (ed.), *Scotland's Welcome*, 1938 (London and Glasgow, Collins, 1938), foreword by the Earl of Elgin and address by the Lord Provost of Glasgow.

55 *Glasgow Herald, Empire Exhibition*, 'The building of the empire; great part played by Scotsmen', by J. D. Mackie, pp. 59–61.

56 Maine, *Scotland's Welcome*, p. 30

57 'Glasgow Empire Exhibition, 1938: Official Guide'; 'Empire Exhibition, Glasgow, 1938: Official Catalogue'; 'Guide to the Pavilion of HM Government in the United Kingdom, Empire Exhibition, Scotland, 1938'; 'Guide to the Scottish Pavilion, Empire Exhibition, Glasgow, 1938'; *Scotland Magazine*, autumn 1938; *Empire Exhibition, Scotland, Bellahouston Park, 1938*, published by the Daily Record and Evening News; 'An Clachan, the Highland Village: Official Guide', 1938; Bob Crampsey, *The Empire Exhibition of 1938: The Last Durbar* (Edinburgh, Mainstream, 1988).

58 Kinchin and Kinchin, *Great Exhibitions*, pp. 53, 93, 125, 166.

59 MacKenzie, *Propaganda and Empire*, chapters 3, 8; John M. MacKenzie, 'On Scotland and the Empire', *International History Review*, 15 (1993) 736–39. See also Raphael Samuel, 'British dimensions: "four nations" history', *History Workshop Journal*, 40 (1995) iii–xxii.

60 Stana Nenadic, 'The Victorian middle classes', in Fraser and Maver, *Glasgow*, p. 288.

61 John McCracken, *Politics and Christianity in Malawi, 1875–1940* (Cambridge, Cambridge University Press, 1977), chapter 1; Sir Harry H. Johnston, *The Story of my Life* (London, Chatto & Windus, 1923).

62 For the wider implications and durability of the Livingstone myth see John M. MacKenzie, 'David Livingstone: the construction of the myth', in Graham Walker and Tom Gallagher (eds), *Sermons and Battle Hymns: Protestant Popular Culture in Modern Scotland* (Edinburgh, Edinburgh University Press, 1990), pp. 24–42.

63 John M. MacKenzie, 'The provincial geographical societies in Britain, 1884–1914' in Morag Bell, Robin Butlin and Michael Heffernan (eds), *Geography and Imperialism, 1820–1940* (Manchester, Manchester University Press, 1995), p. 101; Elspeth N. Lochhead, 'Scotland as the cradle of modern academic geography', *Scottish Geographical Magazine*, 97 (1981) 98–109.

64 Daiches, *Glasgow*, p. 186.

65 MacKenzie, 'Scotland and the empire'.

66 See for example, Sir Charles Wentworth Dilke, *Greater Britain* (London, Macmillan, 1872), pp. 373-4, 533; Anthony Trollope, *Australia* (London, Chapman & Hall, 1873), p. 420.

67 This notion is based on George Elder Davie, *The Democratic Intellect: Scotland and her Universities in the Nineteenth Century* (Edinburgh, Edinburgh University Press, 1961); MacKenzie, 'Scotland and the empire', pp. 722, 732–9; John D. Hargreaves,

Academe and Empire: Some Overseas Connections of Aberdeen University, 1860–1970 (Aberdeen, Aberdeen University Press, 1994); John M. MacKenzie, *Empires of Nature and the Nature of Empires: Imperialism, Scotland and the Environment* (East Linton, Tuckwell, 1997), pp. 65–70.

68 J. A. Froude, *Oceana, or, England and her Colonies* (London, Longman, 1886), p. 116.
69 R. A. Cage (ed.), *The Scots Abroad* (London, Croom Helm, 1985), editor's introduction (not paginated).

CHAPTER THIRTEEN

Sartorial spectacle: clothing and masculine identities in the imperial city, 1860–1914

Christopher Breward

In 1888 the British social realist writer Richard Whiteing published a novel entitled *The Island, or, An Adventure of a Person of Quality* that presaged many of the concerns of the *fin-de-siècle*, particularly those relating to the formation of modern urban identities. While the title of the work itself suggests that trope of exploratory, sometimes futuristic or utopian, escapism employed at various moments of historical crisis by writers as temporally diverse as Daniel Defoe and William Golding, it is more closely reminiscent of those exotic 'colonial' narratives penned around 1900 by Joseph Conrad, Rudyard Kipling, Rider Haggard and H. G. Wells. Many of these authors' works might be described as male romance epics offering the reader spectacular yet safe geographical and psychic spaces for the negotiation of pressing contemporary subjects. What is especially significant here, however, is the contrived familiarity of Whiteing's portrayal of London's financial centre at the height of its economic and cultural power, a site which offers a commonplace setting for those themes of alienation, exoticism and modernity explored by contemporary commentators. In this chapter I wish to consider how *fin-de-siècle* imperial preoccupations, together with an escalating sense of decadence or imminent collapse in the face of rapid social change, related to the experience of the urban everyday and the formation of metropolitan identities. More specifically, I aim to draw out the connections between imperial aspirations and metropolitan realities in the realm of men's clothing and physical appearance in the period between 1880 and 1914.

A focus on men's clothing can help to illustrate the ways in which the increased consumer activity and the enhanced visibility of sartorial practices characteristic of the period indicated deeper social, sexual and racial tensions. Thus changes in the nature and representation of fashion-related consumption can be mapped directly on to the negotiation of cultural exchanges at street level, in a reading of modern city life that acknowledges masculinity as a pivotal, though shifting, co-ordinate. Imperialism, in this sense, should be considered as integral to the formation of new urban identities, another 'co-ordinate' whose effects conditioned the manner in which men consumed and behaved. Here the body and the city seem to merge.

Between 1860 and 1914 London was frequently conceived of as a series of spatial relationships, from east to west and centre to suburb. More pertinently, the contrasts between these districts were often illustrated by recourse to descriptions of clothing, or a suggestion of its metaphorical uses as a marker of boundaries and an indicator of status. In a passage from his impressionistic text *The Soul of London* (1904) Ford Madox Ford elegantly described the varying perspectives involved in an imagining of the modern metropolis. Here architectural style and spatial configurations carry with them all the trappings of the dandy's descriptive repertoire, as much imbued with subjective notions of taste as any critique of the contents in a tailor's window display:

> Speaking broadly, the man who expresses himself with a pen on paper sees his London from the west. At worst he hopes to end with that view. His London of breathing space, his West End, extends from say Chiswick to say Portland Place. His dense London is the city as far as Fenchurch Street, his East End ends with what he calls Whitechapel. The other sees his London of elbow room extend from say Purfleet to say Blackwall. He is conscious of having, as it were at his back, the very green and very black stretches of the Essex Marshes dotted with large solitary factories and small solitary farms. His dense London, his city, lies along the line from Blackwall to Fenchurch Street. Beyond that the City proper, the City of the Bank and the Mansion House, is already a place rather of dilettante trifling. Its streets are tidied up, its buildings ornamented and spacious. The end of the West End is for him Piccadilly Fountain, and this latter quarter of large, almost clean, stone buildings, broad swept streets, and a comparative glare of light, is already a foreign land, slightly painful because it is so strange.[1]

The hold of constructions such as these on the popular imagination was a powerful one, though their reflection on the ground offers up more problematic issues relating to the definition of 'imperialism' itself.[2] My more limited intention here is to interrogate such texts for the signs they reveal of a 'sartorial' engagement with the 'contradictions and tensions' of the imperial city. An examination of the spatial, commercial and social relations implicated in that engagement entails an understanding of the nineteenth-century city that owes much to Lynda Nead's recent revision of debates concerning the circulation of power in the Victorian urban environment. Her comments provide a useful opening framework. She states that:

within the sites of the modern metropolis identity was diverse, unfixed and open to constant negotiation. Subjectivity was not already in place when men and women occupied the streets of Victorian London, but was formed through the encounters, interactions and experiences of that occupation. Social space, in this context, is not a passive backdrop to the formation of identity, but is part of the active ordering and organizing of the social and cultural relations of the city.[3]

'Cog and fly and crank': clothing, crowds and the sublime machinery of city life

Richard Whiteing made 'the active ordering and organizing of the social and cultural relations of the city' an explicit prop for his description of its crowded hub in 1888:

> It was such a sight – civilization in a nutshell – that was what made me pause. I was a part of it, and Apollo was taking a peep at his own legs ... What a scene ! The Exchange I had just left, with its groups of millionaires gossiping, Baghdad and the Irawaddy, Chicago and the Cape; dividend day over at the bank yonder, and the well known sight of the Blessed going to take their quarterly reward; a sheriff's coach turning the angle of the Mansion House (breakfast to an African pro-consul I believe), a vanishing splendour of satin and plush and gold; dandy clerks making for Birch's with the sure and certain hope of a partnership in their early grace; shabby clerks making for the bun shops; spry brokers going to take the odds against Egyptians, and with an appropriate horsiness of air, a parson ... itinerant salesmen of studs, pocket combs and universal watch keys; flower girls at the foot of the statue, a patch of colour; beggar at the foot of the steps, another patch, the red shirt beautifully toned down in wear ... eruption of noisy crowd from the Cornhill corner (East End marching West to demonstrate for the right to a day's toil for a day's crust); thieves and bludgeon men, and stone men in attendance on demonstration; detectives in attendance on thieves; shutters up at the Jeweller's as they pass .... And, for background, the nondescript thousands in black and brown and russet and every neutral hue, with the sun over all, and between the sun and the thousands the London mist.
>
> It was something as a picture, but so much more as a thought. What a wonder of parts and whole! What a bit of machinery! The beggars and occasionally the stock jobbers and the nondescripts to go wrong; the policeman to take them up; the parson to show the way of repentance; and the sheriff to hang them, if need be, when all was done. With this, the dandies to adorn the scene – myself not altogether unornamental – the merchants, the clerks, and the dividend takers, all but cog and fly and crank of the same general scene. What a bit of machinery![4]

In her recent work on British fiction in the 1890s Lynn Hapgood alludes to Whiteing's technique of 'textual disorientation' in this almost cinematic and self–consciously sublime passage. This vitally important narrative moment, when the author looks back from his island refuge to the day of his decision to leave the corruption of the City, realises a complex sense of distance in geographical and chronological space through the stilted language of reportage and the glancing imagery of impressionism. What is not distanced, according to Hapgood, is the psychic impact of the experience, though the two are closely related. She points out that:

> Whiteing suggests that topographical viewpoint – from where one looks – is inseparable from mental viewpoint – what one is open to seeing. Physical and mental viewpoints determine together what one perceives, so that the concrete world cannot be guaranteed to have an objective existence. This symbiotic relationship between the physical eye and the inner eye gives sharpness and precision to the concept of social determinism and reveals both the collective nature of social experience and the struggle of individuals to transcend it.[5]

All, then, was disorientating in Whiteing's London at the close of the nineteenth century; the seemingly ordered machine of empire, commerce and late capitalism, barely containing those notes of unrest and apprehensiveness evidenced through the ever shifting restiveness of the crowd and the fashionable *ennui* of the narrator. Yet at the same time the actors contained in its melee conformed to a fixed and precise hierarchy marked by an outward appearance that confirmed the spectator's preconceptions of class and caste.

Beyond the literary imagination, however, the historical relationship between fashion and masculinity was expressed more tenuously in the fraught and narrow cultural space given over to its manifestation and discussion in the nineteenth century. Though the identification of social origins through the quality of clothing was unproblematic, an assumed association between fashion and effeminacy raised particular problems for the communication of masculine values by sartorial means. Indeed, the social meaning of masculine clothing remains difficult to unearth even now, thanks to the reluctance of Victorian men to record or conserve this area of their lives in any coherent sense, other than to renounce its articulation as a form of social display.[6] Given this perceived 'lack', the richest descriptions of sartorial identities, besides the accidental capturing of cut, style and texture in *carte-de-visite* portraits or street photographs, are offered up through those journalistic or romantic texts on city life of which Whiteing's is a key example. Although their use has presented problems for social historians wary of the subjective nature of representational forms as a source,[7] I hope to use their content here not to make quantitative claims for patterns of clothing practice and urban behaviour, but to suggest that descriptions of male dress and its acquisition in *fin-de-siècle* London contained inflections of empire which are often overlooked.

I would like to focus, in particular, on those 'black, brown and russet figures, the shabby clerks outside the bun shop' described by Whiteing, in order to consider the sartorial roles played out in various literary representations by the professional and semi-professional inhabitants of the London evoked in the prose of 'imperial' texts. These can be placed alongside descriptions of those whose 'exotic' otherness provided counter-performances, showing how descriptive accounts of clothing were instrumental in negotiating simultaneously a sense of national identity, membership of an imperial race, and citizenship of a metropolis that represented both a triumphal celebration of its achievements and a powerful symbol of fears about its decline. This, I would suggest, was a process of negotiation not simply played out between author and reader in the imagination but also subtly manifested through actual clothing choices. The physical manipulation of fashionable identities, and engagement with the spatial formations of the imperial city informed by such texts, influenced the development of a sartorial language for British middle-class men well into the twentieth century, encouraging an inscription of imperial concerns and differences onto their very bodies.

It is commonly recognised by historians of urban life that late nineteenth-century London was often viewed as a collection of highly individualised locales, subsumed within an overriding disparity between the luxuries of the West End and the deprivations and dangers of the East. The exact nature of the relationship between London's regions has been vigorously contested by more recent historians, particularly in those studies concerned with the playing out of gendered and class-based identities in the realms of fashionable and sexual consumption. These debates have largely concerned the extent to which middle-class and aristocratic men and women were free to traverse East/West spatial boundaries, and the manner in which those boundaries were constructed, both imaginatively and physically.[8] Beyond the terrors of the Ratcliffe Highway, however, contemporary commentators seem unsure of the very status of that imagined geography. The journalist Thomas Burke in his London autobiography *Nights in Town* (1915) portrayed the mental division of streets and districts as a more subtle, shifting practice, rather than endorsing the facile moral and political distinctions to be drawn between locales as complex in their similarities and differences as Whitechapel and Westbourne Grove, for example. 'London,' he stated,

> is not one place, but many places; she has not one soul but many souls. The people of Brondesbury are of markedly different character and clime

than those of Hammersmith ... The smell, the sound, the dress of Finsbury Park are as different from the smell, the sound and the dress of Wandsworth Common as though one were England and the other Nicaragua.[9]

Local identity, Burke seemed to suggest, lay more in the convergence of personal habits and the nuances of popular custom (and dress is prioritised here) than in the more programmatic mappings of social reformers and town planners. Indeed, the very impossibility of determining the character of London's regions through fixed signifiers and the dissolving of more established patterns gave him some cause for concern.

> There was a time [he lamented], years ago, when the East End was the East End – a land apart ... But the omnibus has changed all that. It has so linked things and places that all individual character has been swamped in a universal chaos, and there is now neither East nor West ... boundaries are things which exist today only in the minds of the borough councillor ... and the London docks are a region whose chief feature is cockney warehouse clerks.[10]

The old East End as Burke conceived and remembered it offered an intensity of sensuous experience which mirrored that conjured up by Whiteing in the square mile, yet Burke's prose also threw the monochrome gradations of the financial quarter into a still duller relief. The modernising effects of bureaucracy and technology, together with the pervasive strictures of a 'gentlemanly' rhetoric, threatened to homogenise the varied social fabric that Burke believed lent the docks their cosmopolitan reputation and specific character. The two descriptions of the imperial city offered by Whiteing and Burke, differing in their context and readership, yet complementary in their 'colonial' effect, converge in their evocative use of male dress as a categorising device, used to impose order on a potentially overwhelming and socially dangerous *mise-en-scène*:

> These India docks are like no other docks in the world. About their gates you find the scum of the world's worst countries; all the people of the delirious Pacific of whom you have read and dreamed – Arab, Hindoo, Malay ... South Sea Islander – a mere catalogue of the names is a romance. Here are pace and high adventure; the tang of the east; fusion of blood and race and creed. A degenerate chaos it is, but do you know, I cannot say I don't prefer it to the well spun gold that is flung from the Empire on boat-race nights. Place these fellows against our blunt backgrounds, under the awful mystery of the city's night, and they present the finest spectacle that London affords. You may see them at the Asiatics Home ... grouped about the giant stove are asiatics of every country in wonderful toilet creations. A mild-eyed hindoo, lacking a turban, has

appropriated a bath towel. A Malay appears in white cotton trousers, frock coat, brown boots and straw hat ... costumes, people and setting have all the appearance of the ensemble of a cheap revue.[11]

Burke mobilised theatrical metaphors to underline the spectacular appearance of colonial subjects and members of trading nations in London, though his recognition that their exoticism provided a colourful backdrop against which the performance of Englishness could be more clearly articulated remained subliminal. For Burke the cockney warehouse clerk or the golden boat race hearty offered little cause for emotional celebration, let alone sartorial definition, but their inclusion in his narrative denotes a clear set of controlling distinctions in which reticence is pitched against excess. J. S. Bratton's work on empire and theatre offers a useful structure for understanding this presentation of the self through clothing as an act with imperial implications. She suggests that:

> Theatrical and quasi-theatrical presentation whether in music hall, club rooms ... or the streets and ceremonial spaces of the capital, made an obvious contribution to that much discussed national mood ... which has seemed wonderful and reprehensible, inspiring or horrifying, according to the position of the analyst. They played a large part in the creation and propagation of the 'tradition' of the nation, supplanting local, fragmented and potentially subversive histories. Existing communal and personal self-images ... had to be shown to belong within the larger imperial identity instead of standing in opposition to it.[12]

Clerks' clothing and colonial desire

The performance of local, national and racial identities through visual signification was not simply associated with explorations of cultural homogenisation, miscegenation and degeneration amongst the inhabitants of the East End, though its effects may have been more sharply recorded there. As Whiteing showed, the notional and symbolic centre of empire, located between the Bank and the Mansion House, offered its own particular stagings of imperialist rhetoric through a misleadingly uncommunicative set of fashionable co-ordinates that revolve around the seemingly unspectacular figure of the city clerk. The reporter Charles Turner offered a complementary representation of the square mile for George Sims's encyclopaedic account of London life in 1903, which was as pregnant with possibilities for the exploration of physical types as any expedition to the docks, where:

> each centre ... represents an aggregation of allied interest. Of such are the banks of Lombard Street, the shipping offices of Leadenhall and

Fenchurch Streets, the accountants of Old Jewry, the clothes and clothing interests of Wood Street and the narrow ways just east of St Paul's
Cathedral ... the extraordinary maze of irregular narrow lanes and cul-de-
sacs of Austin Friars and Copthall Avenue, where you see an overflow of
hatless brokers from Throgmorton Street.[13]

Thus the Royal Exchange offered 'glossy hats...,well conditioned black
coats and trousers..., expensive waistcoats..., gold watch chains',
Fenchurch Street, the 'voyageur' element, tourists mixed with 'Lascar
seamen'. Mincing Lane and the Exchanges attracted 'hatless clerks,
brokers and salesmen' of a 'negligent' attitude, shirt sleeves and bois-
terous camaraderie alleviated by the presence of a few barge skippers'
wives. Meanwhile the new office blocks of Bishopsgate promised a
more polished version of city masculinity, chipper even, well serviced
by restaurants, barbers, tobacconists and collar and tie shops.[14]

The collar and tie shop, which Turner offered as an example of unac-
customed modernisation in the midst of stultifying tradition, also provided the city worker with a fashionable identity that in many ways
epitomised a shift in the aesthetics of masculinity towards a hygienic,
contained and above all controlled presentation of the professional
Englishman's body. Crisp linen collars, or the wipe-clean xylonite
alternatives, and bright neat sporting ties in profusion represented a
freshness distinct from the confusion of dockside and East End dress or
the complicated layers of silk and broadcloth, the dark textural depth
of the clothing of City patriarchs. The historian Ronald Hyam traces
concurrent shifts in attitudes towards Anglo-Saxon male sexuality in
the colonies, noting an evolution from mid-century

> ideals of moral strenuousness, a Christian manliness, to a cult of the
> emphatically physical ... from the ideals of godliness and good learning
> to those of clean manliness and good form ... By 1914 the whole British
> concept of masculinity ... had been redefined, partly in the name of
> Empire, to mean not sexual prowess and maturity ... but sexual restraint
> and 'cleanness'.[15]

In his humorous novel of life in the Strand and Fleet Street, *The Book
of a Bachelor* (1910), geared towards a knowing young metropolitan
readership, the columnist Duncan Schwann sketched the new imperial type in his portrait of the 'hearty' Clive Massey:

> one of those fresh, clean-limbed Englishmen, the sight of whom makes
> one feel proud to be their fellow countrymen. The product of public
> school and University, he and his kind dance, shoot and hunt through life
> if the paternal income allows. If it doesn't they gravitate into the Indian
> native cavalry, or the South African mounted police, or turn their hands
> to any job they can find in any country on the globe. They have few

ROBINSON & CLEAVER'S NEW PREMISES

IOI, CHEAPSIDE, E.C.— OPPOSITE BOW CHURCH
SHIRTS, COLLARS, HOSIERY, ETC & EVERYTHING FOR GENTLEMEN'S WEAR

Figure 37 The hosier Robinson & Cleaver's establishment in Cheapside presented a restrained facade in this advertisement of *c.* 1900, which reflected the decorum of City dress codes. John Johnson collection, Bodleian Library.

brains of the quality enabling them to pass examinations, and no ambitions, but put them in a tight place in an outpost of civilization. ... commercially their virtues are valueless, imperially and socially they are beyond price.[16]

The cultural historian William Greenslade presents perhaps a more nuanced reading of the manner in which fears regarding degeneration and imperial decline influenced attitudes towards the male body at home, and particularly the body of the clerk, that would favour the appearance, if not the substance, of sporting efficiency. He states that 'the rhetoric of sport, so elementary yet so powerful in associating physical prowess with national pride in imperial success, invoked the call to action and participation', invoking the 'indolent other':

> the annual reports of the Inspector General of Recruiting, first issued in 1901, [were] both a confirming symptom and a constituent episode in the great drama about the fitness of the national body. In Manchester only three out of every eleven applicants for military service in South Africa were considered fit ... Fears prompted and kept alive by degenerationist discourse seemed to be vindicated. The national crisis was, in a very real sense, a crisis of the imperial body.[17]

Though partly informed by the circulation of imperialist and eugenicist propaganda, the tendency for representations of clerk's clothing and appearance to suggest the control of degenerate impulses and the disguise of physical shortcomings should not simply be read as a corollary of a colonial discourse which marked the appearance of overseas subjects as darkly exotic and imperialists as blondly heroic. The rhetoric of empire could also extend to the treatment of domestic social relations. Within the gradations of urban life, the ready-made or cash tailor suit and laundered collars and cuffs also positioned the clerk between the unruly sartorial persona of the East End rough and the over-refined indolence of the dandy aristocrat. In the context of national stereotyping, petty-bourgeois respectability at least denoted a level of civilisation and stability which commentators identified as lacking in the behaviour and image of abutting social groups. The political commentator Charles Masterman, writing on *The Heart of the Empire* in 1901, bemoaned the disregard shown towards the policing of the self by 'the city type of the coming years', a new 'race' given over to 'turbulent rioting over military successes, hooliganism and a certain temper of fickle excitability', upon whose 'development and action depend the future progress of the Anglo-Saxon race, and for the next half-century at least, the policy of the British Empire in the world'.[18]

The indiscipline associated with the bell-bottomed trousers, studded belt, spotted neckerchief and heavy boots of the hooligan offered

40/- Gentlemen's Business Suits, for 13/3

SEE SAMPLES.   SEE SAMPLES.

We have procured a large supply of these strong, durable Cloths, and, as an advertisement offer, we will supply a Gentleman's Suit, consisting of Jacket, Waistcoat, and Trousers, at the ridiculous price of 13/3, Carriage Free.

This Suit is named the "Ludgate."

Square-cut Fronts to Jackets, 1/- extra.
Lined Trousers, 9d. extra.
(Any size up to 44-inch Chest.)

From Photograph.
The "LUDGATE"
13/3 Suit, as advertised.

Please send your Measures on the back of this card   See Samples below

Figure 38   The figure of the City clerk, depicted here in an outfitter's advertisement for the 'Ludgate' suit of *c.* 1895. John Johnson collection, Bodleian Library

much scope for those journalists and novelists keen to expose the results of unchecked drink and jingoism, or illustrate the manner in which the identifying sartorial marks of an imperial elite came finally to rest on the backs of Masterman's 'street-bred people'. Furthermore, the propensity to physical violence encoded in subcultural dress codes could also suggest much potential for reformers who were eager to enlist hooligan energies to more respectable causes, such as Scouting. Pre-empting such observations by several decades, an 1881 edition of Mayhew described the unemployed who gathered for casual labour at the dock gates every morning: 'some in half fashionable surtouts which are bursting at the elbows, and with the dirty shirt showing through; others in greasy shooting jackets, with red, pimpled faces. Others, again, in the rags of their half slang gentility, with the velvet collars of their paletots worn through to the canvas. A few in rusty black, with their waistcoats fastened tight up to the throat; and more with the knowing thieves' curl on each side of the jaunty cap; whilst here and there you may observe a big whiskered Pole with his hands in the pockets of his plaited French trousers.'[19] The barely disguised romanticism with which Mayhew constructed a picturesque version of dangerous East End masculinity clearly denoted a grudging respect for its colourful virility.

Those who laboured manually in the docks and factories of the imperial city, or loitered in its alleyways, thus provided both a marker against which the desk worker might distinguish his own appearance and a form of escapist spectacle, visual relief from the restrictions of life in the square mile. London Bridge, with its uninterrupted view of Tower Bridge and the ports and docks down river, literally framed such promises of alien mystery and foreign adventure. In tourist guidebook photographs the bridge's arches performed in physical and psychic terms as both bridge and barrier between two states of mind, its low walls supporting the crowded elbows of identical bowler-hatted clerks, lost in a lunch-break reverie. W. Pett Ridge, a novelist whose works acted as guardians of the suburban, lower middle-class London spirit in the 1890s and 1910s recalled that:

> On the down river side it has always been a resting place for the Londoner, and he can set elbows on the parapet, and watch the big ships, gaze at men carrying heavy loads, and wait for the Tower Bridge to make a gesture of surprise; it is indeed all much more engaging than sitting at a desk or table. Just before holiday time, City men cannot keep away from London bridge, and clerks with a spirit of adventure try to think of excuses for going in that direction; many count it better than lunch.[20]

Back in the confines of the office, monotony, predestination and the observance of rank seemed to cocoon the clerk from the wider concerns of empire, though leisure pursuits and reading matter offered glimpses of an imperial other-life. In his novel of city intrigue and financial misdemeanour, *The Money God* (1904), J. P. Blake wrote of:

> the rank and file, whose talents and tastes are generally of the mediocre sort. Their recompense is probably amply adequate to the services rendered, and its penchant for halfpenny journals and cigarettes is not to be despised because it is not unpleasant. They spend their leisure in the suburban theatres, in riding omnibuses, and in gymnastics; as they grow older they will possess votes and become householders; but as elements in the competition between nations they are nugatory.[21]

Three years later, in his semi-autobiographical novel *Robert Thorne: The Story of a London Clerk* (1907), Shan Bullock was more explicit in describing the distinct uniforms and cluttered accoutrements of administrative life adopted by those who worked in the civil service offices of Somerset House at the turn of the century :

> dressed carefully in my best – a blue serge reefer suit, striped cotton shirt, red and black necktie, and bowler hat – I had breakfast, and about ten o'clock set out to the Tax Office. [I] walked quickly and abstractedly, in a fever of nervousness. Big Ben was only chiming the half hour as I crossed Waterloo Bridge ... By the door a line of red fire buckets hung under a coiled hose and a row of numbered bells ... the air was heavy with an odour of dust and Irish stew. Presently a clerk, wearing a shabby

office jacket and carrying a novel, a magazine, a copy of the *Times*, and a bundle of papers came down the stairs ... then a messenger, so I judged, burdened with a coal scuttle, a water bottle, a duster, a Bradshaw and two inkpots, came from somewhere ... Then the doors swung in behind me and a personage in black overcoat, silk hat, striped trousers and patent leather boots sauntered in, glanced at me through his eyeglass, and smoking his cigar went across and up the staircase.[22]

In the first few minutes of his employment as a junior tax clerk Robert Thorne astutely surveys those sartorial identities that positioned him within a complex structure of deference and appropriateness, covertly reflective of the broader relationship of City workers to the larger imperial project. His own new suit, spruce, tidy and bright in correct proportion, indicating the ambition and efficiency of the new citizen; his fellow clerks, ground down to assume the workaday dehumanising aspect of clerical labour; with the elite imprint of distinction and authority reflected in the patent leather boots of his superior. These are not perhaps the garments usually associated with the spaces of empire,[23] but their minute gradations and clear differences clearly signalled an unencumbered, carefully calibrated pursuit of imperial objectives, whilst their monochrome visual reticence presented a vivid metaphor for the authoritative character of imperial London itself. Indeed, the head of Thorne's division, whilst conforming entirely to the expected appearance of a bureaucrat in morning suit and top hat, betrayed his colonial connections more overtly in the trappings of his room. As Bullock described it, 'the walls were hung with pictures, photographs, almanacs, maps, and had shelves full of official literature. In a corner stood a bag of golf sticks, a Volunteer officer's sword and helmet case, and a pair of Indian clubs. On the mantel was a date box, a cup and saucer, and a Japanese teapot.'[24]

If the serge reefer suit and the bowler hat marked Robert Thorne out as a servant of empire, constrained and emasculated within the boundaries of London office culture, the windows of the outfitters' shops that his living counterparts passed daily on their route to work, and possibly patronised for the club ties and fancy shirtings that would signal their progressive taste to colleagues, offered one more opportunity – beyond the dangerous exoticism of the East End, the jingoistic escapism of the halfpenny journal, or even the homosocial ambience of a supervisors' room – for an engagement with colonial life. Indeed, Thresher & Glenny's outfitting emporium at 152 The Strand advertised its prime location as 'next door to Somerset House', relying for much of its trade on the passing custom of civil servants, and promoted textiles and accessories adapted to climates other than the London damp in its catalogues and displays. Alongside the Shetland golf coats and white Melton trousers that promised to deliver the requisite athletic demeanour to the deskbound, customers were able to peruse 'Thresher's Jungra Cloth ... especially prepared for shooting suits for the Indian Jungles ... light, durable and impervious to spear grass'[25] or the 'India Diagonal Dinner Suit, made in black and dark grey of a tropical substance yet firm in body'.[26] Such stock could also be relied upon to draw attention from the street. R. W. Shorter, window dresser to Austin Reed in Fenchurch Street, often utilised exotic overseas material in his displays, suggesting in 1910 that should 'you want to show a window of Japanese silk handkerchiefs or shirts, then to pull the crowd up all you have to do is get some Japanese fans, flowers, flags, vases and a large screen for the background, one or two Japanese figures, and there you are. You'll have a crowd all day.'[27] Similarly *The Window Dresser's Diary* for that year isolated Empire Day on 24 May as an opportunity for a 'British imperial display, figures of Britannia and the colonies. Festival of the Empire should suggest ideas. Great opportunity for Scout costumes, riding breeches, leggings, sailor suits, and anything suggesting frontier enterprise and the linking of the colonies with the mother country'.[28]

Figure 39 Clothing for the colonies of the sort advertised by Thresher & Glenny contrasted starkly with the more restrained image adopted for City work yet also embraced the rhetoric of empire. Cabinet photograph, *c.* 1910

In its terse self-confidence the entry in *The Window Dresser's Diary* for 23 April was equally potent in positioning more 'ordinary' masculine clothing as a vehicle for imperial aspirations, stating simply, 'St George's Day – English patriotic goods. Ticket: English goods for Englishmen'.[29] Nevertheless, Robert Thorne, always the epitome of clerkish good form and English reserve, of 'ordinariness', eventually found the tension between the enervating routine of employment at Somerset House and a patriotic rhetoric of masculine endeavour which demeaned all aspects of his life too much to bear, and Shan Bullock's novel ends with his emigration to New Zealand. 'In the main,' Robert Thorne complained, 'what is life but heroic pretence? Our houses are jerry-built, our clothes shoddy, our food adulterated, ourselves not what we are. It is the penalty of civilization. There seems no other way.'[30] Thresher & Glenny's Colonial Outfit List with its 'India gauze waistcoats, calico drawers, straw hat, clothes bag, mosquito trousers, marine soap and sponge bag' offered one version of imperial manliness that would have seemed more authentic to Thorne.[31] Yet the clerk's suit that he left behind signified other equally valid versions, even as its creases and seams seemed to enshroud all the negative connotations of petty-bourgeois conformity. W. Pett Ridge in his 1910 novel of suburban romance *Nine to Six-thirty* prefaced one chapter with some sentimental doggerel that upheld the value of those others. Simultaneously mocking and uplifting, it provides a fitting conclusion to this chapter and suggests the enduring connotations of reticence and introversion that the undemonstrative clothing of the urban desk worker bequeathed to succeeding constructions of male fashionableness and English masculinity. Plain and renunciatory though the clothing of the clerk may have appeared, I hope to have shown how, in an imperial sense, its authority and layered meanings were both more profound and more affecting than that:

> Dear city clerk, I think you have a notion
> That certain folk regard you with disdain.
> If this should bruise, let me apply a lotion,
> Something that may perhaps allay the pain.
> No small talk yours. Controlling land and ocean,
> You see it through in storm, or sun, or rain.
> Without it traffic would be mere commotion.
> You are in truth the driver of the train.[32]

Notes

I am grateful to John Styles, Gillian Naylor, Penny Sparke, Jeremy Aynsley, Tim Barringer, James and Deborah Ryan, Felix Driver and David Gilbert for their advice and support in the completion of this chapter.

1 F. Madox Hueffer [Ford], *The Soul of London: A Survey of a Modern City* (London, Alston Rivers, 1904), pp. 70–1.
2 F. Driver & D. Gilbert, 'Heart of empire? Landscape, space and performance in imperial London', *Environment and Planning D: Society and Space*, 16 (1998), 11–28.
3 L. Nead, 'Mapping the self: gender, space and modernity in mid-Victorian London', in R. Porter (ed.), *Rewriting the Self: Histories from the Renaissance to the Present* (London, Routledge, 1996), p. 167.
4 R. Whiteing, *The Island, or, An Adventure of a Person of Quality* (London, Longman, 1888), p. 1.
5 L. Hapgood, 'Regaining a Focus: New Perspectives on the Novels of Richard Whiteing', in N. Le Manos & M. Rochelson (eds), *Transforming Genres: New Approaches to British Fiction of the 1890s* (London, Macmillan, 1994), pp. 178–84.
6 J. Harvey, *Men in Black* (London, Reaktion Books, 1995).
7 G. Crosswick and H. Haupt, *The Petite Bourgeoisie in Europe, 1780–1914* (London, Routledge, 1995), p. 191.
8 Nead, 'Mapping the self'; J. Walkowitz, *City of Dreadful Delight: Narratives of Sexual Danger in Late Victorian London* (London, Virago, 1992).
9 Thomas Burke, *Nights in Town: A London Autobiography* (London, George Allen, 1915), p. 25.
10 *Ibid.*, p. 91.
11 *Ibid.*, pp. 84–5.
12 J. S. Bratton *et al.* (eds), *Acts of Supremacy, The British Empire and the Stage, 1790–1930* (Manchester, Manchester University Press, 1991) p. 5.
13 C. Turner, 'The City at high noon', in G. Simms (ed.), *Living London*, II (London, Cassell, 1903), p. 126.
14 *Ibid.*, pp. 122–5.
15 R. Hyam, *Empire and Sexuality: The British Experience* (Manchester, Manchester University Press, 1991), pp. 71–2.
16 D. Schwann, *The Book of a Bachelor* (London, Heinemann, 1910), pp. 23–4.
17 W. Greenslade, 'Fitness and the *fin-de-siècle*', in J. Stokes (ed.), *Fin de Siècle/Fin du Globe: Fears and Fantasies of the Late Nineteenth Century* (London, Macmillan, 1992), pp. 47–8.
18 C. F. Masterman (ed.), *The Heart of the Empire* (London, Fisher Unwin, 1901)
19 H. Mayhew, *London Characters: Illustrations of the Humour, Pathos and Peculiarities of London Life* (London, Chatto & Windus, 1881), pp. 357–8.
20 W. Pett Ridge, *I Like to Remember* (London, Hodder & Stoughton, 1925), p. 156.
21 J. P. Blake, *The Money God: A Tale of the City* (London, Heinemann, 1904), p. 32.
22 S. Bullock, *Robert Thorne: The Story of a London Clerk* (London, Werner Laurie, 1907), pp. 33–4.
23 H. Callaway, 'Dressing for dinner in the bush', in R. Barnes & J. Eicher (eds), *Dress and Gender: Making and Meaning* (Oxford, Berg, 1992).
24 Bullock, *Robert Thorne*, p. 35.
25 Westminster City Archives, London, WBA 301/28, E, Thresher & Glenny, Pamphlet for the International Health Exhibition, London, 1884.
26 *Ibid.*, Promotional leaflet, *c.* 1900.
27 Anon., *Publicity: A Practical Guide for the Retail Clothier and Outfitter* (London, The Outfitter, 1910), p. 34.
28 *Ibid.*, p. 38.
29 *Ibid.*, p. 38.
30 Bullock, *Robert Thorne*, p. 249.
31 Westminster City Archives, London, WBA 301/28 C, Thresher & Glenny, Collection of price lists, *c.* 1890.
32 W. Pett Ridge, *Nine to Six-thirty* (London, Methuen, 1910), p. 61.

CHAPTER FOURTEEN

Anti-imperial London:
the Pan-African Conference of 1900

Jonathan Schneer

London in 1900 was the imperial metropolis *sans pareil*, the permanent or temporary home to hundreds of thousands who traced their ancestry to the imperialised territories, the jumping-off place for countless thousands who wished to make a new life abroad, the centre of a government whose decisions influenced the destinies of 400 million people around the globe. This chapter on the Pan-African Conference of 1900 will show that London was also a city shaped by anti-imperialists.[1] It situates the Conference, an epochal event (little regarded at the time), within the larger anti-imperialist movement in which it was embedded.[2] That movement was not monolithic but contained contradictory impulses which were mirrored in the variety of anti-imperialisms articulated at the conference itself. If London in 1900 was the great imperial metropolis, it was also a nexus of anti-imperialisms.

London's turn-of-the-century anti-imperialists were mainly British-born, but also came from Ireland, South Asia, the West Indies and Africa. Briefly consider first the broad array of groups and individuals that made up the British-born component. There were Liberals in Quaker, Positivist and Ethical Societies, the Land and Labour League, the Radical clubs; socialists in the Fabian Society, Independent Labour Party and Social Democratic Federation (SDF); Good Samaritans of all parties in the Anti-slavery and Aborigines' Protection Societies. With few exceptions, however, these anti-imperialists opposed not British imperialism but specific imperial policies which they thought too expensive or ill judged or immoral, and the jingoism which accompanied them, especially during the Boer War. Of genuine human solidarity there was little. In fact most of these anti-imperialists subscribed to a 'scientific' racism which maintained, essentially, that Africans were not fully developed human beings. As the leader of the Marxist Social Democratic Federation, Henry Hyndman, put it in a declaration typical of the pseudo-scientific approach, 'the negro's brain was not constructed like that of the white man. Its convolutions were different.'[3]

London's Irish anti-imperialists held similar views. Organised in local branches of the Gaelic League if they were primarily cultural nationalists, or in the London branches of the United Irish League (UIL) if their focus was mainly political, some favoured revolutionary measures to expel the English from Ireland, although after the fall of Parnell and before the era of 'the great unrest' this was mostly bluster. Many Irish nationalists asserted a more genuine sympathy with subject peoples yearning to be free, or at least with some of them. The *Irish Weekly Independent*, popular among Irish nationalists in London, once commiserated with Finland, 'a gallant little nation struggling to preserve her distinct existence while a great empire is striving to merge it into its body politic'.[4] London's Irish community sent not only sympathy but concrete aid in the form of money and eventually volunteer fighters to the Boers of South Africa. Yet the anti-imperialism of London's Irish nationalists was circumscribed by the same racism which characterised so many British-born anti-imperialists. For example, T. M. Healey, a leading member of the Irish Parliamentary Party, admired the Boers who were resisting incorporation into the British empire because they rightly objected to the 'pleasure of having a nigger as a magistrate probably, certainly as a policeman ruling over them' and all in the interests of 'a number of German Jews'.[5] Healey's were popular sentiments in London's UIL clubs and Gaelic League branches, as a glance at the contemporary Irish press will quickly reveal. Of course there were honourable exceptions, for instance the Irish Quaker Alfred Webb, upon whom the oppressed of every race, religion and sex could always rely, and the SDF activist John Scurr, who lectured UIL branches on the need for solidarity with all victims of British domination. Still, when most London-based Irish nationalists claimed to oppose British imperialism what they usually meant was that they opposed its practice in Ireland.[6]

Attitudes among British-born and Irish anti-imperialists towards the peoples of South Asia were less egregious and self-interested, however. Many believed, again to cite Hyndman, that 'the numerous races and peoples of India [who once had produced a great civilization now sadly decayed] are still capable of great work in every field of human endeavour'.[7] Also they respected Indian nationalists for conducting a well organised campaign to secure co-rulership of India with Britain. The British Committee of the Indian National Congress (BCINC), established with British and Irish support in 1889, ran that campaign.[8] Its model was the Anti-Corn Law League. By 1900 the BCINC, with headquarters in London, was publishing a weekly newspaper, *India*, annually sponsoring hundreds of meetings throughout the country and the metropolis on Indian subjects, maintaining a list of MPs who would ask the right questions in Parliament, lobbying government Ministers and officials. Although the organisation was plagued by money problems, the BCINC's budget in 1900 exceeded £5,000.[9] London-based Indian anti-imperialists were almost as well organised as their Irish counterparts.

Their attitudes towards empire were similarly contradictory. The BCINC wished to limit, perhaps some day to eliminate, British influence in India; it also wished British imperialists would fulfil promises 'to treat Indians exactly like British Citizens'.[10] BCINC speakers argued that Indians deserved this, since they were loyal to the Crown and their country was a vast market for British goods.[11] Moreover, India had been 'greatest of all, long before anyone had heard anything of the oldest States of the West'.[12] Suggest, however, that Indians deserved esteem for general characteristics and achievements and it was a short step to suggesting that other people did not. *India* accepted antisemitic stereotypes. The Boer War would 'make Hebrew millionaires richer'.[13] It distinguished between the 'ignorant and lawless Kaffirs' of South Africa, who were 'savages', and the colony's 'educated and highly civilised Indians'.[14] In short, like most anti-imperialists in London in 1900, many Indians objected not to imperialism, or the imperial world view, but to specific British policies and attitudes; meantime, following in the footsteps of Cobden and Bright, they adhered scrupulously to constitutional methods.

There were dissidents. At an 1898 meeting an Indian student, R. C. Sen, asserted that 'English justice was a myth. English government meant the administration of slow poison. It was a mistake to rely too much on the generosity of the English people. They only yielded when other countries proved by acts their determination to enforce demands,' sentiments which 'did only evoke enthusiasm' from one 'sometimes noisy group' at the back of the hall, according to an India Office spy.[15] And a few BCINC members rejected *India*'s racism altogether. In 1893 the BCINC leader, Dadabhai Naoroji, joined the interracial Society for the Recognition of the Brotherhood of Man (SRBM). His ally, Alfred Webb, a former president of the INC and apparently uniquely colour-blind among Irish nationalist MPs, befriended the pan-Africanist, Henry Sylvester Williams.[16] The Scottish MP, William Wedderburn, another BCINC stalwart, attended protest meetings Williams organised. When Williams convened the Pan-African Conference in 1900, Naoroji sent financial support despite his own organisation's pecuniary difficulties. Finally Joseph Royeppen, a BCINC speaker duly noted by another India Office spy, was 'an Indian born in South Africa (evidently with some negro blood)'.[17] Royeppen's further activities are obscure, but he literally embodied an embryonic alliance of South Asians and Africans.

Turning to anti-imperialists of African descent living in London in 1900, they belonged to a sadly reduced community of West Indian sailors, a few prosperous individuals in the liberal professions, and occasional students of law, medicine or business from Africa, the West Indies or the United States.[18] In 1900 the Anti-Slavery Society and the Aborigines Protection Society, organisational descendants of the anti-slavery agitation, offered this community condescending support. London's modern black anti-imperialists' true origins, however, grew from bonds forged between African-Americans and British radicals after the American Civil War, and in crusades led by black members of British churches, temperance and thrift societies during the same period. They may be discovered also in what Stephen Yeo once termed the 'religion of socialism' movement.[19]

We shall start with the transatlantic links. After 1865 the African-American leader Frederick Douglas paid visits to the village of Street, in Somerset, where he knew the politician John Bright, the shoe manufacturer, William Clark, and a woman with strong convictions about racial equality, Catherine Impey. The friendship with Impey bore political fruit late in the 1880s, at about the time Indian nationalists in London were establishing the BCINC. Simultaneously socialist new unionists were laying the foundations of the modern British labour movement. The conjuncture seems worth noting, if only to emphasise the international dimensions of a movement most historians have considered solely in the national context.

It is worth noting too that, while only a few women featured in anti-imperial London, they played a critical role at the outset in helping to create political space for the movements it embraced. Impey was the main conduit for a stream of African Americans visiting Britain, the most important being Ida B. Wells, the anti-lynching crusader. Impey publicised the British activities of Wells and other visitors in her newspaper, *Anti-caste*. As Vron Ware has shown, Impey, Wells and a Scottish woman, Elizabeth Fyvie Mayo, organised a British anti-lynching campaign too, from which grew the SRBM, with branches throughout Britain and a London governing body whose members included Dadabhai Naoroji and Alfred Webb of the BCINC. The SRBM needed an official organ: Impey temporarily abandoned *Anti-caste*, approached a charismatic African Caribbean, Celestine Edwards, invited him to edit a new journal, *Fraternity*, and become general secretary of the society as a whole. In July 1893 Edwards assumed both posts.[20]

[257]

In Edwards's life and struggles we may trace the second tap root of African-British anti-imperialism, the one running through temperance and Church bodies, and informed by Christian socialism. Born on the island of Dominica, Edwards attended Catholic and Wesleyan schools.[21] He arrived in Britain in the early 1880s already a determined reformer. But what could he do? Native-born Britons joined trade unions or socialist or radical clubs which did not welcome blacks. Therefore, in Edinburgh, Edwards's first British home, he joined the Hope Lodge of the order of Good Templars. Perhaps an organisation aiming to salvage drunkards found it easier to accept black members on an equal basis with whites than did middle-class groups like the Aborigines Protection Society, or organisations composed of class-conscious workers who feared foreign competition, since not only Edwards but, fifteen years later, Henry Sylvester Williams also began in Britain lecturing for the temperance movement. At any rate, Edwards' first attempts at reform were speeches promoting abstinence from alcohol.

Edwards was an extraordinary personality, 'a born orator',[22] but not a demagogue, astonishingly learned, as his lectures reveal,[23] but essentially an autodidact, frank, open and friendly. Even his earliest speeches must have ranged broadly, for soon 'I was requested to lecture upon my country and my people.'[24] Hoping to reach a broader audience, he chose a new platform, the Missionary Committee of the Primitive Methodist Church. Like the Good Templars, a church boasting universalist aspirations proved to be more open than a trade union or socialist society to the young African-Caribbean.

Edwards hoped the Methodists would send him to Africa. They sent him to London. His writings and lectures grew overtly political, condemning the hypocrisy and greed of European imperialists who claimed to be spreading civilisation and Christianity.[25] Expert at the give-and-take which accompanied British public speaking, he became a regular at Speakers' Corner in Victoria Park, a traditional site of East End oratory and a magnet for radicals, socialists and others with an axe to grind. When he was not in London he travelled the country for the Primitive Methodists, but he never tailored his message to his audience. Addressing a meeting of the 'Society for Propagating the Gospel among the Heathen' in Bishops Waltham, 'he hit out, in his usual style, against the effects of the white civilisers who go to Africa for what they can pocket.'[26] His fame grew. Whenever he spoke the halls were packed.[27]

Towards the end of the 1880s Edwards left the Primitive Methodists for the Christian Evidence Society (CES), a nondenominational body proselytising and defending Christianity. He became leader of its East

London branch. During the summer of 1892 he launched a CES news-paper, *Lux*. Published weekly, *Lux* hardly limited itself to articles on Christianity. In its pages Edwards attempted to rebut the exponents of 'scientific' racism and to condemn the imperialist policies which flowed from their attitudes. 'A consistent advocate of Darwinian theory ... can have no difficulty in allowing the obvious truth that, given favourable environment, the Negro race is just as likely to give a good account of itself as the European,' he argued.[28] And: Englishmen 'boast of the Empire over which the sun never sets. How many have been murdered, robbed, and enslaved to acquire that dominion?'[29]

Edwards' anti-imperialism was rooted in Christianity as well as in experience. Reason alone would not solve the problems caused by imperialism, he argued, but reason combined with faith could prevail. 'When would the horrors of the Middle Passage, and with it the slave trade, have been abolished, if men had done no more than think?' he asked an audience.[30] At times he grew impatient with the Church's fail-ure to live up to its universalist prescriptions. 'Why don't missionary societies raise the country against the continual injustices perpetrated against the Negroes in West and South Africa?'[31] Nevertheless, when he accepted the invitation to edit *Fraternity*, and to become general secretary of the society which sponsored it, he maintained his connec-tion with the CES, continued editing and writing for *Lux*. Tolerant of other religions,[32] he never ceased to rail against atheists, freethinkers, theosophists, positivists and Marxists, all of whom he might have con-sidered natural allies of the SRBM in the anti-imperialist crusade.[33] For Christian socialists, however, Edwards made an exception. He wrote, 'Christianity must cultivate that individualism which partakes of the nature of the highest socialism, and the socialism which promotes the noblest individualism. Christianity must maintain the significance of humanity by the continual reassertion of God's grandest affirmative: 'Whatever ye would that men should do unto you, do ye even so to them.'[34]

Editor and chief writer of two newspapers, leader of a CES Bible class, lecturer of renown, Edwards's schedule had become too hectic. References to his haggard demeanour now began to appear in the news-paper. Early in 1894 he collapsed. *Lux* raised £206, on which he sailed to the West Indies to recover his health. A lecture delivered on the eve of his departure conveys a new bitterness of tone.

> Talk about old age pensions: 5s. a week when you are sixty. When I see it in the papers I look upon it as a huge joke. ... Fancy the man who toils all day, and only has 18s. a week, and has to save out of that. ... But I said there was a revolution, and it must come when the labourer will receive not only the equivalent of his labour, but also participate in the profits

derived. Oh! What a hell upon earth for some of our countrymen and women! ... The carrying of the Gospel in the slum has some consolation, but it is poor consolation to a hungry stomach. ... [And] the pulpit has frequently played the coward.[35]

Thus Edwards may have been working towards a more socialist, less overtly Christian, position. But he did not live to develop it. He died in his brother's home in Barbados on 25 July 1894.

Edwards's death coincided with the passing of a hopeful era. The 'new unionism' lapsed; the Liberals languished in opposition. Conservatives ruled for a decade characterised by labour defeats, jingoism and colonial wars. In a London bereft of Celestine Edwards, people of African and African-Caribbean descent were dismayed, but not entirely inactive. This brings us to the third tap root of modern black anti-imperialism in Britain, the small group of London-based men and women who founded the African Association in 1897, and who then, in the teeth of an imperialist gale, organised the world's first Pan-African Conference in 1900.[36]

The founder of the African Association and chief organiser of the conference was another remarkable West Indian, Henry Sylvester Williams, who arrived in London in 1896 to study law. Like Edwards, Williams lectured for a temperance society, and later for a thrift society. Again like Edwards he did not confine himself to condemning drink. 'The British public was not cognisant of ... the oppression and the unrighteous circumstances our people were existing under' in South Africa. This became his main theme.

In 1897 he met Mrs A. V. Kinloch, the native South African wife of a Scottish engineer who had experienced racial bigotry in her homeland. Williams offered her a platform. He had taken a first step towards the African Association and Pan-African Conference. Mrs Kinloch addressed a London-based Writers' Club of progressive women, 'showing under what oppressions the black races of Africa lived'.[37] Jane Cobden Unwin, daughter of Richard Cobden and one of the first women elected to the London County Council, heard her. She would speak at the Pan-African Conference three years later and serve on the executive committee of the Pan-African Association which emerged from it. H. Fox Bourne of the Aborigines Protection Society also heard Mrs Kinloch. Impressed, he engaged her to lecture for the APS on South African conditions.

Meantime Williams met two more figures who would help to found the African Association. One was Celestine Edwards's mentor from Antigua, the Reverend Henry Mason Joseph, who had moved to London and joined the SRBM. The other was a fellow law student, T. J. Thompson, of Sierra Leone. London, the imperial metropolis, acted as a magnet for anti-imperialists too. Joseph, Kinloch, Williams and Thompson saw the need for an organisation to bring the city's African Britons into closer contact and to serve as a pressure group on behalf of Victoria's black subjects everywhere. They were also probably aware of the pan-German, pan-Slav and Zionist movements and hoped for a pan-African movement too. White sympathisers warned that blacks were incapable of independent organisation, but on 14 September 1897 Williams convened the foundation meeting of the African Association.[38] Five weeks later another meeting ratified its constitution and appointed officers: Joseph as president, Thompson as vice-president, Williams as general secretary, Mrs Kinloch as treasurer.[39]

From the start the association's aims were broader than Celestine Edwards's, its tactics more sophisticated, its support more broadly based. Edwards had represented the CES and SRBM, but essentially he had been a lone wolf; he never opposed British imperialism as spokesman for a group of African-Britons or African-Caribbeans. The African Association, however, represented the *organised* expression of African-British and African-Caribbean sentiment regarding the British empire.

As Indian nationalists in London had imitated the old Anti-Corn Law League, so the African Association followed the BCINC, of which it was very much aware. Williams took an office at 139 Palace Chambers, Bridge Street, Westminster, literally next door to the BCINC's offices. It is inconceivable that he did so without consulting BCINC members first. Over the course of the next few years he arranged lecture tours, the publication of books,[40] pamphlets[41] and a newspaper (*The Pan African*,) and the lobbying of Parliament and government Ministers.[42] On one occasion he addressed a meeting in the House of Commons protesting at government policy in Trinidad.[43]

His political views fell within traditional radical categories. He suggested that the principle 'No taxation without representation' should be applied to African Caribbeans, condemned the compound system in South Africa and called for Englishmen to support his positions at the polls.[44] Williams insisted that, like Indians, Africans too represented a vast potential market for English manufactured goods.[45] While taking pains to distinguish himself and his colleagues from 'the raw, uncultured natives' of the bush and jungle (whom he thought unworthy of the vote),[46] he argued that Africans possessed 'education and culture' as Indians did.[47] 'The discovery of the ancient remains of gigantic structures and coinage in the upper Nile, Mashonaland and Matabeleland, now called Rhodesia, tell an African tale which goes back thousands of years.'[48] Thus Africans, as much as Indians, deserved better treatment from imperialists.

Unlike Celestine Edwards, the African Association never condemned British imperialism root and branch. Rather, if England would carry 'the light of Christian civilisation into African lands' instead of ruthlessly exploiting colonised peoples, then the association would offer support. When the Boer War began, Williams volunteered unsuccessfully to serve in the British army.[49] Just as with the BCINC, a contradiction lay at the very heart of the African Association. Insisting that Africans within the British empire should share equally in all rights and privileges accorded to Victoria's white subjects, it simultaneously adumbrated an independent pan-Africa.

The famous Pan-African Conference which the association held on 23–5 July 1900, in Westminster town hall, which brought to London thirty-two delegates from Africa, North America, the West Indies and Britain, was thus a product of a certain milieu and can be comprehended only in context (see Figure 40). The African Association stood first of all upon Celestine Edwards's shoulders but also upon those of Dadabhai Naoroji, and therefore upon those of Cobden, Bright and even Fox Bourne. Since anti-imperial London contained more than one anti-imperialism, so too did the Pan-African conference. The Bishop of London, Mandel Creighton, who delivered the opening address, spoke in the tones of the Aborigines Protection Society, of which, not coincidentally, he was a member. The conference was worthy, he said, because Britons 'must look forward in their dealings with other races ultimately to confer on them some of the benefits of self-government that they themselves enjoyed'.[50] C. W. French of St Kitts, on the other hand, spoke in the tones of the BCINC: 'The coloured people claimed from the British Government just that recognition which they were entitled to as men — namely that under the Queen's rule men of colour should have equal position and place with the white race.' Portions of the conference's 'Address to the World', a document opening with the memorable lines 'The problem of the twentieth century is the problem of the color line,' had been written by the great African American W. E. B. DuBois, who attended the conference, but they could have been written by Celestine Edwards. 'Let not the cloak of Christian missionary enterprise be allowed in the future, as so often in the past, to hide the ruthless economic exploitation and political downfall of less developed nations, whose chief fault has been reliance on the plighted troth of the Christian Church.' It was left to the Haitian Benito Sylvain, an aide-de-campe of the Abyssinian emperor, Menelik, who had defeated the Italians at Adowa, to speak in language reminiscent of R. C. Sen, the Indian student who had so troubled the India Office spy. 'No human power could stop the African natives in their social and political development. The question now was whether Europe would have

Figure 40 Sketches at the Pan-African Conference. *The Daily Graphic*, 24 July 1900

the improvement for or against her interests.' But Sylvain's was an unrepresentative voice.

The conference replicated, too, the implicit contradiction in the anti-imperial campaign mentioned earlier. That it should be held at all suggested the largely unarticulated desire of African Britons for an independent role, but, with the exception of Benito Sylvain, speakers criticised specific imperial policies only, demanding not independence but rather that 'the Imperial government should guarantee protection' to its African subjects.[51]

[263]

Some historians have denigrated the generally moderate tone of conference delegates. 'These were refined men and women who might have caused a character in a Kipling story to regret that they were not white.'[52] This seems wrong. At the turn of the twentieth century few could envisage a world without British imperialism. In London in 1900 anti-imperialists of all races wished mainly to humanise it, to turn it into the beneficent world government it claimed to be. This in itself was a radical notion for the times. Moreover, although anti-imperialists were unaware, the plan to humanise the empire inevitably contained the seeds of more far-reaching changes, just as the policies of *perestroika* and *glasnost* transformed and eventually led to the dissolution of the former Soviet empire.

The conference needs placing within a broader context too. In 1900 Jim Crow laws were at their height in the United States; the scramble for Africa had left nearly the entire continent in European hands; newly strengthened repressive laws bore hard on West Indians and Africans alike in the British empire, and with the Boer War the mood in Britain had turned bumptiously, sometimes ferociously, jingo. In London itself hooligans broke up 'pro-Boer' political meetings and greeted British victories in South Africa, most famously the relief of Mafeking, with riotous, even dangerously violent, demonstrations of patriotic joy. It took courage during an era characterised by racism, intimidation and slaughter to form an African Association, to agitate for better treatment for Victoria's subjects of African descent, to petition government officials on their behalf, to lobby MPs and heads of radical pressure groups. When Fox Bourne learned of the proposed Pan-African Conference he asked Williams to call it off. It took grit for Williams to refuse. 'We must do for ourselves in order to demand and ultimately gain the respect of the other races.'[53] It did not lead to significant practical achievements, but as a gesture, as testimony to the imperialised peoples' determination to 'do for themselves', the Pan-African Conference was a defining moment in the history of anti-imperial London.

It was definitional in another sense. The imperial metropolis contained many imperialisms at the turn of the twentieth century. Most Liberal and Conservative politicians thought that the power emanating from Whitehall defined it; a socialist like John Burns thought a truly imperial metropolis should exalt its workers;[54] a radical like Frederic Harrison thought it should be described by buildings, avenues and vistas embodying 'historic associations'.[55] The 'heart of the empire' as C. F. G. Masterman called London in 1900 was also the product of architects and politicians who wished to make the city look more imperial; of bankers and financiers who believed London's destiny was to reap the benefit of African and Asian labour; of dockers who unloaded ships packed with loot from the colonies and who demanded higher wages not least because their labour facilitated the functioning of an imperial metropolis; of women imperialists who discovered that only London provided scope for their activities. The people of London did not passively accept imperialist ideas brought to them from outside, as some historians have appeared to suggest, but themselves helped to define them, and thus to define the imperial metropolis itself.[56]

But an imperial city is cosmopolitan, and a cosmopolitan city contains anti-imperialists. No definition would be complete which ignored the contribution of London's anti-imperialists. Their multi-faceted approach, their achievements, of which the Pan-African Conference now seems pre-eminent, were a crucial component of the imperial city's identity.

Notes

1 This first Pan-African Conference has not lacked historians. See, for example, Immanuel Geiss, *The Pan-African Movement*, trans. Ann Keep, (London, Methuen, 1974), pp. 174–98; Ron Ramdin, *The Making of the Black Working Class in Britain*, (Aldershot, Wildwood House, 1987), pp. 50–5; Peter Fryer, *Staying Power*, (London, Pluto Press, 1984), pp. 280–7. Nor has its chief organiser lacked biographers. See J. R. Hooker, *Henry Sylvester Williams, Imperial Pan-Africanist*, (London, Collings, 1975); Owen Charles Mathurin, *Henry Sylvester Williams and the Origins of the Pan-African Movement, 1869–1911*, (Westport CT, Greenwood Press, 1976); Clarence G. Contee, *Henry Sylvester Williams and the Origins of Organizational Pan-Africanism, 1897–1902*, (Washington DC, History Department, Howard University, 1969).

2 Historians have examined British anti-imperialism. See, for example, Bernard Porter, *Critics of Empire*, (London, Macmillan, 1968), A. P. Thornton, *The Imperial Idea and its Enemies*, (Basingstoke, Macmillan, 1985), Stephen Howe, *Anticolonialism in British Politics: The Left and the End of Empire*, (Oxford, Oxford University Press, 1993). But for anti-imperialism in London see chapters 6-8 in my forthcoming *London 1900: The Imperial Metropolis*, (New Haven CT, Yale University Press, 1999).

3 *Justice*, 29 September 1900.

4 *Irish Weekly Independent*, 14 April 1900.

5 In a speech to the House of Commons in December 1900, quoted in *New Ireland*, 15 December 1900.

6 See especially the *Irish People*, *New Ireland* and the *Irish Weekly Independent* for antisemitic and racist commentary.

7 H. M. Hyndman, *The Ruin of India by British Rule, being the Report of the Social Democratic Federation to the International Socialist Congress at Stuttgart* (SDF, London, 1907), p. 5.

8 There is no satisfactory history of the BCINC. See, however, Harish P. Kaushik, *The Indian National Congress in England, 1885–1920* (Delhi, Friends Publications, 1991), and chapter 7 of Schneer, *London 1900*.

9 For the financial contributions of a wealthy Scottish sympathiser William Wedderburn, MP, see India Office, Gokhale Collection, IOR POS 11701, Wedderburn to Wacha, 6 May 1901. For the Irish connection see Mary Cumpston, 'Some early

Indian nationalists and their allies in the British Parliament, 1851–1906', *English Historical Review*, 76 (1961) 279–97, and Frank H. O'Donnell, *A History of the Irish Parliamentary Party*, II (Port Washington NY, Kennikat Press, 1970), pp. 413–45.

10 *Dadabhai Naoroji's Speeches and Writings*, (Madras, n.d.), speech at Toynbee Hall on the 'Condition of India', 31 January 1901.

11 *India*, 27 July 1900.

12 Countess of Warwick (ed.), *Progress in Women's Education in the British Empire, being the Report of the Education Section, Victorian Era Exhibition, 1897* (London, Longman, 1898), Professor Gokhale speaking.

13 *India*, 5 January 1900.

14 *Ibid.*, 11 May 1900.

15 India Office, L/P&J/6/66.

16 Webb was a Quaker. See his unpublished autobiography at Friends' Library, Swanbrook House, Donnybrook, Dublin.

17 India Office, L/P&J/6/570/970.

18 James Walvin, *Black and White*, (London, Allen Lane, 1973), p. 199.

19 On the transatlantic links see Paul Gilroy, *The Black Atlantic: Modernity and Double Consciousness*, (Cambridge MA, Harvard University Press, 1993), especially pp. 88–92; Stephen Yeo, 'A new life: the religion of socialism in Britain, 1883–96', *History Workshop Journal*, 4 (1977) 5–56.

20 For more on the anti-lynching campaign and the relationship between Impey and Mayo see Vron Ware, *Beyond the Pale: White Women, Racism and History*, (London, Verso, 1992), pp. 170–220.

21 There is no biography of Edwards. All my information on his life is gleaned from the pages of *Lux*.

22 *Lux*, 27 April 1895.

23 A lecture on 'Political Atheism', delivered on 12 February 1889 to 1,200 people, quoted Voltaire, Newton, Paine, Spencer and Professor Blackie, and referred to Lycurgus, Plato, Seneca, Aristotle, Zeno and Diogenes.

24 *Lux*, 27 October 1894.

25 See, for example, *From Slavery to a Bishopric, being a Sketch of the Life, Struggles and Successes of Bishop Hawkins* (n.d., but published in the mid-1880s).

26 *Lux*, 25 August 1894.

27 During a tour of Bristol, marvelled one reporter, 'Mr. Edwards filled a hall with 1,000 people five nights in the week, and a much larger one three times on Sunday.' *Ibid*, 13 May 1893.

28 *Ibid.*, 10 December 1892.

29 *Ibid.*, 27 August 1892.

30 Edwards, 'Political Atheism'.

31 *Lux*, 10 December 1892.

32 See his lecture 'Does God answer Prayer?' praising 'the Mohammedan, as you call him', and so-called primitive peoples who 'in the absence of priests, in the absence of rites, in the absence of sacrifice, in the absence of holy shrines … perform acts that cannot be called by any other name than Prayer'.

33 See, for example, three pamphlets, *Atheism a Failure; Theosophy Old and New; This Worldism: a Scathing Exposure of the Fallacies and Fraudulent Pretensions of Secularism to benefit Mankind* all published in the mid-1880s.

34 *Lux*, 20 August 1892.

35 *Ibid.*, 12 January 1895.

36 This small circle included but was not limited to the composer Samuel Coleridge-Taylor, the physician John Alcindor, the African-American law student D. E. Tobias, the medical student John Archer, Celestine's mentor in Antigua, the Reverend Henry Mason Joseph, and of course Henry Sylvester Williams. For Coleridge-Taylor see Avril G. Coleridge-Taylor, *The Heritage of Samuel Coleridge-Taylor*, (London, Dobson, 1979); for Alcindor see Jeffrey Green, 'West Indian doctors in London: John Alcindor (1873–1924) and James Jackson Brown (1882–1953)', *Journal of Caribbean History*, 20 (1985–86) 49–77. There are no biographies of John Archer, although as a

local Labour Party activist he later represented Battersea on the London County Council, or of the Reverend Henry Mason Joseph.

37 *Port of Spain Gazette*, 2 June 1901.
38 Geiss, *The Pan-African Movement*, p. 174. Geiss cites the Record of Proceedings of the Pan-African Conference as his source.
39 *Ibid.* Mrs. Kinloch returned to South Africa, however, in February 1898. *Aborigine's Friend*, March 1898.
40 For example, H. S. Williams, *The British Negro: A Factor in the Empire*, (London, published by the author, 1902).
41 For example, H. S. Williams, *The Ethiopian Eunuch* (London, published by the author, 1902).
42 See Contee, *Henry Sylvester Williams*, p. 9. Among Williams's publications were *The British Negro*, *The Ethiopian Eunuch* (1902) and *The Memorial of the African Association on the Distress in the West Indies* (30 March 1898).
43 *Port of Spain Gazette*, 6 April 1899.
44 *Port of Spain Mirror*, 8 January 1902.
45 Williams, *The British Negro*, p. 123.
46 *Port of Spain Gazette*, 2 June 1901.
47 Williams, *The British Negro*, p. 14.
48 *Ibid.*, p. 10.
49 *Port of Spain Mirror*, 8 January 1902.
50 *The Times*, 24 July 1900.
51 *Ibid.*, 26 July 26, 1900, Mr G. W. Christian of Dominica.
52 Elliot Rudwick, *W. E. B. Du Bois: A Study in Minority Leadership*, (Philadelphia PA, University of Pennsylvania Press, 1960).
53 See Williams's letter to Booker T. Washington, in Louis Harlan and Raymond Smock (eds) *The Booker T. Washington Papers*, V (Urbana IL, University of Illinois Press, 1975), p. 570. He wrote on 29 June 1900, 'We are receiving slight opposition from the Aborigines' Protection Society.'
54 John Burns, *The Straight Tip to Workers: Brains better than Bets or Beer*, Clarion pamphlet No. 36, 1902, p. 5.
55 Quoted in Mark H. Judge (ed.), *The Case for Further Strand Improvement*, (London, 1906), p. 6.
56 See Schneer, *London 1900*.

AFTERWORD

Postcolonial times:
the visible and the invisible

Bill Schwarz

In April 1974 many of my generation took the opportunity – of which
there were not many – to travel to Lisbon in order to witness a revolution. For various reasons I never availed myself of the chance, though I
did become an enthusiastic reader, confronting for the first time the
extraordinary history of Portugal. It was another five years before I paid
the visit myself. On seeing Lisbon, eager guides showed the bullet
holes in the buildings (though there were not many of these, either, and
the ones I saw were not entirely convincing). A bit of me, I guess, was
pleased to witness this residue of insurrectionary history, even if from
afar. But, more than that, I was immediately entranced by the city.
Great parts of it had avoided every wave of urban planning, and carried
a peculiarly Mediterranean, pre-industrial feel. The more formal sec-
tors, from the Parque Eduardo VII, down the characteristically Latin
Avenida da Liberdade to the Praça do Comércio, were lavishly baroque,
enough to set the heart pounding. What was most immediately visible
about Lisbon, however, and most immediately captivating, was its
imperial splendour. Even without the street names and statues of dead
heroes Lisbon is palpably, visually, an imperial city, resonating in the
mind's eye with its historic Atlantic wealth: historically European, but
ambivalently so. Yet at the same time, for all its appearance, it is – or
was in the late 1970s – a bankrupt city, testimony to an empire which
for long had ceased economically to sustain the metropolis in the
manner to which its formal structures laid claim. The ancient British
trams and buses were picturesque but from another age. Much to my
surprise, and for all its evident contrasts, Lisbon reminded me of
London – with its historic facades still in place, possessing too a certain decorum, but essentially a post-colonial city on the skids.

As the chapters of this volume attest with impressive verve, to map
the colonial traces still present and visible in contemporary post-colonial cities requires all the skills, and more, of the conventional histo-

[268]

rian. To those with the eyes to see, the urban formations of our own times hold together the inchoate traces of many competing historical times, all jumbled together. Mapping the city has become the stock in trade of many cutting-edge cultural theorists. To read the city on the post-modern turn can gratifyingly confirm that all structures dissolve into their own simulacra. Yet merely to succumb to the confusions of the contemporary cityscape is to reproduce a kind of fashionable myopia. For, despite the apparent chaos of the sights which confront us, the historical times inscribed in the city are organised by powerful logistics. Indubitably, the post-colonial city is hybrid: but it is neither random nor indecipherable.

There is something exhilarating when one travels through the contemporary cityscape and becomes conscious of the different historical zones, simultaneously encountering different times. This is the very stuff of a modernist sensibility, peculiarly part of a collective experience. When I go, for example, to the local twenty-four-hour supermarket, or to the neighbourhood drive-in McDonald's, I enter a historical zone dominated not only by the commodified forms of late modernity but by the colossal Beaconsfield pub and by streets which each carry the names of Disraeli's novels, a quaint reminder of the pretensions of villa Toryism in the high noon of empire. On workdays, in the other direction, I pass public housing dedicated to the memory of C. L. R. James (what he would have thought, one can only guess), go on through the well documented historical locale of Spitalfields and Whitechapel (which, in the terms I am using here, can properly be understood to be *overdetermined* historiographically), cross Tower Bridge, then go down Jamaica Road through docklands which have, to date, been totally insulated from those forces of regeneration which have transformed the opposite bank of the Thames. Compressed in this thirty or forty-minute journey are some conspicuous histories (it is tricky *not* to notice the Tower of London) and some which are a deal less obvious. But it is not only historical time which has been concentrated into these different moments, but also space itself. For the divide between centre and periphery has always been compromised, such that the frontiers separating civilisation from barbarism, us from them, are not only external but run through the heartlands of the native terrain itself. The metropolis is unthinkable without its own internal frontiers.

In part, this is a sociological matter. London, for example, has historically been a cosmopolitan city, creating a home for a multiplicity of aliens (to employ an older idiom) and ethnics (to use a term still in common use). In 1900, as Baedeker noted, London possessed more Scots than there were in Aberdeen, more Irish than in Dublin, more Jews than in Palestine and more Roman Catholics than in Rome. Even before the age of mass immigration from the colonies, there had been small concentrations of colonial peoples in the metropolis for as long as the empire has been in place. Some were white, many more not. From the late 1940s, when immigration from the so-called new Commonwealth took off, so threatened did the divide between white and black appear that there were significant numbers of indigenous Britons who made a concerted bid to re-imagine Britain as a white man's country, reviving the colonial syntax in a post-colonial age. And in our own times, entire ethnic communities, relocated from their native territories, geographically inhabit urban Britain, but live simultaneously in an electronic world which reproduces their native habitats along the mean streets of the inner city. While movements of population have become more rigorously policed, the movement of images has become massively more promiscuous, involving the fracturing and dispersal of the inherited idea of the frontier.

This suggests that frontiers have functioned not only as sociological facts but also as symbolic systems. Frontiers demarcate not only nation states but moments of danger. If, in the imperial imagination of a figure such as Lord Curzon, the colonial frontier represented the truest, most masculine manifestation of the nation, whose virtue was symbolised even in the burning clarity of the sunlight, then there were also locales inside the metropolis which – commensurately – were conceived as dark, decaying, contagious and *alien*. For this reason, the management of the domestic imperial city constituted a political practice steeped in the commonsense idioms of race. Race defined what imperial civilisation was. The public vistas constructed in the heart of the capital – and in the heart of Britain's other cities – provide the visible legacy of Britain's imperial past. But in a deeper sense the imperial city also carries other legacies which cannot so readily be scrutinised by the naked eye.

When, in the late 1940s and 1950s, West Indians started arriving in London, Birmingham, Manchester and so on, the experience – recorded in fiction and in various memoirs – proved dislocating. Many accounts tell of the impossibility, for these pioneer immigrants, of writing home the truth. The climate, the hostility or indifference, the manifold *frontiers* which ran through neighbourly England, became in effect unspeakable, so at odds were they with the imagined expectations which had made these individual journeys possible in the first place. The empire 'at home' proved a far from comfortable place for black West Indians – even when they knew as much about the history of the mother country as its native inhabitants. This incapacity to articulate, at the time, the experience of immigration was powerful, producing a kind of cognitive dissonance, in which all that could be spoken was an emollient, ventriloquist affirmation of private expectations and public, patriotic rhetoric. This incapacity was never merely an individual pathology: unspeakability lies at the very heart of the twentieth-century immigrant experience.

For those indigenous white Britons who did not know the empire, decolonisation was an abstract, distant experience, mediated through stories in the press about far-away places, or in the newsreels, whose early, low-grade Technicolor and bizarre musical scores really did represent the whole thing as if it were a dream. In contrast to the Portuguese experience in April 1974, or to the French, the end of empire in Britain – for those in the metropolis – was a peculiarly invisible process. The principal manner in which it was experienced, I think, was through the dynamics of displacement. What happened in the Gold Coast or in Malaya could indeed be regarded as an abstraction, and passed people by easily enough. But the intensified dramas of ethnic identity, which moved to the centre of public life in Britain in the 1950s and 1960s, was another matter. So far as decolonisation had a domestic, metropolitan dimension, it was within the theatres of ethnic imagining and ethnic longing. To see the black immigrant was to be confronted by the colonial past.

There was, perhaps, an unspeakability about this too. Cognitive dissonance operated not merely on one side of the frontier between black and white, colonised and coloniser. In confronting the black immigrant, *memories* of empire – memories, in fact, of *being white* – were activated in the imaginations of white Britons. In the back-streets of post-colonial Britain, in Wolverhampton and Smethwick, the language of the colonial frontier could be heard again. In a strangely disturbing racial alchemy, England itself was reinvented as a white man's country, the intoxicating figure of the white man re-emerging just at a time when one might have supposed his end had come. And when in April 1968 Enoch Powell spoke in Birmingham, the private reveries of race, in which this alchemy had initially been brewed, crossed the threshold and became public wisdom.

Yet, curiously, it was in part the phenomenon of immigration that *also* created the historical possibility for the colonisers to speak their own history and properly to see themselves, in full perspective. The double-consciousness of the inhabitants of the West Indies – included and excluded simultaneously – worked its way into the urban cultures of the post-colonial metropolis, undercutting the myth of the English as a people peculiarly blessed by providence with the virtue of liberality. The cultural formations emanating from the margins – from the colonies – created new possibilities for the metropolis as a whole, allowing new pasts to be remembered and new futures imagined. This was a historical transformation which carried with it the promise, as one West Indian immigrant put it in 1968, of 'the final demystification of some areas of darkness in the British consciousness'. Or, as James Baldwin described the black colonial arriving in London in those years, 'he had no future in the past'.[1] History itself could be re-imagined, and in this way the invisible – like a photographic image taking shape – slowly came to be visible.

There are in the capital no statues or monuments marking or celebrating the end of empire. There is no statue of Nehru or Nkrumah in Parliament Square, nor even a relief of Harold Macmillan in Cape Town declaring – poised, steely, but ultimately bewildered – that the winds of change were about to blow. In design and organisation London, Birmingham, Glasgow all still signify the imperial past, a past memorialised in the built environment. And yet, of course, within this larger public *mise-en-scène* authentically post-colonial cultures thrive in even the most unexpected locales – not least the Beaconsfield pub. There are no bullet holes which testify to this historical transformation, for it was a revolution which operated deep inside the culture of the metropolis. The post-colonial city has, at last, become home to other memories.

Note

1 Stuart Hall, speaking to the Caribbean Artists' Movement conference at the University of Kent, 31 August 1968, quoted in Anne Walmsley, *The Caribbean Artists Movement, 1966–72: A Literary and Cultural History* (London, New Beacon Books, 1992), p. 162. For Baldwin: James Baldwin and Margaret Mead, *a Rap on Race* (London, Corgi, 1972), p. 48.

INDEX

Note: 'n.' after a page reference indicates a note number on that page.